Working-class writing and publishing in the late twentieth century

Working-class writing and publishing in the late twentieth century

Literature, culture and community

Tom Woodin

Manchester University Press

Copyright © Tom Woodin 2018

The right of Tom Woodin to be identified as the author of this work has been asserted by him in accordance with the Copyright, Designs and Patents Act 1988.

Published by Manchester University Press
Altrincham Street, Manchester M1 7JA, UK
www.manchesteruniversitypress.co.uk

British Library Cataloguing-in-Publication Data is available

ISBN 978 0 7190 9111 7 hardback
ISBN 978 1 5261 4921 3 paperback

First published by Manchester University Press in hardback 2018

This edition published 2020

The publisher has no responsibility for the persistence or accuracy of URLs for any external or third-party internet websites referred to in this book, and does not guarantee that any content on such websites is, or will remain, accurate or appropriate.

Typeset by Servis Filmsetting Ltd, Stockport, Cheshire

For Joan and Alan Woodin

Contents

	List of figures	viii
	Acknowledgements	ix
	Introduction	1
1	Sources of radicalism	12
2	Young people's writing	35
3	The good old days?	57
4	A beginner reader is not a beginner thinker	80
5	The workshop and working-class writing	94
6	Making writers: more writing than welding	111
7	Alternative publishing and audience participation	128
8	Chuck out the teacher: critical pedagogy in the community	142
9	Class and identity	157
10	The mainstream and the movement	176
	Conclusion	193
	Notes	201
	Bibliography	237
	Index	258

Figures

1. Vivian Usherwood, *Poems* (London: Centerprise, 1974/1972) — 16
2. QueenSpark publicity — 21
3. Centerprise young writers, *As Good As We Make It* (London: Centerprise, 1982) — 37
4. Alan Gilbey cartoon, printed in *Writing* (London: FWWCP, 1978) — 41
5. Daisy Noakes, *The Town Beehive* (Brighton: QueenSpark, 1980/1975) — 63
6. Colin Fearnley in *Write First Time* — 87
7. Stephen Hicks, *The Boxer Speaks* (London: Basement, 1973) — 112
8. A Gatehouse book launch, c.1992 — 118
9. Basement Writers' publicity, c.1976 — 132
10. FWWCP booklist, 1985–6 — 147
11. FWWCP black writing booklist, mid-1980s — 165
12. Joe Flanagan from Pecket Well College featured on *Fed News*, 1991 — 190

Acknowledgements

I would like to thank a number of people. Roger Mills, Tim Strangleman and Ken Worpole generously read the whole of the text. Sam Duncan, Mark Freeman and John Hardcastle read chapters. Sheila Rowbotham read early versions of much of this work and provided invaluable support and advice. Eileen Janes Yeo and Paul Kelemen offered useful guidance and ideas. Gary McCulloch also gave encouragement and feedback on draft articles. Of course I take responsibility for the text.

I am grateful for critical discussions from colleagues at various conferences including the British Sociological Association, History of Education Society, International Standing Conference for the History of Education and at conferences held at the Institute for Historical Research, Goldsmiths University, UCL Institute of Education, University of Sassari and the University of Macerata as well as invited talks and seminars in Britain and internationally. The chapters also draw upon articles published in *History of Education*, *Paedagogica Historica*, *Sociology*, *Culture, Media and Society* and the *International Journal of Lifelong Education*.

I have made every attempt to find the authors of the works cited but have not managed to track down everyone; however, I would be happy to acknowledge them. I would also like to thank staff at Manchester University Press.

I acknowledge the support of the archives and librarians at the Bishopsgate Institute, Mass Observation, UCL Institute of Education, Ruskin College, Victoria and Albert Museum, Working Class Movement Library and Liverpool University. Staff at Centerprise, Commonword, Eastside, QueenSpark and Yorkshire Arts Circus provided access to papers and publications. Countless individuals also gave me their archive material for which I am very grateful, notably Rick Gwilt and Mike Hayler. The interviewees who spoke to me and are listed at the end of the book were extremely helpful. I also thank Alan Gilbey, Paul George, Keith Armstrong, Rosa Schling, Laura Mitchison and Guy Farrar.

Most of all, I thank Ella and Eva who have lived with this book, in one way or another, for all of their lives!

Introduction

During the 1970s, working-class writers entered the cultural landscape in ever greater numbers. 'Ordinary' people formed writing and publishing workshops in which they explored ideas, histories and feelings. A great variety of people started writing, including school children, housewives, black and minority groups, unemployed people, retired workers as well as those still in work. Writers of all ages were examining personal experience with fresh eyes and renegotiating their place in the world. Over the coming decades, thousands of publications would be produced, with an estimated readership in the millions. Autobiography, poetry, short stories and drama were consumed avidly by those within the writer's immediate vicinity as well as by more general readerships. In 1976, the working-class writing and publishing groups, which were proliferating across the country, established a national network, the Federation of Worker Writers and Community Publishers (FWWCP or 'the Fed'), that would later add the strapline 'to make writing and publishing accessible to all'.[1] The movement that coalesced around the basic democratic idea that everyone could be a producer of culture released a pulse of energy that still reverberates today.

This cultural ferment was taking place amid growing social and economic instability. Long-held assumptions about social class were being disrupted by seismic political and economic shifts. The post-war consensus cracked in the 1970s, creating a space that came to be filled by the New Right, and which would in turn expedite neoliberal reforms. The historical outcomes of these processes were not a foregone conclusion. The working class came under the microscope as people sought to understand their lives in the past, present and future. Economic and political dimensions of class were being permeated by personal reflections and cultural meanings.[2] The desire to write about material and moral landscapes was palpable. To some extent, they faced the end of the 'traditional working class', and many texts were a means of coming to terms with the demise of a way of life. While the working class had always been diverse and subject to unremitting change,[3] in the 1970s there was a belief that a quiet revolution was eclipsing an old world. This book charts one aspect of these changes. It is not a straightforward organisational history but one that surveys a social formation that coalesced around the need for working-class expression.

In the early twenty-first century, a text about the recent history of working-class writers and writing is not a unique, quirky idea but one relevant to rethinking globalisation, digital technology and the complex cultural interactions that have become commonplace. The relations between these forces have a history. Community publishing itself utilised new technologies and responded to changing urban populations. Gaining a voice and expressing it in writing represented another way of thinking about the world. Writers searched for the means to understand and express the difficulties and contradictions of daily life. They wrote from within a distinct context and also pointed beyond it to more expansive desires.[4] Indeed, the idea of working-class writing is an ambiguous one that cannot easily be slotted into a specific category. It provides an essential window onto the perennial subject of how we live, the so-called human condition; it raises ethical dilemmas and philosophical questions in helping us to comprehend where we have come from and how we might map potential futures.

Working-class subjectivity?

Stories matter. The interpretation and representation of social change is of fundamental importance to the production and reproduction of social structures. Class is not only a material demarcation of life opportunities but is inscribed in, and contested through, symbolic meanings and values that have very real consequences.[5] Studies of working-class literature and writing have illustrated the capacity for narratives to help mould and activate individual and collective identities.[6] Commentators have also worked to explain the apparent inconsistency that, as economic inequality has deepened since the late twentieth century, the ways in which class has been talked about in the public realm have been correspondingly curtailed, not least in literature.[7] Understanding projects that supported the development of working-class voices is therefore particularly pertinent at this current historical juncture, when the tendency towards self-reflexiveness is growing.[8] The expansion of subjectivity has taken many forms. Anthony Giddens has argued that modernity was aligned with a 'reflexive project of the self' by which individuals sustained coherent yet continuously revised biographical narratives. Class, gender and race were seen as partly about access to these potentially empowering narratives.[9] In this context, harnessing and distributing workers' experience was invested with a radical potential. Writing from experience meant that everyone could participate, a fundamentally democratic position.[10] Groups created opportunities for writers and readers who were to become active participants in this expanding cultural democracy.

However, it was evident that these forms of expression had to be built up gradually. Making literature and literacy more widely available, while necessary, was also problematic. A growing sense of individuality among working-class people could be undercut by material shortages. In addition, as Raymond Williams would argue, writing and reading, unlike other forms of communication and art such as painting and sculpture, were technical skills that needed to be learnt through an apprenticeship before taking advantage of them, a fact that helped to explain part of the reasoning behind the Fed.[11] Brian Street provided a different emphasis in stating that writing was not purely a neutral and 'autonomous' technology but was inherently 'ideological' and dependent upon the setting within which it was located. Proponents of 'new literacy studies' would further dissect the situated nature of literacy practices.[12]

In the Fed, technology and context were interconnected. Writing and publishing workshops contained different social possibilities and nurtured self-belief and collective empowerment. Barriers were psychological as well as technical, and the assumption that only certain people could legitimately be writers was not easily expunged. Indeed, sustained organisation proved to be an important basis for writing to flourish, as the contemplative atmosphere of the workshop provided a forum for the development of working-class subjectivity. Technical limitations on written expression were minimised by scribing for others, the use of voice in performance as well as publication via offset litho printing. In turn, the strength and importance of writing helped to galvanise a sense of community and to encourage new writers.

Enriching working-class subjectivity would overlap with the emergence of new constituencies. The dominant position of class within workshops, as in society at large, would be challenged from a number of different directions. At one level, class had always been articulated through a diverse range of experiences. These differences became more pronounced as groups came to assert identities based upon race, gender, sexuality and disability and argued for autonomous spaces in which to write – and, at times, the relevance of class was rejected. The ensuing conflicts led some working-class writers to lose faith in the Fed. Yet class was not abandoned as a personal identity nor as a source of agency, and this was reflected in the writing. Class was also retained as a way of denoting difference and respecting 'other' constituencies.

The supportive structures built around marginalised writers and their communities extended to the reception of written work. A concern of 'community publishing' was that writing should be returned to its originating constituency.[13] A study that removed the 'product' from the 'sources', so that people were unable to see themselves or felt misrepresented, was considered to be an act of violence.[14] This pattern was also seen in the mass media, where stories about working-class people had been manipulated by the popular press, TV talk shows and reality TV in ways that discouraged serious reflection. In recent decades, a penchant for marginalising and laughing at working-class characters has turned into a full-scale frontal attack, based upon demonisation and ridicule.[15]

A comparable process can take place in the more polished arena of university-based research, which rarely gets fed back to the people who are the subjects of study. From the origins of social science, the representation of subordinate groups has been a bitterly contested terrain, often involving more than an element of cultural imperialism in which those being studied have little agency of their own.[16] Rather, people are transformed into 'data' to inform research that may circulate in lecture halls and academic journals, and occasionally influence policy, but not be returned to those 'sources'. This has been closely allied to conceptions of knowledge. Daniel Bertaux described 'symbolic exploitation' which devalues the everyday: 'commonsense knowledge, carrying a cognitive value, is being taken from laymen and converted into social-scientific discourse which can eventually face them as an alien force, exposing them to all kinds of sinister exploitation'.[17] The work of the Fed focused on just this area of 'accumulated experience and reflective communication'. Forms of knowledge were being scrutinised in both intellectual and organisational terms.[18]

Criticisms

The Fed was stepping into a fast-moving stream of contemporary debates on culture, literature, literacy, history and education that stretched back to earlier times. Intellectual arguments were rooted within institutional forms where power, hierarchy and status helped to define cultural practices and disciplinary boundaries. The arrival of these workshops was met with both disbelief and instinctive resistance as certain critics took exception to its work. Indeed, the perspectives that underpinned the FWWCP were to come under substantial critique in the very period in which these groups were forming. Opposition and marginalisation from a cultural elite did not come as a surprise, but other detractors closer to home would soon emerge. There has been very little critical evaluation of the Fed, and the continuous silence itself constituted a form of dismissal. For instance, it has not been uncommon to find sparse mention of worker writers and community publishing in relevant academic works on history and heritage.[19]

In place of the restricted idea of culture as a finished product, 'the canon of English literature',[20] the Fed represented itself as the spearhead of a democratising impulse that might extend and transform culture.[21] The subtleties and nuances of the Fed's cultural practice were at times lost in divisions that came to be called the 'culture wars'. Working-class, feminist and post-colonial positions on culture were being pitted against 'Literature' as exclusive and exclusionary, seen as Eurocentric, middle class and masculine.[22] Others questioned whether literature should be conceived as a body of work at all and, instead, accentuated the practices of reading, writing and communication. From this standpoint, established literary products were being substituted for creative processes and English literature disestablished in favour of a diversity of 'writing'. The proliferation of creative writing MAs testified to this change. Yet commentators in the Fed lamented that such courses tended to attract the already well educated and were isolated from the study of literature, so that the production and consumption of writing were kept on separate tracks with different destinations.[23]

These disputes threw up interesting paradoxes. The Fed was to be called to account by some of those who had pioneered studies of working-class culture, such as Richard Hoggart and Dennis Marsden. Having advanced through grammar schools and universities, they occupied positions in cultural and educational institutions and were inclined to see their own lives as living proof that working-class people should and could progress through education. However, they were upset by the idea that others, without adequate training, were suddenly going to become 'writers'. In particular, Ron Barnes's *Coronation Cups and Jam Jars* caused concern, compounded by the fact that he had received an Arts Council grant. Hoggart referred to it as 'banal; awful rhetoric. He needed to be introduced to the discipline of the craft.'[24] Marsden was also upset by the book:

> In his introduction he [Barnes] says, 'It doesn't take some special gift of genius to write an autobiography, a story or a poem. And of that I am living proof. Writing is not too difficult'. Much as I wanted to agree with him, I'm afraid writing comes harder than this.[25]

While we can agree that writing is difficult, Marsden was reticent to explore the value of the text. Hoggart and Marsden, who both produced groundbreaking studies of working-class life, nonetheless defended standards against a rising tide of relativism and consumerism that, in their view, had undermined traditional working-class culture, a trend that would peak with post-modernism.[26] To some extent, their arguments chimed with the right-wing critics of progressive education in schools, typified in the *Black Papers*, edited by C. B. Cox and A. E. Dyson, which called for a return to 'traditional' educational standards and discipline.[27] This line of thinking also pervaded the Arts Council's allegation that the Fed's work was 'of no literary merit' and only of 'therapeutic' or 'sociological' use.[28] In the 1990s, both Cox and Hoggart would collaborate on a book about literacy and literature.[29]

These criticisms simplified complex social changes. Writing workshops confronted traditions in literature that could alienate working-class people. But this issue was debated vigorously. Writers would come to read 'classic' texts as their own writing improved. Moreover, the question of standards was discussed and groups would develop their own ideas on the criteria for 'good' writing, which could not be set down in advance; they had to emerge over time once the process of fostering, publishing and distributing a large quantity of writing had taken place, 'producing much in order to find out what our "bests" are'.[30] In a letter to the Arts Council, the Fed also quoted Williams, who made the case that the profusion of such initiatives, in the Fed and elsewhere, was a necessary precursor to innovation in literature.[31] Thus, despite the simplifications, many finely graded and subtle arguments over culture took place within the Fed.

Another strand of criticism targeted at the Fed was related to a broader attack on the value of experience. Within workshops, the catholic embrace of different forms of knowledge was matched by interdisciplinarity in the academic world, especially in the humanities, social sciences and cultural studies. Gradual changes of outlook among the socialist and feminist historians' network known as History Workshop, as well as the group surrounding Stuart Hall at the Birmingham Centre for Cultural and Community Studies (CCCS), would influence the debate.[32] They argued for a more theoretically informed approach and became increasingly sceptical about 'bottom-up' history and the possibility of retrieving authentic working-class culture.[33] Indeed, theory was coming to play a much more significant role in intellectual and academic life in a way that would isolate worker writers as less relevant.[34] It was a small step to view Fed work as tainted by an overly nostalgic and simplistic account of the past. 'Therapy' and 'nostalgia' were frequently applied in a derogatory manner to Fed writing, and the mere mention of these words operated as an immediate disqualification from a sympathetic reading. There was a danger that the 'unvarnished autobiographical mode', which was trapped in localised settings, was not capable of identifying real social relationships and wider contexts.[35]

From the 1980s, socialist and feminist historians dissected the idea of working-class experience and thought about the way that discourses could block and constrain the expression of marginalised people.[36] Freeing personal meanings from the institutional frameworks in which they were collected became very tricky. For example, in the past, working-class people have had to give an account of their lives in order to receive welfare and charitable benefits. This form of surveillance has cast a shadow over working-class writing – exposure involves risk.[37] In the cognate area of subaltern studies, Gayatri Spivak asked, 'Can the Subaltern Speak?' Her answer was negative as she doubted the capacity of the marginalised to have a real voice.[38] The critique also drew upon a generation of Marxist thinkers who questioned the notion of class struggle and the progressive nature of the labour movement.[39] Gradually there would be an intellectual shift to focus upon the reproduction of capitalism and its social relations. Education, culture and society became sites for confirming inequalities – a trend that foreclosed active conceptions of class. Writers and autodidacts would be hemmed in by multiple inequalities, a lack of cultural capital and powerful institutional assumptions.[40] This occluded the ability to see working-class writers as significant or as capable of providing a different conception of life.

The Popular Memory Group, in an important analysis of memory and history, applied some of these general arguments to community publishing. They contended that allowing such autobiographies to 'speak for themselves' meant they would be integrated into conservative ideology. Rather, these accounts were to be treated as 'raw material' from which to develop a socialist consciousness through a dialogue with theory and an acknowledgement that contemporary concerns filtered into memory and consciousness.[41] To some extent this was a sophisticated version of the argument that capitalist values and practices were thoroughly embedded in society. For instance, Chris Miller argued that working-class writing workshops were peddling 'reactionary ideas ... They are silent when a writer's understanding is simply a reflection of bourgeois thinking, and fall into the trap that because it's from the working class then it must be good.'[42]

There were a number of problems with these critical stances that treated Fed publications as merely raw material for theory or as soaked in capitalist values. The dismissal downplayed the possibility that working-class writers already held opinions based on protracted experience and critical reflection. Fed groups were very sensitive about the time-consuming editorial meetings, drafts and redrafts that went into the production of texts. Writers became vulnerable in exposing themselves and could not easily be made to adjust their interpretations or widen their analysis. Yet many of these writings were to expand the areas of life that could be written about and made public. Therapy and nostalgia could not be ignored. Therapy encompassed many aspects of life, from resurgence through to pacification, and could exist side by side with other impulses and motivations.[43] Similarly, critique, empathy and the sensitive re-creation of a past were implicated in nostalgia. Celebrated commercial texts often revealed therapeutic and nostalgic strands, so there was a feeling that this was a false distinction used to discredit Fed writing and prevent the active participation of older people in comprehending and framing the past rather than expecting them to accept passively the interpretations of others.[44]

The rebukes also underplayed the validity of distributing texts to a readership who might be able to receive the writing in a critical manner. Given that one book tended to encourage another, it was possible that more thoughtful accounts would accumulate. The Fed was helping to create a movement within which contradictions could be expressed rather than developing a 'correct' theory.[45] In addition, *The Republic of Letters*, an account of the Fed written by activists, maintained that the actual practices and products of the FWWCP – 'co-operative, associative, aiming at two-way (many way) communication, cheap, widely available' – were a democratic challenge to the elitist and competitive notion of Literature.[46]

Critics tended to assume that writers would need to undergo some form of personal transformation before the real meaning of their lives could be comprehended – an analysis that those interrogating this writing did not always apply to themselves. Moreover, complex autobiographical works on class were appearing at this time and were often presented as a norm against which to judge other autobiographies.[47] Such an argument implicitly excluded the majority of people, as academic training would be necessary to write such an account of one's life. At its most extreme, the critique of the Fed implied the need for a kind of 'savage social therapy' that very few people would ever willingly choose to go through.[48]

Histories

These debates were not entirely new and the working-class writer was not an unfamiliar figure in the 1970s. Working-class success stories in literature, drama, TV and cinema had been a feature of the post-war years.[49] The emergence of the Fed helped to cast light upon the past, learning from previous traditions of writing and cultural activity from below. Researchers were identifying marginal voices within the history of reading and writing and the so-called self-educated working class, over prolonged periods of cultural and social change.[50] One of the attractions of radical movements has been the opportunity for self-expression, indicated by the large quantity of poetry found in labour movement journals. Obituary columns bring to light trade unionists and co-operators who immersed themselves in education and literature.[51] Adult education tutors had been exposed to a great amount of working-class writing.[52] The idea of a working-class cultural organisation was not new either and had featured in dreams of a better world. For instance, in the 1970s, the novelist Glyn Hughes interviewed Billy Holt, a councillor, writer and artist who, in the 1930s Communist Party, had been 'more interested in the aesthetic side of life', the 'inner mystery of it all', and had wanted to found 'a league for the liberation of proletarian art, writing and painting and poetry expressed through personal vision, which they were not able to do under the capitalist system of the day'. But the Party would not publish his ideas and informed him that 'You can't revolutionise proletarian art until you've had the revolution. You've to wait for that.'[53] Holt's thwarted vision of a league for proletarian culture was to be partially realised in the creation of the Fed in 1976.

However, historians have attempted to quarantine an earlier tradition of working-class writing which serves to isolate it from more recent cases of worker writing in the Fed. J. F. C. Harrison argued that a British autodidact tradition ended with the First World War whereas Jonathan Rose dates the death at the Second World War, despite continuities in experiences.[54] Those who have regarded the Fed as distinct from older traditions have positioned it as part of a surging relativist tide over the previous four decades,[55] or as focused upon alternative forms of publication, in contrast to the 1930s when mainstream outlets were utilised.[56] The content of autobiographical works and their motivating themes are also seen to be at odds with those of the nineteenth century.[57] Workers' education and culture is portrayed as petering out in the twentieth century in a world that offered opportunities and escape routes for those whose attachments to working-class institutions and communities would be greatly weakened.[58] The Fed was partly a historical reaction to these changes by those 'left behind' in the wake of publicised cases of upward mobility during the 1960s.

While these claims are not without foundation, there remain significant links between the Fed and more distant historical practices, apparent in the very fact of working-class people relating to culture in a serious way as well as fashioning their own. In the 1970s, the lives of some writers did stretch back to this earlier set of influences. The initiators of the Fed were imbued with a consciousness of previous attempts to build radical education and culture. An historical awareness would also help to justify publishing books: working-class writers were to stake their place in history so that, in the future, it would not be all 'kings and queens'.[59] The importance of writing has not always been recognised by historians. For example, Rose's fascinating account of working-class reading, *The Intellectual Life of the British Working Classes*, concentrated more upon what can be learnt from autobiography as a window into the cultural consumption of classic texts rather than viewing working-class writing as a creative act in itself.[60] The singular 'life' of Rose's title and his interest in the 'best' culture downplayed the range of cultural production by working people.

The organisation of writing and publishing among marginalised groups was a feature of the Fed that related to the past. There is always a danger that the term 'autodidact' directs our attention to the oddball individual at the expense of the social circumstances and educational process out of which they emerged. It has been recognised that the nineteenth-century autodidact tradition was based on a network of domestic and associational forms, rather than disparate lone individuals.[61] Furthermore, if we accept that tradition may be an amalgamation of discontinuous moments that require continual remoulding rather than an unchanging practice that is passed on directly through the generations, such experiences can be seen to overlap in important ways.[62] All traditions are to an extent invented and are necessarily selective.[63] Studies of alternative and radical media testify to the enduring significance of these forms.[64] Brecht's poem 'New Ages' struck a chord with many in the Fed who were thinking creatively about the past and the future. His warning that old ways could easily be reproduced and that history was not necessarily a progressive force – 'From the new transmitters came the old stupidities' – helped activists to utilise technology and interpret the past.[65]

Changes

The history of the Fed traverses four broad chronological phases. From the early 1970s, there was a concern to develop writing and personal expression in working-class communities. As writers came together in a turbulent atmosphere, they challenged cultural assumptions and institutions. Their work received affirmation from a number of quarters, and this initial dynamism lasted into the mid-1980s. The later 1980s and early 1990s was a time of growth and debate about the meaning of the movement within the inhospitable climate of Thatcherism, which weeded out alternatives and refashioned British society along more authoritarian and commercial lines. Class movements and alternative ideas came under strain at the same time as new identity groups emerged based upon gender, race, disability and sexuality. However, by the early 1990s, mainstream attitudes mellowed as the Fed became a funded client of the Arts Council and many of its ideas became more acceptable. This period was marked by the development of a looser and more inclusive network of groups. Finally, with the loss of funding in 2007, caused by financial irregularities, the movement returned to a more informal network of writers and workshops, communicating through occasional meetings and online.

The Republic of Letters remains an essential statement, from an early phase of the movement, that presents an oppositional stance to cultural and educational institutions.[66] Subsequent studies were to focus more narrowly on the educational benefits of the Fed, literacy and occupational therapy, or write about specific examples. Although a new edition of *The Republic of Letters* was published in 2009, and while there has been some ongoing interest in the Fed, no broad accounts of the movement have been published.[67] Analyses of radical education and popular history offer occasional glimpses of topics that are of relevance to the Fed but are generally silent on working-class writing and community publishing.[68]

This book has gestated over many years. My involvement with the network of writing and publishing workshops spanned the period from 1990 to around 2005 and provided insights into the feelings and emotions, cultures and dynamics of workshops. Personal experience provided access to invaluable archival material and contacts, much of which was collected in the early 2000s.[69] Material has also been gleaned from listening to people – in meetings, workshops and more informally.[70] It became necessary to step out of the internal debates and place them within a historical context,[71] a process that was helped by writing a number of articles which have here been edited into a new shape.[72] Producing an 'academic' study of the Fed has presented a number of conflicts, many of which have a long history. There is always a danger of 'spurious identification' with a community.[73] Yet all communities are divided and change over time so that, with the passage of years, there are multiple audiences for a text such as this.

I concentrate upon the early phase of the movement to capture the motivations, meanings and complex forces that were in play and how these changed over time. The main story is taken through to the mid-2000s. Chapter 1 analyses the origins of the movement, bringing together the educational and social influences that contributed to the emergence of the Fed. The following four chapters are preoccupied with writing. This is not a random choice. Writing was the core purpose of the Fed and it is worthy of critical evaluation. Professionals commenting favourably on the workshops have frequently maintained that process and organisation have been of more value than the content of the writing. This bears a resemblance to Williams' claim that working-class culture comprised collective organisational structures rather than the creative, expressive and individualist novel.[74] While much Fed writing was experimental, at times ephemeral, it would be an error to assume that it cannot stand on its own. We need to learn how to write about this kind of work and assess it in a way that connects to intellectual currents. Accordingly, Chapter 2 deals with the writing of young people; Chapter 3 discusses the trend of autobiographical writing by older people in the 1970s and 1980s; and Chapter 4 considers the work done in adult literacy groups. Chapter 5 reviews the work of writing workshops and reflects upon Fed writing as a whole. I outline its key characteristics within historical and literary perspectives.

The second half of the book addresses the development of the Fed as a social movement in five thematic chapters. Chapter 6 focuses upon the journeys that writers took and assesses their learning as well as the cultural significance of these personal changes. Chapter 7 looks into the role of readers and distribution in the attempt to democratise culture. Chapter 8 discusses the politics of organisation and its relevance to the theory of critical pedagogy. Chapter 9 addresses class, the element that bonded the movement together – although, as this fractured, intense clashes over identity occurred. Chapter 10 investigates the battles for cultural recognition with the Arts Council and other institutions, and demonstrates that the distinctive identity of the movement gradually waned as ideas that the Fed pioneered gained a foothold across society. Finally, the conclusion draws out the overall significance of these ideas and practices. As a whole, the movement represents an important yet under-recognised cultural force whose impact has been felt for nearly fifty years. In a world of increasingly stark inequalities in which the majority of people feel they have little voice in society, the history of working-class writing and publishing retains great significance.

1   Sources of radicalism

In the 1970s, the idea of working-class writing flared up in the collective imagination. Local areas became sources of creativity that connected to a much wider movement. The local was conceived as both a geographical and a political space that was ripe with democratic potential. Writing and publishing workshops were part of a more general set of social movements, intellectual trends and traditions. They had roots in debates on education, culture, class and the media that stretched back to the late 1950s and 1960s. Writers such as Richard Hoggart and Raymond Williams opened up the study of 'culture' as lived experience, while E. P. Thompson's seminal *The Making of the English Working Class* 'rescued' a rich working-class culture in the early nineteenth century.[1] The idea of the 'cultural revolution', or even a 'long revolution', appealed to those who felt that society needed to be reborn through the creativity of the working class, a term which, even then, meant many different things to different people, encompassing the 'traditional' industrial working class as well as a more diffuse group of people. The growing realisation that culture was material, in the words of Williams, would help to unlock working-class writing as a source of social change.[2]

From the late 1960s, a younger generation of radicals who were mainly but not exclusively middle class allied themselves with what they perceived as a simmering working-class discontent, specifically with writers who were keen to express their experience and frustrations. Creating the means for direct and unmediated communication between working-class people was seen as one vital foundation upon which an alternative to capitalist forms might be built. This interest in the means of communication echoed the radical culture that turned away from formal electoral politics and rejected existing mainstream institutions as outdated and elitist. Instead they asserted the need for democracy, autonomy and self-help.[3] As with other such initiatives, the Fed was set up to meet new needs that could not be accommodated within the mainstream; it was to be an independent space where working-class people could write, publish and congregate.

The Fed's creation in 1976 is of consequence. The moment of formation was to ensure its distinctive stamp. There was at the time an escalating resistance in everyday life as people broke out of the subordinate positions to which they had been assigned. The new forms of resistance did not fit into traditional socialist understandings of struggle.[4] One of these was the Fed. As the post-war consensus came under increasing pressure, a feeling of decline and failure was in the air despite relative prosperity in comparison with the past.[5] While the welfare and corporatist state had brought benefits, working-class people were still excluded. Those who enjoyed improved living standards were moving out of the 'inner city', a newly imported term from the USA. Geographically and culturally they were becoming remote from the old, the unemployed, the unskilled and immigrants who were left behind.[6] Moreover, the rhetoric of the Labour Party that presided over many of these changes was losing traction with the realities of working-class existence.[7] A pessimism about the future was shared by a broad alliance of well-educated professionals as well as trade unionists and many poor people.[8] Some of them also had time on their hands and were keen to contribute to community projects.

The coming together of the Fed was preceded by intense local activity stimulated by radical community politics. It grew out of several areas: schools, adult education and adult literacy, the labour movement as well as newer forms of community campaigning, oral history and the popularity of 'history from below'. Each of them had an educative effect on the others, an outward rippling from many different sources that eventually coalesced into a movement.[9] Although the Fed was in some respects unique, it was propagated within a broad social and cultural context.

Young people

The single most significant event in the emergence of the Fed was a school strike by children at Sir John Cass School in East London, which followed the sacking of Chris Searle for publishing *Stepney Words*, a collection of children's poetry.[10] Searle was to act as a catalyst for educational rebellion, although he would be reinstated two years later by the then secretary of state for education and science, Margaret Thatcher. As with other young radicals in the 1970s, Searle was convinced of the need for both personal and social liberation. Words could be used as weapons in a struggle by conveying a message, and poetry could fulfil people's basic aesthetic need to create beautiful things.[11] He wanted to teach in East London partly because of a strong feeling of empathy with Isaac Rosenberg, the East End Jewish poet who died during the First World War. Searle explained in an interview that, as a young student, he was

> growing up in the mind of Rosenberg ... you almost relive their life, you have a tremendous spirit of empathy ... I wanted to teach in the same place where he had developed his poetic vision.[12]

The reality he was to find contrasted with his vision: his pupils' imaginative creativity had never been given the opportunity for respectful expression. In producing Stepney Words, along with photographer Ron McCormick, he infringed educational expectations. McCormick's photographs helped to bring the writing alive for children and parents, injecting both vibrancy and excitement into everyday life and enhancing the impact of Stepney Words.[13] Searle, imbued with a conviction that educationists should engage with communities, also gained support for the project by contacting parents to present copies and establish a sympathetic context for the reception of the book.[14] The poems published in Stepney Words were about life as seen by the pupils – much of it was unhappy stuff that ran contrary to the 'chirpy cockney' stereotypes favoured by the school authorities, some of whom, decades later, continued to question whether the children had actually written the poetry themselves.[15] The children wrote honest, fresh and vivid poems that disturbed those in power. The collection included Susan Johnson's critical and despondent piece:

The world is dim and dull
My classroom is dim and dull
My teacher sits there thinking
She's so dim and dull
That she just sits there thinking
The world is dim and dull
My life is not worth living.

Susan Johnson[16]

The spirit of the strike spread to many quarters, with well-known figures, Trevor Huddlestone, the Bishop of Stepney, and Jack Dash, the communist dockers' leader, lending their support. The mainstream press took up the story as a picaresque tale devoid of political implications, featuring the front-page headlines 'The Astonishing World of These East End Kids' and 'Please Don't Sack Sir'.[17] Searle, in contrast, insisted that the children were emulating their parents' trade unionism, and other schools even came out in sympathy with the strike. School strikes momentarily became a part of the educational landscape. The Schools Action Union, set up in 1969, was partly responding to the 1968 Lycée movement in France. From 1969 to 1972 a number of school student organisations were formed, such as the Manchester Union of Secondary School Students, and strikes were held by pupils in Manchester and London.[18] This directed attention to a rich history of labour movements and struggles among working people. The great-grandson of the trade unionist Ben Tillett was in one of Searle's classes, yet this history of 'courage, ingenuity and creative skill' hardly featured in history lessons.[19] Later, as the press came to learn that Searle, in Classrooms of Resistance and The People Go Marching On, was encouraging children to empathise with the poor and exploited around the world, the headlines would rapidly change to the horrified 'How "the Class Struggle" is Taught in the Classroom'[20] and

'Teaching Revolution in the Classroom'.[21] This about-turn resulted from a clash of assumptions which had not initially been detected by the press.

The episode created enthusiasm for writing and inspired many of the groups that would establish the Fed. For instance, Searle himself set up Basement Writers in 1972 with some of the pupils he had taught, who met in a basement on Cable Street that carried a symbolic meaning as the scene of the battle with the fascists in 1936 when Oswald Mosley's Blackshirts had been repulsed by an anti-fascist alliance. Searle was not working in isolation. Ken Worpole and a photographer at Centerprise produced a book for use by school children, *Hackney Half-term Adventure*, which proved popular with teachers and pupils who 'were only too delighted to find page after page of photographs of what they recognised only too well'.[22] Worpole came to realise that it might have been even stronger had it been written by children themselves, an insight further stimulated by the weaknesses of commercially produced materials that were

> 'directly relevant to the modern urban working class child,' with breathless titles like, I characterise, 'The Jesmond Alley Crew Go Mugging' … the contents of such readers are very crude and false projections of working class life written without empathy or imagination.[23]

As an English teacher at Hackney Downs School, Worpole had been deeply moved and excited by the poems of Vivian Usherwood, a twelve-year-old 'remedial' African-Caribbean student, and was keen that they be exposed to an audience. His poems, published by Centerprise, mined ambiguous feelings and desires that were both perceptive and emotive. One of the most popular was 'The Sun Glitters As You Look Up':

> The sun glitters, is shining bright!
> The sky is blue!
> The clouds are no longer there:
> It glitters as I look up!
> Bright, it is bright as my sister's face:
> The sun looks like a face without a body,
> Just round, with a nose and two eyes.
> If only that beautiful face would come down –
> It will be mine,
> And I shall shine with it.
> As dim as I am now I will be brighter,
> Even brighter than the sun itself.
> So it shall be,
> And I shall be as dim as ever,
> For it shall stay there for many years to come.
>
> Vivian Usherwood[24]

The humanity of these poems struck a chord and their electrifying effect in Hackney and beyond was reflected in multiple reprints and sales figures which

1 Vivian Usherwood's *Poems* proved to be an enduring success in Hackney and beyond.

would approach 18,000 copies (see figure 1).²⁵ Centerprise itself also reprinted *Stepney Words* and went on to publish a series of publications written by young people. Other teachers, gaining the confidence to develop children's writing, carved out space for it within the curriculum. One of these teachers, Blair Peach, was killed in the Southall Riots of 1979; an anthology of his pupils' writing was subsequently produced in his memory.²⁶ From 1976, the English Centre, part of the Inner London Education Authority (ILEA), also published a series of books written by children, many of them immigrants. In 1966, John La Rose had established New Beacon Books, which would exert a considerable influence on radical politics in the era and bring together established and new black writers as well as young people. Many teachers, such as Anne Johnson, who helped establish the Commonplace Workshop, were closely involved.[27] Children's writing became a normal part of life within overlapping networks that disavowed upward social mobility and provided a culture of solidarity.[28]

This innovative work with schoolchildren built on prominent post-war progressive educational practices.[29] Marjorie Hourd, who had taught Searle at Exeter University, wrote a key text, *The Education of the Poetic Spirit*, in which she maintained that children's writing should be judged not according to notions of grammatical correctness but by its intensity of expression and imaginative engagement. Later, the leading journal *The Use of English*, and David Holbrook's *English for the Rejected*, based on his work in a Cambridgeshire village, were pivotal in fostering self-expression in English teaching. One commentator called the 1960s the 'decade of pupils' anthologies', during which a steady stream of children's writing was published, not least by such figures as Alec Clegg, chief education officer for the West Riding of Yorkshire.[30] There were also moves to make English lessons more 'relevant' and theme based, for instance through the popular textbook *Reflections*, published in 1963, which sold over 200,000 copies.[31] Implicitly the state encouraged these practices. The Plowden Report, *Children and Their Primary Schools*, had given an 'unqualified welcome' to the expansion of 'creative writing' and the 'flowering of children's writing', alleging that 'the best writing of young children springs from the most deeply felt experience'. It stated clearly that 'active and imaginative experience and use of the language should precede attempts to analyse grammatically'.[32] During the 1960s, progressive teachers 'were operating under an invisible license to experiment and explore' and child-centred learning was related to a flexible job market.[33] Moreover, this was becoming the accepted approach in progressive courses at many teacher training colleges.

Radical teachers rejected deficit models of 'cultural deprivation' and the ideas of Basil Bernstein at the Institute of Education that were seen as ascribing a deficient or 'restricted' language to working-class children.[34] In contrast, educationists such as Harold Rosen, author of the pamphlet *Language and Class*, contended that working-class language and speech should be seen as relevant in its own right. For example, Valerie Avery had written her autobiographical book, *London Morning*, as one of Rosen's fifth-form students at Walworth School in London. Rosen, who gained a persuasive voice on the left, reasoned that English teachers

> must engage with working class life and learn to apply our educated ears to its voice, with the same respect, awareness of nuances and human warmth we have applied so readily elsewhere.[35]

He lamented that progressive and socialist opinion had often seen only ugliness in working-class life, complaining that 'more is known by scholars about late West Saxon than about cockney of the Seventies'.[36] In a similar vein, as a trainee teacher in Brighton Worpole had listened to Leila Berg speak about her books for children which embraced working-class life, for example her Nippers series. Both Berg and Rosen had argued within the Communist Party for the cultural recognition of working-class life, and Rosen had resigned in 1957 over the Party's condescension towards working-class culture.[37] Attempting to improve the cultural level of the working class without first examining its configurations and strengths was an anathema to Rosen. Indeed, Party members had long been perplexed by the apparent conundrum that not all the working class had been immersed in cultural activity, yet it was the force that was meant to deliver emancipation.[38] However, in its early years the Fed would be promoted by the Party as part of a new outlook based upon an assertion of working-class culture. Specifically, the Morning Star was the only national newspaper to take the writing and publishing groups seriously, giving a generous amount of space to debate and reviews.[39]

Voice of the people

Young people's writing was not sealed off from older people, who also became involved in Basement Writers and other workshops. Although 1960s radical culture tended to be iconoclastic, stressing an absolute break with the past, it conversely generated an interest in radical traditions. The early years of the Fed were to coincide with an attempt to democratise the practice of history through autobiography, oral history and people's history. More diffusely, the radical culture of the 1960s and early 1970s included a desire to relate to working-class memory. There was an implicit sense of the need to capture something that was vanishing. The specific, everyday lives and thoughts of ordinary people took on great importance. It was an impulse shared by many older people themselves. For instance, this poem was found by a nurse at the bedside of an elderly patient:

Kate's Poem

What do you see nurses
    what do you see?
Are you thinking
    when you're looking at me
A crabbit old woman
    not very wise,
Uncertain of habit
    with far-away eyes
Who dribbles her food
    and makes no reply
...

> I'm a small child of ten
>   with a father and mother,
> Brothers and sisters
>   who love one another,
> A young girl at sixteen
>   with wings on her feet,
> Dreaming that soon now
>   a lover she'll meet.
> A bride soon at twenty,
>   my heart gives a leap
> Remembering the vows
>   that I promise to keep.
> At twenty five now
>   I have young of my own
> Who need me to build
>   a secure, happy home.
> A young woman of thirty
> ...
> But inside this old carcase
>   a young girl still dwells,
> And now and again
>   my battered heart swells.
> I remember the joys,
>   I remember the pain,
> And I'm loving and living
>   life over again.
> I think of the years
>   all too few – gone too fast,
> And accept the stark fact
>   that nothing can last.
> So open your eyes nurses,
>   open and see,
> Not a crabbit old woman,
>   look closer – see ME![40]

Older people chose to express their lives and feelings through poetry and prose, not just autobiography. Experimentation across history, fiction, and poetry was to be a particular feature of the Fed. The willingness to listen attentively and to express this in writing breached academic and cultural boundaries.

A consciously working-class perspective informed new initiatives. Greg Wilkinson, an original member of Commonword in Manchester, produced the Lifetimes series of books with a group on the Partington overspill estate, which included a mix of interviews and writing. A contributor to Lifetimes, 'Sarse', presented an historical viewpoint at a time of momentous social change: 'we'll never come back to the position we are leaving. We are coming to the end of an era.'[41] He had honed a keen sense of history:

> When I was working on building sites I found a number of old pipes and other things. And I would often think 'what were the men thinking who smoked these clay-pipes?' ...
>
> And you can get a middle class person, or somebody from university, who can come along and write about what they assume were the attitudes of working people. But I felt this was an opportunity to record what it was actually like to live, not from an intellectual point of view but from a working class point of view.[42]

An impulse behind Lifetimes was the use of personal experience to challenge professional authority. As a middle-class 'welfare' worker living in Partington, Wilkinson was also sceptical about 'all the surveys, programmes, explanations and theories' that emanated from experts, professionals and even socialists. He called for 'a move to enable working people to define their own experience ... their own words. Not simply to provide raw material for others to refine, evidence for others to interpret, but to find their own forms.'[43] A reviewer in the *Oral History Journal* was to note that Lifetimes did not fit easily into existing models. They were neither simply source material for academic research nor actual histories but rather an attempt to build a sense of community in the present.[44]

The project of recording can thus be seen in relation to concepts of counter-cultural practice in radical circles in the 1960s and 1970s which was to introduce new topics to academic subjects. The Fed was closely aligned with a growing interest in oral history that was stimulated by an uneasy feeling that the past was rapidly seeping out of public consciousness. Jeremy Seabrook described this process in *What Went Wrong?*, a book that fascinated members of QueenSpark in Brighton, who carried out a 'collective review' with the author.[45]

Non-academic work, particularly in radio and theatre, had preceded the 1970s activity in oral history. Examples include Ronald Blythe's *Akenfield* and George Ewart Evans's oral history of East Anglian farm workers which originated with his radio programmes.[46] Tony Parker's interviews with marginalised people offered further possibilities. Charles Parker's *Radio Ballads*, from 1958 to 1964, were innovative in their use of direct working-class speech and song, by Ewan MacColl and Peggy Seeger, to evoke aspects of working-class life, for instance in *The Ballad of John Axon* and *The Big Hewer*.[47] In the 1970s, however, community publishing groups were to apply this approach to a new form, that of booklets with photographs which were essential in unlocking memory (see figure 2). Again these would draw on existing models. John Berger and Jean Mohr's *A Fortunate Man*, for example, had used text and photographs to analyse the life of a middle-class doctor and his relationship with patients in a rural working-class area, the Forest of Dean.[48] Fed books such as *Working Lives Two* (Centerprise) and QueenSpark's *Brighton on the Rocks*, which opens with a quote from *A Fortunate Man*, modified this format, with the latter reviewed sympathetically by Berger. Greg Wilkinson also corresponded with Berger while producing Lifetimes. In addition, the north-eastern group Strong Words worked with photographers Richard

2 QueenSpark publicity inviting people to share their photographs and memories.

Grassick and Sirkka-Liisa Konttinen as well as 'Amber', a film and photography group representing working-class communities.[49]

A more general radical impetus within labour history contributed to the Fed. During the 1970s, the History Workshop movement published research by worker students from Ruskin College and ran yearly conferences that welcomed enthusiasts and academics. The Fed set itself up on a parallel track to this workshop movement, which aimed to draw together a number of history groups.[50]

A conference on childhood in the early 1970s directly led to the formation of a group in Hackney:

> The scales fell away from our eyes; we were converted. We came back to Hackney and decided to start a WEA class on local history that we would call 'A People's Autobiography of Hackney'.[51]

The History Workshop comprised diverse radical clusters, some with direct links to emerging writing and publishing groups, such as the East Bowling History Workshop. Many of the academics in QueenSpark Books were centrally involved and organised conferences in Brighton. Subsequently, these close relations were to dwindle as the History Workshop became increasingly critical of experiential writing and a schism appeared in the way radical culture was conceived by the two groupings.[52]

Labour movement and beyond

A number of Federation autobiographies were written by rank-and-file workers in the labour movement. People in the Fed learnt about cultural traditions through involvement with the Labour and Communist parties.[53] Strong Words was a more politically motivated group that aimed to be openly socialist. In the 1970s, the idea that another depression was looming led activists to interview older people about their memories of the 1930s, published in *Hello, Are You Working?* and *But the World Goes on the Same*.[54] Thus, while the Fed can be traced to the more recent counter-cultural left, it also came out of the 'traditional' labour movement. Yet it was to express dissatisfaction with the limitations and narrowness of the culture of the left. The frustrations of many socialists found an outlet in cultural and expressive spheres of life.

This was displayed in the magazine *Voices*, which Ben Ainley developed from classes he taught on Literature and Marxism under the auspices of the Communist Party in Manchester in 1971–72. Ainley believed in the power of literature and the need to give workers the opportunity to immerse themselves in the very best literature. The aim of the class was 'to discuss literature on the basis of a Marxist analysis, and to encourage free and original expression by the class members'.[55] This was to be the basis for the magazine as well, the first issue of which appeared in 1972. However, *Voices* soon widened its remit and encouraged people nationally to send in contributions. The emphasis was very much on experimentation, although Ainley envisaged the emergence of a literature with a political purpose:

> our writing was not yet a manifesto, or a call to action, but a series of individual utterances. Later perhaps a more unified and challenging character may emerge in future collections.[56]

Voices magazine was sponsored by a long list of trade unionists, academics and politicians, including playwright Arnold Wesker, trade unionist Jack Jones (Transport and General Workers' Union), folk singer Ewan MacColl, poet Adrian Mitchell, sociologist Peter Worsley and educationist Brian Simon. Ainley was part of the Unity of Arts network that set itself up as a response to Trades Union Congress (TUC) Resolution 42. This had called for recognition of 'the importance of the arts in the life of the community and looked for greater participation by the trade union movement in all cultural activities', a resolution that Arnold Wesker had originally convinced the television and technicians union, the Association of Cinematograph, Television and Allied Technicians (ACTT), to sponsor in 1960. Ainley's extraordinary campaigning capacity was one reason for the success of Voices. Rick Gwilt, who was to become editor in 1977, recalled Ainley's pragmatism:

> Ben used to go to labour movement organisations like trade union branches, shop steward committees, co-op member relations committees, maybe even Labour Party branches ... and used to say, 'Resolution 42 calls on the movement, blah blah blah, what we are doing about it is ... what we want you to do is to agree to take twenty copies of Voices, whatever, ten copies of Voices, five copies'. That's what he did. He was brilliant at it. I think one of the strengths of the Communist Party was that it knew that if you are going to do anything, you probably had to start in quite a small way ... find little chinks of light, little bits of achievement to build on. So Ben and people like him were good at creating big snowballs out of little stones. That's what they did turning Resolution 42 into Unity of Arts into Voices.[57]

Gwilt himself was keen to publish material that experimented with personal experience, and he was struck by the work of Scotland Road, which he saw as an authentic working-class group whose writing contrasted with the more convoluted examples being submitted to Voices.

From 1980 to 1984, when it was discontinued, Voices acted as the national voice for the Fed. It also stimulated London Voices, which was initially set up as a reading group for the magazine but gradually developed into a writing group. However, Voices lost its links with the labour movement partly by becoming so closely associated with the Fed and also because, despite informal support from some individuals, such as Norman Willis, general secretary of the TUC from 1984 to 1993, the trade unions never formally developed cultural work.[58] The lack of union response was to be a continuing source of frustration to those in the Fed who wanted closer connections with organised labour.

The trajectory that Voices travelled took it some distance from Wesker's original vision. Wesker himself had been angered by the snobbery of theatre audiences; his response to Resolution 42 was to set up Centre Fortytwo, which aimed to develop working-class audiences for the arts through festivals, and later at the Roundhouse in Camden. Rejecting both the concept of a self-contained 'working-class culture' and the view that the arts were class based, Wesker's festivals included people like W. H. Auden, Benjamin Britten and Joan Littlewood.[59]

Alan Sinfield observed that Centre Fortytwo had the same ambiguous relation to the working class as the New Left subculture of the 1950s and 1960s. Wesker's project consisted of 'relatively political and hopefully accessible instances of high culture' cobbled together with 'bits of current student sub-culture' but only 'uncertain gestures towards the creativity of working people'.[60] This final point was to be taken up by the Fed.

Community organising

For many of the activists in Brighton, leftist political ideas were blended with a range of immediate community issues. They were interested in organising people in a locality rather than a workplace. QueenSpark emerged out of a community-based campaign that successfully prevented the Royal Spa being turned into a casino and luxury hotel; the group put pressure on the council to establish a nursery school instead. In the process, they started a community newspaper to discuss issues of concern. The name 'QueenSpark' was a play on Queenspark, the local park and neighbourhood, but surreptitiously borrowed from Lenin's paper *Iskra (The Spark)*.[61] Several members had been involved in a May Day Manifesto group, which underscored leftist disillusionment with the Labour government, and wanted to federate across socialist groupings. Mothers with young children were particularly active participants who helped to sustain the movement, and the educational focus was in line with their concerns.[62]

The invocation of 'community' which manifested itself in Brighton was also part of a more general preoccupation with 'a yearning for social wholeness, a mutuality and interrelatedness', an ambiguous idea which inevitably took on a retrospective dimension.[63] QueenSpark and other groups consciously occupied this territory. Books were developed out of Molly Morley's compilations of residents' memories in the newspaper, under the heading 'Sparchives'. After the first autobiography sold over 1,000 copies in a few months, publishing developed a momentum of its own. This body of writing would authenticate and promote a neglected version of the past through the prism of autobiography and oral history.

Centerprise was one of the pioneering groups that engaged in community organisation. It was set up in the wake of the failure of the Hoxton Café Project in the 1950s which, contrary to intentions, had isolated young people from their community and even encouraged 'delinquency'. A group of people from this project and the ILEA Area Youth Offices worked out a new vision in 1969. A black draft dodger from the USA, Glenn Thompson, was a key originator of Centerprise who imported ideas from US black and community politics.[64] A quasi-trading context with a bookshop and café in which young and older people would intermix was envisioned. The name Centerprise itself originated from the idea of fusing community activity and commercial enterprise.[65] Very much in the style of the 1960s, the group questioned the boundaries between supposedly discrete activities:

the arts, youth and community work, social work and education itself, are not separate entities invariably requiring different institutions. They are related and interdependent.[66]

In order to break down barriers between different activities, Centerprise would set up not only welfare advice services but also publishing via the People's Autobiography of Hackney from 1972, adult literacy in the Hackney Reading Centre from 1975 and the Hackney Writers' Workshop, which would continue to meet until the early 1990s. Together they formed a mutually supportive cluster.

The bookshop was the only one in the borough, an illustration of the way that culture was geographically demarcated. In 1971, an article in the *Bookseller* predicted the shop's inevitable failure. Yet the first year's turnover was £30,000, which represented sales of 75,000 books,[67] and it thrived well into the twenty-first century. Unlike some other community initiatives, Centerprise catered to a wide range of interests, stocking not just political books. The organisation's 1975 Annual Report included its contribution to the Redcliffe-Maud Enquiry on Arts Patronage and foreshadowed its vision of a bookshop

> as a venture needing assistance so we can get away from the WH Smith model, in which books are simply commodities which are self-explanatory, towards a newer idea of a bookshop as an active outgoing service to the community, as well as a place where people can come along, browse, talk, ask advice and feel at home.[68]

The bookshop was to provide a context in which publishing would flourish. While Centerprise might sell thirty copies of a bestseller, it would shift 1,500 copies of a local autobiography. This created new readers and helped to break down the exclusive image attached to books and bookshops.[69] Another community publisher, Peckham Bookplace, would follow suit by basing its work partly around bookshops. Fed groups also benefited from the mushrooming community and alternative bookshops that were eager to sell their publications.

In developing this work, Fed groups were drawing on a range of radical movements. Ideas of non-violent direct action in India and the USA combined with community organising. For example, Saul Alinsky had outlined models and methods for community organisers in the USA.[70] The emerging black consciousness movements, with their assertion of cultural dignity, also led to an emphasis on the radical potential of cultural activity. The links between personal and political liberation were being actively explored. The US Civil Rights Movement raised the idea of the 'oppressed' asserting a subjectivity and self-consciously using 'I'. This interconnection was also part of the American New Left heritage and was to be taken up by the emerging women's liberation movement. Many of the young radicals involved in the Fed were convinced of the need for both social and individual liberation. Comparable political attitudes cropped up in the leftist organisation Big Flame in 1969, where several members of future Fed groups cultivated their beliefs.

Another inspiration was Danilo Dolci, who had organised poor communities in Sicily to challenge the government and mafia through various peaceful means. Dolci's 1955 *Outlaws at Partinico* had caused a stir with its use of statistics on poverty and ill health alongside the transcribed voices of the people themselves, written in Sicilian dialect. The 'strike in reverse' (*sciopero in rovescio*) drew on popular traditions and organised hundreds of people to mend the roads and carry out other improvements; it inhabited a similar universe to a QueenSpark 'plant-in' at the Royal Spa years later.[71] Both Dolci and Alinsky were a part of the tradition of radical Catholic social action. The worker priest movement, in addition to liberation theology, unlike the Marxist left, placed a strong emphasis on community as a source of personal survival. These views were pervasive across worker writer groups, which looked beyond the state and the market to the community as a source of cultural authority.

Adult education

New forms of struggle, many of which were closely tied to adult education, provided a further fount of ideas for the Fed. Nowhere was this more apparent than in Liverpool, where a rent strike erupted in opposition to the 1972 Fair Rent Act. This campaign galvanised residents to see themselves as initiators of change, writing leaflets in the first instance. Some people were already writing and decided they wanted support with setting up a writing group. David Evans, who had been running free classes on literature at Liverpool University's Department of Extension Studies, was approached by a group of students with a request:

> 'Look, we enjoyed looking at literature, but some of us are writers, and we know you are a bit of a writer, a failed writer like ourselves', I think that was the term, 'We can't read our stuff out in pubs and so on, it doesn't go down well there, and it's not the atmosphere. Could you convene a group in which people brought in their writing, and discuss it?' And that's how the Scotland Road Writers' Workshop started.[72]

Evans was on his own for a time, feeling his way in the dark and learning as he went. The members of the group remained politically active, often abandoning the writing group to attend tenants' meetings, which also served as a recruiting ground for new writers. A pamphlet, *Voices of Scotland Road*, drew in new members and caught the attention of other groups around the country, notably Centerprise, with whom they forged an informal alliance. Scotland Road proudly promoted itself as a pioneering working-class writing group and encouraged many others through visits, advice and support. When a group of working-class women in Liverpool heard about Scotland Road they set up their own workshop. Individual writers from Scotland Road, emulating the success of their parent group, formed workshops around the city, such as Keith Birch who set up Childwall Writers. By the mid-1980s, there was a plethora of writing groups in the region, enough in fact to form the Merseyside Association of Writers' Workshops (MAWW).

In the 1970s, the Scotland Road Writers' Workshop was integrally linked to the work of radical educationalists Bob Ashcroft and Keith Jackson in the Department of Extension Studies at Liverpool University. Their courses targeted working-class adults and engaged in social struggles. They operated in the shadow of Paulo Freire, whose educational programmes, based on the lives of peasants in South America, were outlined in *Pedagogy of the Oppressed* and *Cultural Action for Freedom*.[73] The adult educationist was to take sides with working-class people in an act of solidarity:

> The difference between 'them' and 'us' is not broken down by 'learning to speak the language of the natives' but by becoming one of 'us', not in romantic terms, but on issues that really matter.[74]

A sensitivity to cultural expression led to the long-term development of writing groups among people that had previously fallen outside an educational remit. The adult educationist Tom Lovett noted the importance of oral traditions and anecdotes in Liverpool, which meant that educators made use of 'this descriptive, imaginative, person-oriented characteristic' in order to 'explore ideas, concepts and principles without destroying such qualities'.[75]

Second Chance to Learn, an early form of access course established by Big Flame member Martin Yarnit, was to interact closely with the Scotland Road group. The organisers were determined to avoid the trajectory of the Workers' Educational Association (WEA) classes which, they believed, had been rapidly taken over by the middle classes.[76] In 1980 Yarnit commented that in Liverpool, 'a generation of militants ... for whom education is a priority' had emerged from 'a decade of committed adult education'.[77] Scotland Road and other groups had nurtured 'organic intellectuals' in the Gramscian sense, a concept that was to gain some purchase in the Fed.

With a long history of black immigration, Liverpool possessed more than one strand of radical class consciousness, not least in terms of race issues. For instance, Evans facilitated a writing group in Toxteth, which described itself as 'mainly but not exclusively Black, working class and adult'. In 1976 Dorothy Kuya, a worker at the Community Relations Council, had identified the need for a group to encourage people to write 'stories, verse, recollections, plays and polemics'. The Liverpool 8 Writers' Workshop was then seeded at a residential weekend in March 1976 with the support of the Scotland Road group.[78] The work of a diverse group of 'Black' writers, including Frantz Fanon, Walter Rodney, George Lamming, Sam Selvon and Amilcar Cabral, was read.[79] David Evans himself had spent five years in a South African jail for his anti-apartheid stance.

The association between radical forms of adult education and the Fed existed elsewhere. Bristol Broadsides developed in part out of WEA classes on the labour movement and other groups that recorded people's memories in the Barton Hill area, which led to the publication of Bristol As We Remember It, selling 3,000 copies.[80] This work was stimulated by a boat trip down the canal as a prompt to tape-record the memories of those who had known its past life in servicing iron and cotton industries.[81]

Literacy

During the 1970s, adult literacy was also widening the scope of adult education. The idea of student publishing – that literacy students could write for themselves and other students – flowered in the 1970s. The UK was the first industrialised country to recognise the existence of a 'literacy problem' among a broad section of the population despite the fact that compulsory schooling had been in place for almost a century. A number of individuals and organisations came together around the Right to Read Campaign coordinated by the National Committee for Adult Literacy, including the Russell Committee, local authorities and the British Association of Settlements, and it was given enormous publicity by the BBC, indicative of the growing power of television. In 1974, the Adult Literacy Resource Agency was set up with a grant of one million pounds.[82] Although the issue of adult literacy was marginal, it was symbolic of larger concerns. The 'discovery' of this 'problem' was not just technical but challenged the idea of an 'advanced' society, and the revelation that adults struggled with literacy represented a moment of lost innocence.[83]

Literacy students and their mainly young female tutors were faced with an acute shortage of appropriate reading materials. Many immediately rejected children's books as patronising, for example the Janet and John series, which was associated with failure at school. A few used Centerprise books and other community publications.[84] The only other model was the Liverpool News, which presented issues from the mainstream press in a format palatable to literacy students.[85] In 1974, in order to stimulate discussion about new directions, Sue Gardener called for a 'teaching newsletter for literacy work' that she envisaged would include explanations of legislation and welfare services, topical and political information relevant to working-class people, and student writing based on 'local speech' that would encourage other students and also serve as a means for tutors to keep in contact with each other. Crucially, the paper was to be committed to 'a working class perspective ... worth acting on experimentally'.[86] A number of tutors, dedicated to the idea, self-funded the first issue of Write First Time, a broadsheet-sized newspaper. After numerous fundraising attempts, the Adult Literacy Unit agreed to provide some limited funds for printing and secretarial support – all other work had to be done voluntarily. Alongside the mechanical skills of reading, students needed accessible and relevant material which will talk about their own experience, and help them to formulate their own view of it as distinct from the concepts they inherit from the world's view of them. Only then will we be teaching literacy instead of remedying illiteracy.[87]

Literacy was viewed as a process without end. The urgency and usefulness of the writing, in comparison with the more staid attempts by tutors eager to provide graded reading materials, was rapidly confirmed. The process of writing, often mediated by scribes or tape recorders, was invested with huge potential; it 'transforms you into an active user of literacy and not just a passive receiver'.[88] It was a relatively small step to give students control over the process of publishing as part of the educational process. Tutors and students had to learn these skills together, and the process helped to peel away the 'mystique and authority' of printed texts.[89]

A number of Fed groups would develop this work, including the Hackney Reading Centre, the Peckham Publishing Project and Gatehouse Books. Other literacy groups also started publishing student writing, such as Cambridge House, Blackfriars and CAVE. It is noteworthy that literacy work, specifically the Write First Time group, was started in the mid-1970s and became one of the founder members of the Fed. This created a precedent for other literacy groups to enter later on. A clearly educational and tutor-led national project may have aroused too many suspicions had it attempted to join in the early 1980s.

These tutors had created a unique literacy practice, having started from a practical issue about the availability of reading materials. Many adopted the language experience approach, which utilised the words of students to stimulate learning, and read Freire.[90] They discarded deficit models of education that informed the literacy campaign and the well-intentioned ideas of Peter Clyne, who spoke of the 'adult illiterate' as 'backward' in his evidence to the Russell Committee. Medical metaphors, in which the 'illiterate adult' was afflicted by a kind of illness, were rejected.[91]

In addition, they questioned UNESCO definitions of 'functional literacy' which tended to separate out literacy as a technical skill that needed to be mastered if adults were to function in society by reading notices, directions and instructions. By contrast, 'emancipatory' learning was to take account of the fact that students had a range of skills and life experiences and were able to reflect on political, social and philosophical matters. Gardener distinguished what she called the 'social work approach' from her favoured 'political approach', which saw the student as 'wronged and deprived' and the teacher's job as 'the disturbance and creation of consciousness' to demand 'national recognition of the problem'. She wanted to embrace non-professional teachers as part of a working-class campaign: 'It needs to find a way of creating among students solidarity, mutual help, and the shedding of self-reproach and shame by recognition of a common problem and the growth of indignation.'[92]

Growing up, Gardener had been socialised into the idea of working-class culture; in particular she appreciated the capacity of spoken language to convey a depth of feeling and meaning. Her parents ran WEA classes and Labour Party meetings in their front room and she later drifted naturally to WEA work in Nottingham and Liverpool, where one of her classes made a radio programme using local people's voices. She had listened to the *Radio Ballads* and supported Keith Jackson's view that culture should be a central facet of working-class adult education. From 1975, Gardener would move to Centerprise's Hackney Reading Centre.

Many of the tutors involved in this work were also attracted by feminism, with its focus on talking about personal experience and learning to listen to the subtleties of what people were saying. The idea of organising autonomously in democratically run collective groups became routine in the Fed. Reading the work of writers such as Sheila Rowbotham helped Jane Mace to talk more openly about personal relations, 'validating what you might think of as unimportant or unworthy'.[93]

Technology, culture and tradition

In part these networks had been made possible by the availability of cheap and accessible technology, especially offset litho printers, photocopiers and tape recorders, that would enable 'a completely new kind of history'.[94] Alternative and small-scale publishing expanded in the 1960s and new technologies allowed the past to be re-evaluated.[95] QueenSpark and Bristol Broadsides both developed partly out of community newspapers, which were published with offset litho technology.

The application of new forms of technology was not simply ad hoc. A premise in radical thought was that the media and culture were not neutral in their operation. Marshall McLuhan's *The Medium Is the Message* had a widespread impact in the 1960s, and a similar attentiveness informed Raymond Williams' *The Long Revolution*. Worpole was swayed by the translation of Walter Benjamin's essays 'The work of art in the age of mechanical reproduction' and 'The author as producer'.[96] Overall, the interaction of ideas and technologies fed into the notion that it would be possible to publish 'ordinary' people, and initial experiments were to be successful.

Technological change was attached to a vigorous debate on culture. Mainstream culture was often associated with the middle class, an idea expressed in such books as Nell Keddie's *Tinker, Tailor: The Myth of Cultural Deprivation* and later Sue Braden's *Artists and People*, both of which were discussed in the Fed. Moreover, sociological literature, such as Brian Jackson and Dennis Marsden's *Education and the Working Class*, had documented how educated working-class people entered a cultural limbo because mainstream culture was alien to their working-class background.[97] Writing and publishing workshops assumed that publications would demonstrate a working-class culture that could strip away the distortions of the tabloid press and the elitist arts establishment. For instance, there was outrage when the Greater London Arts Association decided to hold an 'arts festival' by covering Tower Hamlets in posters featuring the work of artists, all of whom were outsiders. They managed to divert some funding to neighbourhood initiatives that included the opening of a bookshop by Tower Hamlets Arts Project (THAP), which would become another Fed member.[98]

Others were not willing to concede that mainstream culture was necessarily middle class. Worpole refused to simply dismiss 'bourgeois culture' and argued that classic authors like Blake, Dickens, Woolf and Auden 'belong to us as much as the contemporary bourgeoisie'.[99] Thus the Fed in its early years echoed the debates of the 1930s, when writers discussed whether working-class and bourgeois culture were distinct or related practices.[100] These disputes were not to find a resolution, and the group that produced *The Republic of Letters* was unable to agree a single position on culture.[101]

Rather than concerning themselves with theoretically coherent statements, in practice groups aimed to widen working-class readership and encourage new writers.[102] Implicitly this notion was informed by the perspective that the working class was the force that would change society and, as such, it was their creativity that should be developed. This implied the acceptance of a variety of overlapping motivations. Tony Harcup, a member of Basement Writers who went on to edit *Leeds Other Paper*, became inspired by the idea of producing culture, a fluid energy that could be channelled in a number of directions: 'Had it been three years later we'd probably have started a DIY punk band instead!'[103] Other writers, such as Alan Gilbey and Tony Marchant, would also adopt a do-it-yourself punk ethic.

In addition, discussions of class and culture were not restricted to small groups of committed socialists. Television was the key medium for reaching general audiences, and new kinds of working-class voices were to be heard there throughout the 1960s and 1970s. Keith Birch, a writer from Scotland Road, elicited the meaning of the *Wednesday Play* for him and his workmates as

> the really good piece of TV that we had, that the working class were involved in ... Everyone used to talk about the *Wednesday Play* ... they felt comfortable talking about it, what they got out of it, and it might be wildly sort of different than anyone else ... it didn't matter. The debate was on. People were being drawn to drama, and its power and everything that it can do.[104]

The use of documentary styles in TV drama by Jim Allen and others, who worked with Ken Loach and Tony Garnett, influenced a new generation of young working-class writers. Jimmy McGovern, who emerged as a playwright from the Scotland Road group, was particularly taken with the plays of Allen, especially *Spongers*, screened in 1978, which challenged the stereotyping of people on benefits.[105]

Though the founders of the Fed situated themselves as part of an ongoing tradition, it became evident that the idea of a continuous working-class culture was overly simplistic. Indeed, subordinate cultural forms have not had a coherent expression; they have been recovered momentarily, surfacing in diverse streams, frequently to vanish again.[106] Roger Mills was a young writer involved with both Centerprise and Basement Writers who avowed that a break in tradition had occurred:

> I think at one time there was the thought that ... that we were carrying on the working-class tradition of writing, going back to Alexander Baron and Bernard Kops and all that. But to be honest, I think the line had been broken, really. I think the people I knew in the Basement weren't really writing as a part of a sense of tradition, they were writing influenced by much newer things, like pop music, pop lyrics, and the Mersey poets, the Liverpool poets, Roger McGough ... And in a response to challenging the things they'd seen on the telly or the films ... I think people create their own art out of lots of different influences from all around them, whether it's from high art, low art or on the buses. Anything.[107]

In reality, teachers were often happy working with popular culture and they emphasised the pupil's urban environment, whereas an earlier generation, including Hoggart and Holbrook, had been critical of it.[108] By positing the idea of a break in tradition, Mills testifies to the fact that experience is not simply transmitted from one generation to the next; rather, it is reinterpreted in new conditions and then related back to previous forms.[109] He offered a fundamentally different approach to mass popular culture which was to find expression in intellectual investigations of football and music. Mills also pointed to a faith in people's ability to break out of the constraints of commercial forms, an assumption widely shared in the Fed.

Building a movement

If *Stepney Words* and the strike provided the spark for the Fed, Centerprise did the most to spread the fire. Chris Searle had set up Basement Writers and established initial contact with the Scotland Road Writers' Workshop after visiting the Scotland Road Free School. Subsequently he went to Mozambique and was not to be much involved in the worker writers' movement thereafter. However, Centerprise had secured funding and created a tangible organisation. It supported people who set up other groups, such as Ian Bild (Bristol Broadsides) and Richard Gray (Peckham Publishing Project).[110] Lydia Meryll (East Bowling History Workshop) attended meetings there as a student, and Roger Kitchen (People's Press) saw possibilities in Milton Keynes after visiting and being impressed by Arthur Newton's *Years of Change*.[111] Brighton's QueenSpark Books adapted Centerprise's work with young people to engage with older people.[112] In the North, Scotland Road and Liverpool 8 had also contributed to a vibrant culture of writing on Merseyside.

From the early 1970s, writing and publishing groups in Liverpool, Hackney and elsewhere were liaising closely with each other. Meetings and readings were complemented by football matches and social activities. After a more informal gathering at Hulme Library in Manchester, the inaugural meeting of the Fed took place at Centerprise in 1976. Each small and seemingly prosaic step in assembling the movement was judged to be tremendously significant to the participants, helping to generate further dynamism. For instance, organising travel so that writers could meet and share their writing was a crucial first step in learning about one another and finding familiarity in other lives:

> very few people actually ever get the chance to travel or to see how people live in other cities or that their experiences are very much in common and so this was terrific ... and it was all done on a shoestring.[113]

The need to express oneself was matched by an interest in listening, and supportive audiences proliferated, for instance, at the E1 Festivals in East London.[114] The launch of *Writing*, the first anthology published by the Federation, featuring contributions from different groups, entranced those who attended. As different writers from around the country read out their work in a range of forms, styles and accents, people gained a cumulative sense of the work being produced. The reading seemingly enabled one to grasp the whole of a movement in its purpose, energy and diversity. The fact that people were reading aloud meant that a real 'voice' infused the writing. The Fed's 1979 Annual Report was enthusiastic about this growing collective impulse:

> readings brought silence. As group after group stood up to introduce its work, the gathering of over a hundred people became electric ... Everyone who stood up to read their own writing was part of a group, and every group was part of a national network. The corporate feeling was unmistakable. Some of the readings were funny; some angry; all, moving. None of the readers were 'professional' writers gaining an income and personal fame from their work. All were gaining strength and illumination from writing. It was an historic literary event.[115]

Infected with this excitement, Worpole sent a postcard to comrades in Brighton suggesting that 'the whiff of an epistemological break was in the air'.[116]

The business annual general meeting (AGM) was incorporated into a weekend of workshops, readings and socialising. The social element became one of the principal factors in sustaining the movement:

> I found it really exciting ... it was the beginning of that culture of sheer enjoyment of weekends away and late nights reading and drinking ... they turned into great festivals, I mean they were great events you looked forward to them all year, it was like a carnival.[117]

Informality became a source of creativity. The workshops were based on what people were doing in their own groups and stimulated dialogue and debate while offering practical guidance. All of these were put on by writers for no payment, which engendered reciprocal learning and an intense interest in the writing:

> people would sit there until two in the morning whilst everyone read, and there was a real thing of, 'I am not going to leave, because you have listened to me, and I will listen to you' ... the early Fed was terribly interested in what everybody else was doing.[118]

Rotating meetings and events around the country helped cement the movement together. Members slept on each other's floors and developed a more meaningful national picture of the writing. Unlike other literature organisations, the Fed included groups from many English cities.[119] Individuals such as Worpole became so motivated and committed that they took personal responsibility for fostering a greater sense of movement, chivvying people to share their work with each other nationally as part of a federated movement.[120]

The personal and political were intermixed. Writing, publishing and organising were part of the personal relationships upon which, in reality, the networks were built. Strong bonds of loyalty and mutual understanding created an environment in which all sorts of relationships blossomed:

> we felt quite welded together by it and you know you could fall in love with each other ... when there is a movement people do find each other's ideas very attractive and do find each other interesting as people ... and so we felt a bit more like a movement.[121]

These energies would sustain a commitment to writing and publication for a number of decades. Writing was always at the centre of the movement, the force and passion that drove people on. Critically assessing the content and value of the work by young people, older people, literacy students and the array of writers in various workshops provides new perspectives on the mental world of working-class people during the 1970s and 1980s.

2 Young people's writing

In the 1970s and 1980s, the work of radical schoolteachers and young people centred upon personal expression. *Stepney Words* reverberated far beyond the school walls throughout society and many other publications followed in its wake. Specifically, it was London, where high numbers of teachers were concentrated within a very diverse context, that provided the focal point for children's writing. Networks of educators, enthused by a love of literature, worked according to the idea that the lives of pupils were a valid basis for cultural expression. As teachers and their networks, such as the London Association for the Teaching of English (LATE), became captivated by writing and publishing with young people, they began to build up a head of steam.[1] Communication was facilitated by the Inner London Education Authority (ILEA), an educational powerhouse that benefited from its scale of operation and supported publishing initiatives. In Liverpool, the Mersey poet Adrian Henri had set up writing workshops as a response to the raising of the school leaving age in 1972, but it proved difficult for isolated practices to gain a foothold.[2]

Educators bestowed great significance upon the writing of young people, which resonated well beyond schools. Its qualitative, linguistic and textual characteristics provide insights into the nature of literacy and subjectivity among young Londoners at this historical moment. Writers highlighted the educational and social contexts of the 1970s and early 1980s through documentary and literary modes of representation. Students explored their local environment and personal and family histories. The tangible nature of the publications helps us to closely observe the ways in which meaning was constructed.[3] Language experience pedagogy fostered connections between life and learning that, when effective, required dialogue and mutual respect among educators and learners. There were significant prospects for free expression in the journey from the classroom to the workshop. In recognising vernacular language, teachers had to negotiate a tricky set of educational issues, even though they were far removed from the tainted stereotype of uninspiring teaching and low standards which critics presented as ubiquitous across comprehensive education.

Let it flow, Joe!

Stepney Words was published in a burst of excitement that is evident in the opening poem, 'Let it Flow, Joe!':

> Let it flow, Joe.
> Let your feelings speak for you
> Let the people know what you know
>
> Tell the people what it's all about
> Shout it out.
> ...
>
> Paul Ritchens[4]

The spontaneity and urgency of the writing opened doors for others. Yet the enthusiasm was blended with feelings of desolation and lack of self-worth. Pupils communicated their reflections on personal and social changes. Apparently simple poetical statements asserted a sense of individuality that was nevertheless based upon shaky foundations. Pat Kirk wrote:

> Me, I'm myself
> No one in this big
> world is like me.
> I'm different from you
> and everyone else
> I'm just plain old
> me.
> ...
>
> Pat Kirk[5]

Identity is expressed directly and plainly and the poem is also constructed to make the writer appear small in a 'big world'. The final two lines, 'I'm just plain old / me', temper the more robust confidence of the opening line and imply a contingent and fragile self. Being different from everyone else exists in a tension with being 'plain', and both carry opportunities and dangers.

Young writers also demonstrated developing personalities in *As Good As We Make It* (see figure 3). Michelle Balgobin felt frustrated with her lack of power:

> **The year ticks by**
>
> The year ticks by
> Slowly but surely
> ...
> My every thought has to be examined
> And cleansed.
> As the year ticks by,
> Slowly but surely

They will realise that I am
Old enough to think for myself.

Michelle Balgobin[6]

Dual meanings of time are employed in the deceptively obvious line 'the year ticks by', which enables the writer to divide a long stretch of time into almost

3 Centerprise young writers, *As Good As We Make It*. Centerprise created spaces for young people to organise and write.

infinitesimally small units, each of which has to be endured. The time frames of the adult and the young person are placed in direct conflict with one another. Balgobin must wait to be able to 'think for myself', which is paradoxical given that clearly she is able already to express these feelings in poetry. The poem uncovers a world hidden from view. The writer complains of being regulated and controlled, but also exhibits self-assurance. It is a call to be listened to while she waits endlessly for the adult world to catch up and accept her independence.

Young writers also delved into their immediate surroundings of school and teachers. Once again, the simple statement could have a wider impact:

The old school

The school is old, and all tumbled down.
The bricks are as black as coal.
The paint is peeling off the walls
And the floors are rotting away.
...

Mary Lyon[7]

This poem bears out the social and psychic impact of the school building and its architecture.[8] It is hard to read this as simply a set of factual statements rather than a critique of schooling. Although the poem draws attention to physical structures, it implicitly questions the meaning of education. Negative uses of the past – the building is 'old' – help to establish that the school has not changed with the times. The claim that it is 'all tumbled down', if taken literally, would imply a heap of rubble, but instead is followed by closely observed material descriptions of the school.

More distant historical events provided a further source of inspiration. Empathy and criticism could be combined, incorporating analyses of wide-ranging issues. The poem 'Soldier' brings together common attitudes about the futility of war with class relationships:

Soldier

I was a soldier
A cockney soldier
A man that was born to die
Only cockney blokes get killed
Stuffy officers stay back safely.

I was a soldier
A cockney soldier
Before I died on the hill
With a bullet in my heart
I clawed my way to hell.

My brother was a soldier.
A bloody good soldier.

He was born to die.
But he died being shot
Climbing over the wire back to our trenches.
We both met in hell.

Colin Graves[9]

The poet positions himself as reflecting back on life. Later we learn he is already dead, yet able to comment on his living self. Cockney soldiers were 'born to die', a despondent thought compounded by the fact that 'I clawed my way to hell'. By mixing up tenses, we are led to ask why he would claw his way to hell before he died. No other choices are offered. It then descends further into an abyss when we discover that his brother, a 'bloody good soldier', has also died: 'We both met in hell'. This is an unexpected outcome for 'good' soldiers, and no escape is available from the class system that predetermined their fate. Despite the fact that the poem is historically inaccurate, that a higher percentage of officers died in the First World War, it nevertheless pinpoints sharp class differences exposed by the war. The writer speaks as one of the damned in cascading destruction, defeat and tragedy and wants to undermine the value of war itself.

In practice, the process of writing was lightened by an embrace of popular culture and the more immediate concerns of the writers. Many texts exude a linguistic freshness, especially for those new to writing. The diversity of spoken language provided a rich resource for writers. The Black Ink collective in Brixton worked with young people who wrote about cultural trends in new ways. The following poem by a fifteen year old reveals close familiarity in describing an African-Caribbean cultural experience:

Domino

Mi enta de club, it waz quiet;
Mi start fe mek me way up de stears
Mi ear noize
Ellis, Brown, Porter an Findley play domino.

Ellis atel Findley fi rub it up
Findley atel im fe shut up;
Brown atel Findley fe play
Porter noh se noting.
...

Rose Porter[10]

The writer is observing the detail of what is, for her, a commonplace experience, and invites the reader to share it. Cultural specificity is directly conveyed through language. The first two lines lower our expectations: nothing surprising is happening, 'me enta de club'. The prosaic and detailed description allows us to stop the clock and look at the world in slow motion while building expectation.

Straight description becomes a creative process. The silence is broken by a noise as we are introduced to a setting suspended in time. The rapid succession of actions, as the four players interact, cleverly mirrors the casting of dominos.

Language was debated in a context where education and culture overlapped directly. While many proponents of young people's writing directly encouraged the use of slang and non-standard language, teachers were also wary of losing contact with standard English. Black Ink disputed this point: the poet Linton Kwesi Johnson argued that vernacular language helped to develop personal identity and demanded recognition for cultural difference, while others wanted translations or recordings to be produced alongside written texts so that readers would be better able to understand how dialect was being constructed and relate it to standard English.[11] This fed into more expansive discussions about the role of vernacular language in education.[12] There were parallels in the approaches to Caribbean poetry pursued by Edward Braithwaite, who broke with European traditions, and Derek Walcott, whose work remained more within mainstream literature although, once again, there were links between the two.[13]

Groups such as the Basement Writers combined linguistic playfulness with an anarchical element of humour that resembled Unity Theatre-style pantomimes rather than Marxist cultural theory. Alan Gilbey remembered one of the performances that did not go down too well with more serious leftists:

> a hilarious Top of the Pops parody sketch ... The audience had come to see hard-hitting, East End poems. They got to watch Chris Searle dressed up as Lena Zavaroni, singing, 'Ma They're Throwing Eggs [Eyes?] At Me'.[14]

Politicised inspiration mingled with an informal youth culture. Gilbey himself was absorbed by comics, preferring to read *The Beano* than attend school. He would produce his own cartoon strips that parodied local developments such as the transformation of Wapping and East London – see figure 4. Later, Gilbey would go on to pursue a successful career in animation.

Other young people adapted ideas and themes from popular culture. Joe Ackerman's *The Kids Are Alright* is a fictional account of a young boy and his daily relationships that incorporates song lyrics. The ending departs from a 'typical' story in that the protagonist does not 'get the girl' and the words in his head eventually become an irritant:

> Joe frowned darkly.
> > *If never I'd held you ...*
> > *My feelings would never sho ...*
> > *Each time I start talking, but ...*
>
> 'Belt up!' Joe shrilled. 'F'r--- sake, jus' belt up, ya noisy bastards!'[15]

The narrator turns in on himself in taking control of the story. How far the presence of teachers influenced texts is hard to judge, though it is not impossible to imagine this outcome eliciting adult approval.

4 Extract from an Alan Gilbey cartoon, printed in *Writing*, critiquing the redevelopment of the London docks.

Writers also adapted the romance format in books, such as Chelsea Herbert's *In the Melting Pot*, where she described a relationship with a new boy on the block to help 'put you in the picture of what goes on in and around our community'.[16] This quote exposes mixed purposes in describing a geographical area through the prism of personal relations. English teachers recalled the enormous popularity of this text among teachers and children.[17] Similarly, in *Teenage Encounters* Stella Ibekwe explored romantic relations but revealed her own learning process in both acting out expected roles and understanding and criticising the way she reproduced them. Elements of fantasy could be grounded in young peoples' lives and frequently merged into documentary styles, in contrast to formulaic romance novels.[18]

Migration and writing

Newly arrived children from across the world were also writing, and they broke with convention in different ways. Initially teachers were surprised that children from immigrant families wrote so much, although they came to appreciate that it was a means for them to come to terms with difficult and life-transforming experiences. The sharp break in the lives of young migrants meant that they immediately had a history very distinct from their current situation. A heightened vision, alongside new perspectives on both old and new selves, arose from such a disjunction. Changed circumstances stimulated comparisons between past and present and a fascination with retrieving the small details and the rhythms of daily life, some of which were already fading out of focus. Arriving and living in Britain and pursuing new life chances while confronting prejudice offered fresh perspectives on the society in which they had settled.[19] As they came to represent their changing experiences through writing, they manipulated language and remade their lives on the page. Personal accounts of movement were linked to events of world significance and even war. Escaping from traumatic events could appear to be almost arbitrary, a matter of luck:

> My life has been sad, horrible and lonely … When we left the city [Phnom-Penh] it was ruined and people were dying and dead along the road. The corpses were starting to smell.[20]

Simply recounting sight and smell was enough to position the young writer in a very different place to that usually associated with schoolchildren. Sensual stimulation was connected to global conflicts which increasingly found their way into the classroom.

The memory of leaving a country could be intensified through the process of recounting and reliving it in writing. The meaning of moving to a new country might not always be understood clearly; it was a leap in the dark for which there were no reference points in the young person's life:

> Mother told me one day that we were going to go to England soon, and I asked her where that was. She said it was a place where white people lived.[21]

Innocence serves as a distancing device, with both nation and skin colour reinforcing difference. Rather than locating 'England' on a map, it 'was a place where white people lived', a statement that helped to conjure up an estranged space. In part this reflected the necessity of helping a child to comprehend wider social forces of which they were unaware.

The divide between past and present was not only an objective determining force, it also offered a basis for an active construction of meaning about the self. Paul George, in *Memories*, recounted his past in Grenada in prose but chose poetry to describe his life in England, underlining the discontinuity he experienced in moving from the Caribbean. His childhood was lived close to nature, with friends, family and stories:

> On the way home we played games in the road. There was no pavements or sidewalks. We walked in the middle of the road and just stepped aside when the cars blared their horns.
>
> When we reached home we did our work: fetch water, get firewood, go to the shop. We did not have pipes in our house or electricity. We cooked on an open fire. Every night we told Anansi stories before sleeping, like the hen, the cockroach and the rice and peas. Bengy used to tell us a lot of stories but Uncle Hayes always said he lied. He always used to frighten us, tell us about spirits and people who came to take children in the night to sell. We always said our prayers before going to sleep.
>
> There was always fruit to eat. If one was not in season another was.[22]

George describes a condition of material shortages in which much time is taken up with survival. Moving away from this past has allowed him to view the routines of a previous existence from a critical distance. It is a bearable life with many consolations in which he and his family are part of nature itself. Storytelling is woven into the pattern of this life, which exemplifies regularity and timelessness. The landscape passes into the people who, in turn, blend back into the landscape. The narration here is reminiscent of George Lamming's *In the Castle of My Skin* or, more diffusely, the work of Thomas Hardy.[23]

In contrast, George's poetry relates to his feelings in a new world while beginning to nurture pride in his heritage, which is now isolated and malleable. He charts the past–present relation in 'Once Upon a Time', with life in England presented as false and dangerous while also offering some opportunity:

> I once walked the road bare feet.
> Now I walk in high heeled shoes.
> I cannot feel the ground under me.
>
> I once climbed trees
> That swayed with the slightest breeze
> Now I climb steps
> That reach to the sky.
>
> I once ate fruit,
> Fresh and pure.
> But now I eat out of cans.

> I once walked the night
> Me and my brothers
> Now I walk my room
> For it is unsafe for I.
>
> I once knew life
> I now know
> Life is what you make it.
>
> Paul George[24]

The short statements juxtapose then and now. Some of George's most poetic phrases, such as 'walked the night', provide continuity with the previous piece of work. Yet the safe and known life has disappeared in England. The movement is not only from the familiar to the unknown in a new country; it also encompasses growing into young adulthood as well as a shift from a rural to an urban environment. In his new world everything is constructed and to some extent false. His situation is insecure, but he recognises the potential to make his own future – an altered emphasis on 'making' things. The final line, 'Life is what you make it', problematises his distinction between the natural and unnatural. He points to a contradictory new world where reality cannot be known, only made. Given the difficulties he has already outlined, we are left to ponder whether this will be possible. Thus, the move from nature and the natural is riddled with ambiguities. On one level, George invokes a long tradition of seeing the rural as pure and real and the city as false and corrupt, which stretches back to Jean-Jacques Rousseau and beyond; however, his writing and life experience brought confusion to the dualism.[25]

The childhoods and communities that were recalled in children's writing bore some resemblance to those found in older people's memories of pre-war Britain, in which community and caring were perceived to be more widespread, a tendency examined in the next chapter. For Ranjit Sumal, in *Back Home*, the privatised and individualised lifestyles in Britain were found wanting in comparison with the extended family and village life in India:

> I remember when we first came to England everything <u>was</u> entirely different. People passed by without a word ...
>
> Sometimes I would cry for we knew no-one. All we were was one small family in the home my father bought when he first came on his own. A few relatives were lodging upstairs but still there wasn't enough of us. Not like it used to be, a big house where you could wander all on your own ... Everything here was full of privacy ...
>
> Everyone in England works as an individual and so keeps everything private which wasn't at all the way our grandparents brought us up ... Here it is not at all a free world. Each one looks after himself and not his neighbour as it used to be in our village.[26]

Sumal is eager to recreate and defend a past based upon receding memories. He connects individual freedom to supportive familial structures that offer physical and personal space and, in doing so, challenges the popular assumption that anonymous urban spaces provide a context for self-determination. This perspective was also exacerbated by the separation of many migrants from their extended families and the exclusion from institutions in the host society that might have provided such authentication and support.

In an isolated context, the family could take on significance as a sanctuary against racism and prejudice, a place where better relations could be lived out and individuals could flourish. For example, in *Small Accidents* Sabir Bandali argued that

> Home was by far the best place. There, I didn't have to obey tedious regulations; I didn't have to get involved in stupid, unpleasant brawls. Everything made sense at home. I knew my right place; I knew what would happen if I so much as swore. Home was always a small, almost ideal society. It wasn't completely perfect because it was made of human beings and these have a tendency to contradict one another a lot.[27]

Clear-cut domestic parameters became confused and potentially dangerous in interactions with other students. Bandali presents the home as an island of peace as well as a utopian space for thinking about the future. It is a safe place away from the overt racism that was more prevalent at this time. Black feminists in particular would develop such arguments against those who associated the private sphere with the oppression of women.[28] Interestingly, Bandali's final sentence is characteristic of his detached and formal style of writing, which reflects different expectations about adolescence and reveals an early maturity in the absence of the youth culture of his peers.

Maturity became a necessity when young people had to take on responsibilities in complex familial settings. Writing could clarify experiences and play a therapeutic role for those faced with handling a new world. For example, when Zohra El Kssmi arrived unexpectedly from Morocco, her relatives 'were surprised to see me because they knew nothing about it'.[29] She did not idealise her past and was glad to leave Morocco, as it released her from difficult family relations. In thinking about her life, she described her relationship with her mother in a detached manner, presenting more than one perspective:

> When I came to England to live with my mother, she was ever so nice to me ... suddenly everything changed for the worse ... She sometimes used to get extremely annoyed just about little things ... Maybe this was because she did not bring me up herself and therefore when she realised I was different to what she had expected, and was growing up in a different way to hers, she then tried hard to assert her leadership by becoming authoritarian ...
>
> Before I became used to her behaviour, I used to blame her a lot for it and the thought of leaving her for ever was forming in my mind. I even had to see my social worker several times for advice in order to solve my situation. I can understand my mother's point of view now. She behaves so strictly towards me so that I can grow up

to be a reliable person, able to face up to hardships on my own, and to be obedient, which might come in handy later on in my life when taking up a career.[30]

El Kssmi has switched roles and is approaching writing from an adult standpoint, seeking advice from her social worker as an independent source of information rather than as a figure of power. The text recalls the shortened childhood faced by many children. She negotiates feelings, emotions and familial relations that are at once public and private. The separation of families meant that relations had to be reconstructed in ways that bridged cultural divides. The fact that it is a written rather than a spoken account amplifies its formality.[31] In addition, for some writers whose first language was not English, their main experience of learning to write may have been largely based on the classroom, and it was sometimes difficult to control the narrative according to the expectations of the host society. Writing 'correctly' took precedence over dialect and accent. The assumed and actual readers were peers, teachers and parents who could all exert an influence over the writer, and an attempt was made to write in an exemplary way.

Longer works

An expanding culture of recognition encouraged young people to take risks with their writing and some produced longer pieces of writing, both autobiographical and fictional. Three of these accounts, *The Gates* by Leslie Mildiner and Bill House, the anonymous *Jackie's Story* and *A Comprehensive Education* by Roger Mills, were all published by Centerprise.

The Gates was written by two schoolboys who did not fit the stereotype of 'good' pupils.[32] Through a partly fictional account, they addressed issues of truanting and 'problem' children. In writing such a protracted piece of work – a real book – the authors staked a claim for the importance of their lives. The novel is both a social document and a work of fiction that provoked a discussion about school phobia:

> When I was ill I remember thinking I was the only person in the world with a problem like mine. So we wrote this book to show phobics that they are not alone, and there is hope ... to show parents that when their child will not go to school ... then he or she will not just be having 'that Monday morning feeling' or 'lazyitis'.[33]

Inevitably, the narrative betrays a tension between showing and telling. The account was personal to the writers themselves, with the use of the third person helping to establish distance from difficult experiences. By transferring feelings and emotions to a fictional character, the writers were able to try out different ideas. Moving to secondary school was a shockwave:

> Geoffrey Moller approached the gates of Elgan Comprehensive School. He hated everything to do with school. How he dreaded those mornings when he sat nervously on the corner of his bed and literally shook with fear ... At one time he had

been safe, safe inside the shell of Stanford Primary School. But now – that shell had opened, and Geoff was released from its womb and let out into the noisy, rough hell-world of Elgan Comprehensive – a world he was not ready for.[34]

The importance of these educational transitions, represented as a rebirth, would gain more recognition in future years. Sometimes the effects of facing the 'noisy, rough hell-world' were both psychological and physical: 'dizzy spells ... attacks of being short of breath ... agoraphobia ... too terrified to step out of the house for fear he would stop breathing and die'. Literally and metaphorically, the large black gates surrounding the school incarcerated the young mind. It was a fear that won over the logical side of David Cook, the other character:

all David could think about as they got closer and closer were those big black iron gates, and the thought of being behind them like a prisoner ... Then his mind went blank, except for one thought. And that was to get away, escape.

He could still remember his mother screaming, 'Come back', and he could still feel his heart racing. It seemed as if he ran forever that terrible day.[35]

Fleeting moments of crisis are relived and exhibit layers of need, guilt and incomprehension. Contrary states of fear and reason wax and wane:

he looked back at the class and shuddered. Should he go in or should he run away?

'Hi' said a voice behind him. He looked round and saw a young man with a beard and long hair and spectacles, smiling at him.

'You must be David Cook', he said in a faint Canadian accent.

'Yes', answered the surprised David.

'I'm Lawrence Dane, the school psychotherapist. I've been standing here for quite a while. You were wondering whether to go in or not, weren't you?'

David looked back at the class.

'Yes I was', he answered slowly.

'Why?' asked Mr Dane.

'I don't know, I just can't seem to go in'.

'Why, what's so bad about it?'

David shrugged his shoulders. 'I don't really know', he answered.[36]

The Gates was based on direct experience that could be outwardly described but not easily understood from the inside. The mystery is sustained as the reader glides over the veneer of characters without being allowed to plumb the depths of their inner psyches. Subjectivity is both built up and contained via stonewalling, which allows for some protection. This helps to portray the turmoil in two boys who are self-aware yet unable to fully articulate their feelings. The well-intentioned professional who is working outside the normal school boundaries is given the benefit of the doubt and represented as a positive figure. As a Canadian, he is familiar enough and, as an outsider to English class culture, he can perhaps be trusted.

The characters are constructed through routine interactions. For example, relations with girls are represented in a way that would have been absent from more formal textbooks, even given an element of fantasy:

> The two girls looked up. They were both about fourteen years old. The smaller one had big blue eyes, a small nose and long brown hair which hung down nearly reaching her waist. She gave a smile when Geoff said the wittiest thing he could think of.
> 'Wanna lick of my lolly?'
> She blushed slightly and looked at the other girl who was also very good-looking ...
> 'What time does your class start?' asked Wendy.
> 'How do you know that I'm in the tutorial?' asked David. 'I could be the plumber come to mend the drains'.
> 'Well I don't see your plunger', she said.
> 'I don't use a plunger, I use my hands'. They all laughed.[37]

The description of fluid social encounters, based upon the preoccupations of schoolchildren, humanise the text and offer a resource for hope in disjointed lives.

The novel also touches on class issues which, although not explored in detail, are introduced through a classroom discussion with a teacher. Individual problems are placed in a social setting:

> Geoff changed the subject. 'How many classes like this are there?' he asked.
> 'There are quite a few. Something like fifty in London. They're mostly scattered around the poorer areas. Like Stepney and places like it.'
> 'Why's that?'
> 'Because most of the problem children come from the poorer areas of London. Not all of them but quite a few.'[38]

The classroom scene enables the authors to return to a documentary style but carries mixed implications. The book finishes positively, with David and Geoff putting on a performance and starting to overcome their fears. They have pride in their school for 'maladjusted' children, recognise difference and confidently reject the notion that they are 'mad'. The process of writing itself had helped to bring about personal change in the authors. At the same time, the class issues raised in the extract above are not drawn out. The reader is left to wonder about the treatment of those in the more leafy suburbs who were not seen as 'problem children', the apparently factual statement pointing to deeper contradictions.

Jackie's Story, written anonymously, details a young woman's life in a 'problem family', truanting from school and her subsequent life in care. She becomes a 'substitute mother' when her own mother becomes ill, taking responsibility for her two brothers while being beaten by her father. After repeatedly skipping school, she is eventually taken into care. In the absence of a family, social workers replace her parents. However, she comes to regret trusting public officials who manipulate informal discussions in unexpected ways: 'I wanted to talk to someone so I told her all of it, stupidly forgetting that last time she hadn't turned out to do quite what I'd expected.'[39] Control over her life is far from assured. Unlike in The Gates, social workers and teachers are presented here as blackmailers who prevent Jackie from seeing her family. On one occasion she is desolate after sneaking out to visit her mother, who turns her away, fearful of the social workers.[40] When Jackie is allowed 'home' for a day she finds herself an outsider, no longer in the family yet not outside it, caught in a limbo between the now alienated private world and the regulated public one.[41]

The book was published with minimal editing. It has a unique style, written as a spoken justification of the immediate past, hardly pausing for breath, jutting from one memory to another, as if everything that is described happened yesterday. The simple past tense is commonly employed by children, yet the experience and feelings recounted here propel the reader into a conflicted adult world.[42] Jackie continues in this manner, describing her life and accounting for daily decisions and actions through a blow-by-blow account in which she lays out precise details of events and her responses to them:

> I went to the shopping centre until dinner time then I went in to get my afternoon mark then I went home. My mum seemed surprised to see me but she didn't ask any questions and the next morning when I came down to breakfast in my normal clothes instead of my uniform she just said she had some shopping for me to do ... My dad got home later ... he walloped me and then he was going to wallop my mum too but there was a ring at the door ... The teacher had wanted to know why I had been to school so irregularly and when I said I didn't like it she said I hadn't even tried it.[43]

This is the narrative of a person forced to explain themselves to people in power and to rule-bound agencies. It resembles a defence, in which she appears as a child witness at her own trial, presenting the reader with the evidence to judge the validity of her case. It is not so much spoken language as an internal voice; having allowed the reader to enter her private thoughts, Jackie then has to work doubly hard to defend her actions and guide her account. There is a naturalistic flow to the text that the author cannot always harness for her own purpose.

Subjective expression was precarious. Survival in this world necessitated self-denial and restraint, partly for fear of getting caught out by arbitrary and unjust officials. In common with many autobiographies by older people, Jackie finds it onerous to express emotion, but it still seeps into her text, as in the following passage where she is deciding whether to attend school:

> my mum said she felt fine and I should go. I didn't want to but she reminded me of the consequences of not going. Nancy [social worker] picked me up and as we were driving along I found I was crying. She didn't say anything but passed me a tissue. I felt embarrassed to be crying in front of her but she didn't seem to mind.[44]

The phrase 'I found I was crying' appears regularly in the text.[45] Going into care, she is stripped of the little power she had and feels intense frustration, turning in on herself while also growing a 'protective layer' and crying herself silently to sleep.[46] She blocks an impulse to open up to her feelings, which are too painful mentally and physically – a visceral and potentially explosive tension. Dreaming is a way of doing this, while putting up the shutters on the outside world:

> I lay on my bed and thought of as little as possible, if I thought of home and the past I wanted to cry and scream and wanted to get out of there so much it made me shake. If I thought of the future I was scared of what would happen, I felt just like a prisoner, alone and locked in, I wondered if my mum knew where I was. So I steered the safe course and thought only about that moment and none other … I lay as I was, dreaming, until nearly three.[47]

Jackie fears stepping out of the present by engaging with the past and future and the dangerous thoughts that such meanderings might engender.

She encounters the different assumptions of other young people immersed in popular culture, which inflects her account with a meditative quality, a feature also present in the writing of young migrants described earlier. Her restricted childhood means she is unable to relate easily to things like popular music, expressed in a more reflective passage towards the end:

> It just seems funny that whereas I'm thinking about whether or not my brother has got beaten up again or even whether or not to go to the Social Studies lesson, they're continually moaning that they aren't allowed to stay out until twelve or that they haven't got the latest jeans. I do think about normal things too and care about clothes but not full-time.[48]

Historically, a constricted childhood might have been seen as 'normal'. By the 1980s, this was not the case; younger writers felt they were entitled to a childhood, and its absence caused a considerable sense of disorientation and unfairness. Jackie is not given the luxury of growing up through a process of graduated independence and support, but rather is plunged into the cold and uncharted waters of adulthood. Paradoxically, when she is finally allowed to leave the home she feels cheated and, with scarce support, is forced to make a sudden jump for which she feels ill-prepared:

> although it might sound funny I didn't want to leave school. Although I'd hated it and still didn't love it I didn't want to go out into the 'big wide world' yet.[49]

Jackie moves into a hostel and enrols on a nursery-nursing course, providing evidence that she is fighting and surviving her childhood. It would be difficult to imagine this book having been written from the perspective of a negative ending, given that the starting point was so inhospitable to personal expression. A certain level of distance and comfort was needed in order to reflect back on these unpropitious circumstances.

In a very different way, Roger Mills's *A Comprehensive Education 1965–75* grew in part out of the supportive context at Centerprise. In writing about his boys' comprehensive school, Mills was influenced by the idea of the collective autobiography and is historically aware: 'Any one of the thousand boys there could have written this story'.[50] He notes the global and social context, a lived experience of schooling, expressed ironically:

> The public schools were so good, one teacher told us, that boys came from all over the world just to be a pupil at even the most obscure of them. Well, it seemed to me that our school must be on some sort of par with them, because we had boys from all over the world at our school too. We had boys from the West Indies, Pakistan, Malta, Italy, Greece, Cyprus, Africa and Turkey, and that's not forgetting the boys from the nearer places – Scotland, Ireland and Wales. Boys, hundreds of them from all over the globe, all sent to Britain and all converging in that one building at the top of Effingham Road in Hackney.[51]

Such concentrations of diverse populations within tight geographical spaces became common in some working-class areas well before the subject entered public discussion. Jocular commentary permeates the text, which is idiosyncratic in places and reveals literary intentions. Mills saw it as a novel which he put through 'the creative mangle ... condensed some characters, left out some other characters, to make it more readable'.[52] Borrowings from popular culture appear throughout the text, such as the pupil who rewrote the western *A Few Dollars More* for an English essay,[53] the appearance of skinheads,[54] and Oz and the 'alternative society'[55] – all references that anchor the text in a particular time and place. Mills's style is informal, which is unsurprising for someone influenced by the 1960s milieu. However, it presents a spirit and way of life that was only partly obtainable. The day-to-day life of the school contrasted sharply with the widely publicised freedoms of the 1960s. A few miles could have been a thousand:

> I felt that school was something preventing me from joining the new 'Swinging London' outside. It was the era of the Beatles, the new Labour government, Mary Quant and the mini skirt. The number one record was 'Satisfaction'
> I can't get no satisfaction,
> And I try, and I try,
> And I try, and I try[56]

The spontaneity of these moments is juxtaposed to the staid, conservative school and its teachers, illustrating the way that old and new collided in the 1960s. Discipline and control were considered essential in order to produce well-regulated children suitable for limited employment in the local labour market. While pupils were closely governed, black children were doubly scrutinised by the school for appropriate behaviour and expected to be 'ambassadors for their race'.[57] One way in which Mills handles injustice is through fantasy, as in this carnivalesque passage in which the authority of the headmaster is undermined in the face of his more responsible pupils. In a dream scene the headmaster had gone loco. With a double barrelled shotgun in his hands and his office door barricaded he would be yelling over the P.A. system 'You'll never take me alive, do you hear me? You'll never take me alive'. The whole school would be listening incredulously as with hideously contorted face he would rave on, teachers panicking not knowing what to do. 'I know you're all out to get me, but you won't though, do you hear? HA HA HA'.[58]

The one-off imaginary moment creates a space where alternative social possibilities can be considered.

Many autobiographies written by people who grew up after the war demonstrate the potential for breaking down the social barriers that were a feature of much working-class writing, even if this remained a distant reality for most. The tension between growing entitlement and the reality of schooling in a working-class area is broached through a pep talk by Mr Harmen:

'Maturity', he expounded, 'is to know your limitations. Maturity is facing up to life as it really is and giving up daydreams. Limits!'

'Lets face it lads', he said, peering benignly around the room, 'none of you are ever going to be rich and famous and you're not going to have a wife that looks like Brigitte Bardot. When you leave this school you'll get an average job, settle down in an average mortgaged house with an average girl. It is from this position and with this knowledge that you must strive to make your life as worthwhile as possible and influence others to do so within these boundaries.'

'Real maturity is knowing, knowing what you really want'.

What I really wanted was to be rich and famous and have a wife that looked like Brigitte Bardot.

I was incensed by Harmen's Smug Sermon and that night I recounted to my mother what he had said, that he had virtually told us we were going to be nobodies. Failures at thirteen. My mother was puzzled by my attitude and was silent for a moment.

'Well?' she said.[59]

Mills struggles to escape the restrictions of working-class life, which are apparently accepted by his parents, without rejecting a working-class identity or simply melding into the middle class. Widening expectations about economic growth were frequently frustrated, a common experience among the postwar working class.[60] Despite his critical stance toward the school, Mills later acknowledged that the teachers were in fact struggling to help the children and were doing what they could.[61] This echoed the debate over whether comprehensive schools were overcoming or reinforcing inequalities. Indeed, teachers were divided on this book, with some on the left venting their concerns.[62] In the 1960s, young radical teachers had gravitated to the comprehensives, then seen as a way of overcoming class divisions. By the late 1960s, some of them were becoming aware that these schools could fail working-class children just as the previous system had. In addition, the leftist critique of common schooling, often with an emphasis on social control, could unwittingly provide ballast for blanket denunciations of comprehensive schooling. Sensing a nuanced range of opinion, Mills is unwilling to paint a finished picture with a 'phoney end', introducing a narrative voice to position himself ambiguously and trying to explain his 'seething anger' as he countenanced a number of conflicting endings:

> I did feel at the time as if I had been promised something by the school ...
>
> I went out last night for inspiration, to the pub and friends of my age who went to similar or nearby schools. I asked them, 'Do you feel you were promised something in school you didn't get when you left?' One said, 'A job'. Another talked about them making our expectations too high. Another said we were promised nothing definite except maybe an ability to apply their ragbag of knowledge to the outside world. The last said that we had been given a fair education in an unfair society and that comprehensives ought to be as revolutionary as the public schools are elitist.
>
> I just nodded at all the suggestions and comments, said I still didn't know what the promise was and that I would have another pint.[63]

The hope associated with schooling was being fragmented among the uncertain possibilities facing young people. The refusal to countenance a neat ending represented a recognition of the complex dilemmas in working-class life. Mills would continue to work in community publishing and the arts for many years and also to write, including a number of novels for young people.

Endings and beginnings

The lives of these young people were indelibly marked by writing. Some of them would go on to become writers – almost all the members of the early Basement Writers group were later successful in a range of cultural activities.[64] Writers received an audience among schoolchildren, teachers, parents, families and communities. Children's writing contested the usual educational limitations: stories, autobiography, poetry and novels were written, breaking out of the 'Toytown measurements' of the examined essay.[65] This educational work represented a serious attempt to value and support children while also inducting them into a wider culture.

Teachers who aimed to engage directly with local communities viewed their pedagogy as capable of widespread adoption and as having an impact on the educational system generally. There was a willingness to learn from the working class as a source for rethinking society. Teachers who read children's writing with care and attention gained insights into students' lives as well the cultural transformations of which they were a part.[66] Significant elements of the 'language experience' approach did enter mainstream educational practice, and its deployment in working-class urban settings fostered the emergence of new work. Allowing young people the space to investigate and to direct their own learning was an overriding concern.

Crucially, personal experience was a key starting point and a place to which writers returned in experimenting with forms and styles and adapting literary traditions. Writing was initiated in the lives of students, their feelings, senses and observations, as well as by empathising with the lives of others. As in the Fed more widely, successful writers remained faithful to the spoken word in developing a literature based in part on the experience of marginality. They tunnelled more deeply into thoughts and ideas and strayed away from directly representational poetry and prose. Imagination and conjecture became necessary to be true to a feeling or experience. Conversely, romance, comedy and fairy tale could also serve a documentary purpose. Yet writing was never entirely free-flowing and could also be directed and channelled by teachers, peer groups and the social and political context.

The expressions of young people could not be classified politically in a straightforward way. While radical teachers agreed on the need to recognise and respect working-class culture, others highlighted the importance of learning the language of power in society, particularly for subordinate groups.[67] Teachers were influenced by various shades of socialism, educational thought and popular culture. This could create thorny problems in classrooms, where critical scrutiny by outside bodies exerted limits on what could be done. The assertion of a radical alternative also made it hard to enlist the sympathy of a significant segment of teachers. Even broadly progressive educators could be troubled by the freedoms granted to young people at Centerprise.[68] Thus, alongside the many successes recounted here, there were also lost opportunities.

Yet over time, these practices became 'normal' and hardly seemed to justify the term radical. In part this reflected the success of such initiatives – it would be unlikely that, in the twenty-first century, a teacher, however angry, would be sacked for producing a booklet of children's poetry, although the content of such writing might still raise eyebrows. Writing continued to be a central and unsurprising part of many English lessons which built on traditions of post-war English teaching, while independent groups published similar work for many years.[69] In 2017, *Stepney Words* III appeared, inspired by the original of almost half a century earlier.[70]

However, the social and political context has changed significantly since this body of work was produced, and the children have now grown into middle age. The historical moment in which these practices took place has long since passed, and the spaces that radical teachers occupied have been closed down. From the passage of the 1988 Education Reform Act, teachers would exercise less autonomy and control over the curriculum.[71] In addition, the openly socialist commitment of some teachers referred to here would not be tolerated by those in power. In the late 1990s, Chris Searle was himself removed from his post as head teacher at Earl Marshall School in Sheffield by Labour Secretary of State for Education and Employment David Blunkett.

Popular culture and everyday life had proved to be a creative springboard for the radicals of the 1968 generation who were interested in the idea of liberating childhood. Centerprise was held up as an exemplary case study of childhood in Colin Ward's *The Child in the City*.[72] Moreover, the widespread use of photographs in the publications surveyed also disclosed a nostalgic concern with the freedom of the child in the past, which was seen to be under threat in the 1970s. The idea of a lost childhood had widespread appeal and highlighted the need to uncover the creative energies of children. Despite the historical and romantic associations of childhood with innocence and nature, in the 1970s young people colonised urban spaces and articulated their experience of urban life.[73]

The whole process of writing raised a dilemma in the history of learning and childhood. While children were respected as different from adults, they were to be treated as mature and capable of operating in the adult world even if their rights could not be fully expressed. Historically, radical groups had rejected a sharp division between adults and children, recognising the significant, albeit limited, roles that young people could play both in adult society and on their own terms.[74] In workshops, young people were appealed to as complex individuals. Their lives were validated as a worthy basis for creative thinking and literary work. A different emphasis was found in progressive education, which posited the uniqueness of the child as part of a developmental process that was now being extended to working-class children. Developmental psychology stipulated stages of growth and maturity, popularised most notably by Jean Piaget, who held that abstract and creative work was more appropriate for older pupils. This could justify the supposition that younger children were not capable of producing creative work.[75] The insistence on recognising the richness of young people's writing meant that it could not be restricted to a phase of growing up, like a skin that would flake away as the mature person emerged. Instead, the writing was worthy in itself and young people were appreciated in the here and now. In chipping away at the idea of developmental stages and fostering solidarity between older and younger people, the Fed was forging links between the learning of adults and young people. The language experience approach, which built upon the lives of pupils, also came to be closely associated with adult education, adult literacy and adult writing groups, as will become clear in subsequent chapters.

Such evidence brings into question the assumed separate nature of adult learning. The claim that adults learn in distinctive ways became widespread in adult education, encapsulated in the notion of 'andragogy'.[76] In relation to the worker writer movement, while the writing practices of young people had some distinctiveness, especially in school settings, broader similarities were apparent. The purpose and context of learning were critical. In adult education, and especially in adult literacy, it was important that adults were not patronised or infantilised. Allowing young people the space to experiment worked in the other direction by nurturing their participation in adult society. Contrary to one tendency in progressive education, creativity was not seen as a trait limited to childhood. In addition, overlaps between older and younger writers were also a fact of life for the movement. For example, as the Basement Writers group expanded, it did so by bringing together different age groups in a critical dialogue.[77] Others were similarly passionate in working with the memories and writing of older people, and the theme of childhood provided a further bond between old and young, each exploring their childhoods, the one contemporary, the other past, but both thinking about the future. Powerful affinities were formed via the writing of these two groups, which was based upon the creative reconstruction of experience and memory.

3   The good old days?

In the 1970s, community publishers worked closely with older people to record their personal experiences in the light of historical changes. The claims of post-war progress and modernity were examined through the optic of their memories of pre-Second World War Britain. Assumptions about what constituted a good life were being transformed by rapid shifts in technology, welfare and travel as well as unprecedented economic growth. Hundreds of autobiographies were written by older people looking back at their lives before the Second World War. Understanding and valuing this work was a central preoccupation of early Federation groups. This writing constituted a substantial category of work produced by the movement, so much so that it was often mistakenly seen as typical of all the writing. Many of the autobiographies were written towards the end of the writer's life and would be their major piece of writing.[1] They served as a durable legacy for authors to pass on their memories, insights and experiences to current and future generations.

Life stories contributed to an interest in the past that critics habitually portrayed as 'nostalgia', tainted with the vagaries of unreliable and saccharine memories. Nostalgia became a keyword in the 1970s, when supposedly less complex pasts were being juxtaposed with the present.[2] The term was originally used to refer to a medical condition of homesickness, dating back to the work of Swiss student Johannes Hofer in 1688, but by the 1960s and 1970s the yearning was not for a place but for the past more generally. Michael Wood sounded a warning bell, fearing a 'rampant, ubiquitous, unashamed nostalgia which leers at us', and academic denunciations followed suit.[3] Detractors viewed the concept of 'community' as an ideological invention, and the idea of 'working-class community' found even less favour, facing charges of nostalgic romanticism about the 'good old days' as well as a forward-looking naive utopianism with no evidential grounding.[4] Later, Simon Dentith and Philip Dodd offered a more sympathetic account, but they argued that worker autobiographies were characterised by 'simple seeing' and had neither the 'sophistication or theoretical reach' nor 'the self-reflexiveness which is a condition for … complex seeing'.[5] They contrasted them with 'two exemplary autobiographies', Carolyn Steedman's *Landscape for a Good Woman* and Ronald Fraser's *In Search of a Past*. Steedman addressed her own autobiographical writing to the perceived limitations of this genre.[6] In addition, while there had long been a recognition that successive generations could repeat nostalgic claims about the past, Joanna Bourke took this to new heights in rejecting the version of community defended in these publications as an entirely 'retrospective construction' with no basis in reality.[7] Finally, Joanna Bornat, in an important essay, reasoned that community publishing systematically marginalised other voices by looking to the past with the inhibitions and prejudices derived from that past.[8]

A related set of arguments in the 1980s attacked what was depicted as a conservative 'heritage industry'. Both Patrick Wright and Robert Hewison held that the decline of manufacturing industry was being accompanied by a process of sanitising and commodifying the past as heritage, sealed off from the present.[9] It was becoming a 'foreign country' unavailable to critical historical analysis.[10] However, in recent years there have been more sympathetic accounts which have paid attention to the complexity of nostalgia and heritage and the multiple entanglements to which they appeal.[11] For instance, Ben Jones, who has looked at working class autobiographies in terms of housing, notes that the emphasis upon nostalgia has been overstated.[12]

QueenSpark books will be considered as providing examples of important autobiographical work, lending this account a southern flavour, although other cases will be drawn upon from across the Fed. The books can be read through a number of lenses. Crucially they help us to apprehend the feelings, thoughts and lived experience of many working-class people born in the late nineteenth and early twentieth centuries. Academic studies have cited these autobiographies, although they were not written to provide 'data' for historical interpretation as part of a 'moment of social history'.[13] Rather, they were interested in a different kind of history in which authors elaborated their own argument from a personal perspective. The writing exposed a tension between the individual and the social context that lay at the heart of the Fed. Indeed, in outlining a subjective being, the worker autobiographers structured their lives around themes including childhood, work, family, individual characters and politics. They were shot through with twin notions of community and poverty. As they narrated a life course, the self partially emerged from the collective and the urge to provide accurate testimony jostled with a desire to enlarge upon creative instincts. Ultimately, the writing resists attempts to categorise it straightforwardly as literature or history.

The self and the social

The autobiographer inevitably deals with their life as a younger person. Childhood serves as a framing device through which a mixture of memory, analysis and argument is fed. Fed writers dealt with oral tradition and stories that had been passed on by word of mouth, part fiction and part fact. John Langley's *Always a Layman* weaves these together in order to paint a picture of early life,[14] sliding from one memory into another, 'sleepy lazy days when we were kids', a phrase that indicates the different meaning of time he had as a child. He evokes an impression of timelessness, a discontinuity compounded by the later transformations of the twentieth century.[15] It was a creative struggle to re-create his childhood based on such fragments of memory.

Divorcing the past from the present helped writers gain distance from their childhoods, which then became amenable to evaluation. Sid Manville, in *Everything Seems Smaller*, focuses exclusively upon his early years, but he cannot escape the growing realisation that inequalities of wealth and power would determine his life. Although 'Dad was law in his own home', 'The Spirit of the Victorian Family',[16] his father's authority was curtailed in the outside world:

> A large portrait of dad used to hang in the front room. There he was with trim waxed moustache, and wearing a splendid jacket with stripes, crowns and all sorts of decoration. I thought he must have been a General at least. What a blow to learn in later years that the jacket belonged to the photographer, and the dignified look belonged to private Alf Manville. We all wanted to be proud of our Dads in those days, but that was not the first time he'd let me down. He told me once that my Grandfather had been M.P. for North Brighton – then I found out that Grandad had been a road sweeper. Dad said 'I told you he was an M.P. – so he was – a mud pusher'. It slowly dawned upon me that my Papa was a bit of a leg puller.[17]

Fathers have often been absent, or unnoticed, in accounts of working-class family life.[18] Through humour, Manville captures the coexistence of shame and pride and reminds us of the constraints and expectations under which his family lived.

By contrast, Manville remembers his mother as the lynchpin of the family and gives a sensitive description of her life.[19] Hard domestic labour was ever present for women, if not in someone else's home then in their own. His upbeat reading contrasts with his mother's unremitting labour, which disrupts the narrative, forcing him to stand back from his story and question uncritical notions of the 'good old days':

> A little 'un in stature was our Mum, but big in heart and tough as nails. Mums had to be in those days. Most of them had large families, and all had seven days a week to get through. Seven days a week with no electrical appliances, seven bucket-and-brush and hass-broom days, seven carbolic soap and hearthstone days per week.
>
> ... the 'Good Old Days'... were not all good for everyone. No posh powders or softeners, Mum's only materials were a twopenny packet of 'Hudson's Powder' and a whacking great bar of 'Sunlight' for the washing and a three ha'penny packet of Edward's Desiccated Soup, plus Sunday's leftovers for the dinner. The rest was just slog, scrub and sweat.[20]

This passage arose from a survey of childhood memories. It nourished an evaluative voice in which personal experience became a conduit for public debates about the past.[21]

Childhood could also liberate imaginative qualities that were suppressed in everyday adult life. The necessarily limited perspective of the child had to be creatively reworked with the benefit of hindsight in order to give meaning to the self and their surroundings. Manville had also been excluded from the adult world and had to be inventive in order to comprehend his past. When describing his mother, he remembered the hard life she led and that time off was severely truncated. 'Losing meself for ten minutes' could be indispensable emotionally. As a child Sid could never figure out why his mother enjoyed reading about the antics of rich people in the papers, but he imagined that it provided escapism, a temporary freedom from drudgery:

> When the kids were out playing and there was a bit 'o quiet to be had, I believe she read herself to sleep – 'Lost Meself' – and for a brief while I think she dressed herself in a silken gown, donned a tiara and waltzed in glittering ballrooms; or strolled among the lakes and flowers in the gardens of a world from which, in her waking hours, she was so far removed.[22]

Bursts of pleasure and excitement played an important psychological role in these autobiographies. The pain of labour which could imprison humanity was never able to extinguish it completely, and moments of physical and mental release were jealously guarded. Amid such tangible inequality, where the working class generally lived and worked in spatially distinct areas, the lives of the wealthy held a fascination and generated feelings that were not always in sync with the rational and political.

A further widely shared impulse was to intervene in debates about childhood and to underscore the strengths of an older way of life. Manville pitied young people because he felt they would have no comparable memories of playing in the street, of making things, of the wide-open road as a place to explore.[23] For Olive Masterson, in *The Circle of Life*, an upturned table became 'a sea of fancy' and source of endless play.[24] She felt the changes when TV arrived:

> coloured television is a far cry from our old wireless. I feel we used our imagination far more. When we listened to a play, it was really interesting imagining what the people looked like. And we really listened, not at all like today. I find I have one eye on the television and the other on something else, so I never seem to know what is going on.[25]

Masterson was not simply reprimanding the younger generation but recognising the complex impact of technology, not least on her own life. These arguments are not too far from what educationists have told us about the 'crisis' of childhood: children 'overloaded' with too many toys – now screens – substitute them for imagination and building relationships, while the fear of letting children play outdoors stifles physical and social development.[26]

But childhood, in its contemporary meaning, was felt to be incomplete for those who faced poverty from an early age. It may have only existed periodically, between the various responsibilities that children had to take on. For Daisy Noakes, in *The Town Beehive* (see figure 5), emotional restraint was a feature of her early years which she could not cordon off from adult life. She was never able to get on with her mother, who struggled to bring up a family of ten children:

> Mum was very strict. We were regimented and no one dare put a foot out of place. I expect she loved us in her peculiar way, but she never showed affection, or had time to listen to us. She kept us clean and tidy and fed us and that's about it. I can never remember having a conversation with her.[27]

Friction between mothers and daughters could be quite common in a context of material deprivation, and there is a regretfulness in Noakes's text.[28] The lack of support for children produced absences, and her fascination with childhood was coupled with ambivalent feelings that could not be fully stated.

The shortcomings of childhood rapidly blended into working life given the limitations of schooling and the necessity to earn an income. School itself not uncommonly receives minimal treatment in these texts. Indeed, other adults played important socialising roles for young people facing an abrupt shift into an adult world.[29] For Langley, whose family life was sporadic, the workplace became a sort of extended family. Some of his strongest emotions are reserved for his mates at work, in particular a Bolshevik who was a vital influence:

> He used to kick me and smack me round the chops for not doing my work right, but I don't think I ever loved a man more because he taught me my trade, and he taught me how to live too.[30]

Like many other working-class men, entering into a trade had been a life-forming experience for Langley that was less conspicuous for apprentices in the 1970s. Violence was a common feature of these hard lives, a part of normal existence for men whose fathers taught them to fight from a young age.[31] The term 'adolescence' was only coined in the late nineteenth century and was still barely discernible in early twentieth-century working-class Brighton. The support and guidance of older people in the transition to adulthood were thus decisive. It is no surprise, then, that intertwined with skilled work was a strong sense of sociability. Talking about work even in leisure hours was an essential part of the job and suffused the whole of life. Alfred Dedman, a lighterman on the Thames, attested to the centrality of work:

> Away from work I classify myself as having been stupid ... I and my mates from around Canning Town used to just meet and drink. We were not even interested

> in girls ... But at work we were proud of what we could do ... Pay and working conditions have improved since then, thanks to the unions, but the job is not so difficult. In the early days, lightermen had pride in their trade. They were skilful men. They worked for their pride, technically.[32]

The appreciation of historical change within living memory was palpable. In adopting the span of a lifetime, the use of 'early days' compressed the textured history of lightermen on the Thames, which stretched back many centuries, into the 'past'.[33] Collective pride in work enabled the individual writer to project himself onto a historical canvas. Improvements in conditions had taken place, but it was a mixed blessing because the meaning of work had been demeaned.

Typically, skilled male workers structured their lives around the workplace. For example, Albert Paul's work as a carpenter and joiner defined his identity. *Hard Work and No Consideration*, his second volume of autobiography, is mainly an account of the different jobs he took on, with bouts of unemployment sandwiched in between. In the style of Robert Tressell, he felt unable to do shoddy work just for profit; his pride was at stake and his sensibilities insulted by 'chancers' who lowered standards and were 'a terrible expense to any builder'.[34] Paul's story is indicative of the value and dignity of skilled labour which was being destabilised by rapid technological change. 'Skill' was associated with male workers, and many of them struggled to reconcile themselves to being out of work and in retirement.

By contrast, women were directed to less skilled work, which tended to be demeaned and categorised as 'low skilled' in any case. Basing a narrative around skilled work was a strategy less applicable to women, even though paid work was a necessity for many of those who worked in a variety of jobs. Langley remembered working with women in both world wars. He considered them to be good workers who could stand on their own, but his brief comment that 'it was a hell of a job getting rid of the women' after 1918 suggests that the gendered nature and struggles of his working life were of consequence.[35] Nonetheless, work takes on distinctive features in these women's lives. 'Going into service', the most common form of employment in the early twentieth century, was experienced as a fundamental life change. Margaret Ward started as a domestic in the village of Rottingdean near Brighton. Having entered a lifetime of hard labour, she realised there was no option but to adjust to the new situation:

> I particularly remember one day, when I was brushing the carpet with a stiff brush. I was so tired, I sat in the middle of the lounge floor and thought, 'I can do no more'. But after a while I got up and carried on because I knew I had to. I was about fifteen at the time.[36]

The necessity of hard toil would become deeply engrained in her mind, so much so that, as with skilled male workers, she felt bewildered when it finished: 'I couldn't get used to retirement, and felt quite guilty with time on my hands.'[37]

5   Daisy Noakes, *The Town Beehive*, an influential autobiography published by QueenSpark.

Similarly, for Noakes as a young girl, starting work as a domestic was a transforming experience that required inner strength and the emergence of a new character. She breaks off her narrative to conjure a new persona in a strange outfit, dispensing with normal sentences:

> Yesterday in blouse and gymslip, today unrecognisable in a costume my mother bought from a neighbour.[38]

Such extracts betray a filmic quality, splicing and sequencing her life in order to observe her childhood from a different perspective. But it was a deeply distressing process; lying in bed on the first night after entering domestic service, she

> lay there thinking about running home, but I knew I would only be sent back, so cried at the thought … from that moment my childhood ended, and I realised I had been launched on the world to earn my own living. 1923. I vowed no more tears but a 'stiff upper lip' was needed from now on.[39]

The effects of an unloving mother, poverty and these work experiences were damaging. Sheila Rowbotham has identified an 'economy of expression' in Noakes's autobiography, for instance, when dealing with the death of her husband: 'When the nurse called one morning, I could not stop my tears they had been flowing since the previous day. I was not crying, yet the tears would not stop.'[40] Ironically this restriction also serves a creative purpose elsewhere in the text, pointing towards a more literary design. Noakes mentions her miscarriage in just a few words, with no explanation or emotion. The text then jumps to a description of normal events and walks in the country. The disparity between the prosaic and the tragic allows the reader to discern the hard times and psychic adjustments that were made. After moving a bed and making batches of cakes, she

> started a haemorrhage. I grabbed a bath towel and sat on it. I was really frightened to move. I went first hot then cold, and hoped I was not going to faint. There I sat till George came home.
>
> There was a lot of to and fro-ing for the doctor and the ambulance which took me to hospital until the crisis was over, but I had lost the baby.
>
> I still took my walks up or down the road, very seldom seeing or meeting anyone, and if a small plane should go up from the airfield, it was something to stand and watch.[41]

Noakes could not afford to dwell on tragedy; nevertheless, the rapid succession of commotion, loss and normality are unsettling for the reader.

Paid work existed alongside other expectations for working-class women, whose accounts tended to integrate more of their private and personal worlds than was frequently the case in male accounts. The family represented a common means of narrating the individual life, for instance in Olive Masterson's *The Circle of Life*. Work is ever present but, when she gets a job, it is related to the needs of her husband and children: 'For the first time in my life, I had a few shillings of my own, and it was nice to be able to buy a gift for Jack or the children sometimes.'[42] Indeed, Masterson sets up a metaphor of herself as part of a family tree in which she finds love, peace and contentment:

> I think of my life as a tree. Our tree, mine and all the rest of the family's, past and present. My branch had been battered and blown by the winds of time, and broken a little, but it is strong in the support of the young branches of my children and their families, and I know it will continue to be so.[43]

Masterson focuses on her extended family, taking a longer-term view of life and the struggle to maintain this institution through turbulent historical change – to create a protective shell that operates over generations. This helps to explain her feeling of stewardship and service to others in which different conceptions of time are intermingled with one another. After the birth of her children, she has difficulty marking the passing of time in the way that male autobiographers might list a series of jobs:

> Life went along quite smoothly. Jack and I had our ups and downs like most young couples do, but he was a loving husband and father, and we overcame the trials and tribulations of early marriage, especially after being parted by war.[44]

> Life drifted along. Times were still very hard in the financial sense. We worked hard to bring up our children. Jack produced a variety of vegetables, which helped our diet.[45]

She skips over parts of her life in order to focus in on others – a transition method to move the life story forwards. Occasionally private history becomes a springboard to discuss public events. Looking back to the late 1930s, the nation is described in language that evokes both family and national identity: 'The country was having problems with Germany and the threat of war was getting serious.'[46]

Furthermore, family was discussed in autobiographies by men. Although the family was part of an assumed background, masculinity did not manifest itself uniformly. Manville took on the role of 'family historian' and devoted the first half of *Everything Seems Smaller* to descriptions of family members, which helped to position himself socially and also signals an uncertain individual identity.[47] Men's autobiographies tended to separate public and private worlds in a way that was less relevant for women. For example, while Paul does mention his wife, she appears only in an isolated chapter that covers countless years:

> We had a very happy married life, combined with joy and some grief, plus little money and unemployment etc. We went through and suffered two world wars, 1914–1918 and 1939–1945, finally being spared to live and enjoy over 52½ years together and nearly 50 years of married life.

> I am very sorry to state that my wife passed away ... Having told you of this very important event of my whole life, I will return now back to the struggles of trying to get a job and unemployment.[48]

Crucial private experiences are glossed over with general statements in order that the main story of work can be recounted. Paul's version is an extreme example of a form of masculinity that does not feature expressiveness. Yet the understated and controlled emotion in the above quote is effective in denoting a deeply loving relationship in the face of hardship – a constant presence. In some male accounts, chapters were added after the autobiography had been drafted in response to requests from editorial groups for more commentary on personal lives.

Autobiographers also tell us about individuals in order to put forward a social message. For those without a skilled trade or strong family network, neither work nor family was an adequate means to delineate self and society. Bert Healey, in *Hard Times and Easy Terms – and Other Tales by a QueenSpark Cockney*, writes that he 'conjured a living' in a variety of ways, from door-to-door sales to taxi driving, while alluding to less honest occupations. Like Masterson, in the absence of a regular job he finds it more difficult to handle transitions, in part because there are fewer of them. Various characters help to organise and perform his version of collective working-class life. For instance, a fly-by-night existence is epitomised by Albert, the wide boy who veers between fiddling by day and frequenting shady and dubious pubs by night:

> Yes, that's how Albert lived, if you could call it living, as most of our class lived in those days ... We lived for today. Who cares about tomorrow? Skint again next day, more scrounging and fiddling, and so life went on. But what a life, what a variety. The films and plays had nothing on our lives, mine, Albert's, and my mates' lives. Ours was true, not make believe.[49]

Healey associates himself with Albert's exciting life, and that of his class, but his writing maintains a safe distance from illicit activities. While the descriptions are 'true', they are also signified as literary and dramatic constructions. Nicknames help to familiarise the reader with his social circle and humanise a harsh environment. 'Spindle', for example, is distinctly 'Pickwickian':

> He was so thin that if you looked at him sideways you could hardly see him. Hence the name 'Spindle'
> ... A character straight out of Dickens[50]

Dickens, more than any other 'serious' writer, entered the popular consciousness and his works became a medium for communicating messages about social life.

The feats and lives of colourful local characters helped writers to personalise social forces. For instance, Manville's second autobiography, *Our Small Corner* includes 'character No 3, in the person of Frank Ingham, Schoolmaster, Town Councillor, and Gentleman', whose 'mission in life was to defend the rights of the working people of Brighton and to ensure that the rest of the Council didn't mess 'em about'. He successfully opposes the Council's imposition of charges at Brighton racecourse, which transpires as a 'one horse race' with Ingham taking on a Herculean status:

broad, stolid, upright and determined, with a bushy moustache and eyebrows to match and this magnificent figure of a man was sustained by a spirit of determination to defend the rights of his fellow-beings. What chance – I ask you – what chance had the few money grabbers on the Council against such odds?[51]

Small victories, embellished in the retelling, were stored as resources and used to critique impersonal institutions. Fed groups would rediscover flamboyant figures whose lives had wide-ranging impacts and who had become part of local mythology, including the chimney sweep Harry Cowley, who ran squatting and other campaigns in Brighton, as well as Dr Jelley, a familiar face in Hackney before the National Health Service arrived.

The labour movement also built solidarities, not only through its material presence but in the popular imagination. In his first autobiography Manville had avoided writing about politics and trade unionism because he thought it would lessen his chances of being published by QueenSpark in the late 1980s.[52] In fact, Fed groups actively encouraged autobiographies by political activists, which make interesting reading because they assimilate politics and everyday life from a rank-and-file viewpoint rather than simply adhering to a party line. Writers provided direct analysis of the political developments of their time, surveying a lifetime of experience and thought.

The process of coming to a political consciousness is a common thread. Socialist understanding did not emerge naturally from the experience of poverty but had to be acquired over time through discussion, reading and participation in struggles and movements. Just as Langley learnt from a workmate, others were influenced by older people whose questions persisted in the young mind. Jack Cummins, in *The Landlord Cometh*, began to doubt his religious beliefs, a process he found unsettling. The parents of a friend turned out to be both socialists and agnostics, which came as a 'shock':

> for after all the Roman Catholic propaganda I had listened to, it seemed incredible that these nice people could not believe in God. I began to think, and my mind began to reach out.

Meanwhile, his troubled intellect digested the eclectic socialist, anarchist and utopian ideas that were circulating at the time:

> I went to meetings, read books that I had never heard of before, Robert Blatchford's *Merrie England*, some pamphlets by the American Robert Ingersoll, poems by William Morris, and the *Rubaiyat of Omar Khayyam*.[53]

Broad-ranging stimuli enabled a re-evaluation of working-class life in the early twentieth century. Cummins discovered a world of learning in London before the outbreak of the First World War, experimenting in a lively political and social ambience:

> I lived in a state of ferment. New political ideas were everywhere and I dabbled in all of them. At various times I found myself associating with syndicalists, anarchists and communists. At meetings I heard Bernard Shaw, G. K. Chesterton, Hilaire Belloc and other famous men of literature speaking. This was all free![54]

The sharp doctrinal differences that were so visible in public debates became blurred in an exciting range of possibilities that were digested by the young man. Cummins wrote articles for The Torch and Freedom, was introduced to ideas of free love at anarchist Sunday Schools, joined the Independent Labour Party (ILP) and spoke at their meetings, all of which forced a showdown with his parents, his father especially angered by his son's support for the suffragettes. Mixing in these circles, Cummins felt the strain of his new identity which detached him from his past, his family and friends:

> we talked for hours about Lamb, Hazlitt, Coleridge and the poets Keats and Shelley. My early education, like that of most working class boys, had been sadly neglected, but my new friends were leading me into a new world full of beauty and pleasure.[55]

The love of knowledge and ideas led him to a realm of discovery and enjoyment but also caused a painful rift with his previous life. However, Cummins cuts off the analysis of his emerging consciousness to give a description of being a soldier in the First World War, after which he returns to a life of socialism and activism. Despite his enduring beliefs, something has been lost and his text becomes more formalised and regulated. It reads as if the war robbed him of a vibrant political and intellectual life: the destructiveness of that experience is replicated in the fragmented nature of his autobiography. Social forces broke up lives which could not simply be stitched back into a seamless whole, even after the passage of many decades.[56]

Les Moss's autobiography, Live and Learn: A Life and Struggle for Progress, was a related journey into politics and a conscious reworking of his beliefs, albeit with a different emphasis to Cummins. A friend's father 'put all kinds of socialist, and especially atheist ideas to me', which encouraged him to start challenging the 'old institutions'.[57] Following these 'preliminary changes' in his thinking, Walter Hannington, the communist leader of the National Unemployed Workers' Movement, presented the 'scientific case' which led to a rupture with his family. Moss's political education changed his 'whole outlook', whereas previously 'I'd just been the ordinary type, had the old bourgeois education'.[58] The alteration in consciousness would become deeply embedded, and Moss's overtly political stance curtailed discussion of his private life. Even though he considered that he had a 'good upbringing', Moss emphasised that it was 'bourgeois' – he had spent too much time in the church and the Boys' Brigade.[59] His aunt was a 'jumped up type' who 'wanted to connect herself with the D'Oyly Carte, the Gilbert and Sullivan people', while his 'mother was entirely under the influence of all the institutions of capitalism, like the church ... the education system and the whole solid system which reflects capitalist economics'.[60] The same framework was turned inwards on his own life. When describing his plans for retirement, it is clear that Moss's identity had become cemented into his strand of socialism:

> I'm a bit of a planner, always have been. After all, a Marxist does plan. Planning is partly economic against capitalist private competition, but it is also personal. That being part of my make-up, I planned what I was going to do in my retirement.[61]

However, while working-class activists felt the strains of political commitment in their personal lives, they could still remain marginal in the political sphere. Moss applied a class-based analysis to his activism in the Communist Party, which was dominated by 'professors and that sort of thing ... secret members' who were 'pulling the strings and we were just the victims of it'.[62] Thus while the labour movement fostered national and international identities and loyalties, it simultaneously reproduced social divisions.

Most of the openly political autobiographies were by men who inhabited a public world of political parties and trade unions less accessible to women. Although Ruby Dunn, author of *Moulsecoomb Days*, was influenced by outdoor political speakers in Brighton and was a pacifist, she did not structure her life in the political ways pursued by her male counterparts; community and home life were more prevalent. However, public and political issues are not absent from her autobiography, and her work in education offers one example. Given an acute shortage of teachers, she was able to stay on at work after the Second World War but lamented some of the ideas that returned with the men:

> Reg made his mark by stating that what this school needed was a bit of discipline. He walked about the room with a leather tawse which he placed on his desk in front of the class ... 'How does he think we women have been coping, all through the war years?' I asked myself indignantly. When I heard him ranting in our cloakroom, I felt almost as scared as my well-behaved Class 3A, and also very sad. Was this the way things were to go?[63]

The war, and the prospect of peace, had given rise to hopes for an egalitarian future in which democratic ideas flourished, yet Dunn describes the closing down of these visions in terms of gender politics. The willingness to countenance wide-ranging political changes was ironically coterminous with the yearning to return to a stable lifestyle in which 'normal' relationships were resumed, which could have contradictory implications.

Female political lives were often structured around areas of experience traditionally associated with women, such as teaching or childbirth. Community publishers did not always tap the area of political experience very effectively. An exception is *Of Whole Heart Cometh Hope*, about the Women's Co-operative Guild, published by Age Exchange, in which the distinction between private and public life becomes tenuous. Home is not simply a springboard for public action but indistinguishable from it:

> Very early in my life, I can remember the Labour Party activities and the Co-operative activities. This is what home was all about ... Other things were incidental – holidays, schooling, even bringing up the family, was all second place to these two activities. My mother was the strongest personality in the house – she was desperately active in both organisations – as the Labour candidate for the Council, and in the various committees of the Women's Guild.[64]

Political and social movements were often underpinned by the commitment and activism of women who formulated a public purpose for the home. The Labour Party and co-operative movement not only helped to support daily material life, they offered a set of beliefs to which activists responded at a gut level.[65]

Class, poverty and community

Despite political commitments, somewhat surprisingly, the open consideration of class was rare in these books although it often meshed with life as a whole. Class awareness became more acute when people came into contact with other social classes. Playing with middle-class children, for instance, could make working-class people mindful of differences in opportunity and wealth. Masterson gives a long description of a 'posh' wedding where she is overwhelmed by the opulence, and while she does not mention class directly, her amazement conveys an awareness of inequality.[66] Similarly, Healey's class consciousness is formulated in terms of the insincere look he perceived in upper-class people's faces:

> a lovely smile and such a pleasant way of speaking to you that it made you feel that the aristocrats were such delightful people ... it was all lies ... they looked down their noses at the working classes and only tolerated them because somebody had to work and keep their properties ... clean and tidy.[67]

In a town such as Brighton, with limited industrial development, the metaphor and reality of almost feudal relationships continued to be widely felt. Healey's description of his struggle to earn an income highlights the sharp contrasts between ways of living, here described in the third person:

> Young men in Oxford Bags had Austin Sevens ... Other young men, thin and lean, wearing plus fours and half-starved, went from door to door, trying to sell Hoovers, Clene Easie brushes, Electric light bulbs, scented soap, floor polish...[68]

In attempting to embody a core idea, he distils his life into an image of class division and collectivises his personal memory in the process. In Paul's account, a common class situation that makes links with a rural past serves as a backdrop rather than something that is consciously described: 'Nearly every house in all the working class districts kept 2 or 3 rabbits, chickens or pigeons in their back gardens.'[69] Divisions within working-class life were equally significant. Commonly 'the street' included finely graded distinctions of wealth and respectability that were all too apparent to the writers when looking back on their lives.

Class experience was never unified when viewed from the inside, even though it sometimes looked that way from the outside.

Moreover, the notion of community was being inserted into understandings of class, which destabilised the claim that traditional forms of community had been replaced with modern class identities.[70] On the contrary, community was both a complement and a substitute for class. The imbrication of class and community was in part revealed through the duality of community and poverty. The inconsistency in describing privation and poverty while valuing the strengths and positive aspects of one's past life can be understood through the concept of a 'structure of feeling'. Raymond Williams expounded this contradictory notion to analyse works of literature:

> It was a structure in the sense that you could perceive it operating in one work after another which weren't otherwise connected – people weren't learning it from each other yet it was one of feeling much more than of thought – a pattern of impulses, restraints, tones, for which the best evidence was often the actual conventions of literary or dramatic writing.[71]

The structure of feeling was to be applied to an extensive range of cultural representations.[72] While the idealisation of a community that no longer exists is a common and recurring theme historically,[73] in the 1970s, working-class writers feared that an older way of life was wrongly being dismissed as irrelevant to modern conditions. The pervasive sense of loss and ending was tinged with regret, which led to a re-evaluation of progress and change in the recent past.

An appreciation that one of the audiences for this writing comprised outsiders who had not lived through the same experiences could reinforce the notion of a community that was formerly cohesive. Writers wanted to educate these readers about the positive aspects of their past; unease about the decline in community was evident when a couple wrote into the QueenSpark newspaper, 'We offer you every success in creating the community spirit that we consider is badly needed today'.[74] A few community publishers did fear that their work might become locked into a 'nostalgia industry'. Strong Words, for example, aimed to consciously challenge 'the nostalgic community ... idea'.[75] However, most worker writer groups occupied this ambiguous space and wanted to value the role of older people, so there was no expectation that nostalgia would be excluded from autobiography.

Rather than driving the whole text, nostalgia could exist alongside other motivations. Activists were sensitive to the nuanced recollections and writing of participants. They were ahead of much academic opinion in recognising the wide uses of nostalgia and its intricate range of potential meanings, from mobilising sentiment to highlighting moments in history when things might have turned out differently.[76] This did not necessarily imply inaccuracy – the People's Autobiography of Hackney aimed 'to provide a nostalgic but realistic picture of the past'.[77] While Doris Hall's autobiography, *Growing Up in Ditchling*, is a rural organic account, she is also critical of the heritage that misrepresented her past. What looked like the 'lovely old house' of her childhood, later bought by the National Trust, had in fact been divided into four cramped cottages: 'I was horrified to find how small was the portion in which we lived.'[78]

Rather than being one-sided evocations of the 'good old days', Fed autobiographies also investigate the 'bad old days', with detailed descriptions of hard work, poverty and neglect and the contradictions of the 'good old bad old days'. John Langley's work combines community, friendship and adversity:

> in those days, because people had nothing – nothing at all – you never knew when your next door neighbour was going to commit suicide. People would be unable to pay their rent, which would only be five shillings for a house, and that shared with two or three families, living in slum conditions, not dirty, but crowded because there was not enough money. You would suddenly find that a neighbour two doors away had drowned themselves or thrown themselves over the cliffs because the burden of life was intolerable, and that was at a time when you could buy a newspaper for a halfpenny ...
>
> My home was very miserable, but it was not the fault of the family, it was the system. We had to beg for tickets for food and tickets to get blankets and things like that from the church. If we were ill we had to go begging round ladies' houses ...
>
> There was a marvellous neighbourly spirit in those years. If you were ill, the whole street was concerned and wanted to do something about it and they did. They took it in turns to make milk puddings and custards out of their little money. Anything they could do to help.
>
> The concern was the same if you did not behave yourself. People used to come up and down outside your house with dustbin lids, banging them to shame you, if you were living with another man or woman, that sort of thing. You had to behave yourself.[79]

Langley's contradictory affirmation of community, material shortages and the punitive aspects of living in close quarters – related to what E. P. Thompson described as 'rough music' – was widely shared.[80] Paul, in *Poverty, Hardship but Happiness, Those Were the Days 1903–17*, employs ironic humour to describe the less savoury aspects of his childhood, such as having teeth pulled without an anaesthetic ('those were the days') and not being allowed to read the Sunday papers ('Proper Victorian days!'). Both hardship and community are contained in many of the simple statements found in Fed autobiographies, for example, 'This was our life then, full of fun and happiness in spite of deprivations, which we took for granted', which pinpoints this structure of feeling.[81]

The themes of both pride and poverty are also perceptible in detailed descriptions. In accounts of daily life, for instance the route taken to a Sunday School outing, readers are given insights into a local place and the richness of working-class life. Relating routines of daily toil, bars of soap, washing powders and brushes was a means of engaging with the reality of poverty and the sheer hard work of it all.[82] At the same time, the particularity of this writing served as an assertion of individual and collective agency which avoided subsuming the individual within abstract historical forces that smoothed the edges of personal experience. Such details were warmly received and picked over by local audiences who had shared a life lived in close proximity,[83] a process of clarification that spurred new writers to action.

Reclaiming the collective past through the minutiae of life was a way of documenting the truth. A. S. Jasper, in *A Hoxton Childhood*, reprinted by Centerprise, noticed that middle-class people often had no idea that poverty had existed so recently and on such a widespread scale.[84] He breaks off from his informal and oral style of writing to introduce a conscious voice and tell us the truth, directly, about conditions in those days:

> I've seen women take an ordinary flat iron, borrow 3d. on it, get 2½d. after ½d. was stopped for the ticket and go straight to the nearest pub and get half qtn. gin. This may seem fantastic in this day and age and if anyone cares to dispute this I can name the pawnshop on Essex Road and the pub.[85]

In the style of a puritan autobiography, the evidential grounding in the naming of the pawnshop and the pub are explicit. The intense concern to comprehend and share experiences added an element of volatility to the autobiographical narrative, as the urge to inform took over from evaluative and descriptive modes.

Ron Barnes wrote two books that illustrate this dilemma in representing working-class life. The first, *Licence to Live*, explores negative experiences and feelings. Readers enjoyed the book but they also noted that it appeared to be a little one-sided and had not fully addressed the more positive aspects of his past; *Coronation Cups and Jam Jars* was the result. The latter text attempts to capture not only the difficulties of life but also the human responses and the communities that people were able to build. Critics were not convinced. Dennis Marsden was troubled by the emphasis on community in a context of virtual destitution: he complained of

> a curious tension between his sententious insistence on the community spirit of the East End as preserved in his grandparents' reminiscences, and his descriptions of violence, vermin, anti-semitism, poverty and ill-health.[86]

One respondent noticed that the tension 'was in the conditions themselves'.[87] It was a view that went unheeded by Bourke, who would marshal evidence of violence, ill-health, unsocial attitudes and divisions within the working class to show that community was a subsequent invention. What undermined Bourke's case was that a large part of her evidence for the absence of community was drawn from these very autobiographies, demonstrating that they could be used to both confirm and deny community, which signified the existence of this contradictory structure of feeling.[88] While Bourke attended to the obstacles to community, by setting up an ideal type she missed the more contingent ways in which practices and meanings of community were constructed and reconstructed. Community was clearly circumscribed by material deprivation, but the spaces in which it was made were very real for those in Bradford, who remembered:

> If the mother of the family was ill, there would always be someone at hand to do the housework, look after the children and invalid, and provide food with no thought of reward. People helped one another as a matter of course in any kind of trouble, especially bereavement.[89]

Although people may have had 'no thought of reward', they also helped each other as 'a matter of course'. Community could take the form of an exchange relation, without which individuals and families could not survive. Helping others in crisis was rational, even if only because one day others might help you. The prospect of surviving on one's own was more problematic. The commercial autobiography by Helen Forrester describes a rare example of a middle-class family fallen on hard times whose problems are compounded the lack of support networks.[90] Those without assistance or resources left few records.

Moreover, the community invoked in these autobiographies often existed on a small scale and might revolve around a few streets, neighbours and relatives.[91] For one contributor to the Lifetimes series, a part of East Manchester could represent the whole world to a child:

> I didn't believe there was such a place as London. The geography books were just picture-books. For me, my own little district, Ardwick, that was the world – I really mean it. As for the pictures, anyone can draw. The wide world was something like God is to me now, you don't know whether it's there or not.[92]

The boundaries of community were flexible and might be expanded temporarily or, at other times, confined to certain neighbourhoods. For Paul, a street party exemplified a 'wonderful community spirit', a widening of community, not a temporary aberration.[93] Indeed, from the 1920s middle-class attempts were made to impose larger community institutions on informal working-class networks.[94]

Debates on community also related to historiographical developments. Rather than dismissing the 'retrospective construction' of the past as contaminating the documentary evidence, historians have examined the formation of subjectivity and memory across time and place. While memory can be informative about the past, it is also affected by the context of remembering.[95] Thus, writers welcomed increasing prosperity and security following the Second World War even if it did not reach everyone. Langley at one point described the world he was living in as some sort of 'paradise' after working in the Labour Party for so many years, but facing the resulting disorientation was no easy task.[96] Noakes knew that the welfare state had prevented her and her disabled husband from ending up in a state of destitution.[97] However, implicitly these accounts cast doubts upon the modernising discourse that the second half of the twentieth century could be interpreted in terms of progress from poverty to wealth and comfort. The issues of housing, 'slum clearance' and eventual gentrification became acute. Groups took up this theme in books such as Centerprise's *The Island*, QueenSpark's *Backyard Brighton*, *Backstreet Brighton* and, from Bristol Broadsides, *St Philip's Marsh, The Story of an Island and its People*.[98] Buildings were tied to people's very identity and their removal hit at the core of their being. Attitudes hardened as residents ruminated over their past lives. The whole language of the 'slum' was contentious, being interpreted as a personal insult to the people who lived there. *Backyard Brighton* includes the notes of public officials who condemned whole areas as 'unfit for human habitation' alongside photos showing streets emptied of people, which were used to justify demolition. Repeated passages reject claims about lack of cleanliness: 'Carlton Hill was supposed to be a bad area, they were supposed to be slums. We were poor but we were clean, we weren't lousy. Their places were immaculate.'[99] The irony is that, from a later perspective, they looked like desirable properties: 'If they'd put a bathroom and electricity in them it would have been lovely, it was such a pretty street.'[100] Ex-residents later felt cheated materially, spiritually and aesthetically, although it is interesting that there were no major objections to slum clearance when it took place.[101] Over time this fuelled a simmering anger and a tacit criticism of political and economic changes.

Healey also wrote about these feelings in somewhat stereotypical terms that drove a wedge between left-wing politics and working-class experience. He wove in polemics against the welfare state, frozen food and hooligans:

> No family allowances then, or your rent being paid by the Social Services ... The 'Welfare State' and the wonderful life as it is supposed to be now under this so-called Socialist, Communist, party who are now in power, was never dreamed of then. Yet we lived and were a hundred times more cheerful and had wonderful food when we got it, not this frozen muck we have now. We danced at the Regent or Sherry's, had wonderful beer at 4d a pint, five Woodbines for 2d and paid 1d on a bus which took you almost the length of Brighton ... by Jingo we had friendship and neighbourly companions, and we could go to a football match in peace, not frightened of the yobbos ganging up and knocking old people over ... everyone going outside the law was given whatever sentence they deserved.[102]

To some extent, this passage sits uneasily with the rest of his text. But he chooses to interpret his experience in conservative ways. His was a 'reactionary' view from which some historians and activists in Brighton and elsewhere wanted to learn:

> There is a depth of feeling against 'hooligans', 'spongers' – even trade unions, and against some of the features of the 'modern' world which make the messy harshness of former times in East Brighton in some sense 'good'. Unless the left can understand this, the depth of feeling will be delivered to an ugly 'right'.[103]

Unresolved dilemmas indicated the potential for alternative meanings and directions. The New Right, of course, were busy attacking the gains of the post-war welfare state. Commonly held ideas about individual worth, responsibility and community were articulated within an authoritarian populism.[104]

Silences

Critiques of community also focused on other exclusions. A number of Fed activists themselves saw the working class as unified by a common culture and common heritage, but this was becoming strained. Conceptions of difference became prevalent, with race, gender, disability and sexuality playing important roles. Community publishers encouraged writers to think about the gaps in their accounts. In this vein, Bornat argued that community publishing groups had been complicit in reproducing versions of 'community' that served to exclude groups of people (disabled, black people) and difficult issues (sexuality, domestic violence).[105] Examples were also taken from a range of community publications beyond the Fed and focused on historical autobiography in particular, whereas within the Fed as a whole, there were frequent interactions among diverse populations.

Community publishers would have found it difficult to discard the whole principle of 'by and for' a community if there had been a requirement for diversity. Groups had been set up with a view that working-class people should control their texts, and a heavy-handed approach to these matters would have undercut the principle of devolving power to authors. Even so, there were cases where Brighton autobiographies included memories of those with mental health difficulties, and editorial groups did raise issues of diversity.[106] They also supported separate publications by 'other' communities, such as *Daring Hearts*, a lesbian and gay oral history of Brighton in the 1950s and 1960s, a community that had been hidden from itself.[107]

In shining a light on new areas of experience, there were, however, inevitable absences. Communities could police thoughts and feelings and cast a veil of silence over some areas of life. For instance, the East Bowling group was, like other groups, very sensitive about discussions of sex, which one writer wanted to pursue:

> there was a sense of not wanting to write anything rude down and Evelyn ... wanted to write ... what it was like in the thirties around sex and she wanted to write about relationships between men and women and how they were ruined by poverty and the fear of getting pregnant and they wouldn't let her, they wouldn't allow her to write about sex ... because it was rude ... some of them ... used to come in a hat ... a bit proper.[108]

The existence of a known and local audience had its drawbacks. At times, writers edited their texts with the audience in mind, perhaps leaving out awkward or offensive material. Margaret Ward, who wrote about the break-up of her marriage, came under family pressure to cut out sections of her text. Some stories simply remained unwritten in order to avoid causing distress to family, friends and community.

Pre-war black experiences were only partly dealt with in this autobiographical writing. Although Bristol Broadsides operated in an area that had a visible black population, the group did not find an adequate way of covering this issue, though some of their collections of writing about the history of Bristol life included post-war recollections of black people alongside pre-war memories.[109] In Liverpool, even though oral history projects were taking place, there was no Fed community publisher that worked on pre-war black experiences. The Liverpool 8 Writers' Workshop included black writers who had settled in Britain in the early 1940s. Their collection, *19 from 8*, depicted black people's contribution to the war effort, their discovery of class differences in Britain, discrimination and the public denial of their existence.[110]

The Ethnic Communities Oral History Project did begin to redress the imbalance with books such as *Aunt Esther's Story*. Esther Bruce, a black woman, lived in a working-class area where she was accepted, and the idea of working-class community permeates her memories of the past. She did face racism, but it came from her schoolteacher, who told the class not to speak to black people. This earlier connection to a community contrasts with her perceptions of the post-war period. As life became increasingly racialised, she was ashamed to be British, an analysis that ties into arguments that a 'new racism' and narrow nationalism had developed after 1945.[111]

External social realities were also experienced in a fleeting manner rather than as a life-long political process. Public discourses and events often skip over the surface of these autobiographical lives without embedding themselves in deeper consciousness. Specifically, the Empire, while an inescapable fact of British life over centuries, makes only brief appearances in this body of writing. For instance, *The Island* contains a picture of a minstrel performer without comment;[112] in Brighton, 'Nigger Minstrels played their banjo's at low tide';[113] in the village of Ditchling, Frank Brangwyn painted murals with 'little dark skinned children' as models, who ran around the village naked 'to the consternation of some of the spinster residents'.[114] The paucity of comment points to the paradoxical role of this global force in everyday life. Writers grew up surrounded by the assumption that the Empire was simply 'there', although its ubiquity was commonly external to personal understanding.[115]

Occasionally the implications intruded into personal lives, as when Ward's mother went into hospital in the 1950s and 'had a very kind Jamaican nurse ... the first black person she had ever met' who changed her mind favourably about hospitals.[116] Empire also had to be consciously taught in schools, and Ward remembers that Empire Day 'wasn't just a day to celebrate; we were taught about the Empire in our geography lessons, which is what made it so special'.[117] However, in general it was a distant idea that was not easily related to personal experience. In fact, the contradictions between Empire and the reality of working-class life could be a salient theme for writers. Manville remembers the empty phrases that meant little to him:

> They had taught us the words and had given us each a paper Union Jack on a stick; they told us how England held 'Dominion over Palm and Pine' and they told us about an 'Empire on which the sun never sets' – few of us could understand a word of it, but they said that we should be proud. So I, for one, held my flag aloft, and as I marched, wondered what I had to do to 'be proud' ...
>
> It was Empire Day, May 23rd, that we marched and sang. I cannot rightly remember the year. But it was around the time that Uncle Charlie stood at the door of the baker's shop to steal bread.
>
> Because his children were hungry.[118]

The idea of a nation without differences of class and race is interpreted as hollow, skilfully conveyed through juxtaposition. Even at its height, empire was an indistinct force sealed off from the everyday experience of the majority of people in Britain. In the coming years, confusion and ignorance would result as the pink swathes on the map were gradually populated with a rich variety of countries, cultures, religions and individuals, some of whom settled in Britain.

Looking back

In the Fed, books were often initiated by a younger generation who were seeking greater understanding. Writers offered personal testimony in a way reminiscent of spiritual autobiographers of the seventeenth century who had sought to justify themselves before God. The texts were also aimed at their peers, for whom they wrote from a position of equality, a fact that helped to foster an evaluative voice and to widen and make familiar the idea of authorship. There was a powerful collective urge to assess an earlier period of working-class history. Dramatic changes were taking place that seemed to mark an ending in personal and societal terms. Writers aimed to represent their past lives accurately and to retrieve a set of values. In doing so, they nurtured a distinction between past and present. The past was imbued with a timelessness and commonality that sometimes collapsed long periods of history into a lifetime. Experience and memory merged with the recollections of relatives in an oral tradition.

Writers faced pressures familiar to all autobiographers: how to make sense of a life and translate that onto the page, distilling lifelong experience into a few anecdotes and events, and which areas to close off as too harrowing or unresolved. In part, writers were struggling to impose meaning upon sketchy memories of childhood with which they intermingled description and analysis. Immersed in the social and political contradictions of the 1970s and 1980s, fragmented lives were nonetheless constructed consciously. They worked on the boundary between the social and the individual and sought to understand collective histories but also to humanise homogenised representations of gender and class. Work, family, politics and community were all summoned to achieve this dual purpose. The critique of Fed publications was in part an uneasy response to the influx of untrained writers and historians. The recoil by some professional historians typified the way in which they were able to separate softer feelings about history, including their own personal pasts, from the harder-hitting analyses which appeared in academic texts. Working-class writers were less able to isolate emotion from analysis in the absence of professional identities and institutional frameworks. It became easy to assume that FWWCP books simply presented uncritical evocations of the 'good old days' in the same way that many commercial publications were exploiting and simplifying this area of experience. Nostalgic and cathartic aspects can be identified, but fluid notions of community were also incorporated into a critical self-awareness. The accounts produced by Fed writers appeared at a specific historical moment even though they were to be recycled by successive generations coming to terms with the long-term effects of deindustrialisation.

Workshops collectivised accounts of social change. The uses of literacy implicit in the production of autobiographies were being extended and reshaped. The scaffolding provided to writers by editorial groups, transcribers and editors was invaluable, although it was at times hidden. These processes were to be consciously applied in the field of adult literacy, where a younger generation of writers were examining their own experiences of the post-war world.

4 A beginner reader is not a beginner thinker

Although the whole worker writer movement was actively reshaping the uses of literacy, a distinctive group of texts were written by adult literacy students. Creative expression was seen as central to taking control of one's own literacy development and educational materials were produced from which others could learn. Students did not necessarily see themselves as 'writers' until tutors introduced them to the idea. Despite the uniqueness of this initiative, there were similarities across the federated workshops and beyond. Adult literacy carved out an independent space for itself, wary of any connection with schools and associated feelings of failure and shame, even though similar pedagogies traversed both schools and adult education. In attempting to overcome the negative assumptions being made about adults with literacy difficulties, student writing was judged as both educational and literary. Peter Goode, a founder member of Pecket Well College, contended that 'a beginner reader is not a beginner thinker', demanding that literacy students should be treated seriously and be allowed to produce real writing.[1] The content of writing responded to changing educational and social environments. The ways that experience and ideas were represented provides a case study of the creative practices in the early adult literacy movement, a considerable part of which overlapped with the Fed. Inevitably, concerns were raised about personal expression, voice and subjectivity. Because the work was read by other students, it enjoyed a significant audience.

First time writers

Write First Time (WFT) was a national body that organised ad hoc editorial meetings around the country in which local students and tutors could take part. As a small group dependent on volunteers, it nevertheless successfully distributed thousands of papers on a quarterly basis. Members were relatively open about their commitment to class politics, providing a national voice and devolving power to students. In short, they aspired to an emancipatory practice of literacy in which the experience of learners was central to rethinking their position in society.² As with other Federation material, the group was keen to publish a diversity of works in terms of style, form and complexity that represented the mix of students who submitted writing. But WFT also helped establish the framework for the form and content of student writing. Its position was outlined in an editorial which is line broken, rather than poetry, in order to help readers grasp blocks of meaning at one time:

> We don't like pieces
> that seem to be written
> in a false voice.
> Some people think you have
> a 'writing' language
> and a speaking language
> that are separate.
> They try to make their writing
> too fancy.
> This may be because of the way
> they are taught.
> Writing does not have to be
> complicated, to be good.
> Nor does poetry have to be
> pretty, or sentimental.
> It is important to find the style
> that comes naturally to you.
> One group talked about this
> at the WRITE FIRST TIME conference:
> 'You wouldn't want to change
> your accent, would you?
> So you shouldn't want to change
> your writing'.
> We like writing that speaks
> directly to the reader,
> and expresses clearly
> the thoughts of the writer.
> Bill said in our book,
> 'Writing helps other people
> to know the person.
> I've read people,
> and I've felt I've been
> a part of them.
> I know what he's gone through'.
>
> Few working class people
> have had the chance
> to write about themselves,
> for themselves.
> Kevin said: 'Class gets into everything.

it gets into writing too'.
In our society many working class people
have been taught to think
that they are not important,
and that what they have to say
is not interesting
or valuable to others.

...

One thing WRITE FIRST TIME never prints
is writing that seems to blame people
for what others have done to them.
We all know things are never
that simple.[3]

This type of editorial helped not only to encourage writing but to channel it in certain directions. The part-time secretary, when typing up the work that had been submitted, claimed she could tell in advance which pieces would be chosen for publication.[4] For instance, birthday card-type verse was unlikely to be printed. The editorial statement stresses the importance of spoken language, accent and dialect, rather than standard English, as a source of authentic expression. It connects to the importance of personal experience and the vernacular voice, reflecting a distrust of fancy aesthetics, an idea with a long puritan pedigree involving suspicion of an elaborated upper-class style. The imputed relationship between writer and reader was conceived of as direct and unfettered – a liberation from wider social relations. The use of 'working class', especially given its subsequent denial, can be seen as one means of 'mobilising' students to have a sense of themselves as oppressed and denied their rights, rather than as victims or patients in need of a dose of literacy. Given that adult literacy students were, on the whole, working class, the emphasis on equality and the emerging discourse of equal opportunities provided further endorsement for marginalised groups. Yet students and tutors selected a range of material in different forms: some writing, on close reading, just 'worked'.

Given time constraints and the effort that writing required, there was a tendency to encapsulate a feeling or meaning in a condensed form. The short statement or idea was published in its own right:

Why I write poetry
I'm too lazy to write page after page of prose, so if I see or feel something that moves me I put it into a poem.
You can describe scenes in people's minds with very few words.
I like that.

Josie Anderson[5]

In the 1970s, Fed groups such as Centerprise, Peckham and Gatehouse published what came to be called 'beginner readers', books of about 500 words with illustrations and photos to help guide the reader, which were popular in literacy classes. Writings typically focused on educational experiences. For instance, the Gatehouse book by Josie Byrnes, *Never in a Loving Way*, contains shortened line-broken text alongside a longer version in prose. She described her childhood, involving poverty and neglect by both teachers and parents, which struck a chord with many readers. Byrnes's spoken and simple style of address allowed readers to respond on a human level:

> I know what it's like
> to be poor and hungry
> and to have no bed.
> Yes, I can see it now,
> as my mother used to lay us down
> on the floor
> with coats for a mattress
> and coats over us
> for blankets and sheets
> and even one for a pillow,
> a coat rolled up.

The lack of literacy was central to Byrnes's position.[6] The extract has the feel of a flashback in which she is both present and removed – 'Yes, I can see it now'. With poor eyesight and lack of support, she was always the 'lousy headed little girl' who made no progress. The reader is prodded into dialogue: 'I suppose you'll be saying by now, "Well, what was the point in giving you an education if you wasn't going to be helped at home?"'[7] Byrnes momentarily escapes from her surroundings by dreaming about a 'green world' where she has things and is clever, which turns the world upside down:

> I tell you something else. We used to pretend, my sister and I, that my mother and father wasn't our mother and father! They was our auntie and uncle! Oh, we came from America! Oh, what our father and mother would do if they knew, only knew how our uncle and auntie were treating us! They would go mad! Another favourite was that I had a wardrobe and I had lost the key and we couldn't get our new clothes out of it.[8]

At a time when absolute poverty was no longer ubiquitous, Byrnes knows her family is not 'normal' and feels wronged. She wrote her story when she was in her forties, and it ends with a faith expressed in education as an enabling and potentially equalising force, although her hope appears to have shaky foundations:

> I've learnt a lot in forty years. Most of it since I've been married. Well, how did I help my children? Well, I haven't. I failed them as a mother for the simple reason that because I did not know this and I don't know the other, I haven't been able to speak or to read properly. Oh, I'm learning and I'm going to learn. But I hope that by

learning I'm not going to be hateful to some of them who haven't got an education. I hope I can still see folk for what they are and not make fun of people.[9]

The post-war world, which trumpeted 'secondary education for all', equality and material progress, paradoxically induced internalised feelings of failure on a widespread basis as it became clear that these benefits had not touched everyone. Learning was by no means an inherently positive experience. Educational journeys for the marginalised were much more hazardous than was indicated by the public image. Byrnes's repeated self-reproach is a case in point. She has clearly suffered from the negative judgements of others but is determined that the process of learning will not lead her to treat others with the contempt she has received. In addition, the impact of books on readers could be overwhelming. Sharing painful lives through literacy was a first step in building confidence. Sue Torr, who went on to write an award-winning play, remembered learning to read from Byrnes's text as a literacy student:

> I looked through *Never In a Loving Way*, reading the words I could read and looking at the lovely pictures – there's one of a girl on a swing – and thinking about my childhood. Even though I couldn't read every word in the book I was engrossed with the pictures and print and I was getting a good feeling in myself. I wanted to tell everybody: 'Look, I've just read my first book!'[10]

Jane Mace would later discuss the isolation and neglect felt by students as a motivating force behind the literacy movement. There was a fear that students were being presented as if their lives were thoroughly blighted by a lack of literacy, whereas in reality they were capable of leading fulfilling and complex lives – a position also accepted by Mace, who had originally connected her argument to class inequality.[11] This debate reflected a predicament in the way the concept of deficit was understood. Although working-class writers often chose to highlight adversity, when their writing was taken out of context and incorporated into official discourses, divergent meanings emerged. 'Disadvantage' could be used to emphasise shame and isolation at one moment and exploitation at another, while some writers found that sharing memories with peers was a form of consciousness raising. It was hard to maintain a clear division between these positions, which would continue to re-emerge in new guises.

Indeed, the idea of deficit could be put to multiple uses. Having difficulties with reading and writing did not always equate with unhappiness. *A Good Life* by 'Alan' is a story about a man who was ignored at school and never learnt to read. As a result, he was not able to set up a bank account. Instead, Alan gets rich by buying houses for cash earned in the mines as a 'Bevin boy'[12] and on the docks:

> I work on the docks, right.
> I work long hours.
> I have money off the job
> ...

> I don't know what to do with it.
> I can't put it in the bank,
> because I can't read,
> or write a form out
> to put money in
> ...
> What can you do with it?
> You can either burn it,
> or do something with it.
> ...
> I saw a house,
> I bought that house
> ...
> When the house was done up,
> I let it off.
> Got some more money off the docks,
> with working hard.
> Bought another house,
> and that's how it kept on going.[13]

Not being able to read was an inconvenience, but Alan subverted social expectations by benefiting from a lack of literacy. At a time of virtual full employment and rising wages, it was possible to navigate one's life successfully with limited formal education. Alan's vernacular style appealed to a wide range of students and *A Good Life* would be reprinted many times.

'Negative' experiences were also counterbalanced by more 'positive' aspects of working-class life. Student publishing aimed to utilise the personal experiences of learners in a way that gave them control over their literacy development. Selecting specific areas of experience could further this purpose. For instance, in *Every Birth It Comes Different*, published by the Hackney Reading Centre, women and men from different cultures contributed their experiences of childbirth. Books such as these successfully made the student the 'expert' by drawing upon rich experience and knowledge. This book also shared different traditions and cultural ideas relating to childbirth, communicating across differences. It even gained an additional audience beyond the literacy group, being used on nursing courses for a time.

Politics of literacy

While Alan's writing was implicitly political, others explicitly responded to the public issues with which their lives were entwined. Indeed, political writings, many by learners, were featured in *Write First Time*, including articles on rent, landlords and employment law. In the mid-1970s, an editorial explained that workers would not be getting pay increases under the Social Contract, questioning: 'What do the bosses have to do to keep the social contract? / Nothing. They are not in it.'[14] Other student-written *WFT* editorials criticised cuts in education. When making a case against nuclear weapons, Robert Carson revealed a canny distrust of the powerful:

> I can't read and write
> but I do know what's going on.
> The people in power,
> they know what's going on as well.[15]

The statement occupied a liminal space between everyday and political worlds which validated similar attempts by students to write about political and social issues. This was queried by some readers who feared bringing politics into education and that tutors might be seen as foisting their political views onto students. In reality, writing on political and social subjects was problematic. Only tentative steps were made towards documentary and political modes of argument and writing. WFT organised a week-long summer conference on 'writing beyond the first person', influenced by the School Council's *The Development of Writing Abilities (11–18)*, led by James Britton, which classified writing on a scale from transactional through expressive to poetic, along which, it was claimed, learners were capable of moving.[16] WFT explained:

> Most writing by adult students is mainly expressive ... there is not enough published work on ... how adult learners move from the expressive to broaden their range, without losing the integrity of their expressive writing. There are also not enough models of adult learners' own writing to suggest to others forms and modes of writing they might try beyond the expressive.[17]

The question could not easily be answered in adult literacy and would become the source of a major problem as external forces were brought to bear in an altered political climate.

During the 1980s, student writing would be closely scrutinised through a newly politicised lens. As the hold of the New Right became firmer, so the Fed found itself having to operate in an inhospitable setting with constrained funding opportunities. From 1979, Thatcherism was systematic in its attempts to locate and eradicate actual and potential opposition. While the Falklands War and the Miners' Strike of 1984–85 had very real implications in themselves, they also symbolised the narrowing of the parameters of acceptable political debate, rejecting one version of class analysis in favour of a new nationalism and a class politics wielded from above.[18] Community and voluntary organisations were not immune to the changes.

The political context also affected the relationship between WFT and its funder, the Adult Literacy and Basic Skills Unit (ALBSU).[19] In 1982, a major controversy was sparked by a vivid poem by Colin Fearnley about the impact of Thatcherism (see figure 6):

6 Colin Fearnley's controversial poem in Write First Time, an innovative paper mainly written by and for adult literacy students.

> Come, Mrs Thatcher
> Let me lead you through this desolate land –
> The land you have laid so bare.
> See all the dead factories left there.
> See the old, the sick the young
> Shuffling round, heads bowed with despair,
> Asking is there no-one who cares.
> See the Nation's body laying there
> Blood flowing from its wounds.
> Cut by a surgeon with no care
> Of the body held there.
>
> Her coat once blue, now red
> From the blood of her dead.
>
> Colin Fearnley[20]

The poem exposed an anger and a sense that the nation had been irreparably damaged. It reworked the patriotic language of Thatcherism in order to encapsulate a mood of betrayal.

However, a Norfolk tutor complained about the poem to her MP, who then informed the Department of Education and Science (DES). It was suggested informally that a literacy student could not possibly have written this poem and must have been directed by a tutor – literacy students were, and are, seen as vulnerable and easily led.²¹ William Shelton, then a junior minister in the DES, was quoted in the Sunday Times under the title 'Write First Time "getting it wrong"':

> The poem was in jolly bad taste. I thought it could upset a lot of people. You have to realise that if people are using Department of Education money, then we are responsible. It was a repugnant poem ... I think it's a good magazine. It's not a question of me going for it politically. A lot of it is very anti-establishment. I don't mind that. I don't think they are exactly writhing under censorship.²²

This quote displayed a growing right-wing confidence in attacking the legitimacy of others' political positions while denying that their own intervention had anything to do with censorship or politics. No formal complaint was ever made to Write First Time so it was not possible to have an open discussion about the matter. WFT were forced to read between the lines, and the minutes of their meetings disclosed a confusion about how to represent the paper in public: 'keep our heads down' with a 'long-term strategy for clarifying and adjusting the way we are described in the press'.²³ ALBSU imposed a number of new conditions: no further articles were to be commissioned that were 'not in keeping with the philosophy of the paper'; editorial 'checks and balances' were to be set up; 'senior people with wide experience of education and its management' would be appointed to the management committee; and the DES was to be sent future editions. But funding continued 'in view of the potential value of the findings of the (temporary) Writing Development Project'.²⁴ The collective were in no doubt that they should keep future issues 'trouble free'. At one point it was decided to cut two lines from a piece of writing that was deemed too political. 'A card carrying conservative' present at the editorial meeting wrote a letter bemoaning the 'creeping cancer' of 'censorship and oppression'.²⁵ In this changed atmosphere the Sunday Times commented that the paper had 'heeded the warnings'. A section of the paper, 'You and the Law', was 'now occupied by a charming story about a parrot'.²⁶

In 1985 ALBSU cut its funding for WFT and other national literacy organisations. Alternative voices were no longer to be encouraged by the state and the Fed's version of literacy was seen as unacceptable. In 1985 Alan Wells, head of ALBSU, had insisted that WFT should consist solely of student writing 'uninfluenced by tutors', in keeping with the ideas of the paper.²⁷ By 1991, however, ALBSU's position on student publishing had become increasingly strident. The tide had turned so much that Sue Slipman, who herself had moved rightwards from the Communist Party, accused tutors of using student writing 'as a way of confining students to an educational ghetto' and dismissed student publishing as the '"valium" of basic education – an excuse for lack of planning and rigour and a poverty of expectation', an almost exact opposite of the aims and practices of student publishing.²⁸

Writing in new times?

Literacy groups negotiated the representation and sharing of student experience. Even though adult literacy became less openly political in the 1980s, groups such as Gatehouse were able to continue working in this restricted climate. It mined the seam of positive aspects of writers' lives, commonly with a humorous element. Similar stories would proliferate as Gatehouse published beginner reader books, many of them anecdotes about commonplace events: looking after a dog, going out for a drink and starting a new job. In place of stereotypes about illiteracy, writers presented themselves in normal situations. This was not only a response to narrowing political parameters. Students and tutors became cautious about accentuating shame and neglect at the expense of normality and humanity.[29] For instance, in *The Cardigan*, Chris Curley charts a man's relationship with his wife through an argument over an old cardigan:

> About fifteen years ago
> my wife went to a jumble sale.
> She bought a few things for the house,
> plus the scruffiest cardigan
> I've seen in my life.
>
> I said to her, 'What's that for?
> Is it for the dog to sleep on?'
> 'No, it's not. It's for you',' she said.
> 'I wouldn't wear that thing
> if I were stark naked
> in the middle of town
> on a January morning,' I said.[30]

Curley employs a storytelling format to build the prosaic details of a relationship and to establish common understanding. This ordinary scene is then disrupted by lively dialogue that allows Curley to befriend his readers. Domestic relations appeared less frequently in student writing by men. In addition, on the first page we find the word 'scruffiest'. While beginner readers did not use overly complex language, sometimes longer words added to the story and could be a familiar part of speech.[31] In general, books written by students aimed to avoid the stilted and repetitive language of graded readers which could speak down to the audience.

The Cardigan served as a new model of creativity and helped to open the floodgates to a whole series of comic stories at Gatehouse. As the volume of this writing increased it became the norm, each book serving as a model for the next. The suggestion arose that Gatehouse books were becoming sanitised, avoiding awkward issues. In part this reflected the tendency of students to see themselves as less 'political' in a world where politics was being compressed into ever more restricted spheres. One group of students discussing the setting up of a student magazine in 1994 felt it was important to avoid all mention of 'religion or politics'. Moreover, funders could influence outcomes: a regeneration board in East Manchester enquired about editorial policies, worried that a magazine they funded might actually criticise them.[32]

Unavoidably, issues relating to social justice started to seep back into arenas of public discussion. While party politics was out of bounds, there remained vast areas of experience, often divorced from class analysis, that could be exploited in writing. For instance, both *My New World* by Georgina Conway and *The Body Builder* by Charles Carrington focus on bullying.[33] This issue had been aired in public and so became more available and acceptable for open discussion. Carrington outlines how he became a loner after being bullied and sidelined at school, partly because he could not read or write. With his parents' support, he joined a boys' club where he discovered a passion for weight training and a way of being in the world:

> I still go weight training to this day.
> I go to classes three times a week.
>
> I am still a loner. I have got used to it.
> I like my own company.
> I go to reading and writing classes
> twice a week. I am now a lot better
> at reading and writing than I used to be.[34]

This was not a clear-cut 'before and after' picture of improvement, but it did show the individual writer successfully inhabiting the world. The articulation of personal experience could thus be mediated by dominant social and institutional frameworks.

Moreover, 'risky' and challenging writing did not always arise spontaneously but came from workshops that had been specifically developed for this purpose. Targeting new constituencies helped to challenge ideas of what could be written about. A project working with prisoners produced writing on crime, while collaboration with Asian women led to a range of bilingual texts touching upon disability and migration.[35] An earlier example was the group of African-Caribbean writers who produced *Just Lately I Realise*. Over three years, the writers came to trust Gatehouse staff, built up a group identity and gained the self-assurance to write about settling in Britain.[36] For instance, 'William' relives his experience of getting a job as a driver's mate and his testing time at the Trueshine factory works canteen:

> When we went to the canteen
> There's about six hundred
> of us there,
> and I'm the only one coloured
> and they call a strike

> just through me.
> Everybody line up
> and them all looking
> looking round at me.
> Everybody be looking and talking.
> The stacka-truck driver,
> he's a shop steward,
> and he say to the whole canteen,
> (excuse the language)
> 'That black bastard
> not getting served here.'
> ...
> When we finish our break
> and we came back to the load
> I pull my cigarette out
> and I give one to him,
> the man who drive the stacka-truck
> and he took it,
> yes, he took it off me.
> He said, 'Ok'.
> My mate said to him,
> 'What you done man?'
> He said well he got to do that
> to suit his people
> because if him don't call a strike
> them throw him out of the union.
> That place was called Trueshine.
> No black guy work there.[37]

This spoken text was not written as a poem but reads like one. Remaining faithful to the voice, it is a very effective literary text that reaffirms the close association between written and spoken forms of address. It builds tension to the crescendo of the directly racist language, emphasising everyone 'looking' at him repetitively. The short staccato lines jolt the reader into feelings of outrage at the racism of the workers and their union which forced a division between traditional class politics and the migrants arriving from the Caribbean. Yet William stands tall, searching for communication and understanding, uncovering the hypocrisy of the driver and the trade union structure. There is a degree of dissonance between his ability to communicate on an individual level and the collective muffling of his voice. By invoking an actual and known place, he writes in the style of Langston Hughes but with echoes of William Blake, who encouraged us to 'see the world in a grain of sand'. The factual statement, 'That place called Trueshine', anchors his exposure of racism within an exact location which reverberates beyond the local.

Aesthetic judgements were wrapped up with social and political arguments where educational issues could become contentious. As with young people's writing, within adult literacy there were ongoing debates about whether publishing non-standard language was a useful way into literacy or whether learners needed to be taught standard English as the language of power or even as the 'correct' way. *Who Feels It, Knows It* included writers from the Caribbean who had lived in Manchester for a number of years; their language was a mixture of Caribbean and Manchester styles and grammar, neither one nor the other. Some black groups were critical of the work, claiming it implied that the African-Caribbean community were stupid and that it would be used by racists to justify separating out black children in schools. However, the book was funded by the Commission for Racial Equality, and black groups were split on the issue. The writers were happy with what they had produced, and to have corrected the writing would have meant imposing from the outside and taking the text away from those who were not yet able to work in standard English.[38] Opposing positions could dissipate into finely graded arguments.

Moving on?

Student writing and publishing continually sought avenues out of the 'literacy ghetto' as part of a broader movement of working-class literature.[39] Some writers aspired to go beyond the educational limitations of student publishing. The association with the growing network of writing and publishing groups enabled connections to be made to wider cultural practices. For example, students began to develop their work in more literary directions and joined writing groups. John Small in Liverpool and Pauline Wiltshire in Hackney both moved from literacy classes to writing workshops. Kevin Higgins was another writer with a clear sense of his own voice whose poetry was published by WFT in *The Seed Is Me*:

> If the seed is me
> And the part I play is cold and dark
> When will the seed grow into a bloom?
> ...[40]

An urge for literary expression and growth was shared by Goode, whose idiosyncratic book, *The Moon on the Window*, was transcribed from speech and contains a mixture of thoughts, stories, poetry and one-liners such as 'the truth is not always on wanted posters'. In reaching out, the writers working within adult literacy came into contact with the varied activities of the Fed.

Higgins and others were confronting their marginalisation, and they rejected certification in favour of engagement with circles of writers and educators who were able to work more openly and creatively with those struggling with literacy. At times, it was not always possible to meet expanding personal needs. One student who was moving into writing groups was upset at being encouraged to edit out a reference to the Cold War that he had slipped into a story about waiting for his dad at a bus stop, thus weaving a political context into his childhood, which was seen as less appropriate for readers.[41] Literacy groups could create obstacles for aspiring writers ready to explore and experiment. Moves to push writing in new directions included not only WFT's writing beyond the first person but also Gatehouse's work of fiction, *Telling Tales*. The latter was completed at a time when adult education was being restructured and accreditation introduced, which made it difficult to disseminate the approach. The attempt to give full recognition to everyone was not always successful. Writing workshops offered an important outlet beyond the sphere of formal learning where literary aims could be further explored.

5   The workshop and working-class writing

The workshop served as a testing ground where prolonged commitment to writing was facilitated. Initial attempts to get something on the page produced eclectic results and could not be categorised easily. Those unaccustomed to writing sometimes felt that existing literature did not provide them with adequate models. Such a body of writing could appear daunting. Working-class writers struggled to connect their experiences and emotions to what was on offer and needed to search for new ideas. Even published working-class writing was not immediately available and there was no ready-made path to follow. Personal experience and memory provided starting points and would be edited and revised in the light of advice and deliberation. Writers explored autobiography and moved on to short stories, drama, poetry and occasionally novels. Surveying this work will represent the final case study before turning to the overall characteristics of this body of working-class writing.

Forms of writing

Autobiographical work that arose from workshops bore the marks of a more literary approach than other texts published by Fed groups, which might have involved an editorial group working with a single writer. In writing workshops, complex, onerous and prolonged feedback on multiple drafts ensured this was the case. Liz Thompson's *Just a Cotchell: Tales from a Dockland's Childhood and Beyond* has many of the hallmarks of a novel. Thompson developed her book through involvement with Basement Writers, which provided a launch pad into a creative exploration of her past. She developed a series of characters and incidents that reveal the fault lines and tensions in East London life. It bears some similarity to Pat Barker's *Union Street*, which was discussed sympathetically in the Fed although reviewers were unhappy with its unremitting despair.[1] Strength, pride and humour are more noticeable in *Just a Cotchell* than in Barker's dour novel. For instance, 'Fag Ash Fanny' is viewed through Thompson's nine-year-old eyes:

Fag Ash Fanny would drop into the papershop for her twenty fags, and then spend her day prowling about in tottery stilettos busting with her corns, and a slowly moulting fur jacket ... 'The Bermondsey Bike' said my cousin Lee. He was twelve and feeling his age obliged him to prepare us for the wicked world.

'There isn't a bloke in the Borough she hasn't given a ride to eether', he said.

'Why don't you ask her for one then', said Derek, my other cousin who was ten. 'I bet you wouldn't walk under her window and whistle'.

'Bet I would'.

'Go on then, let's see ya'.

We all wanted to see this, so off we ran.[2]

The child's eye lends a simplicity to the story based upon limited knowledge of the adult world. When the plan goes wrong, the children scarper but the protagonist slips over and Fanny, desperate for company, invites her young tormentor in for biscuits. When she returns to her mates, they are annoyed at hearing about the prosaic details of Fanny's life, but the story shows Thompson as a young girl becoming attentive to gender relations:

'You're Jim Hankey's granddaughter, aintcher?' she said ... 'I used to know 'im. You ask 'im if he remembers me' ... but even at that age, I knew I wasn't going to do THAT.

I got to go down to the yard, and the other kids pounced on me.

'Wot she DO, Liz?'

'Wot's it LIKE up there?'

'Red hat no drawers', carolled Lee, forgetting the ignominious retreat he'd led earlier.

'We 'ad ginger biscuits, and she was saying about her son, and her cat dying, and that.'

'You're useless', said Derek ... 'Bloody girls. I dunno why we bother with ya.'

'She could tell ya why ya do, old Fanny up there', I snapped. 'Why don't you go up there and ask her.'[3]

Autobiography was being deployed creatively to construct characters who also advanced a social understanding. While Thompson is discovering and describing her past, she also paints a picture of growing up and defying the expectations facing a working-class girl. As a child she is alert to her own intellect, and she wants to get a job and become an independent woman. However, her portrayals of working-class life are neither negative nor celebratory. It is a book in part about the struggle to assert a self without denying class and family, in contrast to an earlier generation of working-class writers who had a diffident, and at times negative, attitude to their pasts.[4]

A second example is Arthur Thickett's *Deckhand, West Pier*, an autobiographical exploration of his time working on Brighton's West Pier that reworks the QueenSpark model considered in Chapter 3. Thickett was born in pre-war Hull but spent much of his life in the army and travelling. He weaves together work on the pier and his nomadic life and connects up the pre- and post-war worlds.

For instance, he watches 'a few older people shaking their heads' at the flower power generation smoking pot but then links to memories of an anti-Vietnam war demonstration, so that personal reflections are complemented by external commentary:

> I grinned to myself; they were harmless enough even though some of their elders certainly did not approve; 'harmless', no that really wasn't the word. The young these days might appear frivolous, way out, but many of them, workers and students – as well as, fair to say, some older people, were trying to stop a war.
>
> They poured into Grosvenor Square, banners flying, the human tide swamping over the green, swelling into every corner, chanting – chanting: 'Ho, Ho, Ho Chi Minh'.[5]

In fact, Thickett hovers above the local backdrop rather than it being an inherent part of his character. As a soldier/traveller, his life story draws on previous international and political experience. He threads his past into the texture of a neighbourhood scene using flashbacks:

> Saturday night (and Sunday morning): Saturday nights I would contrive to get away 'early' – 9.00pm ... I'd finish up at the Belvedere, located right on the sea front ... Frankly, a somewhat sleazy place, it was my usual destination Saturday nights.
> ... with the aid of the old 'white logic' beginning to percolate, I philosophised: First the indulgence of playing back a few vivid reels of my life; what a life! Wars, strange lands, dramas ... and dramas within dramas. Love, plenty of that though never enough. My story, eventful and dramatic in the extreme at times, though I did not plan it that way at all, nor at the time did I see it that way ...
> World War Two ambushed us all, then struck at random. Many it hardly affected at all (rationing hurt nobody); some, whatever they experienced were barely touched; some ... it transformed totally. For me The War and the series of personal dramas it wrought upon me shattered my otherwise bland enough life for ever. It had the further effect of shoving me into a flood of graphic events, both personal and climactic; this state then continued to feed upon itself – potentially dangerous and dehumanising for me though I was not aware of this in 1970 or for some time afterwards.[6]

The passage borrows from *John Barleycorn*, Jack London's own autobiographical account of his struggle with alcoholism, while alluding to Alan Sillitoe's classic *Saturday Night and Sunday Morning*.

Even though Thickett was born in 1928, having been influenced by the 1960s and attracted by expanding personal freedoms, he is more willing to explore relationships and his inner feelings and mental health. Wider social forces circumscribe his individuality and constrain his ability to recount his story. Thickett's drunken dreams elucidate this ambiguity about the autobiographical form:

> 'I', am but a fragment and My Story ... is not mine ... I've only to look back to realise that I did not invent my story to-date, had very little to do with its construction and

incident, very little, largely it just happened to me. Still, I do strive, there is an input, however minute.[7]

Thickett's personal exploration leaves him struggling to identify his own agency, and encourages us to rethink the way in which individual identities are created and sustained over time. In examining his life in a critical, reflexive way, the narrative of the powerful individual begins to dissipate amid the powerful forces which partly determine his classed existence.

It was a small step from autobiography to fiction. Writers took up the short story quite naturally by elaborating and reordering their experiences. At readings, people did literally stand up to tell a story and speak about their lives. Colloquial language could be easily assimilated into the form. Sources were extracted from the lives of the writers and those around them, which could work on the knife edges of daily life. Jimmy McGovern remembered one story that stood out for him,

> about a woman with a gang of kids. Her husband comes home from work and treats the kids to sweets and gives her some money, insisting, absolutely insisting, that she treat herself to a bar of chocolate rather than save that money for something else. It was a great short story. It summed up poverty. The husband insisting on a little bit of pleasure despite everything, the woman utterly pragmatic.[8]

'I Fought Norman Snow' by Eddie Barrett was also recalled by many writers as a good example of the form. Barrett sets the scene with working-class scousers living off the reputation of the Beatles in 1960s London. The central character publicly shames Charley, an old man basking in his past (imaginary?) glories as a boxer, claiming to have fought Norman Snow, a better-known fighter. However, he redeems himself by supporting Charley in a brawl. The old man is stabbed and dies but not before having his claims accepted as authentic. The memory of Charley lives on, with the story expressing a faith in ordinary lives, and redemption feeding into a class awareness. Barrett ends his story in a pub next to the Old Vic, where he is speaking to a theatre producer who

> needled me straightaway. 'Oh, you're from Liverpool are you?' he said, speaking so far back his voice was coming from behind him. 'I suppose you're a great friend of John, Paul and Ringo?' I felt like giving him a belt ... 'No' I said. 'I never knew them. But I knew a fellow who fought Norman Snow'.[9]

The story was performed many times and the written version accurately reproduces the spoken word, introducing sections with 'I'll never forget' and inserting diversionary quips which tightens the narrative, such as, when a fight breaks out, 'even though I'm allergic to violence (I come out all cuts and bruises) I had to make myself busy'.[10] Overall, 'I Fought Norman Snow' has a classic structure with a scene setting, a fall from grace followed by ultimate deliverance along with a new understanding and richer appreciation of life.

Jean Archer's 'The Collector' is another short story based on a common theme, that of living in urban flats and tower blocks.[11] Archer's characters illuminate aspects of working-class life within a brief moment in time. The narrator is dragged around through freezing winds by another character, Rita, to collect money to buy a wreath for the recently deceased Ivy. She had not wanted to go along, but Rita insisted as other possible candidates had gone away for Christmas. The author is understated and provides a contrast to the strong-willed Rita. Indeed, the narrator's guiding voice is stitched into her own poverty: Rita 'knew I'd be available. Like they say the poor are always with us.' Her control over the storytelling is at odds with the way she is manipulated in the text itself. The solidarity of writer and reader is established in opposition to Rita, who holds disagreeable attitudes. Entertaining dialogue and commentary on Rita and her neighbours are well managed: 'It was just her sort of thing. A good chance to clock other people's carpets and curtains and whether they washed the window ledges.' Rita's concerns are exposed as they come to a house with similar curtains to her own:

> We spent a lot of time at that door with Rita topping up her local knowledge. This was even better than finding out in the local paper who'd married who, who was being buried and if you were really lucky who'd been nicked, appeared in court and been banged up. She was appalled to the point of being irritated at the poverty of my acquaintance. I almost felt like apologising.

Hardship and loss are interwoven with comedy. The pair are grieving for Ivy, a good friend. As one woman makes a contribution for Ivy's wreath she leers into the narrator's face and comments:

> ''Ere you're a widow now too encha? I used to see 'im coming along, your 'usband. Nice looking bloke 'e was too, someone told me and I thought …'
> 'No she ain't a widow!' Rita jumped in in her usual multi-decibel voice. ''E went off with another woman didn't 'e'.

At times Rita becomes an overstated and inhospitable character. Halfway around and undeterred by howling winds, freezing temperatures, poor lighting and neighbours who didn't actually know Ivy, Rita comments, 'Marvellous 'ow people 'elp one another round 'ere ennit?', although regarding immigrant families she complains, 'Trust them! … Always the same, ennit? "Me no understand English!"' To another person who had not known Ivy:

> I opened my mouth to attempt a description but Rita got there first. 'Oh you must've known 'er!' she insisted. 'Very clean she was – always kept 'erself respectable'.

The ending is almost a non-ending, with no witty catch or twist in the tale, just two simple sentences that bring us down to earth and slow the pace once the narrator arrives back home, sheltering from the winter: 'It seemed incredibly warm in my kitchen after the cold outside. My eyes and nose began to water at the same time.' Becoming alive to her senses, she conjures up a momentary meditative state in a conflicted world.[12]

The use of language was of central importance in worker writing, as were dialect and dialogue. As a member of Heeley Writers in Sheffield, Renee Crofts resisted the tendency to associate dialect writing with comical characters or to use it as a way of getting recognised by adding local flavour. One example is a fly-on-the-wall piece set in the prime minister's bedroom in which the onlooker's voice is in dialect and the spoken parts are in standard English, an imaginary transformation of the traditional social investigation. In place of the middle-class observer, she views the private life of Margaret and Dennis Thatcher:

> She slithers off bed an' drapes this silk sheet round her. ''E stands watchin', pickin 'is nose – miles away 'e were.
>
> 'I will contemplate' she seys, wavin' him away, an' sits at this dressing table, beautiful dark oak wood it were; she hadn't got that from MFI I can tell yer. Then she starts slurpin tea an' you could 'ear ev'ry swoller – just like a navvy, I didn't know upper-crust did that.
>
> 'A theory, an invention to ease the gigantic burden of the prosperous'. ''E'd gone missin', but she rabbited on to 'erssen. She draind 'er cup an' she yelled aht.
>
> 'Get my financial secretary'.[13]

The depth of feeling, often personal, about Thatcherism and what was perceived as the politics of destruction was a source of inspiration for writers. Even though there is a clear political message in the text, it is grounded in the writer's hushed excitement in viewing daily life away from the public gaze.

Dialogue was a further preoccupation, not least at Scotland Road, where it was seen as a way of reaching a larger audience. The workshop included people who had, or would have, some involvement with acting, and writing was frequently acted out in the workshop. Barbara Shane's 'Another Kind of Union' is an example of the kind of short plays that were written. She charted a growing responsiveness to gender relations in working-class life by dramatising the friction between a married couple, the man an active trade unionist always out of the house and his wife arriving back from bingo:

> Mary: Hello, luv. What time did you get in?
> Eric: (Irritably) I've been in for hours and my tea's ruined, Where've you been?
> Mary: What dy'a mean your tea was ruined? It was ready at five. I can't stay in every night you know, luv. I only went down to the bingo with Teresa. You can't begrudge me that little bit of pleasure.
> Eric: There you go again. No-one's begrudging you anything. Always jumping. All I meant was you think with all this trouble at work you'd realise that I'd be late sometimes.
> Mary: Sometimes? I never see you these days. I was just telling Teresa that.
> Eric: That's another thing. Keep away from that Teresa Smith. She's no good, that one.

Mary: What'ya mean, no good? She's been good to me. Just because she likes a bit of fun now and then.
Eric: Never mind that. I don't want you going out with her, that's all. She's got a bad name and I don't want you to get one as well.
Mary: There's not much chance of that, is there, stuck in the house all day? With no-one to talk to.
Eric: Where's the kids?
Mary: They're over at me mam's.
Eric: What again? Why don't you keep them there? You haven't got all that much to do that you can't look after two kids.
Mary: That's not fair. You know my ulcer's killing me. Oh, I'm sick to death of all this picking. Every time you come in you have another moan. Aren't I entitled to any life at all? That bloody job of yours is getting me down ...[14]

Drama forced people to stick to vernacular speech. As they developed, writers would learn how to translate talk into text, 'showing not telling', while curbing a natural desire to educate an audience. Moving from oral storytelling to writing presented a number of challenges. Sometimes alternatives had to be found when what was written down appeared inauthentic.

The voice was also incorporated into poetry, which proved to be one of the most popular forms of writing for those busy at work and with multiple commitments. Workshops limited the attention that could be devoted to any one writer, which further encouraged shorter pieces. Through poetry, writers could celebrate the everyday, often explicitly in opposition to literary assumptions, as in 'No Dawn in Poplar':

> When the sun comes up in the morning
> rising slowly
> the sun comes up
> it's the sun coming up.
> There's no dawn in Poplar.[15]

Poetry was a familiar form, especially rhyming poetry that eased writers into the craft. One example of how rhyme helped to capture common experiences is *Shush Mum's Writing*, from a much-quoted book of the same title, published by Bristol Broadsides:

Shush Mum's Writing

Sit down be quiet read a book
Don't you dare to speak or look
Shush Mum's writing

She's left the dishes in the sink
All she does is sit and think
Shush Mum's writing

Nothing for dinner nowt for tea
And all she ever says to me is
Shush Mum's writing

But what's all this Mum's wrote a book
Why not buy one have a look
No need to shush now we can shout
And tell our friends about
MUM'S WRITING

Pat Dallimore[16]

Not only was this a popular poem, it also inspired many in the feminist movement where activists were assessing personal experience and recognising the creative talents of those who had been previously silent.

Poetry was often produced with a view to performance. Gladys McGee's irreverent poem 'Empire Day' is an example of how writing groups fostered critical accounts of the past via comedy:

Empire Day
I'd been picked!
I'd been picked!
My arms were a flinging,
My heart was a singing
'Cos I'd been picked!
It was for Empire Day
I'd been picked,
My teacher said I was
A good reader
And I could dress up
As the leader
Of the Empire
We had then.
I'd wear a bronze helmet
And be draped
In a red white and blue flag
And reign over all other lands,
That's what an Empire meant then.
The day came nearer,
I was getting excited,
Teacher spoke to me,
Then my day was blighted.
She realised I was too small
To reign.
She wanted someone tall and striking,
Who looked like a Viking,
Holding a shield and looking
Across the sea.

> I was already weedy,
> Then I felt rather seedy,
> And asked if I could go home
> 'Cos I was in pain.
> She said I could
> Do this part when I
> Grew older
> But how could I?
> Silly old cow.
> We ain't got no
> Empire now!
>
> Gladys McGee[17]

The incongruous desire to be a ruler was thwarted by her position as a weedy kid in the school. She places herself in an impossible predicament. The hopelessness of her cause uncovers the hidden ties between class and imperialism in a light-hearted but critical way. Such poems were written with the spoken word in mind, and, as an older woman dressed in a gold lamé suit, McGee would electrify audiences.[18]

Workshop members also wrote reflective pieces, such as this example by a member of Heeley Writers which beautifully mines ambiguous feelings about the decline of heavy industry:

> **An unemployed steelworker in the middle of a zebra crossing stealing a diamond**
> When I worked
> I was lost
> In noise, explosions,
> Danger and boredom,
> Given values and
> Metal tokens in place of joy.
>
> My sky was contained
> By iron,
> Peopled with white hot stars,
> Soaring rubies,
> Diamonds of light
> From whirring stones,
> And the roaring mouth
> Of furnace.
>
> I stand now
> Aimless in the city savanna
> On this flat, inanimate creature
> Designed to keep us moving
> Prising the eye from a rubber cat
> With a screwdriver
> And holding it

> High, High
> To the moon's gleam
> Trying to remember
> The bright harshness
> Of my once controlled life.
>
> Peter Whittingham[19]

Whittingham plays on a dual notion of experience as invoking both the immediate senses and longer-term reflections on the past. By locating himself at the heart of a number of ideas, he brings to the surface contradictory feelings about deindustrialisation. Older, 'traditional' working-class jobs are not simply eulogised – the worker had been offered only 'danger and boredom', 'metal tokens in place of joy'. Thus while the fascination with 'diamonds' and 'rubies' signals the excitement of the steel industry, his 'soaring sky' is still confined. Looking back, the poet is left standing on a burnt-out 'city savanna'. Seemingly purposeless destruction is his only means of connecting with the past, his 'once controlled life' and its 'bright harshness'. Grasping for purpose and agency in the present, he can neither relate to his previous life nor leave it behind. The attempt to reoccupy a previous experience is ultimately bewildering.

Finally, it should be noted that community publishing groups published very few novels, with only a handful appearing by the end of the 1980s. Groups found it difficult to publish and sell novels which were often seen as individualistic, when their main purpose was framed in collective terms. In theory, a novel was much harder to write than a short story and involved a lot of work, usually over a number of years, which excluded many Fed writers from this form. It was a development that did take place, but it often had to be done away from the constraints of a writing group. Yorkshire Arts Circus and Commonword published novels and, to some extent, this move coincided with an acceptance of publishing writers who might not fit with the traditional image of community-based writing groups. Examples of Commonword novels included *A Matter of Fat*, English teacher Sherry Ashworth's comical take on the slimming industry, and Cath Staincliffe's *Looking for Trouble*, which follows a self-consciously middle-class female detective around Manchester. Mike Duff's *Low Life* related a shady world of shoplifters to his readers, somewhat reminiscent of Irvine Welsh's work. David Evans's novel, *A Touch of Sun*, was also published to some acclaim.[20]

Working-class writing?

The early work of the Fed and its groups encompassed a heterogeneous mix of content, forms and styles. As this writing was being composed, evaluated and published, there were simultaneous conversations about its characteristics and meanings. The question of whether Fed writing was distinct proved to be contentious from the beginning. People were unsure about how to assess it and whether it was right to do so. Writers experimented with a range of shifting opinions. Ken Worpole was worried by the tendency to see the emerging body of young people's writing as special, in a way that might see it ostracised as 'community writing' alongside 'community development', 'community arts' and 'community education':

> It is not 'anything writing', it is writing. No special cases, no different standards. What these young people are writing is literature … and ought to be judged in exactly the same way as we judge all writing. The well-travelled road is the best road with all the old dilemmas unresolved: naturalism versus critical realism, documentary realism versus allegory, and so on.[21]

The need to appraise could lead to dichotomies of good and bad. As a professional playwright, McGovern, looking back, expressed the view that the value of the Fed lay in the process that allowed working-class people to start writing and to develop their skills. But he applied standards:

> [The] Arts Council insisted that the stuff coming out of such groups was 'not of a sufficiently high quality'. The counter-argument was, 'Look, this is a different type of writing: working class writing. And you should judge it with different criteria'. I never really agreed. Good writing is good writing is good writing. And many of us, myself included, were only just finding our voices. Some very good stuff was produced. But a fair bit of shite as well. Especially the ever-rhyming poems.[22]

McGovern would, however, support the idea that working-class writing could be defined in terms of the actual people writing and, to some extent, the content of the writing. By contrast, in 1978 Rick Gwilt had expressed the view that working-class writing was, in many respects, unique:

> Working class writing is not an area of inferiority where marks are awarded for 'trying'; neither is it something which is 'good enough' to get into 'Reader's Digest'. Working class writing is simply different, both in content and style.[23]

Gwilt found it hard to outline a precise definition but thought it became clear in the magazine *Voices*, where he was dissatisfied with the 'intellectual', 'individualistic' and esoteric writing that had appeared in some issues, often sent in via radical networks.[24] Distinctions were made with both 'popular' and political writing, which Gwilt found wanting. He favoured explorations of experience that were generated in workshops and attuned to the needs of working-class writers. However, drawing attention to these differences raised a danger that the writing could be judged to be of lesser worth, which was strongly resisted.

Debates were rarely articulated as absolute positions; rather, they were part of a common stock which could be grafted onto changing arguments according to the context. Those who wanted to link up with mainstream understandings of literature also drew attention to its special traits, while those who accentuated the differences did not want to isolate it completely from wider critical attention.

Embracing contradictions allowed claims to be made for both the singularity of Fed writing and its relevance to historical traditions. Writers with different priorities and interests could locate themselves at points that suited them. The following cautious summary from 1978 was to be a prescient comment on the work that would be produced over the coming years:

> No attempt has been made so far to define what is meant by working class writing. We feel that the answer is implicit in this and other publications … while we do not see good bourgeois writing and good working class writing as utterly distinct (such matters as a feeling for words and a sensitivity to the nuances of life are common, for instance), we are agreed that they are recognisably different. Working class writing is the literature of the controlled and exploited. It is shot through with a different kind of consciousness from bourgeois writing. Whatever its subject matter, working class writing, when it is any good at all, must contain in its tissues and exude through its pores, working class experience. Politically, the class struggle would be felt and communicated … even if the writer has no such design on the reader.[25]

Direct personal experience and empathy with working-class characters was to infuse working-class writing with a certain authenticity, and this was supported by the use of everyday language. The quote above, written by Worpole, points to a transitional moment in class relationships when the politics of class struggle was losing some traction. Elsewhere he had himself recognised the strengths of 'bourgeois' writing, which had consistently incorporated literature written by outsiders such as John Clare or Thomas Hardy, a process discussed by Raymond Williams in *Culture and Society*. At times, in order to force a division, writers in the Fed would refer to examples of 'boring' themes and writers – tea on the lawn or surreptitious middle-class affairs – as uninspiring literature. But these were selections from a vast array of work, and a complete break between bourgeois and working-class culture was not easily sustained.

Nevertheless, classed relations would continue to foster feelings of separateness. Fed publications constituted a form of life writing that could not easily be assigned to neat categories but rather cut across disciplinary boundaries. While Fed writing often revealed a strong 'materialist aesthetic' and a desire to understand the world,[26] it also engaged in literary representation. Writers blended styles, forms and devices, including storytelling and anecdote, conversation and speech, reflection and analysis, in order to communicate with an audience. Autobiography employed documentary and literary styles, just as poetry was used to convey a message and get a grasp on historical experiences. In part, they were returning to earlier definitions of literature, when its meaning extended beyond imaginative works to generic practices of reading and writing.[27]

The detailing of specific memories opened up new interpretations. Intensely personal, celebratory moments, sometimes with an element of fantasy, were invested with tremendous symbolic importance. Filmic metaphors assisted in this endeavour – writing one's life onto the big screen was indicative of the way in which this technology had enabled and altered self-perception across the twentieth century. Writers and readers gained a critical distance and considered the world anew. The desire for accuracy and to bear witness existed alongside the desire to interpret a life creatively, which could affect the veracity of these texts: 'I never try to make out that I remember things exactly right', wrote Sid Manville.[28] Writers' factual insights about work have been be valued by historians, but a less generous opinion might be extended to the widespread belief in ghosts and myths.[29] Even Arthur Exell, an important and perhaps over-used 'source' in the History Workshop movement, attended a writing group where he wrote a story about a mythical mandrake.[30] In addition, the unfinished nature of some texts, especially from a historical point of view, could also contribute to a literary effect. The experience of poverty was not a comfortable one: displacement, fragmentation and transformation all stimulated people to write but could mean that such experiences jutted out of neat narratives which jolted the reader into a richer appreciation of a life. Truncated experiences, scaled-down memories and distancing techniques left a silence that suggested a depth of feeling about painful episodes in the past.[31] However, in much Fed writing, personal difficulty was blended with spontaneity and humour, a trait that earned the incredulity of critics.

The promiscuity with forms was aided by exchanges between workshops. Writers had the idea that they were starting from scratch, with a blank page, and wanted to demolish artificial distinctions between forms of writing. Centerprise embraced autobiography, creative writing workshops and writing by adult literacy students. These various practices were held together in an exploratory tension and the result was to be a cross-fertilisation of forms for the expression of working-class experience. Mirroring this concern with dismantling artificial barriers, the first Fed anthology was simply called *Writing* and included autobiographical extracts, poems, short stories and cartoons. Roger Mills was keen to dispense with false categories:

> In practice, the Federation has never differentiated between autobiography/local history, poetry/prose and adult literacy. We have broken down the barriers that elsewhere still exist between these written forms.[32]

Fed worker Al Thomson concurred that 'the artificial distinctions between history, autobiography and fictional writing often blur as people write about their own lives and the life about them in a range of different styles'.[33] This necessarily involved a fair amount of experimentation:

> everybody was writing something different … some of the stuff that people were writing, there wasn't a name for it, really, it was just an expression of themselves. There were bits of poetry, bits of songwriting, plays, and part of the function of that group was to help them to fit it into a category wherever possible, whatever suited them.[34]

The breaking down of forms could also be overstated. What was often happening, especially in workshops, was that writers were trying to find a way to express their experience. Preliminary work led to a discovery of literary models, and this was a moment of assertiveness as writers looked outward from the haven of the workshop.[35] Through trial and error, some writers found the forms that suited them best: for instance, Joe Smythe was clearly a poet, McGovern became a playwright and so on.[36] Workshops also encouraged specialisation, and most were less ambitious in setting up new projects than Centerprise. They focused on certain forms, partly because restrictions existed in activists' heads as much as in society at large. QueenSpark concentrated on autobiography and local history although it subsequently developed writing groups; Scotland Road mainly pursued creative writing and drama despite some interest in local history; while Gatehouse worked exclusively with adult literacy students.

Subjectivity and the social

Each of these forms served to expand the terrain of working-class subjectivity as new models of apprehending experience and history became available through texts that served as prototypes to emulate and adapt. Writers broke with convention by capturing experience in fresh ways. They worked around tensions between the individual writer and the classed contexts in which they were located. Young people's critical exposition of their own lives, experiences, environment and culture represented one breakthrough. Another was the writing by adult literacy students who blended their experiences of learning and life and worked through negative feelings of shame. Exploitative relations, humour and an assertion of normality were all mechanisms for self-representation. The third key area was older people's nuanced examination of past and present, self and community. The experiences retrieved were not just random memories but carried an implicit critique of the loss of community. Describing a life of poverty became a means of highlighting the individual within a broader dimension.

Writing was viewed as integral to personal and social transformation. The marginal position of Fed writers lent their writing a critical edge but also conveyed an uncomfortable sense of self in relation to accepted culture. Carving out a subjective existence within a context of material shortages was no easy task and individuality could be circumscribed by social expectations. Working-class writing has often been seen as furnishing a collective purpose, with roots in everyday life, places and historical moments.[37] Although Manville thought that his autobiography would only be of value to his family and some local people, the critical attention paid to his work made him realise that his writing was not 'provincial' but that 'a working class childhood is much the same wherever it may be lived'.[38]

The choices facing individual writers were also apparent across workshops. During the 1970s and 1980s community publishers viewed autobiography as a form of collective representation. For instance, books published by the Yorkshire Arts Circus carried the subtitle 'A people's history of Yorkshire'. Individual lives were regarded as significant precisely because they related to social experiences and collective pasts. Worpole, in mulling over the work of the Centerprise publishing project in the 1970s, explained that they were not celebrating the 'unique life':

> We felt it important to weigh the quality of expression against the extent to which a particular individual's experiences could clarify, express with precision, stand for and carry the weight of the typical and common experiences of a much larger group of people who could find and recognise large parts of their own lives within a particular autobiography ... a life rooted in the localised and common experience of the majority of working class people in Hackney.[39]

Fed groups developed the idea of the collective autobiography and published books with many contributors on collective themes, such as Centerprise's *The Island*. Publishing 'experiences which people had in common' based upon key themes of work, home and leisure was favoured over individual autobiographies. In time this track would lead to the very successful *Working Lives* volumes.[40]

Groups initially published discrete contributions by individual authors all on the same theme of work or community. Later the prominence of individual contributors was reduced further by pasting together short extracts grouped into themes. Collective histories proved to be popular with readers and allowed many more writers to be published, allaying fears that too many resources were being devoted to single writers. Given the potential commercial returns from publication, some groups would also move towards joint copyright, shared between authors and the group.

The second book published by East Bowling History Workshop, *East Bowling Reflections*, was to take the collective form further by removing names from the text and simply listing all the 'Members ... associated with the production of this book' in alphabetical order at the end. This was a logical step that gave equal significance to everyone involved in the book and mirrored a radical interest in collective cultural production.[41] East Bowling was one of the few workshops to take this step. As a self-help working-class organisation, it lacked the publisher–writer relationship that characterised some community publishers.[42] Elsewhere collectivising authorship might have been considered an elitist imposition and a denial of the individuality of authors. For instance, at one point the community theatre Age Exchange adopted this practice, and it was less inclined to treat those who contributed their memories as writers.[43] This policy did not go unnoticed. Sally Flood, as a member of the FWWCP executive, once rejected an application for membership from Age Exchange on the grounds that individual writers were not given the recognition they deserved; subsequently, this position was changed and she herself would be employed there.

Over time, the innovations in writing and publishing could become derivative. Historical and generational alterations also meant that existing ideas were less valid for new cohorts with different life experiences. During the 1990s, the collective impulse declined as writers came to challenge assumptions that they believed were becoming set in stone. Ciaran Lynch of Northside Writers reasoned that they could be in danger of imposing restraints by focusing too exclusively on social identities:

> write of working class experiences; write on working class issues; write poetry or short stories that take the establishment to task. All very commendable in their own right but overbearing if such issues are confined to by the entire memberships. In fact if we are to confine our writings to such things the term writer should be replaced by the term propagandist. If we are to be true to ourselves about writing, then one must accept that we cannot put restrictions on it ... If the term *worker writer* conceals some hidden prerequisite as some people suspect then it can only be a *Manacle*.
> ... I will be classless in my judgement of writers as I am in my assumptions of individuals and life, assessing writers on the wealth of spirit they give working class topics when they write, rather than their wealth of means or lack of them.[44]

Working-class, black, gay and women's writing groups and writers all negotiated whether their writing would be fairly judged or whether it would be ghettoised and devalued. Separate spaces allowed for ideas to be developed and worked up with sympathetic listeners, but it left them open to negative judgements. The debate disclosed one of the drawbacks of collective experience – that it could impose a so-called 'burden of representation'. Writing as part of a social constituency related to class, sex, race or disability lent power and importance to texts and provided purpose and identity, although it also posed the danger that writers might limit themselves. Being tethered to a collective group could stifle individual expression, 'deeper probing ... imagination, fancy and speculation'.[45] For example, Sabir Bandali's book *Small Accidents* was subtitled 'The Autobiography of a Ugandan Asian', implying that he should represent a social group.[46] Consciously breaking with experience or embellishing it for literary purposes posed an additional dilemma for the writer with some responsibility to a larger constituency. As a result, writers pursued both general and specific experiences in negotiating the divide, a tension that remained at the heart of working-class writing.

While experience was a starting point, writers were to forge divergent paths. The respect accorded to individual writers ensured that individualistic accounts gradually became more pronounced. The uniqueness of individual voices and close personal relations within writing groups meant that each person's style and writing felt different. Despite the collective tendency of Fed groups, workshops attracted people who wrote in their own styles and forms: 'It has not, as some outsiders have jibed, become a muddy sea of uniformly produced work where you wouldn't know or be able to remember if you had written a certain poem or somebody else had.'[47] Indeed, a key theme that emerges from this analysis is the sheer potential diversity of working-class writing in terms of forms (poetry, prose, autobiography, drama, song, storytelling), purpose (bearing witness, protest, therapy, nostalgia, literary aims) and content (historical contexts, housing, work, politics, social movements, community and so on). Workshops widened the range of issues that could be written about from a working-class perspective. The male worker had been a central figure of working-class literature in the past and still attracted attention, yet writers in the Fed were producing a more diverse set of characters as part of rapid social changes. This is a journey often taken by working-class writers. For example, the novelist James Kelman discussed art in terms of breaking down the 'general characteristics' of class and race and the construction of individuality:

> When we perceive a member of a class we are not perceiving an individual human being, we are perceiving an idea, an abstract entity, a generality; it is a way of looking that by and large is the very opposite of art ...[48]
>
> So within the process of art more and more human beings start being 'discovered' as particulars, witnessed as individuals, specific folk, persons; and within the process of society more and more human beings start making discoveries themselves, and in the far-off future there won't be any racism, no sexism, no prejudice, no imperialism.[49]

Kelman's aspiration is difficult to apply to a working-class writer. Even his own impressive body of work cannot escape its collective mooring in the Scottish working class. Writers in the Fed were not all willing or able to let go of the bigger picture, which provided meaning and sustenance for their idiosyncratic expression.

The dominant image of a lone and creative genius remained elusive. Individuals in the Fed were sustained by organisation. They came into being as writers through a warren of workshops that spread nationally and unlocked new opportunities for learning. Internal organisational structures fostered participation and were tied to the external promotion of working-class writers. This led to close encounters with mainstream cultural and educational institutions – and, at times, direct conflict. Readers, book buyers and listeners at performances were a further critical link in the work of the Fed. The avowal of the working-class writer was, however, to be severely tested. It is to these debates that I now turn.

6 Making writers: more writing than welding

Writing was not conceived as a technical process but involved significant personal and social change. People would learn a considerable amount in these groups and some would be completely transformed as writing became central to their lives. Paradoxically, the 'educational' effects of workshops could be more profound than those of formal classes, and Fed groups came to realise that effective learning took place in non-educational settings.[1] This point had not been fully recognised previously. Despite the fact that the Fed had roots in education, writers often had negative experiences of school and were reluctant to evaluate their development in educational terms. A common cause was promoted over personal development and many activists felt workshops should be independent of formal education.[2] In the mid-1980s, Gerry Gregory usefully outlined the early developmental trajectory of writers in making a case for 'community publishing as self-education'.[3] He argued that the changes writers went through were best seen as a precursor to education, 'early moves' in 'collective self-education'.[4] At that time, Gregory was not able to analyse the longer-term transformation of individual writers within a broader social context. From the vantage point of the early twenty-first century, it is possible to amend this picture. Charting the intellectual journeys of writers reveals rich social histories and a sustained engagement with literacy. Indeed, participation in writing workshops served as an alternative to education for some, while for others it could become a complementary influence.

Complex odds

It has been a common assumption within Fed groups that cultural expression serves a basic human need. Stephen Hicks, in *The Boxer Speaks* (see figure 7), captures this feeling: 'It seems that somewhere within me a silent voice now and then says, "Hurry please, let everything be, and pick up your paper and pen".'[5] Through writing a people could express pain and hurt and 'make sense of it all',[6] comprehending life and the troubles that were thrown in their path.

7 Stephen Hicks, *The Boxer Speaks*. Hicks was a popular character with the young writers in Basement.

Yet the opportunities for cultural expression and education available to working-class people had been scarce. In 1980, Tillie Olson's book *Silences*, which spoke of the 'complex odds' facing aspiring working-class writers,[7] struck a chord with many in the Fed. Workshops and groups were based on the assumption that marginalised people needed organisation at every step: to write, read, edit, publish and distribute each other's work. *The Republic of Letters* declared, 'we know the talent is there', but the supportive context in which writing could flourish was often lacking – writing needed to be 'read, understood, supported, answered, propagated and built into culture, without being in some measure stolen from you and from the world that has given rise to it'.[8]

Belief in one's capacity to write and in having something worthwhile to say was a crucial starting point. A lack of self-esteem could tip the balance against ever writing, or at least showing it to another person. The anonymous *Jackie's Story*, discussed in Chapter 2, initially had been started at the suggestion of a social worker but was left unfinished. The writer needed external validation, and a bit of luck, to complete it:

> I was going to chuck it away as there wasn't much point in keeping it but then I saw a play on television that was about some children in care and I thought maybe I should finish it off.[9]

Once the manuscript was written, the author still felt very unsure about its value, reflecting an ambivalence about her whole life: 'If you don't want to publish the story I don't want it back so feel free to throw it away.'[10] Communities could also frown on aspirations to read and write. Jack Davitt, who became a shipyard worker in Newcastle, had a fascination with words as a young boy but testified to a shared experience when he remembered that poetry was considered beyond the pale:

> I was just trying to write as a child you know and eventually I managed to put some of the words so as they rhymed and then I threw them in the dustbin and the fire because we cannot really be a poet amongst football mad kids.[11]

The impulse to write often remained latent until a significant event led people to ruminate on the purpose of their lives and/or provided the opportunity and resources to write. Time was a severe constraint for potential writers, whose energies were mainly focused on work and home life. Retirement or unemployment could spur people to write. After finishing work as a bus driver, Fitz Lewis attended an English class in Manchester and was pointed in the direction of a writing group.[12] In addition, trauma or personal crises such as the death of a close friend or relative exposed raw nerves that could turn an inclination into a strong desire to write or join a workshop. Writing helped people create something more permanent in the face of the temporary nature of life. For Liz Thompson, a member of Basement Writers and author of *Just a Cotchell*, writing helped to focus her energies after her grandfather and her father died in close succession. The loss of these relatives coincided with what was the end of an era for East London, the decline of the docks and gentrification of Wapping. She saw her writing as an attempt to preserve on the page what was being lost from her life:

> the sort of working class geography of the area was being obliterated and other things were being superimposed on it and it was as if a whole lot of stuff had never existed and it was literally like a blank page where you couldn't see what had been there before. And I found this a bit of a frightening concept so that kicked me off writing political poetry.[13]

Writing about her family was a way of comprehending and dealing with both personal and social transformation while also asserting some control. The connections between 'personal troubles' and 'public issues', in the words of the sociologist C. Wright Mills, were explicit.[14]

Despite the obstacles that working-class writers faced in the world, many were able to draw upon elements of their experience that facilitated rather than limited creative expression. Thus writing and personal expression could arise directly out of working-class life; it was not something perceived as alien to lived experience. Thompson grew up in a post-war East London family, where the idea of performing or doing a turn was a familiar one:

> Within the family there was this kind of tradition where there would be parties … if you wanted to stay up with … the grown-ups, you had to do a turn … at that stage it was singing which was like the acceptable little girls' party piece … and I only did it so I could have an excuse to stay up and watch everybody swamping back the booze … it was a happy childhood artistically, I didn't feel stupid about myself or anything but I just didn't make a big show outside the home … it was very much the case of having … a public face and a private face.[15]

Creative expression was commonly a part of home life, although it was more problematic in the public world. Domestic restrictions on young girls could also stimulate cultural expression and growth. As a girl, Thompson had found it was less of a problem to be seen reading by others, as it was 'sort of a female thing to do'. In any case, reading was supported by her self-educated father who had truanted from school to visit museums, itself an interesting comment on the perception of schooling. Her mother provided a role model in being one of many 'strong women' in her family and would actively contribute to the political conversations of her husband and his mates who worked on the docks.[16] Thompson was also fortunate in finding supportive listeners at the E1 Festivals, where a sympathetic audience was drawn from the areas about which she was writing.[17] Similarly, workplaces could provide a supportive atmosphere. Davitt, quoted above, who destroyed his poems as an embarrassed child, would later find a welcoming reception among his workmates in the Navy and on the shipyards, where his writing 'went down very well and … at the finish I was doing more writing than welding'.[18] Being published by Strong Words would help to establish him as a writer and, in turn, make poetry more acceptable to working-class readers.

Coincidence and luck played a role in getting people to start writing and in bringing creative desires to the surface. Some texts remained in bottom drawers until writers chanced upon local publishers.[19] Eddie Barrett took up the pen after his wife bet him a fiver that he would not write a story, but clearly there was a pre-existing urge to do so. Growing up in Liverpool, he had a strong local identity to which a mix of experiences were added as a merchant seaman. He consciously traversed Walter Benjamin's distinction between traditions of storytelling based on settled communities and on that of travellers, as he reflected on the impulse to write:

> storytelling has been the great thing in Liverpool for a long time ... there's always been a tradition of storytellers from farmers, people from the land, and also the tradition from people who are at sea ... I went to sea myself, and telling stories in the mess room at about five or six o'clock after tea, that was traditional ... all the different people who came to Liverpool, from all over the world ... Most of them had stories to tell. All in all, it became a place where if someone could tell a story, that gave them a sort of prestige and kudos, so it was a good thing to tell a good story. It still is, I think. So that's the way I got into it.[20]

Political activism could also ease people into writing, particularly those immersed in socialist politics and the major social transformations of the twentieth century. The early political writing found in *Voices* magazine endured throughout much of the Fed's history. Although the Fed had reacted against agit-prop, politicised forms of expression continued to be attractive. For instance, Lawrie Moore, born in 1923, had been a member of the Young Communist League and was later involved in Unity Theatre, a left-wing-inspired theatre movement targeting working-class audiences. His poetry was thoroughly political, for example this parody of Margaret Thatcher:

> I used to be a fascinating witch
> My friends and I are quite, quite rich
> I bashed the unions and I soaked the poor
> I closed more hospitals than ever before[21]

Similarly, Kay Ekevall, born in 1911, lived a politicised life supporting struggles from the Spanish Civil War to the US Civil Rights Movement, and had known and disagreed with George Orwell. She wrote a poem each year on 6 August in memory of the atomic bombing of Hiroshima.[22] Writing also arose directly out of struggles and campaigns. People came together to fight for a cause, but in circumstances that cultivated reflection and the discovery of something new. Rick Gwilt completed his first 'writing', a leaflet, during the 1972 builders' strike.[23]

The organisation of expression

The momentum created by the Fed would help to fracture the taboos on personal expression and entrench a sense of entitlement to personal expression among working-class people. Given that writing was often done under extreme time pressures and with little encouragement, writing groups offered much-needed validation. Regular meetings energised writers and counteracted personal anxieties and social barriers. Workshops fostered long-term friendships and commitments, supporting members during barren periods when they did not write but were still welcome to attend. Writing on one's own could be difficult to sustain without this support and feedback, something many professional writers continue to take for granted. Being in a writing group and performing also introduced writers to wider networks. For Fitz Lewis, ceasing to write would be a betrayal of his community:

> I'm still quite active in the writing game ... once one is involved in writing for over ten years like myself, to pack it in, forget about it, it's like committing a crime because when you meet other writing colleagues they ask you, 'What you are doing – are you still writing'. How do you say, 'No I am not', they want some explanation you know, so to me it's like committing a crime.[24]

Fed groups actively sought out new work. At Centerprise, Ken Worpole was the first person to whom Roger Mills showed his writing as he was shy and wary about sharing it. As a secret writer, discovering books by 'local' people at the Centerprise bookshop had been a revelation:

> So I bought those two books [Vivian Usherwood's *Poems* and Ron Barnes' *Licence to Live*] and took them home, and was fascinated by them, because both of them would mention places in Hackney that I knew very well, and the poems were about subject matter like dreams, and looking to the future, and school, experiences ... they changed my life, in a way. The fact that I was holding two books, one by a schoolboy and one by a taxi driver, was amazing. Because these were exactly the sort of people I didn't think were writers, and that altered my view of who could write or what people had to say and how they said it ... I sort of got a vision of the future. People telling their own stories, expressing themselves, in very ordinary everyday language ... I was astounded.[25]

The very existence of these groups and their books communicated a basic humanity and showed that it was possible to write oneself.

The first time a writer attended a group was often remembered as a turning point, after which they gradually overcame their apprehensions. That moment was commonly burnt into the writer's memory, as it was for Alan Gilbey in London and Keith Birch in Liverpool:

> on a very cold, November evening, I walked up and down outside about nineteen times before going in.[26]

> I'd joined the writers' workshop in Scotland Road on the same night as John, we both stood outside trying to pluck up courage to go through the door and join. We did, and we stayed firm friends forever after that, and still are.[27]

Patricia Duffin attended the Home Truths writing group in Manchester. As a Gatehouse employee who worked in adult literacy, she gained an insight into the world of the students with whom she worked:

standing outside and feeling really really scared and thinking, 'Oh my god this is what literacy students feel like before they come in ...' through the door of the adult ed centre to sign up.[28]

Within workshops, writers were able to learn and experiment. Pat Smart attended an English class in Liverpool after her mother died. She disliked the formality of the class, which was reminiscent of her school days. On becoming part of a writing group, however, she discovered the freedom to express herself because grammar was less important than content and the ability to communicate:

> I've always told children's stories and made up funny rhymes for them but never written them down. I decided to go to a night class, but found it was exactly like it was in school, sat behind a desk with the teacher in front, saying things like, 'Don't drift off the subject ... you'll be sitting an exam soon'. The pressure was awful! ... where to put full stops and commas ... and then big red crosses ... and notes at the bottom like, 'try again'. But going to the writers' workshop, nobody saw what I'd written. I'd just read it out so all the pauses were correct, where I wanted them to be ... and the spelling didn't matter one iota, and that pleased me ... the teachers thought I was soft ... before I discovered the Fed I would have agreed with them, that I was a 'stupid girl'.[29]

Formal education and the workshop were worlds apart. Writing would often be read out loud, putting the 'voice' in control in order to connect with an audience. However, the thought of reading to the public was received with much trepidation. Most participants remembered the first time they read: sweating, shaking, even being sick, before overcoming their fears and gaining confidence. For Lewis, public reading was a precipitous plunge into the unknown but he went on to steal the show at a poetry slam:

> it was a long programme and I was last to go on. I waited till I was sick, I sweat and try again you know, I got nervous and regained my composure and yes, you know, waiting ... I read 'Lizzy' and you wouldn't believe it, it was like a stampede, when I bowed and said thank you it was like a stampede to the stage, I couldn't get off, people were mauling me, honestly, people were mauling me.[30]

Book launches for literacy students (see figure 8) were also powerful and dramatic events as many first-time readers performed their thoughts and feelings, sometimes struggling to read the words that they had written. The first time one woman from Gatehouse read at a book launch she was sick, but eventually she overcame her nerves and, in time, compèred such events with great skill.

These moments of elation had their source in a safe group – the workshop. A culture of equality was created in many workshops and included people who were coming to reading and writing for the first time, while coping with physical impediments. In such situations, participants would scribe for and record each other. Language experience was not simply an educational pedagogy, and

8 A Gatehouse book launch, c.1992, led by adult literacy students. Doreen Ravenscroft on the left, Chris Barrett on the right and Sheilagh Tynan seated.

people wrote for each other as an act of camaraderie. In discussing Scotland Road, Keith Birch spoke of

> The old woman who joined the group, in her 70s, could barely hold a bloody pen in her hand – because she'd worked in a laundry all her life and her hands were like ragpicker's hands, the joints were all swollen and all the rest of it. And people used to help her to write. But she told terrific stories ... Bloody fascinating ... the difficulty would be putting that into writing and trying to retain that same passion and humour and warmth that was in the storytelling.[31]

Within the culture of the workshop, technical and practical problems were inseparable from the challenges of representing oral stories in text. Despite differences of interest and skill, it was possible at times to build a workshop culture that valued everyone while also enabling people to develop. Scotland Road helped to provide a

> Balance ... of arrogance and humility. That was a wonderful opportunity in the workshop. You were never allowed – [Jimmy] McGovern included – you were never allowed to feel that you were any better than anybody else. You were respected for what you did, but everybody was equal, everyone had equal opportunity and equal time.[32]

This was a fundamentally radical position rarely found in cultural or educational activity: allowing everyone the same time and attention in workshops and insisting on equal worth while also recognising differences in ability and allowing people to grow and develop. There was no reason why 'better' writers should receive more attention. It was a model of democracy that questioned educational and cultural hierarchies.

However, as writers gained confidence and became more proficient at writing, they started to come to terms with the idea of criticism as a natural development emerging out of workshop discussion. Being able to separate feedback on a piece of writing from a comment about oneself was a vital first step. Barrett recollected his own development when he realised that 'criticism was a good thing. Because the way we were brought up, certainly myself, if someone was criticising you he was having a go at you ... People did learn ... to take criticism.'[33] The discipline of writing and rewriting enabled writers to gain distance on their lives, resulting in greater reflection and a marked improvement in the work produced. Workshops were able to address issues such as rape, racism and violence, which could ultimately lead to more nuanced writing. Occasionally there were strong disagreements that could not be contained,[34] but most workshops welcomed debate and developed their own criteria for good and effective writing, a point endorsed by virtually every writer to whom I spoke.

Fed writers bought each other's books and attended the same workshops and performances where they learnt from different people. Lotte Moos, a woman in her seventies, once thanked a teenager for helping her to approach writing anew;[35] Lewis recalled a workshop run by a Sheffield-based writer, Mike Hoy, as an important influence on his own writing as well as that of Manchester poet Steve Waling; and Alan Gilbey highlighted a Jimmy McGovern workshop on playwriting that was an inspiration for his own development.[36]

Reading would also become essential for those who wanted to improve. Writers were keen to encapsulate their experiences and feelings with greater precision after early attempts had been only partially successful. Nick Pollard, from Heeley Writers in Sheffield, argued that

> you are never going to be able to write decent poetry unless you actually start taking somebody else's work to pieces and find out ... what makes that tick ... you have got to have that kind of curiosity.[37]

Some started to read as a result of joining groups, while others altered their reading patterns. Keith Birch would later become a lecturer at Liverpool University and write the *Mersysiders*, dramatising the experience of adult education for local radio. He had always read but, after joining Scotland Road, he expanded his range and became more discriminating:

> I was reading stuff that other people were talking about, books I'd never heard of before. 'Why don't you try that, you can get that in the out-of-print, you can get this, and you can get that.' And I would avidly read all the stuff that the Fed was producing as well. And there was tons of it, which was brilliant! [laughs] So yes, I

was reading, but more selectively, and I wasn't reading for pleasure any more, I was reading in a more critical way ... And looking at different styles and all that. I was reading as a writer.[38]

The writer and critic Blake Morrison, who visited Fed groups on an Arts Council fact-finding mission in 1979, testified to this literary exploration. At Scotland Road, he was struck by the reading that was informing people's work:

> The level of reference in the group was extremely impressive: though knowledge was never paraded for its own sake, there was reference over the evening to issues diverse as Brecht's 'Verfhemdung' theory, Shakespeare's language, Nancy Mitford's 'U and Non-U' and the nineteenth century novel.[39]

Similar exchanges were assisted by the Fed and other black and working-class cultural and educational initiatives that provided a gateway for writers to meet and hear from each other. For instance, Centerprise and Hackney WEA brought writers Ngũgĩ wa Thiong'o and Raymond Williams to Hackney to speak.

As is often the case with self-educated people, so-called 'autodidacts', influences were eclectic and did not immediately correspond to school learning or academic disciplines. Smart read comics as a child, particularly *Bunty*, and, after being involved in a writing group, started to unpick its class and gender messages:

> these four girls going to this high class private school in beautiful uniforms ... one of them ... always had tatty hair, she was a scholarship girl and every week in that comic in that story they mentioned her being a scholarship girl.[40]

Being in a workshop gave Smart the confidence to read Dickens, whose plots she found unconvincing.[41] Writers rejected the class nature of British culture and searched further afield. Worpole suggested in *Dockers and Detectives* that during the 1930s working-class readers had found American crime fiction an attractive genre – this was to be repeated to some extent in the Fed. For instance, Rick Gwilt read American writers such as Langston Hughes, James Baldwin, Ralph Ellison, John Steinbeck, Ken Kesey and Meridel Le Sueur, while Eddie Barrett enjoyed Damon Runyon; McGovern and Liz Thompson also mentioned Steinbeck.

Workshops acted as a conduit into formal education, where writers were exposed to assorted influences. In 1970s and 1980s Liverpool, despite the reluctance to view workshops in educational terms, there was a symbiotic relationship between writing groups and educational provision. For instance, David Evans, sensitive to the developing needs of writers at the Scotland Road Writers' Workshop, which he had helped to establish, was able to attract members to his literature classes at the university where a number of demanding writers could be introduced to those who were ready and confident enough to engage with them:

So you can put a Yeats or a Brecht or even a Shakespeare ... in the creative writing courses I ran I was much more dogmatic because I felt people ... having been through the workshop experience ... could listen to some of my preoccupations. So I'd ram a bit of Beckett down their throats. Amazing how people would come round ... But to say to people 'You've got to read all the models'... that can terrify. You present somebody with a very successful difficult writer, usually middle class, and say 'You have to write like that'. It's intimidating.[42]

Poets who wrote in a simple and uncluttered way while also communicating a message effectively proved popular, among them Bertolt Brecht; Adrian Mitchell, the Mersey poet who once visited the Basement Writers; and the war poet Wilfred Owen. Evans spoke fondly of his tattered copy of Brecht's poems, which had been passed around the Scotland Road group over a number of years.[43] Examples of writers using other poets as models include Mary Casey borrowing from Brecht, as well as Terry Lee borrowing from Andrew Marvell:

A working woman reads history
...
Records of hidden stories
That tell of unknown lives
In papers so rarely taken
From dusty archives;
...
I'll dip my nose into the past
To seek the hidden glory
Of unsung heroes and lowly folk
Who have no cenotaph

Mary Casey[44]

Come live with me and be my love
Come live with me and be my love,
And we will all the pleasures prove,
That unemployment and the bomb,
Won't bother us for very long.
...

Terry Lee[45]

A related example from 2001 was Alvin Culzac's *Nandralone Highjumper* CD of poetry, whose style derived in part from the music and lyrics of Gil Scott-Heron. Interestingly, Davitt, the shipyard worker, was always attracted to poetry that rhymed, and he admired Pam Ayres even though the content of his work contrasted with that of Ayres. He wrote with the tools he had to hand rather than as part of a writing workshop in the Fed, which might have pointed him towards other possibilities.[46]

Within most workshops, a tension developed between new writers who needed encouragement and those who wanted to challenge themselves. Some were just starting out or were satisfied with their writing and had little desire to develop and communicate with a larger audience. Writing could be a form of leisure and enjoyment, rather than a means of becoming publicly successful. This aspect of Fed workshops influenced even the more experienced writers. Rebecca O'Rourke wondered whether

> one of the ... legacies of the Federation that's maybe less positive perhaps is that I've never been ... single minded about publication, I mean I like to write and I quite like to sort of share writing but I ... don't measure success by publication and I don't particularly pursue it.[47]

Nevertheless, as individual writers improved and developed, workshops could become limiting. Alan Gilbey drifted away from writers' groups because he felt they 'blanded out' into reading circles, with members afraid to make critical comments. For this reason, new workshops were set up so that writers could branch out. Gilbey himself started Controlled Attack, a punk-influenced theatre group that performed to more critical audiences.[48] A playwriting group was started at Liverpool University as a result of pressure from the Scotland Road workshop.[49] Others set up novel groups. O'Rourke, Mills and Anne Cassidy often read each other's work in a more detailed and critical way than was possible in a workshop setting and all three went on to publish commercial books.[50]

Intense personal relationships fed into the production of more critical and lengthy texts. As writers became more discerning, they started to edit their own and others' work more effectively. Leslie Mildiner and Bill House, authors of *The Gates*, discussed in Chapter 2, found that enhanced literary skills of composition and editing were necessitated by the novel. A friendly spirit of emulation pushed the schoolboys to complete *The Gates*:

> I didn't take him seriously ... then one day he turned up with the first part of 'The Gates' and I'll be truthful, I thought it was terrible, and that was how we started. Being bigheaded I thought I could do much better, and I wrote my idea of the first chapter, and for the next six months that's how it went ... Sometimes a chapter would have to be written four or five times until we had it right.[51]

Making it?

Some of those who struggled with writing would go on to reap rewards. The TV playwright McGovern was nurtured through the Fed and its writing workshops, and his path to success manifests many of the themes and processes outlined above. Before taking up writing seriously, he was infused with a latent political anger that was unfocused but based upon a general dissatisfaction with life and what it had to offer:

> I'd been writing ever since I was a teenager. Bad poems mainly. By my mid-twenties I was married with three kids and I had a shitty job – warehouseman ... I was also gambling much more than I could afford. And I was angry. Always angry. An angry

young man. My wife and I managed to secure an 'improvement grant' ... and the builders moved in. I had a row with one of these builders. He was quite taken aback by the extent of my anger. He decided I needed help and he took me along to the Scotland Rd Writers' Workshop.[52]

Word of mouth and a chance encounter played a role in introducing McGovern to the workshop, which was becoming a part of everyday working-class life, and it would support his writing. The solidarity of the workshop, and the importance of publishing, gave McGovern the strength to handle feedback from mates. He was 'immensely proud' of the first magazine:

I gave a copy to a docker-friend. He read it and said to me, 'You're no Arthur Miller'. He was right, of course. Much of what was in there wasn't that good. Mine especially. But ... many of us were trying (though we didn't know it at the time) to find our own voices. And there's nothing quite like seeing your stuff in print, with your name beneath, to help you find that voice.[53]

Becoming a published writer gave him a psychological boost and egged him on. It was a common experience for writers in the Fed to have their initial writing published as part of an ongoing process, marking out a stage in an apprenticeship.[54] Although writers might later look back with horror at some of their early published writing, the very fact of appearing in a book meant that they had progressed. The obverse could also be true. After having a collection of poems published at a young age, Tony Harcup decided to try something different and moved into journalism, working for many years as the editor of *Leeds Other Paper*.[55]

The national network of workshops supported aspiring writers. McGovern was impressed by *Voices* magazine and by Gwilt, who 'imposed a bit of quality control. It was always a boost to get a story in there.' Indeed, McGovern came to believe in the importance of judging and valuing writing with no special treatment given to working-class writing.[56] He also drew inspiration from his experiences and his surroundings as well as the subtleties of working-class language. For instance, he wrote a story that helped launch his career after his wife noticed

a woman across the street confined to a wheelchair. Her husband, who had to care for her full time, had a heart attack ... his wife stopped eating in an attempt to lose weight and reduce the burden on her husband. Terrifying and noble ... I wrote it as two monologues. Not quite drama but not a short story either.[57]

McGovern followed the trajectory of Fed writers who searched for new ways of formulating problematic experiences. He was fortunate that his writing found exposure in forums that provided stepping stones to critical attention. Unity Theatre toured with his twenty-minute monologues as well as other work from Scotland Road:

> Luckily Pedr James, who had just taken over the Everyman Theatre, came to see it. He liked my piece and he asked me to do a Scouse version of Dario Fo's *Can't Pay? Won't Pay!* So I was IN. And I began to take it seriously then.[58]

The content that McGovern produced at Scotland Road would be reworked in his later professional writing.[59] He went on to contribute to Channel 4's *Brookside*, a second apprenticeship, before launching a successful career in TV drama which included *Cracker*, *Hillsborough*, *The Lakes*, *The Street* and *Broken* in addition to writing films such as *Priest* and *Liam*.[60] Moreover, when writers were successful, it was celebrated by the Fed. In 1987, Virago's publication of O'Rourke's novel *Jumping the Cracks* was met with collective excitement and support:

> when anybody got published by the mainstream … it kind of reflected on everybody … it wasn't just a kind of individual thing … it was like 'We've made this … we've produced writers who are being published in the mainstream' … the Federation sort of coming of age almost and … proving its worth … proving that it was supporting writers who could hold their own with anybody else.[61]

Of course, the few people who 'made it' were the tip of an iceberg. Many of those involved in the Fed and its groups for any length of time forged new identities or evolved and progressed in some way. Betty Battle, of Prescot Writers and later Heeley Writers, and Barrett, quoted earlier, both learnt administrative and facilitator skills, which helped them to secure employment in voluntary organisations and education. Similarly, Hazel Marchant in Brighton not only learnt about writing and poetry, but became chair of QueenSpark, an able administrator and workshop convenor.[62] However, organising groups could soak up an enormous amount of energy and some 'writers' became so involved in running groups that their own writing was put on the back burner.[63] Gwilt speculated – perhaps ruefully given his own experience as editor of *Voices* – that 'the energy that people might otherwise have put into writing their own stuff, goes into editing and they never write the stuff they should have written themselves'.[64]

As these changes took place, new relationships were built. Marriages, partnerships and friendships all gestated in the Fed, as did break-ups and divorces. Some long-term relationships became both political and personal alliances, which enabled people to commit time and energy to the Fed. One popular story that many people told me is how an unlikely couple came together in the mid-1980s when a Fed AGM coincided with a local magistrates' and chief constables' conference:

> John still worked as a labourer on the building … and he met a local magistrate on the first night … they just clicked, the two of them. She was from Crosby and he was from Huyton … And they lived together. They set up home together. I just think that's a wonderful story. This is what it did for John, to enable him to mix as he did, and get to know this woman who was from a completely different world.[65]

For some the change was sudden and climactic, verging on a religious conversion. This was the case for Julia Young, who became aware of herself as a woman with power over her own and others' history. She wrote in her autobiography about a course at Northern College:

> That night I went into the grounds. As I walked through the trees I started to cry. I cried for those wasted years. I cried because it had taken me thirty-three years to realise that I was an individual. I cried for the women who couldn't see further than the hoover and the duster. Standing there in the dark overlooking the motorway, I cried till I ached. Not just for myself but for the thousands of women like me who had never had the chance to breathe. 'Let each man's hope be in himself', my dad had said. It took me a long time to understand what he meant, but now I understand I'll pass the message on to my daughter. 'Let each woman's hope be in herself.'[66]

Writing and publishing also carried risks associated with the loss of anonymity. Neighbours might shun writers whom they viewed as spies.[67] One man had his arm broken in a pub by someone who objected to a book he had written, while in Liverpool another writer went into hiding after having criticised the wrong people.[68] While these experiences took place not in the Fed but in related groups, they illustrate how exposure to an audience beyond the sheltered space of the workshop could be fractious. Moreover, there was always a danger that recognition would not follow on from publishing. Even those very close to you might not understand or agree with the idea of writing for a wider public; the ever-present complex odds were never far away. Birch's parents were confused by his writing and were unable to offer him any support:

> the first short story that I got published – I took it home to my parents ... and I took them a copy each, in a plastic bag [laughs] ... and I plucked up courage and got the books out and gave them a copy each, and said, 'There's a short story of mine in there, you know.' I don't think they even opened it, they sort of looked at it ... I suppose it doesn't matter how old you are, with your parents – and you're the same with your own kids – you're always looking for that approval, aren't you. I suppose I was looking for something like, 'By God, lad, there's your name in print here' [laughs]. And they didn't know how to cope with it ... I was so bloody persistent, I ended up taking the bloody book off them and I read part of the first couple of chapters [laughs] ... my mother was just sort of just looking into the distance, and dad was looking at me, but he wasn't looking at me. Then he turned to my mother and said, 'You know that woman I told you about ...' and started talking about something completely different! I suppose that in a way encapsulates what the whole working-class thing was, if you're coming from that kind of background – it's not their fault, it's no blame on them whatsoever – they didn't know how to cope with it. Anyone who aspires to be a writer from a working-class background, where all the main activity was to do with putting food on the table and keeping a roof over your heads, it was very difficult. Extremely different. So you felt alienated, that the people who you loved the most, closest to you, you weren't able to discuss the thing that you loved most, that was taking over your life, that became so important to you and

the activities you were involved in. Because years later, I'd be talking to my dad ... and I remember him saying so many times, 'Tell me again, lad, what's it all about? What are these meetings about?'[69]

Moreover, prevailing class and educational forces impinged upon the ability of writers to feel absolutely secure. They remained outsiders on the inside and were plagued by a certain amount of self-doubt:

> I still sit here sometimes, engrossed in doing something, and there's a knock on the door, and for that split second it's ... 'Come on, we've sussed you, you're out, on your way!' [laugh][70]

Birch's concerns bear some resemblance to those of the interviewees in Brian Jackson and Dennis Marsden's *Education and the Working Class*, which uncovered the conflicted identities of educated working-class people. The support provided in workshops became a vital means of assuaging such feelings. The writer was not conceived as a solitary character but as part of a movement that nurtured their development.

Writing workshops articulated the energies of people who either had a passion for writing or wanted to reflect upon their lives. Individuals were respected for their own visions and ideas even when these had not been fully formed. Within a culture of mutual respect, writing was central to interlocking processes of learning, volunteering, organising and campaigning. Learning often took place through activities that were not viewed as specifically educational. Despite the lack of formal structure, growth and change did take place, sometimes incrementally and sometimes in leaps and bounds, as people broke free of both external and self-imposed restrictions. The Fed actively countenanced the idea that writers could indeed create important work without the kinds of apprenticeships and certification that are commonly assumed necessary. Nonetheless, dissatisfaction with early literary attempts fed a craving to improve and try out new ideas. Fed writers provided one set of models, while others were discovered through reading and exposure to eclectic cultural influences. Some writers would make significant progress and search out affirmation and possibilities beyond the security of the workshop. But everyone was treated equally irrespective of the quality of their writing, and equality coexisted with a diversity of individual experiences and abilities.

'Successes' did not appear ready-made from a vacuum, rather they were sustained by a network of groups. Outsiders from the margins are habitually represented as unique, as one-offs, and occasionally as geniuses. The possibility that such 'creative' people might be a normal part of working-class life and progress from collective workshop experiences finds only rare acceptance. While all writers are born, they also have to be made. From the beginning of the Fed, activists were aware that literature is structured by power and institutions. The Arts Council, commercial publishing houses, universities, reviewers and literary criticism all influence what gets written and published, and by whom. Years of education, support and money from parents and friends have helped to launch more than one talented career. Aptitudes and abilities are not independent of institutional and familial support.

It remains ironic, then, that working-class writers have themselves obscured these processes and may have become complicit in downplaying the support they receive. At least one interviewee complained to me of people in workshops who gained some success and were never seen again. To continually feel shackled to one's past might serve to undermine artistic freedom and allow others to stereotype your writing as a certain type or genre, for example in the way the BBC attempted to label Joe Smythe, a rail worker, as a 'railway poet' – something he resisted fiercely. Competing in a world of strong-minded individuals, where talent and originality are the going currencies, makes writers all too aware that the term 'community', 'worker' or 'black' can easily be interpreted as a weakness. This is one reason writers from marginal spaces need to navigate apparently contradictory arguments.

Writing was not pursued as an isolated activity separate from reading. The nature of commitments and friendships naturally blended into promoting the writing widely. Writers communicated with audiences in new ways through publication and performance. Building spaces for the reception of Fed work was crucial. As with all culture, a production was not complete until it entered the lives of a public who were able and willing to receive it.

7 Alternative publishing and audience participation

Writers and publishers in the Fed responded to known communities. Previously working-class writers had been absorbed into traditional patterns of consumption and readership that reinforced hierarchies. Fed groups were aware that accounts of working-class life had not been read in significant numbers. For example, the growth of labour studies had not necessarily led to a more historically conscious labour movement.[1] Mainstream cultural and political institutions had ignored writing about working-class experience, exploiting it for purposes contrary to those intended.[2] These tensions have been expressed by playwrights in drama, for example Arnold Wesker in *Roots* and Jim Cartwright in *Prize Night*. Enabling working-class voices to be respected and understood before launching them onto an unknown market posed a challenge.

The origins of the Fed were tied to conscious attempts to remake the relationship between producers and consumers of culture. The templates of private patronage, state funding and market demand were all problematised in favour of working with, and responding to, the needs of local communities. From the 1980s, these initiatives had to contend with the diffusion of market ideologies. The connections between writer and audience was to become a contested arena in which multiple conceptions of the market became evident.

A new reading public

Passive audiences were galvanised into active communities as part of a process of cultural and social change. By establishing workshops in working-class areas, Federation groups were attempting to cultivate cultural activists, rather than launching writing onto an unsuspecting market. In bringing new readers into existence, the Fed would adapt the idea of 'a reading public'. In the 1930s, Q. D. Leavis had outlined the emergence and disintegration of 'the' reading public, but her concerns had been with a cultural elite.[3]

Workshops aimed to make the process and products of publishing accessible to new readers. For example, QueenSpark in Brighton successfully linked the rarefied world of publishing to a working-class readership by nurturing new forms of interaction and dialogue. The writing and publishing of books came to be seen as an extension of everyday life, stimulated by the intense interest that outsiders were starting to show in working-class history. The development of Albert Paul's autobiography *Poverty, Hardship but Happiness: Those Were the Days 1903–1917* is a good example of how cultural bridges were created to enable unknown writers to reach larger audiences. Paul's first 'audience' comprised the workmen who had exposed an old flint wall in Brighton during the improvements following the 1969 Housing Act, which sparked many memories. Radio Brighton recorded his recollections and a local historian encouraged him to write them down.[4] After reading the QueenSpark newspaper, Paul took his first tentative steps in writing; he would complete his manuscript on days when his wife was out of the house. QueenSpark then took a risk in publishing this experimental work. An initial print run of 1,000 sold out within a few months, necessitating a reprint.

In fact, many early Federation publications would articulate common experiences and this was reflected in the sales figures. In the early 1980s, it was alleged that the intensity of QueenSpark's work made 'the sales of Harold Robbins worldwide look rather lacklustre'. Some Centerprise publications sold over 10,000 copies, while Strong Words in the north-east could shift 3,000 copies of a book with only minimal sales and marketing effort.[5] Raymond Williams has written of

> those specific and historically definable moments when very new work produced a sudden shock of recognition. What must be happening on these occasions is that an experience which is really very wide suddenly finds a semantic figure which articulates it.[6]

The 1970s was one of these definable moments when people were listening to marginal voices. The explosive 'shock of recognition' confirmed the numerous readers for community publications and testified to the fact that the books represented just such a shared experience at a time of political and economic turmoil. In this case, the 'semantic figure' was the individual working-class writer whose personal history was steeped in a collective consciousness.

Actual readers far exceeded the number of books that were bought. The passions generated by sharing life experiences ensured that books were passed around and discussed in groups and families as a new reading public formed. Mrs Y. Turner wrote to the QueenSpark newspaper about Daisy and George Noakes's books:

> 3 books ... were loaned to me quite by chance. My mother was talking to a friend who referred to these books written by Mr and Mrs Noakes. Apparently she had borrowed them from a relative who had borrowed them from a friend etc, etc ... Anyway many people had been privileged to have the loan of the books – somewhat like a library but I didn't know who owned the set.[7]

The book format itself gave kudos and recognition to the memories and thoughts of local people. The durability of the books ensured they were passed on for a long time – even acquiring the status of a 'library' – in contrast to newspapers that rapidly became dated before being thrown away. The pressing need to spread the message and share books meant that use became more important than ownership. Furthermore, popularity was a major reason to continue producing them:

> socialists and community activists were much more used to small meetings and hacking away and thinking you were a minority. And it was quite energising really to realise that what you were doing seemed to be wanted by a very wide range of people.[8]

The opening up of new audiences among working-class readers created an impetus and momentum which carried campaigns and informal groupings into writing and publishing. Although involvement in struggles would continue, the emphasis slowly changed as cultural activities gradually became the core purpose of Fed groups. Indeed, the development and circulation of working-class expression was given great urgency and placed at the core of this emergent cultural movement. In their eagerness to link up with readers, they found cheap ways of publishing that bypassed the normal requirements of publishing a book. The spaces, resources and technologies available within institutions were exploited by such self-help initiatives. For instance, one member of Basement Writers managed to reappropriate his workplace resources:

> [publishing] was done by that bloke … in his lunch hour … every week he'd come with a box of about 500 print run of poems … We thought this bloke was a miracle worker![9]

Richard Gray, writing about the Peckham Publishing project, noted how books tended to be sold informally and promoted by word of mouth. Comments about and corrections to previous publications arrived on the order forms, and people regularly came in to discuss books and to share writing. Gray argued that they were challenging the traditional passivity of the audience or readership: 'The frontier between consuming and producing the printed word, so jealously guarded by commercial publishers … began to look passable'.[10]

Audiences and marketing were not terms in common use, nor were they separated from other activities. Indeed, the idea of 'publishing' itself encompassed an eclectic mix of practices, including books, pamphlets, magazines, readings and more informal means of communication. It became hard to distinguish writing, production and publishing from consumption, marketing and distribution, which blended into one another. Community publishers provided a considerate first audience for the writer, while a more extensive range of readers would be developed over time. Groups made books accessible, cheap and easily available to people through a variety of direct means. For instance, in the 1970s

QueenSpark sold their magazine and books door to door in East Brighton; at one point, they even made a principled stand against selling through bookshops.[11] The informal distribution of Jack Davitt's poems in the shipyards of the north-east over a number of years created a reputation and readership for his work that would make them into good sellers; fellow workers had copied 'tons of poems' and distributed them among his workmates on the shipyard.[12] In the late 1970s, Mike Kearney, the Fed administrator, realised that he was in no position to sell their first anthology, Writing, through established outlets but that distribution had to be carried out informally; it was

> a book that needs to be 'passed on' where possible, personally. Writing is an idea and not a commodity. It breaks down the barrier – the myth – that says, only the 'educated' can write or express themselves.[13]

Writers and community publishers emphasised the importance of building long-term and ongoing close relationships with readers. From the moment of conception, actual and perceived audiences played a role in the production of books.[14]

Readings and book launches became a further important means of distributing work – see figure 9. Basement Writers' roadshows found young people proselytising poetry to groups around East London. In contrast to the staid launches of commercial publishers, these events aroused great excitement:

> if it was a Jewish autobiography, there'd be all kinds of kosher food and there'd be klezmer music, great! ... such wonderful celebrations of the life, and people had their families and grandchildren, and there was live music. That act of celebration of the book, made the book, not like a conventional book, you know, WH Smiths, God, this was blood, sweat and tears, this way, you know, 'my life!'[15]

The success of these events meant they became established fixtures. If run well, they were also an opportunity to sell literally hundreds of copies and to keep the whole of the cover price. Launches enabled direct communication with audiences, who had been nurtured over many years alongside the writing and production of a book.[16] They bonded the writer to communities who, in turn, became book buyers, readers and, in some cases, writers. The process of building audiences around collective cultural identity felt like a world apart from the impersonal and individualising trends of the market.

Even more impromptu 'performances' took place. Rick Gwilt grabbed the mic to read a poem at a Shakin' Stevens concert and started off-the-cuff readings in pubs.[17] Sally Flood once claimed she never got on a bus without trying to sell a book of poetry while in the queue,[18] while Tony Harcup stuck up poetry posters around East London and others distributed leaflets through doors.[19] Nick Pollard, as editor of Federation magazine, remained an advocate of this enterprising promotional activity.[20] The evangelism created new readers in significant numbers and broke through the shell that separated people from the world of reading and writing.

9   Basement Writers' publicity, c.1976, drawn by Alan Gilbey. The Half Moon Theatre was a popular venue for writing groups.

Groups realised that what they were producing did not fit easily into existing book-buying categories. There were some attempts to sell through established outlets, in particular WH Smith, but this proved difficult.[21] Kearney called on bookshops to form a 'People's History and Local Culture' section which might increase sales and 'help pull together the various autobiographies, local histories, novels, anthologies of poetry and plays related to working class experience' which were otherwise randomly scattered throughout shops.[22] However, Fed books looked and felt different to mainstream books and could not easily be sold in bookshops. Looking back on his experience at Centerprise, Ken Worpole argued:

> The only thing worse than not getting your books distributed by WH Smiths is getting them distributed by WH Smiths. It's a false hope, a diversionary tale. They may agree to take them, demand a high discount, then 4 months later send the lot back unsold. Our books simply don't sell well in mainstream bookshops; they're different kinds of books. They sell locally and through libraries where there is already a keen interest in the subject or the authors.[23]

To some extent, this contrasted with Worpole's rejection of the uniqueness of 'community writing', indicating the ways in which arguments could be strategically deployed according to the context.[24] Many Fed books were designed collectively and became material artefacts, featuring photographs of the author, who was represented as a 'local person', and the books were often priced cheaply. A contact address for readers wanting to discuss the book or to get involved in other ways was also prominent and contributed to the overall message that 'you can write too'. Thus, from the beginning, these books were created with a known reader in mind.

As well as being hawked by Fed groups in their immediate vicinity, books were distributed beyond local areas. The labour movement itself was one avenue that had been targeted successfully with a Fed booklist. Rick Gwilt, as a trade union arts officer in the early 1980s, was able to make use of unions in developing his work; he recalled

> in 1982, going for a meeting with the [Leyland Motors] shop stewards ... they could invite me as an outsider to their meeting in works time and arrange for me to put this [performer] on the shop floor.[25]

Similarly, Joe Smythe was supported by the National Union of Railwaymen (NUR) to produce a book for the 150th anniversary of the Liverpool and Manchester Railway, and the *Transport Review* heralded him as 'probably the first trade unionist to receive sabbatical leave for creative work'.[26] In addition to the established labour movement avenues, there was a widespread radical network of alternative presses, book fairs, festivals and events at which books could be reviewed, publicised and sold, and writing could be performed. The Fed itself had roots in the radical milieu of the late 1960s, a period closely associated with a counter-cultural movement that combined creative expression and social responsibility, not least in the alternative press.[27] Mutual interest and joint understanding emerged from the encounter between these constituencies.

Having an external and interested market, a listening ear outside of local communities, was very important in providing external validation for community publishers and writing groups. For instance, almost 500 Federation books were sold at the 1980 History Workshop in Brighton.[28] A roving Federation bookstall was stored at the London History Workshop centre, where the Fed helped to organise a session on 'Working class writers of the 1930s'. In the mid-1980s, an Exploring Living Memory event in London brought together a large number of history and reminiscence groups, where the Fed sold a substantial number of books, especially to those who had moved out of the city but wanted to retain contact with their pasts. The Centerprise *Working Lives* books were widely reviewed and hardback editions were produced for libraries. This also helped Fed groups make the case that their books were of more than merely local interest. Within a decade of its formation, Centerprise estimated it had sold over a million books, more than 40,000 of them bought by the Swedish WEA, where it was observed that 'Bus drivers (both men and women) in Enkoping, Sweden, have said how fascinating they have found accounts of Hackney people's working lives'.[29] In addition, certain Fed groups were themselves national organisations, such as *Voices* and Write First Time, the latter distributing 7,000 copies of its quarterly literacy magazine at its peak. The education sector was one source of readers, including teachers and pupils as well as the patchwork of interested people within ILEA and myriad adult education classes.

The hidden hand

However, this radical culture was to change rapidly in the 1980s as it became enveloped by a hostile political environment. With the rise of Thatcherism, socialists and radicals commonly shifted their focus of attention away from 'alternative' structures and worked to defend and transform existing public services, often from within the Labour Party.[30] Over time, academic interest in class politics would be shaken by economic and social changes and the rise of 'new' identity groups. Even within the History Workshop movement, the interest in 'experience' abated in favour of new theoretical paradigms as energies were refocused away from participatory conferences and towards the academic journal. The effect of these shifts meant not only that FWWCP groups lost some members but also that part of their 'market' was reduced in size. In educational settings, writing by schoolchildren was stifled by changes in policy, especially after the 1988 Education Reform Act. Adult literacy tutors could feel dispirited by the critique of language experience that also reflected tutors' insecurities about using the pedagogy.[31] As a result, the Fed became more isolated from the broader movement. This coincided with the waning of the labour movement that had served as a market for books and a source of publicity. Gwilt's earlier work with trade unions and the worker's magazine *Voices*, struck him as unimaginable twenty years later:

> the decline of the big workplaces ... and the loss of the shop stewards committees, increasingly the trade union movement lost its foothold in the workplace ...
>
> That sort of era is gone ... that fertile ground that *Voices* was able to grow in really started to get much less fertile towards the end of the 70s.[32]

Already by the 1980s 'working-class writing' was beginning to appear outdated and this tendency was to become more marked.

Moreover, strong connections with particular communities was not manifested across all groups. Commonword, for instance, had never managed to sell books in the quantities achieved by other community publishers. General books of working-class writing did not always sell in high numbers, especially anthologies of creative writing rather than autobiography and oral history. In responding to the politics of equal opportunities, black, women's and gay/lesbian writing workshops were established and Commonword was more able to target these growing markets. An internal discussion document commented on the contrast between the seemingly amorphous notion of 'working-class writing' and the more specific new identity groupings:

> 'Nothing Bad Said', Commonword's first short story collection ... cannot be said to be of a lower standard than, say, the Northern Gay Writers anthology. But its sales figures are low, whereas Northern Gay Writers has done really well.
>
> One conclusion from that might be that we should concentrate on specific markets – a market for gay writing, a market for women's fiction and so on ... Perhaps it is simply the case that there is, at the moment, no large and evident market for working class writing.
>
> Where working class writing has done well as such, is where it appeals to a definite audience within the working class – the labour movement, a local community interested in local history and the experience of local people, steelworkers, groups (such as in Wales) with a strong regional and class identity. We need to think seriously about that.
>
> ... ideally we should reach a compromise where more commercially successful publications subsidise those which (through no inherent fault) sell slowly.[33]

In a commercial atmosphere, where each market had to produce a high enough return, the final statement would become difficult to justify.

The availability of grants decreased for some groups but for those that retained them, the strings attached became tighter as part of a cultural swing towards accountability and marketisation. Commercial pressures dovetailed with a radical critique of informal organising. Indeed, the think-tank Comedia argued that radical ventures were failing due to their lack of structure and unwillingness to prioritise marketing.[34] Community publishers found that certain books did not sell well and printing too many copies left a bitter aftertaste as people's attics became storage space for unsold book stock. The urge to expand, or even maintain, the audience for Fed books also nurtured a focus on 'marketing'. Customers could not be taken for granted. Groups with paid staff, such as Commonword,

Gatehouse and Yorkshire Arts Circus, wrote marketing into job descriptions, eventually creating dedicated sales and marketing posts.

Backed by North West Arts Board, Commonword widened its remit to the whole of the north-west and started to embrace professionalism more overtly. In the mid-1980s, staff were discussing the need to gain larger sales in order to break into national markets and access audiences through bookshops and libraries.[35] Dave Parrish became convinced of the need to develop mainstream distribution, spurred on by the experience of trying to get commercial outlets to stock their books:

> a Forbuoys or a small Smiths ... we gave them the spiel ... 'these books are written by marginalised people – people who haven't had the chance to develop their writing in the past but Commonword brings them on and gives them the opportunity to write' and this newsagent guy said, 'So what you are telling me is it's crap, it's worthy but nobody actually wants to buy it and read it' ... we were both stunned and shocked and upset ... I just thought is that the image we are giving off – that because we have some sort of social purpose to our publishing that people assume that the writing itself is crap – that it's sort of patronising.[36]

This version of populism, which was associated with an expanding consumer culture, generally did not provide a sensitive context for community publications.

As market-like relations impacted upon voluntary and community groups during the 1980s, Fed groups would adapt a range of business practices. Commonword would set up the Crocus imprint, which emulated mainstream publishers by introducing brands, barcodes, books with spines and glossy covers more suitable for bookshops, as well as carefully crafted blurbs aimed at a conventional audience. This was based on a more traditional idea of marketing and was related to the concern with the 'customer' that was extending throughout society. To some extent, in place of the earlier activist fervour, the product was shaped to the needs of an existing market 'segment'. As bookshops became more important sources of income with the shrinking of informal networks, there was pressure to produce quality books on subjects that could sell. In particular, Waterstones colonised the spaces once inhabited by informal radical practices, organised readings with authors and devoted a huge amount of floor space to displaying books, which had the effect of squeezing out their smaller radical counterparts.[37] In addition, informal distribution could be seen as archaic, with complaints about 'old men who wanted to make pamphlets to sell in pubs'. In tune with this concern, some writers became frustrated with selling small publications informally to a familiar audience.[38] Stephen Yeo later mused about the lost potential for co-operative business development on a larger scale than was conceived as feasible or desirable at the time.[39] In his new guise as a consultant working with voluntary organisations, Gwilt looked back on his time selling *Voices* as 'sheer blood, sweat and determination and cheek, but not much finesse or thinking about marketing strategy'.[40] These debates reflected the ways in which the meaning of markets was being contested.

In a changing atmosphere, community publishers were to develop a greater sense of professionalism. Parrish emphasised the potential improvements that also fitted in with the priorities of paid workers who wanted to develop their publishing and design skills:

> I think the purpose is sacred and sometimes you have to update the methods ... the modernisation or professionalisation which some people were uncomfortable with but others weren't ... it was no longer absolutely grass roots with people doing it in their spare time after coming off night shift and ... all that sort of stuff which can get a little bit too romantic I think but it was paid workers from a grant ... why shouldn't we use professional marketing techniques to sell more books to give writers a bigger audience but there is always a suspicion that comes with that.[41]

This point of view also held that books should be sold at standard prices so that they would be seen as 'real' rather than 'worthy'.[42] The associated focus on producing quality books that looked good did find widespread sympathy, and many groups had always aimed for quality in order to value the writer and to make a statement to the audience about the work. As a literacy group, Gatehouse had produced a durable product that could be reused in classes. Centerprise had effectively brought together these twin tendencies of professionalism and informality, but in the 1980s they began to diverge. In fact, the change represented a new angle on a long-term tension about how to represent marginal groups. It paralleled the views of the Wesleyans in the eighteenth century, who believed that cheap or free books would be perceived as worthless.[43]

Drawbacks

Adopting more established means of distribution and promotion raised a number of snags. Recalling earlier fears, there was no guarantee that bookshops and distributors would welcome the opportunity to sell these books. In fact, they frequently demanded over 50 per cent of the cover price and did not actively promote them. Depending on the mainstream press for publicity had always been difficult and carried no guarantee of success. The Fed anthology *Once I Was a Washing Machine* received very few reviews despite being a significant collection of working-class writing. Even Alistair Niven, literature director at the Arts Council, was dismayed at the muted national response to the book. After sending three copies to the *Guardian* and making numerous phone calls, the incredulous Fed worker was told to 'send it to the reviews editor and if it's good enough it will rise to the top, the cream rises to the top'.[44]

Aiming for national distribution proved to be a costly and convoluted business. Using distributors was not a successful strategy in the early years of the Fed, although Commonword made use of Password Books, a distributor for small literary presses. The Publications Distribution Co-operative, established in part by Glenn Thompson, was utilised by some groups but did not suit the needs of all, especially those that operated on a smaller scale. Attempts at a national Federation book club came to nothing in the early 1990s due to the scale of such an undertaking, and attempts at regional distribution met the same fate. Similarly, Write First Time concluded that support for writing in adult literacy should go into distribution, seen as a key point of weakness. However, its request for funding from the Adult Literacy and Basic Skills Unit was turned down. Building such projects faced insuperable difficulties and lent weight to the arguments of the Minority Press Group (MPG), which complained of a restrictive British distribution system in contrast to the more open French one.[45]

One danger of focusing on the needs of an established audience, coupled with the increase in price, was a creeping conservatism in publishing policy based on a notion of 'quality', a position the Fed had originally rejected in favour of democratic participation as a precursor to making such judgements. The need to sell to an established audience could lead to a diminution of the distinctiveness of some Fed writing. For instance, Dim Sum was a collection of short stories by British Chinese writers published by Commonword which considered drawing in writers from beyond their already-extended catchment area of the north-west. In justifying the case to the Arts Board, the new language around quality and markets was employed:

> there is a greater and greater financial imperative in today's publishing market to launch only the highest quality writing. We would therefore like the latitude ... to publish British Chinese writers from outside the North West ... should we find insufficient North West Chinese short stories of sufficient quality.
> This is a 'safety net' strategy to ensure a book of the highest quality is launched.[46]

The fears expressed here must be viewed not only in relation to the audience but also to another 'market' – the funder. It is ironic that marketisation and the adoption of business ideas were expedited by public subsidies and grants. Being seen to produce a certain type of writing might help to secure grants, but this approach dismantled the bridge to first-time writers, who would feel less welcome among those who aspired to be 'professional' and 'critical'. It was not always possible to contain all these interests.

Similar tendencies would have different consequences at Centerprise, where the link between literacy and literature would be severed. In the late 1990s, Calabash magazine, published by Centerprise literature development workers, declined to review Gatehouse books because they worked in 'literature not literacy'.[47] But the focus on quality and literature could create problems. For instance, in the mid-1990s, Centerprise published Maurice Beckman's The 43 Group, about the activities of a Jewish anti-fascist group in the East End of London after the Second World War. However, they were overwhelmed not only by the labour to edit and publish the work but also by its huge success, which generated income yet took up much time and effort in distribution. It was difficult to justify such expense on just one project. Only a handful of books were published each year, and it was hard to envisage a community publisher sustaining itself entirely from sales. Delivering large projects from a standing start was problematic and groups were reluctant to accept that they had a 'break point' as opposed to more familiar discussions about breaking even.[48]

Formal methods of marketing were also diffused through informal contacts. Centerprise staff became interested in the changes taking place at Commonword/Cultureword, which had adopted a

> more 'commercial' profile – less explicitly rooted in established ideals of 'working class' writing. They still, however, work within the boundaries of publishing work by 'others': black writers, women, lesbian and gay writing. But their emphasis is certainly upon 'quality' writing, literature that will appeal to a wider market ... how much do we want to perhaps 'compromise' our historical ideals in order to sell books?[49]

Subsequently, Commonword worker Pete Kalu produced a report for the London Arts Board in which he proposed setting up literature development provision across the capital. He noted the high staff overheads in producing quality books that would sell well and also argued that publishing 'pamphlets' was becoming obsolescent, which caused retail outlets to de-stock some Centerprise publications. New technology, particularly desktop publishing, meant that self-publishing had become more feasible for individuals. Kalu also pointed to the growth in commercial and semi-commercial alternative presses, especially for black writing, which meant that the need for Centerprise publications had declined.[50] As a result of this and the scarcity of grants for publishing, Centerprise stopped publishing and initiated a literature development project. This gave rise to feelings of guilt, but Centerprise insisted it was not simply jettisoning its past – it had 'just transformed itself ... we are getting a lot more people published than if we were a publishing house'.[51] The organisation became a resource for an increasing number of writers, some of whom aspired to be published in the mainstream. But it also meant that other people felt excluded who did not immediately fit with the emerging categories and the perceived market demand.[52]

I have emphasised this development in order to illuminate the tensions within alternative publishing. The groups attracted to quality, professionalism and marketing did not suddenly become part of the mainstream and they retained a vision of championing the expression of marginal voices. In fact, some groups that argued for quality would later be sidelined by the same arguments emanating from policy circles.[53] Workshops also embraced differing versions of marketing. While only a few were able to scale the heights of semi-professionalism that often depended upon funding, others would choose very different paths by remaining committed to low-cost production, distribution and performance. The search for self-sustaining and creative ways of distributing writing proved to be an ongoing struggle for most writing and publishing groups.[54] Moreover, informal and experimental methods of production and distribution resurfaced in the gaps created by the professionalisation of voluntary action, spurred on by the desire to publish experimental work by a range of writers.[55] For example, in the early 1990s QueenSpark found itself depending on printing two quality books a year, a development activists felt was starting to skew their core purpose:

> QueenSpark had been led into high printing and binding costs, print runs that were overlong for our distribution resources and a costly, labour-intensive process of planning, publicity, marketing and sales. We were being led back towards the elitist economics of publishing from which we wanted to break away.[56]

'Market books' were developed in order that more writers could be published. They resembled pamphlets, which had cheaper production costs. In 1991, these were sold for a pound. By the late 1990s, they had become the main publications produced, featuring photos and glossy covers while still selling at the cheap price of about £3. Again, this was enabled by technological change and helped to refute the claim that they looked amateurish. Commonword also published pamphlets that could be sold at performances and informally by writers, very much as would other small presses which utilised all available means of distribution just to stay afloat. Those without access to resources have continued to develop creative ways of distributing writing. In the early 2000s, the internet became a means of sharing writing and a way to engage those who could not easily travel. In 2017, the Fed continued to organise an online monthly writing challenge as a way of connecting its various groups and writers. While the internet has reduced the visibility of community writing, its use has become essential for virtually all writers.

Moreover, moments of early popular participation were to be repeated in areas where there was a contested sense of community. During the 1984–85 Miners' Strike, ideas of working-class community would be formulated in radical ways.[57] Over a decade later, in 1996, Gethin Jones, a member of the Maerdy writing group, explained to me how, as he took a big pile of copies of the writing group's new pamphlet to the library, he was beset by people coming out of their houses to buy one; it took him a number of trips before he managed to arrive at the library with any copies at all. Maerdy was a Rhonda village with historical Communist Party leanings and despised by the Tories, who informed the village of the closure of the mine on Christmas Eve and then levelled the winding gear and other evidence of the mine in early January, wounding the identity of the local people. Locals felt this devastation of a working-class community was 'Tory revenge' for previous militancy.[58] Williams' explosive shock of recognition could thus return at unforeseen moments.[59]

Remaking markets?

According to this reading, markets are not neutral arbiters of popularity, an ever-present force that must be accepted. Rather, evidence from the Fed helps to illustrate how they are forged and contested over time. The whole counter-cultural trend from the 1960s had questioned professional knowledge and power in the hope of establishing a more equal and democratic society that met the needs of all. The diverse responses by Fed groups were a sign of how alternative market relationships were being developed based upon solidarity with working-class readers and writers. It is ironic, then, that the New Right critique that professionals had captured public services and civil society for their own ends subsequently led to the restriction of relationships with communities and readers. Indeed, in the 1980s, a singular ideology of 'the market' was imposed upon assorted social activities. Quasi-market relationships seeped into the public sector and civil society where they took on a new shape. In many ways, this was a political decision and 'the market' could be a blunt ideology used to justify restricting the ways in which communities engaged in cultural activity. Enforcing market thinking served to close down certain relationships while favouring others.

Our understanding of markets should thus be decoupled from neoliberal ideas based on the dominance of transnational corporations. As the historian Fernand Braudel argued, capitalism and markets are not synonymous nor are they historically coterminous.[60] Markets also operate at multiple levels. The actual marketplaces found in cities and towns historically operated as a form of 'commons', communal spaces where struggles over ownership and rights took place. Similarly, the Fed represented an example of a moral economy that created unfettered communication between readers and writers.[61] Audiences were articulated as potential friends, comrades and allies with whom long-term relationships were built. Professional forms of marketing could be allied to a concern to represent working-class writers in a positive light and to promote their work among wider audiences. The issue became further confused with the emergence of new identity groups and the rise of professionalised marketing. Holding together these contradictions in a productive alliance was a process replete with difficulties. Alternative publishers faced choices and dilemmas about how to respond to the assertion of cultural entitlement and the need to sell more books. Clear-cut options tended to blur into pick'n'mix methods of sustaining readers and audiences.

External relations with audiences were mirrored by internal arrangements in the way that workshops were conducted. Debates over organisational form would be analogous to those surrounding the changing nature of audiences. The ways in which 'grass-roots' writers and readers were sustained through inclusive forms of organisation became a vexed issue in the Fed. Indeed, the effects of transforming workshops into service delivery vehicles sparked another set of debates that had further implications for understanding social change.

8 Chuck out the teacher: critical pedagogy in the community

Writing and publishing workshops contested the processes and forms of organisation. The democratisation of writing and publishing was one element in a radical vision of social change. A great deal of discussion and work went into the development of alternative structures as a means of building solidarity with local people. Ends and means were interrelated and process was seen to have major implications for product. For example, the Centerprise Annual Report for 1978 highlighted the desire to 'engage with needs, demands and possibilities that were not included in the programmes of parliamentary politics or directly allied to industrial struggles' and to 'remain distinct … from the local state and its services'.[1] In particular, relations between writers/students and organisers/tutors were questioned and debated. As such, the early Fed constitution defined community publishing in terms of producing and distributing writing in co-operative ways mainly for a working-class readership. These ideas would come under strain in the 1980s and 1990s, although they were not wholly extinguished.

The concern to recognise and value writers was linked to developing theories of radical or critical pedagogy. One of the clearest crystallisations of these ideas was to be found in the work of Paulo Freire, whose *Pedagogy of the Oppressed* had an international impact and remains a classic statement on critical pedagogy.[2] His approach probed the traditional divisions of labour between leaders and led as well as teachers and taught. Through a dialectical process of mutual learning, teachers and students would change both themselves and their society by bringing together theory and practical experience in a process of 'praxis'. Initiating the educational process from the experience of the marginalised, as a basis for creating knowledge and fostering social transformation, was contrasted with depositing layers of disembodied knowledge in a previously empty and uneducated person – the so-called 'banking' concept of education. Through dialogue, Freire argued, a stage of 'conscientisation' would be reached whereby the oppressed would become self-aware of their position in the world, recognising the forces that limited their human capacity as well as those that might free them. Concepts of 'cultural action' and 'cultural revolution' highlighted the need to work with social movements and community groups.[3] Similarly, Henry Giroux called on progressive educators to 'form alliances with parents, community organisers, labour organisations, and civil rights groups' in order to help democratise social structures.[4] Freire's ideas were inspired not only by Marxism but by an eclectic mix of religious and cultural influences, a fact that helped to ensure that his ideas would resonate internationally despite a number of critiques, not least from feminists who questioned Freire's notion of 'humanisation' as denying the fissures that divide any community.[5]

Critical pedagogy has inspired continuing debate and discussion.[6] Although Freire's focus was 'education', he foresaw an all-encompassing process of social change. This was familiar ground to community publishing and writing groups which confronted comparable dilemmas and contradictions. At times these two worlds came into contact with each other. For instance, Freire was a major influence in the early years of the Fed – a sort of 'guru'.[7] He also appeared on television in 1990 commenting sympathetically on British literacy, history and publishing groups.[8] As a result, even though community publishing operated outside the formal educational sphere, its history helps us to comprehend critical approaches to pedagogy. Freire himself advocated building 'culture circles' on the basis of local understandings. However, he gave limited attention to the role of cultural and social organisations in his writing.[9] In part this may have reflected the difference between the state of civil society in Brazil and Chile in the 1950s and 1960s and the configurations found in British cities since the 1970s.

Destruction of the student–tutor relationship

In developing working-class self-expression Fed groups aimed to undermine traditional notions of education and leadership. *The Republic of Letters* reported a widespread fear of, and opposition to, the 'professionalisation of cultural production', a rejection of the idea that activism and commitment should become a paid occupation.[10] For instance, in 1977, the minutes of a meeting in Manchester recorded the concern that 'an administrative strata would take control of the burgeoning movement' and that a rift would open up between 'working class writers and white collar working class administrators'.[11] Commonword in Manchester only issued temporary contracts in order to prevent the formation of an elite, and some proposed that the Fed should elect staff on a yearly basis in order to ensure an organic connection with members.[12] Such defensiveness helped to safeguard that paid organisers were sensitive to charges of 'taking over' a movement that was owned by the writers. Many middle-class radicals helped to bring these groups into existence and fostered their growth, but a strong counter-pressure developed to ensure that staff and leaders emerged from among the working-class activists. It was felt that insiders understood the nature of the movement and would be able to enlist the support of local people. One person at Tower Hamlets bookshop noted:

> The surprise people felt and expressed at seeing a local person working in the shop – the others seen as 'weirdos' or 'commies' or 'hippies'. How important it was to have people from the borough working there.[13]

The Manchester adult literacy group Gatehouse appointed an ex-literacy student to a paid full-time position, demonstrating faith in the capacity of so-called 'illiterates' and making a statement about how literacy should be organised. This also meant that the staff were strengthened with a range of relevant experience and understanding. In the short term this might mean giving considerable support to a student, but in the long run they would be able to hold their own.[14] The person involved, John Glynn, would go on to work in a range of settings, including the adult literacy group Pecket Well.[15]

Working-class people gained the confidence to overturn educational expectations about their role. When a group of women from the Knowle West estate in Bristol, part of the Bristol Broadsides group, decided they wanted to form an English/writing group, they requested a tutor from the WEA and drew up a detailed specification: they thought a man would be more sympathetic than a middle-class woman, and he had to be middle aged with children. Maureen Burge recognised the value of a tutor but insisted on retaining control: 'We thought that if we felt he was putting us down, we'd chuck him out. We told him exactly what we wanted: he was the tutor but we directed him.'[16]

The adult literacy network Write First Time also delved into these educational relationships, particularly at residential writing conferences where more time could be spent with students informally. Positive relations were developed and, in 1977, a tutor referred to 'the destruction of the tutor–student relationship',[17] although a student from the same conference was probably a little more realistic when he identified a moment of equality: 'the sing-song was good, everybody's equal in a sing-song'.[18] Tutors such as Ursula Howard were inspired to cast doubt upon educational thinking:

> the limitations of a structure where students are still marginal, their appearance on committees largely token ...The exclusion of the learner from the discussion of the ideas behind teaching, seemed to be EXPLODED at the conference.[19]

By the same token, Sue Gardener argued that if a student 'starts to speak for her or himself, we as tutors have to change how we respond, plan, work out initiatives. It isn't comfortable, but surely it's necessary.'[20] Giving permission to students to redefine the learning agenda, and creating space for it to happen, gave rise to new understandings and pointed to the possibility of altered ways of working. One tutor was 'completely thrown' when a student turned the tables by interviewing her and wrote it up into an article.[21]

Across the Fed, middle-class activists found they needed to become learners and offer up their own personal experience. This involved more than simply finding out about the lives of working-class people or appearing humble in a tokenistic manner. Writers were given the confidence to question leaders and teachers. It was a common experience that professionals/tutors were expected to write in response to demands for equality within the group.[22] Centerprise, which positioned itself as a democratic alternative, applied this to its internal relationships.[23] By forming a collective they aimed to provide 'checks' against 'powerful individuals being drawn into alliances that turn out to be against our interests or those of Hackney people'.[24] But more than this, internal organisation could prefigure the future and show in microcosm that a different sort of society was possible:

> our co-operative working pattern ... is a political statement in itself, prefiguring and demonstrating the possibility of forms of working life and social organisation that give hope for a future state of society.[25]

Workers at Centerprise were all paid the same wages and jobs were rotated to help them understand each other's roles and be better able to support and guide people making enquiries. The physical and social setting was orchestrated to create a welcoming atmosphere, which included banning workers standing in the bookshop loftily discussing important issues which alienated people.[26] Members aimed to democratise divisions of labour; for example, at the People's Autobiography of Hackney, it was a rule that any member could interview any other. The WEA accepted that tutors for classes could be appointed on the basis of experience and knowledge rather than qualifications and that groups could be engaged in social action.[27] Indeed, the Fed tended to distinguish workshops from writers' circles, where middle-class people were portrayed as putting their own individual needs over those of the group.[28] While valuing individual differences, workshops were a means of forging solidarity among writers and communities rather than a space for 'local opportunists who are only concerned with their own work':

> It is a good idea to emphasise that a workshop means that people help and learn from each other, that the group is more important than the particular success of individual members ... Everybody who writes must be convinced that their audiences are also potential writers.[29]

Prefigurative form was thus invested with an inflammatory radical potential in which human relationships, when organised democratically, might generate social change.[30] According to Stephen Yeo, activists 'did think that the production of history, the production of books, the production of people's writings, in the right way, would have the capacity to alter dominant meanings'.[31] Working practices were dissected at a microscopic level and tied into social issues so that, for example, 'editing' went well beyond the technical aspects of working on a text. The traditional interventionist role of the editor as clarifying meaning was treated with suspicion amid fears of the writer losing control over their words and, by extension, their life.[32] It provided an opportunity to forge more equal human relations. With this in mind, community publishing groups transcribed the words of older people whose recollections could then be edited by the writer, often with the support of an editorial group. John Langley's *Always a Layman* started as a series of recordings in 1972. In the following passage Langley communicates a personal reticence about the validity of putting his life in print but goes on to express, quite poetically, a deep faith in the relevance of this work. Sandwiched appropriately between these contradictory views is a recognition of the enabling role of the group:

> I trust I have not bored you with my story. It would not have been told but for the intense interest of the group who so patiently listened for so many hours and then transcribed it into something reasonable ... One of the important lessons to be learnt in life is to listen to people when they talk to you. You then discover they have a philosophy which you never dreamed they possessed and you find you have so much in common.[33]

In this way, Langley connected personal experience to a social and political arena.[34] It was just this sort of mix that community publishers aimed to develop.

Changes

Contradictions inevitably surfaced. Over a period of time, some groups changed in ways that negated their earlier aspirations and practices. A number of obstacles would arise which considerably complicated the radical claims that were being made. As a conservative neoliberal hegemony infiltrated British society during the 1980s, the energising rays of light from a wider radical culture diminished.[35] The number of sympathetic academics also dried up as intellectual trends became increasingly critical of the notion of working-class experience, leaving the Fed more isolated.[36]

Generational changes also affected alternative practices. Groups metamorphosed as older members were gradually replaced by newcomers. Commitment and voluntary activity could only be sustained for a limited time, and many of the initial cohort of activists born in the late 1930s and 1940s were moving on to new pastures by the mid- to late 1980s. Groups had demanded a huge amount of work, commitment and emotion from members and politicising daily life could be wearing. In an honest comment, literacy worker Maureen Cooper admitted that she was worn out by the voluntary work:

> I was relieved when Write First Time ended in a way, because I felt very guilty about it, I felt very exhausted, thinking, 'I can't actually give any more time and energy to it', and felt very guilty about that. So it just finished.[37]

10 FWWCP booklist 1985–6, illustrating the diversity of writing produced in the movement.

This was a painful process for people whose work and personal lives had been wrapped up in these workshops. In the late 1980s, the writing group Scottie Road '83 lost members as experienced writers found new outlets for development. The group started to change, attracting 'a different type of person', and the original dynamic faded.[38] Keith Birch had, by then, gained paid teaching and writing work, although it was not easy to cut the ties. He remembered trying to 'rescue' the group when numbers dwindled. After a time, Birch felt he and others were damaging the group:

> what we were doing now, or attempting to do, was to impose our values on this new group of people ... we were becoming a crutch ... as soon as we step aside it's all going to fracture, because it's not their values, it's ours ... So we stopped going, and the workshop eventually just fell apart.[39]

Within groups, internal pressures soon became visible and cut across any simple notion of empowerment, a term that was gaining in popularity. Although the theory of prefigurative form held that such 'cells' might expand rapidly, in reality ensuring survival, let alone growth, proved to be an uphill struggle. Some collectives became more focused on the staff rather than the extensive constituency of writers and community:

> there is a conflict between ... whether we are other directed; i.e. taking our directions from outside the collective and responding to needs expressed by our users; or whether we are self-directed; i.e. taking responsibility for our own needs first and prioritising 'the collective' in terms of who is in it, how it conducts itself etc above what it actually does.[40]

Equivalent debates in the women's liberation movement mulled over whether they were a movement for the liberation of women or a movement of liberated women.

The aspiration to equalise power differences could be severely compromised on occasions. Les Moss's *Live and Learn: A Life and Struggle for Progress* was a collection of recorded memory, written autobiography and contemporary campaign material, published by QueenSpark. A number of taping, production and editorial teams worked on the book. Moss's initial concern was to campaign against his mistreatment by the health authority, but QueenSpark was more interested in producing an autobiography about his life as a whole. As a result, the sections of the book are somewhat disjointed. At one meeting the writer felt alienated from such an intricate process and claimed the book

> had very little to do with him. He knew little about it ... it wasn't his book ... if he had done the book himself it would have been different – but he couldn't have done it ... the book was based on answering questions.

His powerlessness was apparent alongside his eagerness to be published; later in the same meeting

> Les was asked if he wanted the book to go ahead and he replied that of course he did. He was upset that anyone should think anything different.[41]

Checking recorded memories and rewriting transcripts was here perceived as very different from being in total control of a text. Lack of ability, time and enthusiasm could all prevent a writer from playing such a role, especially when power relations of class, race, disability and gender meant that community publishers were grappling with multiple and conflicting communities.

Voluntary groups faced a series of common problems with collective working, including a lack of individual responsibility, poor accountability, lengthy meetings and protracted consultations prior to making decisions.[42] As a result, some radical groups started to recognise the value of structure and management.[43] Previously workshops had not been realistic about the unequal distribution of organisational skills among activists, writers and staff.[44] The Popular Memory Group also pointed to the reproduction of unequal relations within groups, which raised serious doubts about the radical hopes for them.[45] Others, more sympathetically, would later draw attention to the continuing power of the tutor in adult literacy groups.[46] At QueenSpark, there had been complaints that not everyone's voice was heard, where 'the eloquence, intelligence and confidence' of an 'in-group' intimidated others.[47] Critics of community politics had noted that divisions in society could easily be reproduced in collective groups and even work to 'tyrannise' members with the least power.[48] In evading the issue of paid work, already privileged people with time on their hands benefited further, which suggested 'a leaning towards the nineteenth century concept of the "gentlemanly amateur", or a public school idea of "service" '.[49] One disgruntled participant characterised QueenSpark as 'a sort of Fabian set-up'.[50] Indeed, these tensions and criticisms corresponded to a general critique of critical pedagogy which argued that power relations were not fundamentally altered, despite the assertions of advocates.[51]

The positions of paid staff illuminated additional problems. From the inception of the Fed, paid workers had faced dilemmas given the large amount of potential work to be done with extremely limited resources. It proved difficult to treat this sort of work as a 'job' given the expectation that workers were merely paid activists. Moreover, writers without appropriate skills and experiences found they had to learn fast when taking on varied responsibilities. There was a potential danger that employing people without adequate support and training could confirm stereotypes about a lack of ability, although this was rare. Roger Mills, as a Fed worker, claimed that his job description included 'just about everything short of showering the nation with Fed publications from a hand glider'.[52] Personal life could also come into conflict with the demands of employment. Olive Rogers, another Fed worker, felt caught between two worlds,

> the one world being that of a woman originally almost unschooled in literature, coping with a demanding and tiring job, the other being a working class woman with a husband and family still basically working within the traditional circumstances. The two are not always compatible and I have great moments of stress.[53]

Paying people the 'rate for the job' became an important principle in some groups and mirrored a growing concern about not exploiting staff in the voluntary sector as a whole. However, a dependency on grants also weakened the willingness of writers and organisers to see their work as part of a movement or campaign as opposed to a job of work. In 2000, Alan Gilbey remarked that

> before grant aid became a big deal, there was more like a sense of, 'Well we'll just do some things voluntarily', and I think we all got a bit trapped in being dependent on grants ... it was like, 'Sod it, I'm a professional, I'm a professional community artist.' We were very low paid, and when they cut that, you used to think, 'Right, I won't do it anymore'. But before that, it was a do-it-yourself culture ... It was crusading.[54]

Funding and support brought unintended consequences. In Liverpool there was a direct link between the Fed, Merseyside Association of Writers' Workshops (MAWW) and wider creative writing provision. Some members went on to get paid work in cultural and educational activities, and it was ironic that apparently favourable developments could lead to the depletion of workshops. The huge growth in writing groups under the MAWW banner led to a successful campaign to get a writing liaison officer based in the libraries. Pat Smart felt this may have unintentionally led to the replacement of voluntary provision. They had successfully campaigned for a writing liaison officer, but 'he became so good at his job and sorting things out for writers in Liverpool ... the Merseyside Association wasn't required anymore because they could get everything they wanted through ... the libraries'.[55] In the longer run there was no guarantee that institutional support would be renewed: 'the libraries started taking less interest in the writing groups and more interest in arty groups, the writing got left behind again'.[56] When the libraries started closing in the late afternoon, many writing workshops were left without a place to meet in the evening.

These developments could be exacerbated when paid staff were seen as representatives of groups rather than enablers of writers. Formal contact was increasingly filtered through staff, in some cases weakening the bonds between writers within the national movement. The zeal of activists who took paid jobs contributed to the Fed, but this 'work' was not often incorporated into job descriptions. For new staff not socialised in these ways, especially those with children and outside commitments, the prospect of attending Fed events as an 'extra' was not always appealing.[57]

Expectations escalated in relation to the role of paid staff, the 'development' of a group and the level of skills required. As groups grew more complex, so more expertise was required from an 'elite ... workforce ... of a particular educational and political background'.[58] Outsiders were also appointed to jobs in order to gain staff with the right skills. During the 1980s, administrators needed to have a portfolio of specific organisational skills; commitment, experience and understanding were no longer adequate on their own. Funders also demanded transparency and openness in employment practices according to the burgeoning discourse of equal opportunities. In the early 1980s there were only a handful of paid staff positions in Fed groups, but by the late 1990s it was estimated that they numbered about 140. From that time, there would be a gradual decline in numbers. One effect of this was that it became increasingly difficult to 'trust' volunteers with 'delivering services'. Instead, activists might be demoted to 'clients' and 'beneficiaries' rather than owners and controllers.

Moreover, employing members threw up intractable problems. Scotland Road Writers' Workshop was unable to handle internal conflicts after it secured funding to employ staff. Although workers were appointed from within the writing group, mistrust soon burgeoned into a full-scale split, with most of the writing group reforming as Scottie Road '83. That two employees were related to one another, as were some of the members, was perhaps unsurprising in a Catholic working-class area, but many in the writing group suspected wrong-doing when they were outvoted by a newly established oral history group.[59] Members had been unable to develop organisational structures beyond the personal relationships from which the workshop had originally emerged. The resulting ill will was a further reason why groups started to appoint external staff rather than looking internally. Bristol Broadsides faced many of these pressures in an extreme form. An array of workshops had been successfully built up around the city, but when a charismatic worker left, the staff were unable to unite everyone and aroused suspicion by encouraging the formation of new workshops and black writing groups. The paid workers were perceived as taking over. Emotional outbursts led to violence and one writer receiving a prison sentence. The regional arts board, stung by the incident, moved its funding to the safety of a literature development officer, removed from community control.[60]

Changes were often precipitated by a crisis. In the early 1990s, a lack of accountability led to fraud and corruption at Centerprise and, under pressure from funders, it was forced to appoint a manager in 1992, relinquishing collective working and pay parity.[61] In 1990, Gatehouse responded to these trends by creating a fundraising and marketing post, following the departure of the ex-literacy student. While this brought necessary stability to the project, it had to be done at the expense of employing a student. As the organisation progressed and took on extra projects and staff, pressure mounted to appoint a manager. However, when this eventually came to fruition, the group was ill-equipped to manage the manager. Existing staff were accused of theft and the manager subsequently bought the book stock and traded as a private commercial venture for profit.[62]

While strong leaders could help to contain conflicts and develop new initiatives, they were not always a panacea. From 1992, the Fed appointed a paid worker who became increasingly influential over a changing executive committee, particularly in dealing with funders, the media and on foreign visits. Around the year 2000, a few people complained to me of his 'chief executive' status although most welcomed the active administrative role. But in 2007, with the disappearance of tens of thousands of pounds, he was dismissed. The Fed lost its Arts Council grant and reverted back to a more informal body.

Handling contradictions

The pressures encountered by radical practices did not undermine the entire approach. While the focus on management had strengths, it also ignored a number of drawbacks in relation to democratic participation. Indeed, there was no single road to development for groups that thought through the implications of funding and employing paid staff. Some bypassed these issues entirely because they had no desire to 'develop', or were not able to do so, and maintained the original group dependent on writers and volunteers. This allowed members to concentrate on writing rather than setting up organisational structures. For instance, Basement Writers, established in 1972, continued to exist for decades with members taking responsibility for the group. Likewise, East Bowling History Workshop, a history group of older people, also remained as an informal voluntary group, writing and publishing until members died.[63] Moreover, despite the lack of an explicit handing down of experience, organisational continuities were to persist. In the 2000s, a new recruit, Grimsby Writers, closely resembled Fed writing groups from the past as did Newham Writers, formed in 1986 and still going strong in 2017.[64] Others rediscovered older ways of working after having embarked on a more professional course. Both Hackney Writers and QueenSpark writing workshops at one time returned to less structured forms, replacing paid workshop coordinators with volunteers.[65] In the 1990s, Ethnic Communities Oral History Project formed ad hoc community groupings that were given the resources and responsibility to develop and produce books.

Staff were a necessity for certain activities and provided continuity when voluntary enthusiasms waned. Some groups that chose a developmental route managed to diffuse conflicts, and the process of 'professionalisation' could not simply be represented as a failure. Employing staff meant relinquishing some power, although in practice this loss could be tempered by the way in which they carried out their work, fostering and supporting writing and voluntary activity rather than replacing it. Generally, workshops became more alert to the way in which power relations might resurface. For example, in the mid-1980s QueenSpark Books was declining as active members were suffering from burnout after years of hard work and political and emotional commitment. The group was reformed on a more corporate basis, with spaces for less confident members – 'Structures … for continuity, that don't depend on individuals' – including a constitution, management and democratic structure so that people were 'encouraged to get involved and can see ways that they can influence decision making'.[66] This helped to ensure the long-term survival of QueenSpark, which would continue to produce autobiography and creative writing and, later, develop online publishing with support from Sussex University.

Pecket Well College, which ran a residential college for adult literacy students, proved to be a fascinating example of a group that actively grappled with bringing together participatory and service delivery approaches. Literacy students controlled the organisation and were fully involved at every stage, even though this required many long meetings where, if necessary, every detail was explained. An instinctive fear of professionals 'taking over' led to the exclusion of staff from many meetings, which at times weakened communication and made working relations prickly. Funding from mainstream providers forced compromises between the demand for classes with clear outputs and detailed information on clients on the one hand, and the desire to run experimental, democratic and open workshops, in which students contributed to teaching, on the other.[67] However, those involved gained tremendously in skills and confidence and remained fiercely loyal to the college. Smart, who worked as both a volunteer and a paid worker, commented in 2001:

> people here are not afraid to say what they think anymore and some people say, 'Oh Pecketwellians don't really run the place'. They bloody well do. OK the expertise might be coming from somewhere else but they do they run this place.[68]

Such experiences were far from uncommon among Fed groups. Ultimately, the residential college folded, but people continued to meet informally and charted Pecket's history.[69] As the college retreated, some members regretted the loss of a vocation and purpose in their lives as they were forced back into socially assigned roles.[70]

Marrying structure and organisation with informality and spontaneity was testing. Structures emerged from a variety of sources. For instance, those influenced by participation in the labour movement would also bring with them an awareness of the importance of structure, which Keith Birch valued when he arrived at Scotland Road Writing Group:[71]

> A lot of people think 'It's a working-class organisation run by the working class so it's going to be bedlam, there's not going to be any order'. But in actual fact it was really well run, there was lots of self-discipline among the people who were members.[72]

Multiple traditions overlapped within the Fed as new and old social movements melded. The free spirit of writing workshops had been imbued with an older tradition of organising based upon trade unionism, tenants groups, co-operatives and social clubs. In addition, one response to the difficulties of editing for community publishers was to develop writing groups where structured and regular support could be offered by other writers. For instance, Hackney Writers' Workshop established more equitable relationships which the People's Autobiography of Hackney had found difficult when working with writers.[73]

However, this inventiveness with working relationships proved difficult to sustain in the face of internal contradictions and external pressures. It became clear that old hierarchies and structures could not be completely banished. Fed groups came to realise that structures could enable as well as inhibit. Many activists learnt that ethos was as important as structure in determining the nature and success of a group. In fact, at a time when other radical community-based ventures were dying out, a crucial reason for the longevity of the Fed was the way in which different groups promiscuously adopted a range of organisational forms in order to build avenues for working-class expression. The Fed itself grafted together both collective, non-hierarchical models and more structured, trade union-influenced modes of organising. The groups that set up the Fed created a federal structure with autonomous groups, but at the same time they established a formally run AGM, with standing orders and an elected executive committee who carried out the nuts and bolts of organising and were accountable to members. This mix of structure and flexibility created the potential for working-class people to play effective roles, and each year a range of people from different areas and with varying amounts of experience were elected to the executive committee. The claims of management gurus such as Charles Handy that the idea of federation is somehow a non-British practice is thus brought into question by the Fed.[74]

Rethinking critical pedagogy

The Fed moved radical pedagogy onto new terrain as part of a democratic impulse by marginalised people claiming a voice. Community publishing and worker writer groups were passionately concerned with process and method and forged new forms and structures through dialogue and communication.[75] The boundaries between tutor and community organiser were crossed. Worker writers were also free to undermine the authority of tutors and organisers and did so regularly. The idea of the tutor in the Fed was treated with scepticism and was constantly scrutinised, repackaged and replaced with volunteers and activists, often later to reappear in new guises. At times, the facilitator was viewed as a function rather than residing in a particular individual, so that many different people could take on this role according to the needs of a workshop. Although it was found that inequalities could not simply be abolished, relations and roles were debated and remoulded.

The Fed levered genuine learning opportunities and avenues of 'empowerment', enabling participants to achieve personal and social change through writing and publishing. While activists drew on Freire in expressing solidarity with working-class people, their practices contrasted with some of his writings in which the role of the tutor/organiser takes on a rather fixed quality, despite his claims of teachers becoming teacher-learners and learners becoming learner-teachers. He never quite envisaged that there might be a situation in which it would be advantageous for the two to merge or even swap positions. It is true that he warned against any simplistic role reversal between tutor and student, favouring instead a fusion. However, this approach often underplayed the potential agency of subordinate groups acting on their own initiative with teachers/ leaders playing a secondary role. Freire was clearly committed to education and social change beyond the classroom, but the continuing power of the tutor echoed quietly throughout his writings.

Although the idea of critical pedagogy was informed by the urge to amalgamate theory and practice – praxis – within the Fed, it was not envisaged that major changes in consciousness would take place in the short term. Rather, community publishers placed these processes within a longer-term perspective in which popular expression, participation and communication were crucial. They were clarifying and learning from experience more than they were transforming it. Moreover, the communication of experience was not envisaged as an initial deposit to be overlaid with theoretical sediment but rather as an ongoing process capable of generating new meanings among an ever-widening constituency. Theory might be utilised insofar as it helped to disseminate and develop popular understanding. The internal relations within groups were valued and debated and contributed to books and readings which promoted public dialogue, well beyond the control of any tutor/organiser. Durable and permanent local institutions provided for 'local accountability for the accuracy and sympathy of the work ... the context in which the study of history, local and national, can be socialised and politicised'.[76] It is unsurprising, then, that many different points of view were given a public airing.

Stereotypical, racist and sexist views were directly challenged, but the evaluation of experience was complex and time-consuming. This contrasts with some interpretations of critical pedagogy that underline the need for considerable refashioning of subordinate groups to clear away the deadening pall of capitalist ideology within which victims are trapped.[77] The Fed downplayed the tendency to view working-class people as deluded – or, in the words of Freire, that 'the oppressed, having internalised the image of the oppressor and adopted his guidelines ... have adapted to the structure of domination in which they are immersed ... have become resigned to it'.[78] Activists contested the notion that working-class people were socialised by dominant discourses in such a one-sided way, and the context of publishing and writing workshops were living proof of this.

Only limited attention has been given to one of Freire's central ideas, that the existing culture of marginalised groups should be the foundation for education and learning. Many people in the Fed subscribed to the idea of a 'cultural revolution', but they did not assume that marginalised people would necessarily come to an awareness similar to that of organisers and tutors. This would be to deny the relevance of previous experience, an assumption implied by the concept of banking education. A readiness to listen to people pervaded workshops. As a result, developing popular dialogue was privileged over producing theoretically rich forms of knowledge. Indeed, experience was coupled with expertise as a way of fostering new writing and challenging power relations. It was not a straightforward celebration of working-class life at the expense of a more searching analysis advocated by critics. In consequence, while radical pedagogy aimed to bring together theory and practice, community publishing, with its emphasis on the depths and strengths of reflective practice, illustrated the considerable scope to implement these twin objectives in different ways.

A range of voices and experiences were nurtured by workshops. The idea of (working-class) experience continued to inspire large numbers of people and involve them in dialogue. Although versions of working-class identity were disputed and broadened, class would not be jettisoned as a concept as it was in other areas of social life. However, a range of identity groups would complicate the focus on class and these debates would become fraught within the Fed.

9 Class and identity

The issue of class and identity gave rise to perennial and at times acrimonious disputes. At an AGM of the Fed in 1991, I found myself in the midst of tempestuous emotions. In the bar on the Friday evening, a man was shouted down at his reading for attempting to parody a racist by using the term 'darkie'. An Asian man read a poem about the need for a laundry to get the workers to do their job properly. A disabled working-class man found that offensive – he later told me he did not bother with formal procedures but sorted it by telling him what he thought of his poem and calling him a 'cunt'. Throughout society, issues relating to class, gender, race, sexuality and disability were bubbling up and, in the Fed, they would erupt into open debate.

The emergence of working class-writing and publishing groups was, ironically, in part a response to the decline of one version of class politics and organisation built around the contours of heavy industry. The movement was imbued with a sense that something had been lost, that a way of life had passed away. This was expressed in cultural terms in a poem by Joe Smythe:

Small world

Outside the fair at Ardwick Green
hot potatoes from the hot-potato man
stay like a taste for the old exotic.
The hot-potato man, the organ grinder,
the knockerupper thieving dreams,
the donkeystone with dollyblue man,
the foggy tram conductor's cough,
the policeman with his street wide feet,
the local burglar with apprentice,
the man who fought Len Johnstone
the length of Brunswick Street,
Preaching Billy Arbuthroyd in flight
From nightwork husbands,

> The born lights of singing pubs
> That small world's ending.
>
> Joe Smythe[1]

The 'small world' of East Manchester, an area that had undergone considerable decline and depopulation, symbolised the degeneration of a working-class tradition.[2] In the 1970s, it was this fixity that was crumbling amid tectonic capitalist transformations. By the 1980s, spurred on by the success of Conservative governments, the nature and implications of the decline in the traditional bases of the labour movement were to be interrogated. Links between labour and social movements were becoming weaker as the unions were forced into retreat. The divisive politics of the 1980s fuelled hatred on both sides. At a time when class language and analysis were being suppressed in public discourse, Thatcherism was wielding a class politics from above. Just at the moment when turbulent change was radically transforming the working class, it was being silenced. Indeed, many class analyses subsequently concentrated upon middle-class individuality within the marketplace.

It became less tenable to unite a diversity of groups under a class banner as gay, black and women's groups affirmed their own identities and needs. Class came to be seen as archaic and irrelevant to modern conditions.[3] Moreover, issues of class and identity began to take on a dichotomous character. Chantal Mouffe and Ernest Laclau posited the idea of 'new social movements' being opposed to older forms of labour organising. This position was to be popularised by the Communist Party journal, *Marxism Today*, which had an impact well beyond its ostensibly leftist audience.[4] It was accompanied by a rush of ideas from 'new' movements that further undermined the focus on class.[5] For many intellectuals and writers, the rationale for using the term disappeared; 'farewell', class was 'dead'.[6] Others did not go quite so far but recognised only scattered shards of a once dominant presence. In its place a range of other identities assumed unassailable positions; class had been subsumed or irrevocably fractured by more specific loyalties, accurate measures and precise categories. However, this was a partial development and class would continue to be defended on objective grounds,[7] or in connection with life history and desire,[8] as well as in terms of negative stereotypes.[9] Detractors of class, such as Anthony Giddens and Ulrich Beck, characterised it as a monolithic historical formation which could then be contrasted with the present, an example of 'dualistic thinking'.[10] The idea of a homogeneous historical actor, which prevented other forms of identity from developing, became a popular view of history.[11]

The Fed became a key arena in which these conflicts over class were played out, giving rise to disagreement, animosity and a number of splits. Groups from Ireland, Liverpool and Bristol either imploded or decided to leave the Fed, arguing that it had travelled too far from its working-class roots. Having said this, the Fed continued to be populated by groups arguing for the relevance of class while trying to comprehend the changes. Consequently, by investigating writing and publishing workshops it is possible to discern how wider conflicts panned out in a specific context. The Fed constituted a social microcosm that, when examined, demonstrates how complex these debates were in practice. Wrangles over whether the Fed should be an organisation specifically for working-class writers or for the writing of marginalised groups in general contained, on closer inspection, a range of nuanced opinion that blurred the divide.

Class awareness

While many people came to the Fed with a strong working-class identity, others shied away from the term 'worker writer' as something to be avoided. The members of East Bowling History Workshop in Bradford were largely 'working class' but 'didn't have a sense of a class loyalty to the working class ... they would never talk about themselves in that way'.[12] However, through discussion and participation in the movement many would develop an allegiance to a classed identity. Peter Goode was introduced to the Fed through adult literacy but had little experience of labour movement organisations and had not tended to see his identity in terms of class. He described to me a process of gradual immersion through which he came to understand the positive side of being a 'worker writer', as something in which he could take pride rather than it being a mark of shame. Another set of experiences was brought to the movement by those who lived out the contradictions of being both educated and working class. They would be deeply moved by the supportive culture that enabled working-class people to speak and express themselves in a creative way. In the late 1980s, the photographer Jo Spence was taken aback by the camaraderie at Fed events:

> I could only stand and gasp at the solidarity, non competitiveness, friendliness and pleasure that I saw going on when members came together to share their writing ... the cultural skills amongst working-class people are exciting and amazing.[13]

The Fed was also a refuge for many broadly political people in the 1980s who kept returning despite their differences. Roger Mills summed up the value of the Fed for people who felt marginal to the mainstream culture – a group of teachers to whom he had been speaking had met him with 'hostile criticism' and

> all the usual crap ... the idea that once you start to articulate then you're not working class anymore ... their tone was scornful and some individuals actually became abusive. Loudly ...
>
> I sit here writing this with a half empty bottle of wine at my side that I bought on the way home to help drown my sorrows. Wine? Are working class people allowed to drink wine?[14]

The Fed marked out an arena in which positive class identities could be expressed, where a sense of entitlement was often couched in class terms. This was in contrast to later research studies that would probe into the negative way that working-class people viewed themselves, compounded by continued stereotyping in the media and other institutions.[15]

Writers were also distrustful of outsiders, echoing a long tradition of dissent. In 1981, one workshop challenged the role of middle-class people and raised alarm bells about 'working class writers–middle class managers?' Rick Gwilt locked horns with Greg Wilkinson at Commonword. Wilkinson believed there was a 'common cause' between those excluded by the dominant culture and those, like himself, who rejected it:

> The emphasis on WORKING CLASS writing is a move to right the current class imbalance – in cultural as in political spheres. But this does not mean that all of us are working class, or that writing can be confined to this or that side of the lines in the class war. There's fighting to be done, but unless we can look to some prospect of humanity beyond, there is nothing to fight for.[16]

Gwilt was more concerned with countering the influence of middle-class people such as Wilkinson whose vision, he reasoned, resembled that of an 'encounter group' rather than a self-organising association of working-class writers.[17] Similarly, Eddie Barrett learnt skills from middle-class leaders but then challenged them to step aside:

> Which didn't mean to say that we just ousted everyone who was of a middle-class persuasion [laugh] ... But we said, 'If you really believe what you're doing, when you think your job's done, you should step aside, and let us start doing the job ourselves. Even though we appreciate what you've done ...' It's possible that some of them were quite hurt about it, and I can understand that.[18]

Within Scotland Road the fact that David Evans was South African, rather than English middle class, probably made it easier for him to be accepted into the Vauxhall area of Liverpool where he could be less easily placed in class terms.[19] Evans was a sympathetic facilitator who would only visit officials when accompanied by another member of the workshop, which helped to build a collective spirit. But when Scottie Road '83 reflected back on the rent strike, from which the group originally emerged, members became distrustful about 'middle class joy riders' who 'appeared on the scene with notebooks and gusto, threw themselves into the fray, picked, in the process, the brains of hundreds of working class people, then retired to universities and polytechs to write their PhDs ... This particular type of infiltration or entryism was to be stopped.'[20] From the beginning there had been uneasiness about middle-class people joining workshops and potentially 'taking over'. One writer feared the 'embourgeoisement of the writers' workshops' with the appearance of 'unemployed, academically trained middle class people':

> So those who have not had the experience of learning might feel shy, less able to cope. It is us and them again. I think the process of discovery is important for all people, but there is a great need to share, not for middle class people to dominate.[21]

Further confusion ensued because 'working-class people' were not always recognised as such, a fact that stirred difficult emotions. A local East London boy was once told to 'fuck off back up the road to Cambridge' because he appeared too middle class, which caused bitterness.[22]

Deciding whether workshops should be given membership sparked additional anxieties about class dilution. A rigorous procedure was developed to ensure that groups were comprised of working-class writers. In 1978, John Small argued that

> a desire to grow shouldn't lead to laxity about credentials; there was a danger of middle-class entrepreneurs becoming dominant in the movement on the strength of working class writing which they assembled, selected and controlled. Ken [Worpole] was troubled about other-worldly dilettantes who saw in working class groups a chance to explore and exploit personal visions and idiosyncrasies.[23]

It was contended that where middle-class people predominated, working-class people would 'dry up'. For instance, the executive committee were unsure about a writers' group from Runcorn despite the fact that they claimed to be '99% working class'. Varying criteria were applied which emphasised working-class writing as an alternative to dominant literary practices:

> we had doubts if members had really sorted out exactly why they are writing. There was a lot of references to established authors and a hesitancy to actually criticise their own work in a way that implied style was generally more important than content ... we were ... unsure of their commitment to the worker writing ideals.[24]

At a later meeting the minutes demanded further evidence of devotion to the cause: 'a commitment to working class writing can't be assumed, it had to be remade at every workshop and performance that the group took part in'.[25] The constitution stated that groups had to publish their work. Part of the reason for this was that the writing could then be vetted for evidence of middle-class writers.[26] This led to the anomalous situation where writing groups with just a few middle-class members might be found wanting, whereas community publishers or adult literacy groups with middle-class people firmly in control could be more easily accepted because they were publishing working-class writers.

The working classes?

The Fed regularly questioned the meaning of 'worker writer' and 'working-class writer': should the 'worker' be dropped from the title of the organisation in order to broaden the appeal, or should it be retained to keep a focus on working-class writers? One faction claimed the 'worker' helped to position the Fed in opposition to mainstream culture while also accepting any marginalised group.[27] Comparable arguments were taking place in the trade unions and in the Labour Party and for some they were a sinister echo of those debates. Keith

Birch, at the height of the Blair years, identified an erosion of the class base of the movement,[28] and saw it as indicative of changes taking place in the Labour Party: 'I saw that as the beginning of the end of the Fed ... in actual fact was the end of the Labour Party as we knew it, as a socialist party'.[29] The Fed was also affected by the Miners' Strike of 1984–85, during which many groups held benefits, with representatives attending 'one every week'.[30] But there was by no means a complete consensus. Writers were sceptical of Neil Kinnock's policies in the Labour Party but also envisaged an alliance between class and social movements in solidarity with the miners. In the early 1980s it still seemed possible that the activities of other social movements could complement rather than replace class.

Divergent and at times divisive understandings of class were in play and often arose in response to how groups had been formed. For example, the Scotland Road workshop had been set up as a consciously working-class group in an area that had been fundamentally defined by the Liverpool docks. Strong Words in the north-east was mainly focused on mass industries, including coal mining and shipbuilding, and their view of class derived partly from these material factors.[31] Gwilt's idea of class was, by and large, based on the notion of a unified experience. But he would become embittered by challenges to this 'common culture' during the 1980s:

> Groups joined the federation from places like Oxford and Wimbourne, and some of them may have been window-cleaners but they seemed so different from us they could have been company directors.
> ... the southerners aren't going to expel or restrict themselves, and there's no obvious reason why they should. They're a sign of the times.[32]

Class took on a spatial aspect and became associated with a north–south divide that was becoming more noticeable in the 1980s: southerners who did not fit into a perception of a 'common culture' were often assumed to be middle class, which might be far from the truth. Moreover, the bulk of southern groups were from London and were influenced by the politics of equal opportunities and the work, and funding, of the Greater London Council (GLC). To some in the north this seemed like an alien culture. Equally there was concern at the sheer number of London-based groups within the Fed, and, at one point, in elections for the executive committee, some maintained a 'vote north' policy.[33]

Regional variations were explicit in contrasting books such as *Working Lives* (Centerprise) and *Hello, Are You Working?* (Strong Words), which inhabited discrete universes, although both were about work and were written by working-class people. In Hackney, it was argued that the experience of industrialism and trade unionism was less relevant than 'housing, education, welfare rights, health, unemployment and the special problems of the black community'.[34] Centerprise would distinguish local class experience from its image in the popular imagination:

were we reaching the ordinary working class, we were always being asked. No, we replied, because there is no such thing as the ordinary working class, only working class people with a variety of interests, coming from a variety of geographical and religious backgrounds, who from time to time in an area like Hackney, in a tenants' dispute or an industrial dispute, act in a highly self-organised and collective way.[35]

Age was clearly another factor in delineating aspects of social class. Autobiographies by schoolchildren would strike dissimilar chords to those by retired dockers which made it difficult to pinpoint a unified working-class experience.[36] Meanings of class were thus complicated by the fact that 'the working class' was never homogeneous and was undergoing significant change from the mid-1970s.

The flexibility around the term 'working class' was subjective as well as objective. The almost puritanical views of class were constantly being enlarged with the emergence of groups staking out an 'identity', which was welcomed by many in the Fed. Class operated as an umbrella category that provided shelter for an assortment of people. By the 1980s, identities were becoming more sharply defined and distinct. This contrasted with the fluidity that had existed in the 1970s. The early Fed included women and black writers who either identified themselves as working class or felt at home in working-class groups. Write First Time included many educated young women who were drawn to feminism at the same time as being influenced by a class analysis; this was a common approach within 1970s socialist feminism. Similarly, Peckham Publishing, Centerprise and other groups included black writers. The minutes of the Fed executive reported that Liverpool 8 was 'committed to being a black group, while solidly committed to working class struggle'.[37] The Fed constitution purposely proffered wide-ranging definitions of class and community:

> The term 'Working Class' is open to various definitions and this is a matter essentially for member organisations to determine, subject to the right of other members and the Federation as a whole to question and debate. We favour a broad definition. By 'working class writing' we mean writing produced within the working class and socialist movement or in support of the aims of working class activity and self-expression. By 'community publishing' we understand a process of producing and distributing such writing in co-operative and mutual ways (rather than competitive and private), primarily for a working class readership ... the Federation positively works to provide a forum for the discussion of issues connected with working class writing, racism, sexism, disability and age.[38]

The embrace of multiple positions created a home for a diverse range of people as well as offering opportunities for new groups to join whose primary focus may not have been on class. One early draft of the constitution by David Evans had even proposed the words 'We favour a broad definition [of class], to include, for instance, Black or Feminist groups'.[39]

The definition of class was constantly problematised by women's, black and gay groups who organised separate workshops throughout the 1980s, and the politics of these groups would influence workshops. A growing critique of class politics was seen as denying the specific situation of other marginalised people. Autonomous workshops would nurture ideas and writing on issues that could not easily be raised in mixed groups. Gatehouse and QueenSpark organised women's groups and, in 1982, a women's writing group, Women and Words, joined the Fed. John Gowling set up Northern Gay Writers in 1980 and the group was invited to run a workshop at the Fed AGM in 1983.[40] Under the influence of these developments, Worpole and Sue May wrote a press release:

> It is Federation policy that women-only workshops and black writers' workshops are automatically eligible for Federation membership as they represent specific sections of the community which have been particularly repressed culturally and linguistically.[41]

In fact the whole question of separate groups was to be a hotly contested issue.

Widening differences

Change was not accepted by everyone. Commonword set up the Home Truths women's writing workshop as a space for women to address issues they could not raise in mixed groups. The personal experiences of women could appear threatening to men. Patricia Duffin struggled to return to a time when forming a women's group seemed like a radical thing to do:

> I find it quite hard now to kind of grasp this because it seems so crazy really … I don't think it was just as crude as you should be writing about class issues but you shouldn't be indulging in personal experiences and talking about how you feel … writing about like being in relationships that were violent and the men in particular … felt very threatened by all of that, they took it really personally … like anything that criticised men was attacking them as well.[42]

The growth in consciousness of new groups could also lead to the running down of 'working-class' workshops that had previously served as a canopy for diversity. Hackney Writers had always included an eclectic mix of people, but the rise of women's and black writing groups contributed to its decline:

> This had the knock on effect of both depleting the numbers in Hackney Writers and making it a pretty boring, male white and slightly odd ball place to be.[43]

The 'working class' had apparently dissipated into an assortment of oddball survivors – a residual status that was perceived as extremely threatening by some Fed members.

Black writers within the Fed added to the critique of class. During the mid-1980s, a black consciousness emerged from a fresh set of circumstances, different from the earlier radical culture.[44] In 1986, Commonword established

11 FWWCP booklist promoting black writers, mid-1980s.

Cultureword, with its own staff devoted to working with black and Asian writers. Black writers were less tolerant of what they perceived to be the racism of working-class organisations and the placatory attitude of an older black generation. Indicative of this consciousness, the Moss Side People's Writing Group changed its name to the Black People's Writing Group, 'as this is its identity and there is a felt need for a black writing group … any past members … would … be given information about alternative writing groups'.[45]

Tensions were fuelled in part because the arrival of women's and black groups coincided with a struggle over resources. Being able to muster an 'identity' was beginning to serve as the basis for funding by local government, complicating the meanings of gender and race in community politics. The Fed was no exception. Centerprise, for example, was faced with demands to set up a black literature post in a context of decreasing resources and a deepening gulf between black and working-class politics. The black writing workshop Words, Sounds and Power protested against the introduction to Monica Jules' *Wesley, My Only Son*, which they argued adopted a condescending attitude to black people, especially the claim that 'Monica's writing is unusual among the Worker Writer Movement in that it is not about her own life, but about the life of her son, Wesley'. They rejected links with the Fed as irrelevant to black writers: 'We would like to know what the Worker Writer Movement is, and what it has to [do] with Monica as a black person?'[46]

They also pointed to the much lower proportion of books published by black writers as opposed to white writers. In common with earlier class criticisms, they picked up on the unequal power relationships within literacy work: black (or working-class) writers should not have their expression mediated by white (or middle-class) tutors. In the mid-1980s, Maggie Hewitt, a worker at Centerprise, was criticised for her editorial work on *Living and Winning* by Pauline Wiltshire, a black disabled women. The book won the best autobiography/popular history award from the Socialist Bookfair in 1985, but it was also accused of being 'at best patronising and at worst as exploitative and oppressive'.[47] This clash between black and class politics put the workers in a state of deadlock and held up publishing to such an extent that the workers felt it was 'very difficult for us to know how, if at all, we are to work with Black writers'.[48]

By the late 1980s relations were wearing thin. Al Thomson, then a Fed worker, was excluded from a meeting of black writers that he had himself helped to organise. He noted, sympathetically, that some black writers have 'identities and interests which are different and sometimes even opposed to those of the white working class' and that 'activists in black writing and publishing projects are wary and sometimes hostile' to the Fed.[49]

A clash of assumptions ensued, with some white writers invoking integration against assertions of an autonomous identity.[50] For their part, black writers were unwilling to tolerate what they perceived as racism and did not see it as their role to start educating people, the feeling being that they had waited long enough. Commonword worker Lemn Sissay, for example, resigned from the Fed executive committee, complaining of tokenism.[51] As a young and angry writer motivated by a black consciousness, Sissay viewed the Fed with much suspicion. One writer gave this graphic account of a reading at a local Federation event when it became impossible to communicate across barriers:

> A young man ... arrived in the theatre ... and indicated he would like to read ... His opening gambit was to enquire if any other black writers had performed that day, when informed to the contrary, he then went on to say, 'That is typical of the Federation and its policy' ... [He] then demanded that I remove myself from the stage ... He spoke with much hostility and aggression and asked if anyone had ever read to a black audience, because he said he hated reading to a white audience. When members of the audience tried to win his friendship he said, 'Don't patronise me' ... After a final piece on the more gentle topic of mother and child, he leapt from the stage and hurried out of the theatre, it must be said to a number of shouts and protests ...
> It was felt he had used the event as a platform to criticise the wrong people.[52]

These bruising encounters related to a political dilemma for the left: how to recognise specificity and still maintain universalism in organisation. In the late 1980s, Nick Pollard noted that black writers were 'suffering a crisis of neglect' and being told that 'we are all worker writers, that nothing should divide us and nothing should distinguish us'. Contrary to this, he reasoned that 'our most oppressed members' should have greater influence.[53]

Debates

It was difficult to distinguish a desire for autonomy from a claim for completely separate groups, in part because one section of the Fed refused to consider any diversity. Throughout the 1980s a significant current of opinion argued that the Fed, as a working-class organisation, should not permit women, black or gay groups. At one point almost a third of the membership voted against a women-only writing day.[54] Across the Fed, a few were even unwilling to countenance the possible existence of working-class homosexuality and there were misgivings about working with prisoners and people using mental health services.[55] Scottie Road '83 wrote an article entitled 'Separatist Groups' in which they warned of 'the temptation to dilute and spread, thus giving the impression of growth whilst in reality thinning and weakening', leading to 'a lack of direction, to a loss of common purpose'.[56] It was alleged that umbrella groups such as Commonword were unconstitutional because they evaded the rigorous entry procedures by establishing separatist workshops. The Fed welcomed 'gays, blacks and women' as individuals but they should all be united by 'class: above all, they are working class women, working class gays and working class blacks'. Black, gay and women's groups each had magazines that catered to their exclusive needs and the Fed should follow this lead:

> Working class people ... only have one outlet: the Federation; and we will jealously guard it. We will not stand by while some form exclusive groups and ban other working class people from membership and use the one medium that those working class people have and publish material that could just as easily appear elsewhere.[57]

The article rejected robustly that they were acting in a discriminatory manner and stressed the need for education through participation in writing groups:

> Now the working class are not all intellectual socialists; they are not all socialists; they are, unfortunately, multi-prejudiced. However, we still have to attract them to the movement and hope that, through the shared experience of workshop writing, they will lose these prejudices. What we cannot do, though, is impose our own enlightenment upon them. If we do that, they will never join in the first place.[58]

Simultaneously, feminist ideas were being portrayed as middle class and inappropriate to working-class men and women. Eddie Barrett recollected the altercation that occurred on one occasion from a 'culture clash' with feminist groups who were 'essentially middle class'. He argued that they all had similar ideas but 'we spoke different languages':

> this feller said to our group, 'Come on girls'. And one of the women from another group said, 'They're not girls, they're women' and 'what are you talking about?' But they addressed themselves as girls. And away it went then. So it was quite a big thing.[59]

As Barrett indicated, this was not an exclusively male point of view. It also troubled working-class feminists, who noted that some women in the Fed had internalised media myths and were unable to identify with women's liberation.[60] This was in spite of the fact that they might have been aware of unequal gender relations, which formed the subject matter of their writing.

Women themselves discussed the merits of meeting separately against the need to educate men in mixed workshops.[61] There were also a number of working-class women who were sympathetic to feminism and were applying it through a class lens, such as Olive Rogers. Following a women's writing day organised by the Fed, Rebecca O'Rourke countered the claim that women-only groups weakened class identity:

> All of us in the Fed ... define ourselves as working class people committed to developing a distinctive working class voice in writing. But those of us who bring other life experiences and identities with us can't leave them at the door when we come in ... Those of us who have the power that comes from being men, heterosexual or white have to recognise that women, blacks and gays have the right to meet as WORKING CLASS PEOPLE with those who share their particular experience. It's not an either/or situation: it's being both and all at the same time.[62]

Writing about personal experience compounded visceral arguments. Class was closely bound up with personality and identity and had to be experienced to be understood:

> An ordinary person does not need a description of working class, it is there with them, in their accents, in their feelings, in their dependency on regular income, even in their social security, in their background, in their hang-ups and their fears.[63]

Jimmy McGovern recalled the fractious class feelings that were continually aroused, on this occasion through a friend:

> Brian, a Scouser with a real Scouse face and a thick Scouse accent. Together we sat through a lousy story read by a black man. The well-meaning white liberals applauded it enthusiastically. Brian found this patronising and said so. 'They're only clapping like this because he's black,' said Brian. It was overheard. An hour or so later, at the bar, nearly everyone is discussing Brian's remarks and declaring him racist. But Brian ... is putting his kids to bed ... Brian returned and there was a row. He tried to defend himself but no-one listened. He had a skinhead, you see, and a lived-in working class face and a thick Scouse accent. He was everything they secretly hated, secretly despised, and now they had a chance to put the boot in and they did so.[64]

The body and voice were called upon as a marker of class in opposition to what was perceived as the growing liberalism and political correctness of the middle class.

One tendency was to reformulate class in terms similar to those of their opponents, viewing it as a specific identity rather than a collective social force or general category. Societal developments and the onslaught of Thatcherism nourished this embattled consciousness. It looked as if both the left and the right were united not just in undermining class as a category, but in attacking working-class people. Again, McGovern articulated this sentiment most clearly and sharpened his own identity as a white working-class male. Rapid historical changes were being reworked through the prism of experience and subsequent reflection:

> 1979–1989 was a bloody awful time to be a white working class male ... The trade unions (built largely by white working class males) were smashed. The factories and mines and shipyards (staffed largely by white working class males) were closing. Feminists were telling us we were sexist pigs. Blacks were telling us we were racist bastards. Gays were telling us we were homophobic bigots ... The trendy left ... had a mental image of us: a foul-mouthed fascist skinhead with a tattoo on his arm and a spanner in his hand ... And quite a few people in the Fed thought something similar ... I think that's why I packed the Fed in ... In the future, I decided, my identity would be 'white, working class male'. I would still attack racism and sexism and homophobia, yes, but I would be a white, working class male and other decent, white working class males would be my true brothers.[65]

Class was being reconstituted, not only through social and economic forces but in terms of individual identity and a politics of recognition.[66] Personalised understandings could thus mirror the identity politics of opponents.

These feelings became acute in writing workshops. In developing a literature based on working-class experience, writers had to be free to express themselves around other like-minded people. This was not possible in a diverse grouping where 'sexist' or 'racist' language would be shouted down too easily:

> Some members of groups were feeling intimidated to open their mouths in case of saying something that was racist, sexist etc. yet the working class naturally had many such features.[67]

McGovern observed that working-class men in Liverpool used 'tart' in an affectionate way to denote 'wife or lover', which was misunderstood: 'The feminists couldn't understand that. They couldn't accept our culture … The Fed forgot what it was there for: the promotion and encouragement of working class writing, warts and all.'[68] This line was potentially a productive one – analysing the use of language and freedom of expression. For instance, writing in racist or sexist ways would be poor writing, but accurately portraying racist and sexist characters was sometimes necessary. The editors of *Fed News*, favouring greater diversity, also made a move in this direction:

> Not many of us in the Federation would use clichés/stereotypes to describe working class men. We know that working class men do not all wear cloth hats, have hearts of gold or take pride in poverty … But how are Women and Black people perceived through the language we use, through the characters we create? Often in a deeply insulting way; a way that excludes them from the solidarity of a working class position.[69]

Discord was stoked as people rarely stuck to one issue but roamed among them freely. Duffin remembered that arguments over writing could be motivated by an 'aggressive … political style' that discouraged participation:

> there were a lot of clashes and a lot of the blokes thought that their good writing was being attacked unnecessarily and possibly sometimes it was but … given that these were tough blokes that got up and shouted at everybody else I suppose it was hard to feel that you weren't allowed to make those retaliations.[70]

Writers took individual positions on shifting topics. Rick Gwilt was not against separate groups but was concerned that admitting them to membership could act as a funnel for the middle class. There is some evidence for this although it is not straightforward. The radical black movement in this period was divided on whether to aim at the mainstream or create alternatives.[71] The Fed already occupied an alternative space, and many black writers were apprehensive about 'community-based' and 'grass-roots' initiatives which they saw as ghettoising writers rather than giving them opportunities for development, breaking into the mainstream and even earning an income. In the mid-1990s, the Fed supported a black writing day on the theme of 'Breaking out of the Black Writing Ghetto (without sacrificing your principles) – workshops on "how to get out of the ghetto of anti-racist/anti-oppression work towards a wider and greater audience"'.[72] In addition, the more professional groups most actively took on equal opportunities in part because they were funded and had more scope to redirect resources to favour black writers.

The prevailing discourse of equal opportunities within funding bodies meant that class was often ignored whereas minority groups were not. The whole purpose of the Fed was to be open to all, and targeting resources at specific groups weakened this aim. Some socialists, furthermore, believed that equal opportunities policies were a means of undermining the labour movement by purposely excluding class. Concerns about middle-class domination were intensified at a time when the language of class was being sidelined just as newer identities were emerging, often in opposition to class. The writer and photographer David Hevey appreciated notions of multiple identity. He noted that, as the 'male monolith of Labourism' cracked, outsider groups could self-define:

> These groups are all linked by ... the throwing off of the oppression from the body to the social order ... they are also linked by the denial of class politics ... the successes of these peoples within Equal Opportunities and access has, in reality, meant the success of their respective middle classes. It is my experience that New Orders as much as the Old Orders silence the proles.[73]

The issues were never resolved but with the passage of time, perspectives altered.

As the dust started to settle

Within the Fed, the predominant 'position' was to support groups that organised autonomously. Writers such as Mills were happy for working-class groups to coexist alongside, and mix with, women- and black-only workshops:

> I sympathised with the people saying all the groups should be open to all working-class people, but ... I didn't have any problem with women-only groups coming in ... their politics were the same ... they could see a strength in coming together as women ... a lot of the groups that wanted to stay specifically black were doing it for the right reason, because they felt they were addressing questions and debates in that community. I never saw that as a problem.[74]

This was a common position held by the majority of members who were not rejecting class but thinking about how it could be incorporated into other standpoints. 'Working class' was extended to include anyone who found themselves in a problematic relation to the dominant culture. Certainly, a commitment to diversity gradually became less controversial. The equal opportunities policy, agreed in 1992, noted the 'need for specific groups in the community to hold closed workshops and training that offer positive action to help further their development and equal status'. Black and women's groups, which might include middle-class writers, were increasingly welcomed. In the year 2000, Mills detected that the Fed felt 'so strong ... in its identity that people add to the mix rather than trying to take over'.⁷⁵ The value of surviving conflicts and supporting writers through difficult learning processes had been immeasurable. Pollard argued that the Fed had been able to support and change people with 'unrefined attitudes',

> making people aware of different ways of coming together, of the need to be in this kind of co-operative ... we've all got to be a bit thick skinned I suppose and not walk out of the room, slam the door and throw a wobbler ... most of the time people do talk through these things you know ... that's why people say it's like a family because ... for a lot of us anyway we've actually been there, we've been through all these disputes and stuff, you know, seen people at times in pretty ragged states ... and still welcome[d] back even if they have been quite awkward.⁷⁶

It was an attempt to support people from a position of equality rather than talking down to them.

Within the Fed these discussions thrived in open debate with few restrictions, in contrast to other networks and organisations that suppressed them. No 'line' was ever arrived at; this would have been alien to the whole culture of the Federation. Early in the 1980s, the executive committee had shied away from adopting political positions when writers with the 'wrong' opinions on the monarchy and Northern Ireland had been brought to task on a tour of the USA.⁷⁷ The focus on personal experience helped the Fed to bypass much of the divisiveness found in leftist groups. Debates were not clear-cut and writers often agreed with seemingly contradictory viewpoints, refusing to take sides. Alan Gilbey had mixed feelings and shifted from one argument to another, declining to settle in any camp as he watched others become polarised. He was uncomfortable with the 'violent' statements against middle-class people who had made sacrifices in support of the Fed; equally,

> you can understand why ... a low-paid, badly educated, working-class guy being told by a paid middle-class community worker that he was oppressing her ... hard to empathise with, like, 'All men, you are keeping me down' [laugh] ... It didn't have to be as shouty as it was ... So it was a bit like, 'Yea but ...' I was a bit middle-of-the-road on it all really.⁷⁸

Although these could be destructive debates, protracted exposure nurtured reflectiveness as responses became more nuanced. Pat Smart arrived at an understanding over a number of years. At first she distrusted groups who wanted to form autonomous workshops but, after listening to the debates, came to support them in certain cases, such as where women had faced violence. But at the AGM she

> couldn't quite fathom out why they still wanted it to be women only ... this was a time to open up and let other people understand what has brought you together as a single sex group or a black group or whatever, I thought that would educate other people, bigots ... I thought a bit more about it in recent years, yes they should have

been allowed to come to the Festival so other women from other groups could join their women only group or black only group.[79]

Later she favoured the idea of two workshops, one open and one closed, which might serve alternative functions.

Disagreements could also be handled amicably. 'Floyd' was impressed with the way issues were openly discussed. Instead of a bland consensus, the Fed AGM showed 'that despite the heat of the argument people were always willing to hear each other out ... If we continually bit our tongues for fear of offending each other we'd only make ourselves voiceless.'[80] The poet Steven Waling reported that writers were learning to be more sensitive about their writing, and one man who was met with complaints of sexism 'actually apologised and said he would be more aware of the issue in future!'[81] What is most surprising is that these differences were contained for so long. As a result, views gradually became more thoughtful and, at times, quite profound learning was fostered. In part this was due to the fact that the Fed remained a friendship network. Despite the harsh disagreements, McGovern wrote warmly about some of his adversaries:

> Rebecca O'Rourke, a lovely woman ... whom I had one or two rows but I thought she was great ... And Anne Cassidy who always used to speak up for us poor misunderstood men.[82]

In fact, solidarity across differences had always been an aspect of writing and publishing workshops. Scotland Road and Liverpool 8 met on many occasions, holding joint events from which new understandings and friendships developed. At first, David Evans had been reticent and knew that 'to be working class is not necessarily to be anti-racist'. But his worries were soon allayed:

> They got on wonderfully. One member from Scotland Road who talked about 'coons' and 'niggers', meaning no harm by it, was radically transformed by meeting the Liverpool 8 group. He liked some of the writers, one particularly, he liked his stuff, and they started knocking round together. And the guy, his vocabulary on race changed. He'd never been a race hater, but he just had what we call a politically incorrect vocabulary ... he went on marches and demos, and became a fierce anti-racist. So those things were the kind of interaction that was exciting.[83]

In the 1970s and 1980s, activists were able to engage with openly racist language in a way that would become much more difficult as time passed. Even in the school classroom, Chris Searle had encountered open racism which he could deal with through discussion.

As some of the venom drained out of these interactions, exclusive workshops became less frequent in any case. In 2002, Centerprise ended the position of a black literature worker that had been created in the late 1980s, leaving just two generic development workers. While targeting specific minority groups created spaces for development, it always entailed the danger of hardening lines of identity and marginalising writers. For instance, it could mean that all black writers would always be referred to as the 'black worker' rather than being welcome to participate in all groups. While Fitz Lewis attended the Identity Workshop at Commonword, a black group, he wrote for all people and rejected the idea of writing solely about black issues. Others preferred to write in open groups in order to gain feedback from various points of view. Sarah Richardson, an Eastside writer, appreciated working with the opposite sex when creating male characters.[84] By the year 2000, Mills had noticed

> a lot more mixing in groups, which obviously is a good thing ... the Tower Hamlets Writers Group, you find Asian people, black people, white people, Jewish people. And that's not planned that way, it's just the mix of people you get.[85]

During the 1980s and 1990s, the blossoming of Survivors' Poetry added a further ingredient to the mix. These groups argued that the experience of mental distress could form the basis for an identity that was sometimes more significant than other markers of inequality. The term 'mentalism' was willingly incorporated into the Fed's equal opportunities policy as an attempt to recognise the situation and experience of those in mental distress, and *Federation* magazine published a special feature on the theme.[86] Unsurprisingly, class, race and gender tensions remained apparent within the Survivors' Poetry Network and middle-class people often played dominant roles. For instance, Joe Bidder utilised his marketing and business experience as the first manager of the London group, and Larry Butler played a similar role in setting up Survivors' Poetry Scotland.[87] Class continued to attract vibrant discussion with many defenders, not least among survivors. The specific realities of a classed existence remained a theme in much of the writing. In the absence of public debates about class, ideas about the 'hidden injuries of class' also became more relevant to the British experience, an example of psychic damage and shame, just at a time when unrestrained loathing was being directed at the poor.[88]

The definition of a Federation of 'Worker' Writers was repeatedly discussed but, for many years, there remained considerable allegiance to retaining the 'worker' in the title. Dona Campbell from Survivors' Poetry Scotland argued that it was useful just because it had the capacity to link up groups of people in contrast to the 'breaking down of working-class community into differing strands (identities)' which 'creates opposing interests and narrow mindedness' and weakens 'resistance to infection'.[89] The Fed thus continued to convey a class focus and opposition to dominant assumptions about who can and should create culture. However, after the financial fiasco of the Fed, writers finally dropped the 'worker' from the title so that it became The Fed – A Network of Writing and Community Publishers, in part to help attract 'ordinary' people. Nonetheless, the Fed remained a shelter for working-class writers. The fluctuating meanings of class within the Fed were tied in with the way that external institutional arrangements were confronted. Working-class identities clashed with the dominant organisation of culture as the Fed mounted an assault upon elitism. Wranglings over class were thus connected with attempts to nurture change in the wider society.

10   The mainstream and the movement

The Fed mounted an assault upon British cultural institutions while attempting to live out a democratic vision. The mainstream, both commercial and public, was accused of excluding working-class people and denying them expression at a time when the parameters of the debate on culture were unstable. On a broader canvas, this was a period in which the exclusiveness of national institutions was being put under the microscope. The pressure was not coming exclusively from below. The unleashing of transnational capital in the 1980s and the rapid spread of commercial forces also destabilised the distinction between high and low culture. Differing conceptions of the popular were undermining long-held cultural assumptions. Following the trail of these developments within the Fed highlights the unique path the movement took as well as important variations in the ways culture was being conceived.

Mobilising for change

A crusading collective purpose infused the early Fed, a sectarianism that was inherent in the trajectory of the worker writer movement and the local cultures on which it was based.[1] It resembled a sect in its singular concern for popular participation. Working-class writing and culture were defended at all costs. Attendance at the AGM was originally made compulsory in order to help cement together a united movement.[2] Groups failing to attend, or to provide a good reason for non-attendance, automatically lost their membership and had to reapply by sending an explanatory letter. Inner integrity went hand in hand with challenging external practices. Accessible and democratic workshops, based upon a supportive culture and ethos, were contrasted with the stifling practices found elsewhere. Yet over time, the very institutions that stood accused of exclusivity would mirror this image back to the Fed by presenting it as small scale, inward looking and isolated from common histories and traditions. These were not simply organisational issues but provided grist to the mill of writers. Keith Armstrong incorporated politicised sentiments into poetry:

You will say, no doubt, that 'this is not poetry'
So <u>you</u> talk about 'freedom',
but only <u>your</u> own,
sit at <u>your</u> little writing desk
burrowing into <u>your</u> innermost thoughts,
preparing harmless images for limited editions
and the applause of one or two friends
and the Arts Council
and the gnomes of Faber & Faber.
...
<u>We</u> say to <u>you</u>
that there <u>is</u> hope,
that there is no love without it,
that the bomb can be destroyed,
that <u>we</u> (the world together) can create
the most beautiful poem –

but <u>you</u> will say, no doubt, that 'this is not poetry'.

Keith Armstrong[3]

The personal experience of writers, as well as the collective purpose of the Fed, fostered a general mistrust of outsiders. In 1980, the FWWCP minutes reported that a 'Macmillan rep is prowling around groups',[4] an apprehension that many people today would find hard to understand in their eagerness to be published. Nor was the opportunity for television coverage always welcomed. There was concern about a request to film a tour of Ireland, with members worried that it would compromise the writers: 'Feeling of the meeting was that film would change the nature of the tour. What we did would be determined by what the cameras wanted.'[5] Similarly, the offer of a slot on Reports Action ITV was unsettling: 'doubtful ... fearing that our intentions would be compromised by media presentation, by last-minute editing etc; sceptical about the value of this sort of commercial/charitable approach: would it bring the sort of people we want to interest?'[6] Activists were also not afraid to question authority. In 1975, Trevor Glover from Penguin wrote to the *Guardian* to complain about an article by Ken Worpole which he considered to be unduly harsh, especially given that the company had donated £400 to Centerprise for shelving, extended credit, contributed to fundraising campaigns and supported it on TV.[7]

The identity of the Fed was to be brought into sharp relief in its relations with the Arts Council of Great Britain, exposing a great deal about the changing nature of cultural policy. Initial reactions to Fed requests for funding for a national development worker were unsuccessful, with the acerbic and outspoken literature director, Charles Osborne, leading the way. The panel were unanimous in judging 'the whole corpus of little, if any, solid literary merit ... sympathetic as they are to the community value of the Federation'. It was asserted that the Fed 'was successful in a social, therapeutic sense, but not by literary standards'.[8] Some argued that there was 'little point' in national organisation as 'the whole strength of the work lay in its stimulation of <u>local</u> activities and interests, and in binding the people of a certain locality together'.[9] The panel member and novelist Margaret Forster opposed the application vigorously and asserted that the focus on working-class writers made the cause 'not literary but political'.[10] This snub from the Arts Council confirmed the fears of writers about the exclusive definition of literature. It was to prove useful, however, for marketing purposes: *The Republic of Letters* celebrated the rejection and carried the back cover blurb, 'GUARANTEED. No solid literary merit – The Arts Council of Great Britain'.[11]

This episode in fact signified much more than a minor skirmish in the attempts of disgruntled writers to gain funding. The decision came at a time when elitism and hierarchy were being confronted in many areas of life and the application for funding could not be easily disentangled from these bigger issues. Fractious personal encounters manifested a disorientation about how cultural institutions should respond to disputes over access and inequality. The Arts Council's assumptions on literature were thrown into confusion as it stood accused of marginalising subordinate groups.

The contention that Fed writing lacked 'literary merit' was met with incredulity and confirmed suspicions of elitism though the Fed was directed to reapply in six months with samples of writing in order that the Council could 'judge the value of the work being done'.[12] No definition of literary quality was forthcoming, and none would be, even though this had been held up as the reason for the negative response. The Fed wrote repeatedly to ask for clarification. Jane Mace, chair of the executive committee, kept the topic alive, while Worpole requested an I. A. Richards session on analysing Fed books.[13] Fed writers were convinced that judgements were a cover for the personal and class-based predilections of those involved with the Arts Council. By contrast, Osborne, recalling his time at the Council, lamented that 'every talentless lout who fancied himself a poet' had been 'howling' for his blood.[14] It was ironic that in 1973 Osborne had supported Centerprise publications, finding both Vivian Usherwood's *Poems* and the *Houses in Between* to be 'touching and impressively produced'.[15] By 1980, he was assiduously avoiding any definition of literary criteria while at the same time stoking the fires of discontent by driving a wedge between democracy and culture:

> It may seem to you unfair that some people are more talented than others and indeed it is unfair; however, it remains a fact that talent in the arts has not been handed out equally by some impeccable heavenly democrat ... It is important that we do all we can to increase audiences for today's writers, not that we increase the number of writers. There are already too many writers chasing too few readers. Although the real writer will always emerge without coaxing, it is not so easy to encourage new readers into existence.[16]

These confrontations made plain how the specific case of the Fed was being understood as a local example of a more expansive set of cultural forces. Greg Wilkinson protested against the interests of a leisured class who were out of touch with the life and language of the majority. He emphasised the need for new standards and drew attention to the interconnections between popular and elite culture, noting that jazz had informed classical music and 'primitive' works had influenced modern sculpture.[17] Osborne brushed him off in defending cultural standards.[18]

Officials were embroiled in Kafkaesque circular arguments. Literary merit had become an article of faith in the Council, not least for the secretary-general, Sir Roy Shaw: 'The Federation's reactions to the Council's decisions indicate an unwillingness to accept the Council's criteria of literary merit, but the Council can't accord the Federation immunity from artistic assessment.'[19] He modified the terms of the debate in avowing that the educational purpose of the Fed was beyond the remit of the Council: 'the need for someone to be engaged at a fee to stimulate people into writing was simply not recognised as valid'.[20] Behind the scenes Osborne also realised the advantages of administrative obfuscation rather than open debate: 'they are a noisy and belligerent bunch of people, so w'd [sic] do well to hide behind our bureaucratic pronouns!'[21] At another point Shaw and others became confused about the Council's decision-making process, which had left some panel members in the dark over why the Fed application had been rejected.[22] The Council approach betrayed a nervousness about how to counter the cries of injustice. The writer and broadcaster Melvyn Bragg, who chaired the Literature Panel from 1977 to 1980, found the Fed to be a 'powerful pressure group', which led him to reconsider the policy of aiding individual professional writers.[23] At one point Bragg mused whether the Fed might indeed nurture new readers, much to the chagrin of Shaw, who asked his people to form a united front and warned that 'they represent a source of lots of trouble'.[24]

The issue could not be contained and drew national attention, which added fuel to an already explosive situation. During the post-war years, a number of working-class writers and cultural workers had risen to prominence and a section of them objected to the Council's decision. A collective letter argued that the Fed was a new cultural force and was creating readers, partly by introducing new content into literature, for instance relating to racism or domestic life. The letter was signed by writers including Jim Allen, Sid Chaplin, Caryl Churchill, Barry Hines, Bob Leeson and Jack Lyndsey; the folk singers Ewan MacColl and Peggy Seeger; the poets Adrian Mitchell and Linton Kwesi Johnson; the historian A. L. Morton; and the MP Audrey Wise. Arthur Clegg, the veteran left organiser, journalist and poet, in rebutting the panel's decision, emphasised the dual purpose of the Fed:

> How does your Literature Panel know that the Federation will not produce another John Clare or unearth another Ragged Trousered Philanthropist? Besides, there is the question of promoting the enjoyment of and participation in literature.[25]

Others weighed in, with Eric Appleby from the National Federation of Voluntary Literacy Schemes stating that the Council was ignoring a 'mass of undeveloped creative potential'. Roy Jackson from the Education Department of the TUC was convinced that the 'latent talent' of working-class people was considerable.[26] Similarly, Reuben Falber of the Communist Party complained that the criterion 'literary merit' was too narrowly defined, an approach supported by the Morning Star.[27]

The Arts Council itself had invited in external opinion but, once again, judgement was not favourable. Jim McGuigan, a sociologist, whose report on the Literature Department's work was censored, concluded that the Council was complicit in reproducing a literary hierarchy based on a narrow social foundation and that the notion of 'serious writing' was being used as a 'kind of shorthand legitimation for the tastes of individuals appointed to the Arts Council'.[28] The Fed represented a challenge to the whole idea of 'serious writing', and McGuigan reproached the Council for its 'socially blinkered' response to the attempt to facilitate a wide-ranging entry into literary production.[29] As a result, the Society of Authors called for the resignation of Osborne, who later dismissed sociologists as 'witch doctors' and countered that McGuigan had himself imposed a 'blinkered' view on the facts.[30]

Behind these tense exchanges lay fluctuations in the recent history of social class. Sir Roy Shaw himself had a background in adult education, having worked under Sidney Raybould at Leeds University where debates on workers education and standards in adult education had flared up in the 1950s.[31] Shaw and others symbolised a strand of adult education from which the Fed had diverged. Attempts to woo Shaw by appealing to the connections between adult education and working-class literature were unsuccessful.[32] Shaw was clearly not ignorant of social class but maintained that social mobility had wrought positive changes:

> Writers already come from all social backgrounds: it is simply no longer true to say that there is any section of the population in which talent is stifled because of lack of opportunity.[33]

Similarly, Osborne was critical of the Fed for its 'arrogant assumption that there is a working class which cannot appreciate the best in literature, music, theatre or painting and has to be fobbed off with something less good but somehow more "relevant"'.[34]

In fact, the Fed misconstrued its detractors as a traditional cultural elite. Critics of the Fed exhibited the thinking of a generation of 'scholarship boys', and girls, who were proud of their achievements. Shaw could be placed alongside Bragg, Richard Hoggart, vice-chair of the Council, Forster and even Osborne, the key figures in this fracas, who all came from working-class backgrounds of one sort or another.[35] They were devoted to the arts, were proud of their achievements and were more likely to see mainstream institutions in meritocratic rather than pernicious terms. To them, culture implied education and work and they supported elitism based upon merit. In part, they had emerged from a tradition of culture and education brought vividly to life by Jonathan Rose's *Intellectual Life of the British Working Classes*. They did not try to hide their class heritage; on the contrary, they wore it as a mark of pride. This could be uncomfortable at times; for example, an official at the Council had referred tartly to Shaw as the 'provincial educationalist'.[36] Hoggart was himself repeatedly negotiating his own class position in public; as assistant director-general of UNESCO in the early 1970s, he had suffered class put-downs from stuffy British civil servants – one reason why he 'banged on' about class.[37] This class fraction was keen to mark out and defend its dominance of the working-class cultural space. The Fed was seen as a cultural trespasser that might destroy their hard-won position and undermine the hierarchy from which these capable individuals had benefited. The Fed may also have brought this group uncomfortably close to personal lives that, in different circumstances, might have been their own – a world they had escaped.[38]

Further institutional strategies diverted the Fed when its application was passed to the newly established Community Arts Panel, with Osborne declaring that the Fed 'was of more value in the community level than on a literary level'.[39] *The Republic of Letters* would make the case that the Fed refused to apply for funding from the Community Arts Panel on principled grounds, not wanting to be marginalised as something other than literature. In reality there were mixed feelings about applying to this body: it was an important strategic argument to make, but writers did make contact and funding may well have been accepted from Community Arts had it been offered.[40] Internally, dealings between the Literature and Community Arts panels, the latter led by John Buston, had been uneasy. In fact, Shaw was troubled by the rise of community arts and commissioned a number of reports into community-based developments in various art forms. For example, Sandy Nairne, later director of the National Portrait Gallery, looked at art, and Blake Morrison, then working at the *Times Literary Supplement*, was to research literature. Morrison soon gained the impression that Shaw was hoping for a negative outcome, but their reports were to be more nuanced.[41] Indeed, Morrison provided grounds for support for the Fed as one of the few growth areas of contemporary literature:

> As yet the bulk of the work it publishes is of indifferent standard; but a significant proportion is not, and the prospect of better work to come seems a real one. I would strongly recommend the Literature Panel to consider with greater thought and care any subsequent application made to it by the Federation.[42]

Although Shaw remained opposed, further campaigning succeeded in securing limited funding for a worker with the condition that Arts Council representatives would sit on the recruiting panel and that the person appointed should have knowledge of 'literary traditions of the past'.[43] By this time, Forster, a strong critic of the Fed who had 'fiercely' opposed the application, had left the Council and had been replaced by more agreeable voices, including the writer

Marghanita Laski, who 'pressed' the decision upon the 'reluctant panel' that she now chaired.[44] Despite the Council's about-turn, opposition still had not dissipated by 1982 when Shaw reaffirmed that 'there hasn't been a change of heart in the Director'. Rather, it was the influx of new members onto the panel that explained the U-turn.[45]

Once a grant had been agreed, other members of the panel started to warm to the worker writers. A few publications were seen as 'appalling', but much work, including that of Centerprise and *Voices*, met with support. It was argued that the Fed had previously misrepresented itself in appearing 'aggressively political'.[46] The idea prevalent in the Fed, that everyday life was political, had been incomprehensible. However, workshops were not in a conciliatory mood. The executive committee required 'precise information' about the role of the Council in appointing and monitoring the new person before coming to a decision about whether to take on the grant.[47] It denied the need for national advertising, the submission of CVs, for applicants to have qualifications or for them to be 'well-grounded historically in the literature of the past, English and foreign'.[48] Instead, electing staff from among those who had already shown 'commitment and ability' was favoured.[49]

With a partial truce, the oscillation between warmer and frostier relations would persist in the coming years.[50] Trust was built when Laski and the person appointed to the position, Olive Rogers, ended up getting on well, corresponding with one another and exchanging notes on their reading. Rogers wrote about her insecurities in making the transition to a paid position and provided details of courses she ran using work by Dylan Thomas, Keats, Shelley and Shakespeare as well as women's writing.[51] In fact, Rogers's reports would help to win over other members of the panel as well.[52]

Worpole furnished further evidence about the value of the Fed. Writing in *City Life*, he critiqued community arts and the way in which the GLC and the Arts Council had both established community arts panels in order to preserve traditional cultural divisions. He argued that working-class history suggested 'a strong desire to incorporate the experiences of the great bourgeois traditions as well as developing its own forms'. By contrast, community artists claimed that 'all previous traditions are redundant, that our cultural future lies in firework displays, street theatre and dressing up once a year. It's unbearable.'[53] Laski shared this piece with Council colleagues and identified a 'considerable shift towards ... workable-withness'.[54] Other coverage followed in the *Daily Telegraph* with a well-disposed article on Rogers.[55] Small victories such as these created room for manoeuvre and the Fed came to be seen in a more sympathetic light. It was reported in 1982 that the Council now had a 'modus vivendi with the FWWCP, but it is a fragile one'.

Contact continued to be somewhat edgy and the earlier history could not be simply wiped from the slate. McGuigan, in the *New Statesman*, cautioned that the 'resilience of elitism was exemplified by its ability to make small concessions'.⁵⁶ Indeed, distrust could easily be re-ignited on both sides of the divide. When observing the appointment of a southern development worker, Council staff were directly confronted with the sectarianism of the Fed and rapidly resorted to class dismissals. This provided an example of the way in which purportedly neutral institutional processes shrouded the arbitrary judgements of officials. In later years, the concept of institutional racism would help us to understand the potentially malignant effects of supposedly impartial practices. One official argued defensively that if 'the quality of work' did not improve, 'we do not renew the grant after the first year',⁵⁷ in the expectation that funding must have an immediate effect on the quality of writing in the outskirts of Liverpool or the East End of London, rather like the effect of switching on a light bulb. Council representatives were taken aback by the committed positions of activists and found it hard to suppress their disdain, complaining about 'a large black lady ... whose name I forgot', 'a nondescript personality', one who was 'dull' and another of whom it was noted, 'I couldn't see her organising a children's tea party competently'.⁵⁸ The steadfastness of activists was impenetrable and was interpreted in terms of 'militant inwardness' and a 'prejudice' against outsiders. The main criterion was perceived to be how much applicants knew about the Fed – 'they were boring to a degree in their working class bias and commitment'. The charges of 'exclusivity' were countered by Fed activists, who insisted on the need to retain an identity, and there was little understanding across the rift. ⁵⁹ But these comments were not broadcast beyond the Council. Sporadic and limited Council funding was given reluctantly from 1980 but it did not signal a total endorsement of working-class writing.

Interactions with the Arts Council and other institutions had been a defining feature of the early movement, yet the overall circumstances were in flux. In 1984, the Council's *Glory of the Garden* would announce baldly that literature did not need to be supported or developed because the commercial publishing houses already fulfilled this role. As a result, funding for all literature was cut, confirming the gut feeling of sceptics about the elitist credentials of the institution. As an active movement sustained by volunteers, the Fed weathered this storm. Its sectarianism was not only idiosyncratic but also released the energy and enthusiasm necessary to a voluntary movement.

The corporatism and fixed institutional settings of the post-war world were being shaken by the winds of Thatcherism and its injection of commercialism into the social fabric. It was not only the trade unions that were under scrutiny; many public bodies were subjected to it as well. From the inside it regularly looked like the world could fall apart; 'we've got to keep our limits or else we lose all sense of coherence', Bragg is reported as saying at a meeting.⁶⁰ It was this coherence that was being eroded from different angles. The denial of public funding for literature was a part of these changes but it was not to prove a permanent arrangement. While market ideologies were becoming more influential, their dominance was never complete and public subsidies for literature would in time be restored.

Changes in the mainstream

During the 1990s, the Fed was to be propelled into a new relation with key institutions as attitudes softened. This was partly because the radical movements that had been part of the Fed's milieu dwindled, but also because there had been a shift within the mainstream. Though the Arts Council did not take on board the political aims of the Fed, it was to become more accommodating to community-based writing and publishing, leading in turn to some funding for workshops but making it harder for worker writers to guard their distinctive agenda and values.

The Arts Council Literature Department was to undergo considerable change, in part with the arrival of Alistair Niven in 1987.[61] In dealing with competing pressures of quality and access, he was more apt to speak of a 'spectrum' of writing as opposed to a hierarchy and was himself interested in writers from the Commonwealth, having previously managed the Africa Centre in London. He conceived of community writing as watering the roots in order that 'good' writers might grow from a vigorous culture of writing. Niven was critical of the claim that literature could be viewed solely in commercial terms. He noted that, at one level, everyone is an author who manipulates words and he aimed to

> Recognise the amount of community publishing which flourishes ... and strengthen the support system ... for writers who do not necessarily seek publication and acclaim for their work.[62]

A Raymond Williams Prize for Community Publishing was instituted, out of an acknowledgement that community publishing is 'the bedrock upon which all other literature grows'.[63] The initiative was an attempt to develop a national audience.[64] Survivors' poetry and prison writing projects were also funded under this new regime. The Fed itself received revenue funding in 1992 that enabled it to appoint a worker four days a week. Niven's approach was to be continued by his successors, and funding for the Fed, albeit at a low level, gradually increased despite a restructuring of the arts funding system.

The new spirit was signalled by Violet M. Hughes in a report commissioned by the Arts Council titled *Literature Belongs to Everyone*. Hughes interviewed trade unionists, educationalists, arts agency staff and writers, eliciting their views on barriers and access to literature and writing. In tune with the times, she welcomed groups such as the Fed that supported people in creating their own culture, but stressed the need to shed an overly inward-looking approach and warned of the risk of being 'enclosed within their own ethos' with few external links:

> It would be ironic if such radical ventures in the very business of attacking barriers were to be in any way, perpetuating the divisions between 'elite' or 'highbrow' culture and the 'popular', between 'creating your own heritage' and possessing the huge heritage that should be commonly owned.[65]

This criticism was valid, although it underplayed the extent of closure on the part of key institutions. The reviewer in the *Fed News* welcomed the report for its openness and, most crucially, for its willingness to countenance that class was a factor in the organisation of literature:

> This report is in fact a small milestone in our struggle with the hegemony of the state. Until now any demand to start to discuss class and culture has generally met with a brick wall of silence and fear.[66]

These changes were debated extensively in the Fed. Some averred that they were a matter of chance, depending on the appointment of certain individuals, rather than a transformation in Council policy. The subtleties of the Fed's approach might easily be swept away as 'mere relativism' if the tide were to change back in favour of traditional hierarchies in the arts.[67]

Moreover, the maintenance of a well-defined identity would be compromised by the cumulative effect of minor accountability measures. The Fed learnt to present its work in terms of 'service delivery' and 'business planning', which could erode the sense of it being a social movement.[68] In 1995, the Arts Council chose to carry out an appraisal of the Fed, an unusual move for a group with such low levels of funding. The assessors described the democratic aspirations of their client, in which workshops were organised for mutual benefit, as archaic:

> the organisation has a particularly hermetic dimension; member groups decide what services they need and these are often provided by other member groups.[69]

In addition, the Fed was becoming a company limited by guarantee, a common legal form for charitable and voluntary associations. The appraisers welcomed this development because it separated the Fed from its constituent groups:

> The largest proportion of income now comes from ... funding bodies which means that the Federation is essentially a service provider to its member groups undertaking tasks agreed in advance with the funder. The move towards company status will take this one step further since the board will be duty bound as directors primarily to safeguard the operations of the organisation as opposed to the membership as is the case now ... The team believes that this may change the nature of the Federation ... this is a good thing ... this process of change may not be easy for the organisation and [the team] urges them to manage the process carefully.[70]

The Arts Council actively nurtured a sharper division of labour between writers and professional administrators. For instance, when the Council agreed to provide funding to develop an 'educational policy', the Fed's proposal that the research be done by trained members of groups, who, it argued, had the sensitivity to carry out this work, met with a negative response; instead the money had to be spent on one consultant to provide an 'independent' and external point of view.[71] The Fed had always been about learning and it supported extending access to arts funding. But the movement would be hoisted on its own petard when subsequent education policies forced a further element of professionalisation as new hierarchies were formed around access.

Differences of opinion operated at a detailed level below the radar. Compromise and negotiation were the order of the day. Disagreements tended to be over matters such as the meaning of the 'mutual and co-operative' eligibility criteria for the Raymond Williams Prize and whether this competition should include local authorities and colleges with multimillion-pound budgets or small commercial presses – an oral history published by Greenwich Community College had won the prize in 1996. The Arts Council was also quite prepared to utilise its funding of the Fed for ulterior objectives: in the late 1990s, Lord Gowrie, then heading the Council, mentioned the Fed's grant of around £20,000 when justifying the multimillion-pound lottery grant to the Opera House – a sum that totalled more than the combined budgets of the Literature Department during the whole of its existence.

Acceptance?

These developments were indicative of cultural changes across society that were more receptive to community-based writing and publishing. Increasing approval came in part with the reconceptualisation of culture in terms of employment in a 'cultural industry'.[72] In the 1990s, cities adapted the traditional literature festival as a celebration of reading and writing - Off the Shelf in Sheffield, Writing on the Wall in Liverpool, the Reading and Writing Festival in Birmingham and the Manchester Poetry Festival. Although they brought in big names, local writers and community-based events were also encouraged. This stimulated work among local theatres and libraries which had long been enthusiastic about local history.

The once clear division between alternative and commercial publishers became blurred by changes in the publishing policies of commercial publishers and new presses more able to cater to the 'quality' end of community publishing. For instance, novels by Pete Kalu, a Commonword/Cultureword worker, were taken up by X Press.[73] Fed writers were to be published by the Women's Press and Sheba, while Virago adopted Joyce Storey's autobiographies which had been first published by Bristol Broadsides.[74] Centerprise initiated a competition in which the winner would be considered for publication by Jonathan Cape.[75] A Centerprise worker, Kadija Sesay, went on to co-edit a Penguin collection of new black writing in Britain.[76]

The growing popularity of performance poetry also connected the Fed to wider developments where it had a substantial impact. Performance was perhaps the most important aspect of the Fed and many members, including Gladys McGee and Patience Agbabi, became accomplished performers. Janice Fullman, active in Tottenham Writers workshop and previously a chair of the Fed, helped to set up the performance poetry agency Apples and Snakes in 1982. This group, which joined the Fed in the mid-1990s, actively promoted performance and worked with semi-established poets. Liz Thompson organised a women's performance night in London, popular for a number of years in the 1990s.[77] Thus the expansion of popular writing meant that some of the people active within Fed groups now had a range of choices about where they could write or perform.

Indicative of the diminishing distinctiveness of the Fed, building partnerships came to be seen as necessary given the need to gain funding and have a visible impact. The Fed itself promoted 'literature development' within a network that included the National Association for Literature Development (NALD), the National Association of Writers in Education (NAWE), Writernet (developing writing opportunities through the internet), and Lapidus (using the literary arts in personal development) which attracted funding to train and support literature development workers. The Fed brought its voice to bear in this partnership and effectively argued for the inclusion of all writers in the scheme, not just professionals who made their living from writing, residencies and workshops.

The participatory ethos of the Fed would also be curtailed in a changing educational context. For instance, the fluctuating priorities of funding agencies posed both dangers and opportunities for adult literacy groups. Resources and formal recognition for adult literacy programmes came with the arrival of the Skills for Life policy.[78] Some activists from the 1970s literacy campaigns were promoted to positions of power and did link up with younger professionals who became interested in publishing student writing.[79] Despite these alliances, however, the concentration on economic and deficit models of literacy created difficulties for unorthodox and 'emancipatory' projects such as Pecket Well College and Gatehouse. In addition, many adult and further education centres developed creative writing courses that to some extent competed with workshops. The Poetry Society and Arvon Foundation ran schemes for poets in schools and writing courses from which the Fed benefited. The Poetry Society had itself been pushed in this direction after a critical report from the Arts Council and a cut in funding.

In higher education, there was some acceptance of the Fed; for example, the Open University adopted Evelyn Haythorne's *On Earth to Make the Numbers Up* as a text for one of its courses.[80] Universities and their English departments had previously been considered suspect for separating the writing of literature from the critical appreciation of it.[81] While this trend continued, creative writing mushroomed, with Malcolm Bradbury's course at the University of East Anglia frequently cloned. For a time, widening participation in higher education enabled people with fewer qualifications to progress to university, usually after studying for one year. Some of these may have fulfilled a need that was at one time met by the writing group. Ultimately, access courses with a liberal or radical agenda would be squeezed and the expansion of higher education would have mixed results for working-class people. In addition, academics within higher education were less able to support workshops as they had to meet rising obligations within their institutions, concerned with 'bums on seats', running accredited courses and publishing work in academic journals for the Research Assessment Exercise (RAE) which affected university funding.[82] Tricia Jenkins, a university worker involved with the Merseyside Association of Writers' Workshops, had developed a popular course on training writing workshop leaders, but this support became less possible over time.[83]

A weakening movement and a growing network

Incremental alterations in the Fed were closely associated with ongoing institutional changes. While the movement gave the impression of being localised and dispersed, it drew much of its strength from interactions within a national forum. The festival remained central in the annual calendar but its relative importance was downgraded in comparison with new activities, running training courses and regional events. For most people involved in the early phase of the Fed, bringing writers together, primarily at the AGM, was the essence of the movement and costs were kept to a minimum.[84] In the early 1980s, the Fed was fortunate to receive £1,500 from *Breaking Through*, the Channel Four programme about writing groups in East London in which writers retained editorial control, and this would be used to fund places at the AGM.[85] When that source dried up, a minimum charge of £5 was 'reluctantly' introduced.[86] In the 1990s, the AGM was renamed a 'Festival of Writing' in order to help broaden its appeal. Yet even comparatively cheap semi-commercial rates proved to be beyond the means of many. Subsidies were only available in some areas and were subject to the vagaries of regional arts boards which were not keen to fund small-scale ventures. The Fed was reluctant to subsidise members out of 'core costs' although the annual meeting, workshops and readings endured into the twenty-first century. In 2017, the Fed was continuing to arrange an annual event and local groups were gaining strength from being part of a movement.

The definition of membership within the Fed was relaxed. In the 1990s, the early restrictions on membership slowly evaporated as less appropriate to changing conditions. The practice of compulsory attendance at the AGM was to lapse without a debate as the Fed metamorphosed into a looser, more inclusive network. Potential members were more actively solicited and the way in which these groups were visited and vetted became more haphazard in comparison with earlier prescriptions. For instance, Yorkshire Arts Circus was admitted to membership in the 1990s, whereas previously the Fed had disagreed with what it saw as its overly directive publishing and editorial practices. New types of non-voting membership were introduced to help expand the movement.

'Reciprocal membership', based on sharing information, brought in groups such as Soundsense, a professionally run community music venture. More groups were able to 'try it out' for a year, before applying formally to join, through a system known as 'first chapter' membership.

Separating the work of Fed groups from community arts became problematic as divisions blurred. Rhonda Community Arts, which organised writing groups, was approved for membership in the 1990s. Similarly, Fed members Forest Artworks in the Forest of Dean and Corridor Press in Reading both described themselves as community arts groups, and individual community artists received a sensitive hearing in the Fed.[87] In the mid-1990s, the Fed became a member of the Voluntary Arts Network (VAN), which made good use of the Fed to establish kudos with other, more radical groups likely to question the idea of the boundary between voluntary and professional arts. This stirred memories of the Fed's long battle in the 1970s and 1980s against the Arts Council's statement that they were 'amateur' writers and therefore unworthy of support.[88]

Passing on a collective history to new members was a common problem for radical groups. In the 1990s the Fed produced explanatory leaflets for newer recruits, who were unfamiliar with the Fed's history and the values it embodied in its early years. Nonetheless, the movement was supported by a core of people who had been active for ten to twenty years and were immersed in its practices and values. At the AGM, despite the claim that 'people were there as themselves rather than with a group or representing a group',[89] there were a sizeable number of activists whose commitment kept alive a basic common purpose. Again, this was visible in 2017.

Of course, the active membership of the Fed did change gradually. Fewer young people joined and the movement's age profile rose. Those young writers involved from the start of the Fed grew up into middle age. As a result, the relative importance of different types of groups varied at different points. For example, in the 1990s, literacy groups within the Fed, particularly Pecket Well College (see figure 12) and Gatehouse, filled a larger space as some of the working-class writing groups, which held sway over the spiritual centre of the movement for many years, either folded or left. Ironically, given the earlier criticisms of tutors as 'middle-class managers', literacy groups ensured a continuing presence within the Fed of working-class people who had not been successful in formal education. As a result, groups with an educational slant once again became more acceptable. Shorelink in Hastings, initially supported to establish a literacy class by the Centre for Continuing Education at Sussex University, recruited members for a Fed writers' group.[90] In turn, as the funded literacy groups struggled in the early 2000s, so writers' workshops again became more prominent. Following the financial collapse of the Fed, it also opened itself up to individual members.

Some of the most noteworthy groups to join the Fed in the 1990s and 2000s were connected to the flourishing Survivors' Poetry Network, just as the Care in the Community policies were having their full effect. Survivors' Poetry

12 Joe Flanagan from Pecket Well College featured on the cover of *Fed News*, 1991.

attempted to re-categorise writers who had been in distress at some point in their lives as 'survivors'. For instance, the book *Beyond Bedlam*, published by Anvil and edited by Ken Smith and Matthew Sweeney, included selections of poetry chosen from 5,000 entries alongside contributions from other 'survivors' – T. S. Eliot,

William Blake, Sylvia Plath and Jean 'Binta' Breeze.[91] One older member returning to visit the Fed was struck by the development of survivors' poetry, seeing it as concentrating on individual pain and healing at the expense of social issues; the spectre of writing as therapy was thus to return to the Fed. This was countered by those who viewed such writing as inherently political given the marginalisation of those facing mental distress. Indeed, within the Fed, Survivors' Poetry groups were welcomed as 'the right sort' of group to join.

Ethnic Communities Oral History Project (ECOHP) had emerged in the late 1980s, in part reflecting the growing forces of migration and globalisation. Councillor Ahmed Aftab, influenced by the television series *Roots*, became aware of the need to chart the lives of migrant communities in Hammersmith and Fulham and succeeded in gaining local government support for the project. The group aimed to both celebrate specific communities and educate the public through a series of books produced and written by ethnic minority groups, a term interpreted widely to include 'Asian', Irish, Polish, Greek, African-Caribbean and others. For over ten years this innovative group survived on a shoestring with the active support of a 'paid' worker, in reality more of a volunteer.[92]

With the surge in homelessness, writing groups formed among homeless people; the Big Issue Writing Group became members of the Fed for some time and other writers also addressed the issue of homelessness. In the changed circumstances of the late 1980s and 1990s, Towpath Press in Lancashire published local people's writing but tended to avoid 'religion or politics'. Conversely, politically motivated groups emerged, notably Working Press, set up by Stefan Szczulkun as a national group to support self-publishing by working-class artists.[93]

Recruiting and visiting international members was prioritised, including groups and networks from Ireland, South Africa, the United States, Canada, Mauritius, France and Germany. In a globalising world, communication and travel became easier and international radical networks came together under the banner of global civil society, notably via the World Social Forum. In the 1990s, Northside Writers from Cork became full members of the Fed, bringing a sense of purpose and large numbers each year to the annual festival. Other international members were more distant 'associate members', although there were Fed visits to the USA, Canada, France and Germany. The Fed met an echo of its past self in the activism of poverty action groups such as the Kensington Welfare Rights Union based in Philadelphia. Interest in working-class studies had been developing in the United States since the 1990s, and like star-gazers who see the light from a previous time, perhaps viewed the Fed as more focused on class activism than it actually was.[94] Nevertheless, support across national borders provided external validation and, in some cases, material support.[95] Prior to Nelson Mandela's release from prison, contacts existed with South Africa where cultural issues were debated, for example in the collection published by Buchu Books, *Spring Is Rebellious: Arguments about Cultural Freedom*.[96] The group Ledikasyon

Pu Travayer, from Mauritius, sent a Mauritian kreole dictionary, translations of Shakespeare texts, poetry and tracts on cultural issues.[97]

Supporting actual writers and writing remained central to the movement and was nourished by a spirit of openness and tolerance as well as friendships between writers. Free workshops enabled writers to share skills and ideas. The cost of paying writers would have been prohibitive, a fortunate consequence in terms of participation.[98] Despite a more restrictive political and economic climate, a way of working within and against institutional conceptions of culture was maintained. While other comparable movements folded, the survival of the Fed has been significant. It successfully negotiated a transition from an alternative and oppositional sect focused on working-class writers, through the Thatcher years, to engage productively with mainstream artists. What is most surprising of all is that the Fed survived the loss of funding in 2007. As one writer expressed it, the Fed had been knocked down and dazed but had got back onto its feet and was recovering.

Conclusion

Working-class writing and publishing workshops are an underexplored phenomenon that has featured very little in contemporary debates on culture. They have offered spaces for people on the margins of society to articulate their feelings, beliefs and experiences. The contours of the movement have been determined not only by power, resources and institutions but by a shared commitment to democratic culture, an inheritance that remains a resource for the future. The advent, development, successes and defeats of these workshops represent an important phase in the history of working-class creativity.[1] As democratic spaces, they were innovative in diffusing practices of reading and writing, and they have had a major impact in the way poetry has become a means of popular communication, now incorporated into digital technologies and even commercial advertising.[2] By introducing original subject matter and blending experience, analysis, reflection and critique, writers transgressed the boundaries between literature and history and also facilitated greater participation in historical practices.[3]

The Fed built solidarity at the intersection of multiple generations that were claiming a voice. It emerged from a counter-cultural impulse that addressed new needs and broke with existing frameworks. From the late 1960s, social movements and radical groups were becoming interested in working-class life and they began to engage with communities in a sustained way. Alliances formed across generations. Activists looked to the past in order to comprehend the future, and they found older people disoriented after decades of relative prosperity. Unprecedented material wealth had bypassed some and disregarded the strengths of an older way of life. Writers melded memories of material shortage with a set of human responses that retained notions of caring and community. Later in the twentieth century, the universal promises of the welfare state and allied policies of full employment would be undercut by poverty, divisiveness and international conflict. Nowhere was this clearer than in schools, where the hope of 'secondary education for all' had resulted in the marginalisation of the majority of the population, as 'failures', an emotional scar that would cut deep. It was a trend that, in future years, would swell the numbers of adult literacy students, who used their experience as part of a learning process. In addition, the young people whose actions and writing sparked the movement drew inspiration from their own lives at a time of political and cultural change but also became involved in a range of causes, including community development and punk rock. For them, the experience of comprehensive education continued to highlight the felt tensions between a promised future for all and the rationed opportunities they faced in daily life. Other young writers migrated from the across the globe and brought with them different ideas and assumptions, some of which bore a striking resemblance to the preoccupations of the autobiographers who were investigating a much earlier period of history. These young writers met older people in their families, in the streets and in writing groups, where an active dialogue was initiated that stimulated fresh modes of representing experience. It was the listening, communication and connections between age groups that had such an electrifying effect across Britain.

The socially mobile working class had already been recognised as a force for change in the post-war years, but radical groups extended this to the entire class. It pointed to a significant intra-class division that had been less noticeable prior to 1939 when fewer educational and social opportunities were available. After the war, the educated and aspirant, although relatively small in number, were the dominant presence in terms of representing the working class. However, from the 1970s, pioneering ways of writing about working-class life materialised from writing and publishing workshops, which were more inclusive.

Expressive impulses mingled with the urge to document the truth. A variety of tactics were deployed to capture contradictory social experiences. The personal nature of writing ensured writers stayed close to actual lives and focused on the ambiguities of experience rather than the political and social issues that inevitably intruded. Everyday life was explored in many facets – in families, neighbourhoods, communities and workplaces across the twentieth century. Moreover, the autobiographical urge so apparent in the Fed encompassed different motivations. The need to put the record straight, to detail one's own life trajectory, was a form of testimony about the past that enabled a re-examination of the present. Aspects of life were also interrogated as writers shifted between the documentary, literary and poetic in order to seize hold of their history and experience on the page. Some of the best writing built upon the specificity of vernacular language.

Cultural growth depended upon breaking down old barriers while navigating new ones. Although it often appeared that writing could be free-flowing, spontaneity was tempered by external and internal restraints. Young people and adult literacy students in particular worked within educational settings where their writing drew attention to the contested nature of subjectivity. Meanings were channelled and constrained by personal desire, technical ability and the influence of authority figures, teachers and parents. Adult literacy students negotiated the experience of poverty and poor schooling in a wealthy, well-educated society. As part of a movement for cultural recognition this could be powerful as students identified themselves as writers, thinkers and performers. They searched for stories that would accurately convey complex emotions to an audience, while incorporating humour and humanity. Yet providing opportunities for writers to represent their lives and assert their humanity was not straightforward and could unexpectedly be used to confirm negative messages. Writing from a certain identity could also become limiting artistically. The collective impulse to represent a shared experience through personal writing was valued, but it was discovered that fixed expectations could curb expression. In response, writers redrafted their personal experience and delved into heterogeneous readings and influences. It was not a once-and-for-all development, and writing from an identity was often integrated with individual expression.

Expanding cultural horizons involved judging and evaluating work, but this took place within a particular environment.[4] 'Classic' texts would be consumed as writers improved their technique and enriched their knowledge. The Fed actively grappled with the notions of high and low, quality and popular, and aimed to replace simplistic polarities with more complex approaches. Writing and publishing groups would actively debate and develop their own ideas on the criteria for 'good' writing. One commonplace view was that the selective tradition of 'the canon', or indeed any canon, should be dismantled in the name of democracy and equality.[5] They argued that there should be no restrictions on the right to beauty, expression and self-development. The idea that 'anyone can be a writer' and 'everyone has a history' appealed to Fed groups as a way to recruit more members and project an image of their workshops as places where all writers were respected. It was a tension that made space for newcomers but allowed for the extension of critical thinking.

Workshops were integrally linked to individuals' development. A culture of mutuality and equality, irrespective of talent or ability, formed the basis for deep learning and searching discussions.[6] The workshop was a launch pad for some writers but not at the expense of the rest. In time, worker writers would influence the mainstream, contributing their own voices and experiences. The purpose of the Fed was never simply to develop such writers; rather, they were an outcome of democratic practices and involvement in workshops. Paradoxically, during the period when the Fed was at its most oppositional to the mainstream, it nurtured a significant number of successful writers. The list includes not only playwrights Jimmy McGovern, Bridget O'Connor and Tony Marchant, but also the novelists Rebecca O'Rourke, Anne Cassidy and Roger Mills. Bafta-winning Alan Gilbey now writes for animation, Henry Normal received acclaim as a TV writer and poet and Roberto Bangura went into film and TV work. Sandra Agard, Patience Agbabi, Pete Kalu and Levi Tafari all achieved success as writers and poets.[7] The punk poet John Cooper Clarke had been published in *Voices*. Some writers from Scotland Road went into acting:

Bernadette Foley had a part in *Brookside*, Eddie Barrett was involved with the theatre and Chris Darwin would go on to play 'Snowy' in Alan Bleasdale's TV drama *Boys from the Blackstuff*. That someone like Lemn Sissay could be elected chancellor of Manchester University in 2015, be invited to British embassies and read a poem on BBC 2's *Newsnight* on National Poetry Day would have been unthinkable in previous decades.[8] In 2015, Edexel adopted Mary Casey's poem 'The Class Game' onto its GCSE syllabus. Furthermore, the movement stimulated originality in other areas; for example, David Hevey produced groundbreaking work on representation and disability.[9] The Fed and its groups acted as a seedbed for these writers, though outwardly the movement was suspicious of career building. Thus, Richard Hoggart's association of the Fed with relativism was an oversimplification, although his position did soften in later years.[10]

Even those who were not intent on becoming 'famous writers' learnt much and developed ideas about value and quality. The Fed supported significant numbers of cultural and educational workers who would contribute to arts agencies and educational institutions, from primary schools to universities and adult education. Few other organisations could lay claim to such active and self-organising member groups. Indeed, there are elements of familiarity in the movement's grass-roots and accessible community focus to which many contemporary educational programmes have aspired. Some people from the Fed went on to enrich these very schemes. Workshop practices have been discredited as both utopian and antiquated, yet within the work of the Fed it is possible to glimpse ideas that the mainstream would later adopt as pragmatic, associated with lifelong learning, community-based education, family learning, widening participation and other initiatives. The Fed contributed to the establishment of playwriting courses in universities and literature development agencies, and brought writers into schools and adult education.

Working-class people were given significant control over the direction of their work and learning. In the 1970s, the autonomy of teachers and educational institutions allowed for experimentation and personal expression. The contrast with the contemporary situation is stark: teachers, tutors and facilitators are highly regulated and need to meet specified outcomes and accountabilities. Indeed, just at the point when varied forms of learning were receiving an official stamp of approval, not least from UNESCO,[11] they were either being starved of funding or confined within league tables, regulatory frameworks, instrumentalist testing and high costs that made sense according to 'market' thinking but stifled freedom and imagination. It creates a contradiction ripe with potential to build associations in which self-directed learning and personal expression play a central role. It is an awkward problem because contemporary learning regimes, by focusing on standards, have effectively re-articulated the radical idea that everyone can be educated to a high standard.[12] In addressing this challenge there is a need to recognise both standards and diverse interests and needs while avoiding exclusive hierarchies.

At a time of deepening inequality, elites have been reformed in a very visible way. Cultural and educational institutions are still nurturing 'stars' that speak and write to a passive audience and, in 2017, a much more unequal audience, many of whom find themselves once again cut off from mainstream cultural life. In the early twenty-first century, the middle-class 'cultural omnivore' has attracted attention, stepping into areas once closely associated with the working class, not least popular music and football.[13] In spite of the proliferation of manipulative TV shows such as *Britain's Got Talent*, the majority of people remain positioned as outsiders, consumers rather than producers. In addition, the dramatic disappearance of working-class writers, actors and cultural workers from public positions makes the search for alternatives pressing.[14]

From the 1990s, a culture of acceptance harboured new curbs on working-class expression. The pendulum swung towards a notion of culture as a restrictive circle — repeated waves of cultural activism had only led to limited long-term changes.[15] For policy makers eager to break down elitism, the problem of cultural democracy could become one in which 'good' culture was disseminated to wider audiences. For instance, Chris Smith, as secretary of state for culture, media and sport in the late 1990s, adopted this distributive model in his book *Creative Britain*.[16] Although the idea of 'creativity' was being diffused as a universal good, much like 'community' or 'education', the idea that marginal spaces could be a source of cultural advance went unheeded. While there were jobs in cultural industries, proper culture was often to be funnelled in from the outside for consumption by passive audiences. It was one way of marrying quality and access but allowed for the return of a narrow version of 'the arts' that would be justified as funding became tighter.[17]

In the Fed, the interest in culture had been partly born out of the ending of one version of class politics related to political attacks on working-class institutions. As class language was being erased from public discourse, the Fed offered a protective cocoon, sustenance against the brutal destruction of the Thatcher years. The psychic aspects of this social transformation were considerable as people attempted to sustain classed identities. The Fed played a considerable role in nourishing those at the margins. It was a haven for people committed to a class perspective. Organisational support and social frameworks all transformed a vague sense of injustice, marginalisation, self-hatred and experience of poverty into a deeper class identity of which one could be proud. It may be true that working-class expression, indeed working-class culture, requires an organisational structure in a society where so many forces either stigmatise it or are unwilling to tolerate it.[18] It was an achievement of the trade unions, co-operative movement and other working-class institutions which allowed commentators to speak and write of working-class culture with such confidence. As these movements stalled or were undermined, and had to re-invent themselves, so the public airing of class wavered. Changes in identity were thus closely associated with the Fed as a collective force.

Writing workshops stretched the meanings of class in a number of directions as nuanced understandings became necessary.[19] In the Fed, class was used to assert personal identities and collective solidarities, to validate the marginalised, to retain an oppositional stance to mainstream institutions and to hold up the potential for future social transformation. Furthermore, from the 1970s, the ubiquity of class was augmented with the recognition of a diversity of experiences as well as the influx of different constituencies. Women, gay and lesbian, black and disabled writers had always been part of the Fed but for many of these groups identities sharpened in the 1980s, partly in opposition to class. Whereas 'new' groups could identify some positive trends in society with the appearance of similar groups elsewhere, working-class groups felt cut off. The result was a conflict over resources and the increasing isolation of sections of the working class. Protracted debates ensued, with mixed results. Some felt betrayed or disillusioned and worn down by endless disagreement. But most of the time the Fed contained these contradictions and straddled the dichotomies between class and other forms of identity which, by the 1990s, were becoming less contentious.

Class had been demoted from its commanding position, and a process of 'fracturing' took place.[20] For many years insufficient attention was paid to the ongoing significance of class alongside other markers of inequality.[21] It became clear in Fed writing that class was experienced in multiple and divergent ways according to factors including geography, age, work, gender, mobility and race. Explicit class consciousness only ever became noticeable at times of heightened struggle or awareness. However, many academic accounts assumed that class had always been a monolithic and/or exclusionary category. The fluidity of lived relations and meanings could be lost in the translation into fixed categories. It was difficult to make use of 'confused and vague' ideas as a basis for hard analytic models.[22] Yet, separating academic discourse and the everyday risks a permanent divorce between the two. The evidence from the Fed suggests that we need to explore further the ways in which class continued to have meaning in conjunction with other identities as people learned to live more consciously with messy ideas that could not easily be abstracted out of the tangled undergrowth of lived experience.[23]

Moreover, class did not disappear but, in the shade of dominant discourses, it transmogrified into unfamiliar shapes. The silence over class became so pronounced that the questionable notion of the 'white working class' effortlessly seeped into official policy and this also made sense to some in the Fed. The political evacuation of class during the New Labour years even allowed right-wing politicians to step back into the lacunae and claim social class as their territory, for instance, in Iain Duncan Smith's Social Justice Unit or the work of Ferdinand Mount, an adviser to Margaret Thatcher, and subsequently in Prime Minister Theresa May's rhetoric claiming to address inequality.[24] In the wake of the Brexit vote, it has been much commented upon that people felt alienated by the political system and that no one was listening.

In generating dialogue around class identity, the organisation of the workshop appropriated old and new in a way that confused the claim that this period witnessed the unproblematic rise of 'new social movements'. Books were produced and distributed in participatory, informal ways. The processes of writing, publishing and distribution were not just a means to an end. Working-class people were becoming involved in associated forms of production which rearranged divisions of labour. Fearing middle-class manipulation, writers worked to secure control and experimented with more equal relations.

In the 1980s and 1990s, a number of external and internal pressures brought about change. Some groups folded or had their funding cut. The survivors came under pressure to introduce elements of structure and hierarchy in their organisation while learning to be less political in public statements. The role of paid staff could pose problems for informal democratic processes, which would be further undermined by the decline of radical networks. Mainstream 'marketing' methods became more common as groups responded to commercial expectations and prioritised the archetypal customer. Consequently, the links with grass-roots writers could become more nebulous. It is a pattern that reflects the professionalisation of participative voluntary associations, which has been one factor in the onset of a democratic deficit afflicting many societies.[25]

However, personal contact and friendships, which were the building blocks of the Fed, remained at the core of the movement. Workshops frequently stayed small and flexible with the focus firmly on supporting each other to write. Those that adopted professional forms of organising often did so at the same time as encouraging inexperienced writers. The Fed itself provided a supportive structure that nourished smaller workshops. Although claims about the ubiquitous nature of power lent credence to the notion that inequalities could not be eliminated or remoulded, writing workshops have served as a space where collaboration and understanding have been developed across differences.

The experience of the Fed also helps to illuminate contradictions in more formal areas. Successive governments and policy makers have argued that output rather than organisational form should be the basis for developing social policy and allocating resources. Critics have presented this as a funnel for the profit motive and in tune with partial versions of democracy in which people choose between elites who compete for power.[26] The continual shake-up of the educational system has been a means of centralising state power at the expense of local alliances. The policy attachment to the constant reform of public services has been underpinned by the celebration of capitalist business practices.[27] In reality, a range of organisational forms, some of which relate to co-operative enterprise, have kept alive the possibilities of accountable and responsive public services.[28] Documenting, generalising and theorising previous experiences of democratic forms is one way of contributing to this agenda. For instance, alongside the Fed, the co-operative movement has developed the democratic potential of schools and universities.[29]

The survival of these workshops has been significant. Their ideas and practices could still have a much greater impact in more propitious circumstances. Rising material inequality combined with the suppression of people's voices will ensure a continuing need for expression by those who find themselves at the bottom of society. Small-scale projects may also become fused in a greater movement. It is relatively easy to identify a widespread urge for public expression and independent working-class education. An abundance of writing and performance can be found on the internet, a stream of alternative publications continues to be produced, the active contributions of people living in poverty has been recognised, emancipatory literacy practices have found new homes in developing countries and marginalised workers continue to produce poetry.[30] The man who recently handed me a photo poem on the Euston Road in London and refused to give two to the same person, expressed a spirit of equality and openness familiar to the Fed. Working-class writing and publishing has provided cultural tools to imagine a different future. It is a creative process without an end.

Notes

Introduction

1. Since 2007, it has been known as the Federation of Writers and Community Publishers. The 'Fed' is used as an umbrella term encompassing the movement in general.
2. J. Kirk, *Class, Culture and Social Change: On the Trail of the Working Class* (London: Palgrave Macmillan, 2007), p. 5.
3. B. Rogaly and B. Taylor, *Moving Histories of Class and Community: Identity, Place and Belonging in Contemporary England* (London: Palgrave Macmillan, 2009).
4. Cf. J. Rancière, *Proletarian Nights: The Workers' Dream in Nineteenth-Century France* (London: Verso, 2012).
5. For instance, R. Williams, *Problems in Materialism and Culture* (London: Verso, 1982); B. Skeggs, *Self, Class, Culture* (London: Routledge, 2004); A. Sayer, *The Moral Significance of Class* (London: Routledge, 2005); E. O. Wright, *Understanding Class* (London: Verso, 2015).
6. P. Lauter, 'Working class women's literature: An introduction to study', *Radical Teacher* 15 (December 1979), 16–26; P. Hitchcock, *Working-Class Fiction in Theory and Practice: A Reading of Alan Sillitoe* (Ann Arbor, MI: UMI Research Press, 1989); J. Zandy, *Hands: Physical Labor, Class, and Cultural Work* (New Jersey: Rutgers University Press, 2004); Kirk, *Class, Culture and Social Change*.
7. R. Wilkinson and K. Pickett, *The Spirit Level: Why Equality Is Better for Everyone* (London: Penguin, 2010); D. Dorling, *Inequality and the 1%* (London: Verso, 2014); L. Driscoll, *Evading Class in Contemporary British Literature* (New York: Palgrave Macmillan, 2009).
8. M. Archer, *The Reflexive Imperative* (Cambridge: Cambridge University Press, 2012).
9. A. Giddens, *Modernity and Self Identity: Self and Society in the Late Modern Age* (Cambridge: Polity Press in association with Basil Blackwell, 1991). See also C. Waters, 'Autobiography, nostalgia, and the changing practices of working-class selfhood', in G. K. Behlmer and F. M. Leventhal (eds), *Singular Continuities: Tradition, Nostalgia and Identity in Modern Britain* (Stanford, CA: Stanford University Press, 2000), p. 180.
10. S. Yeo, 'Whose story? An argument from within current historical practice in Britain', *Journal of Contemporary History*, 21:2 (1986), 259–320.
11. R. Williams, *Culture* (London: Fontana, 1981).
12. B. V. Street, *Literacy in Theory and Practice* (Cambridge: Cambridge University Press, 1984). See also D. Barton and M. Hamilton, *Local Literacies: Reading and Writing in One Community* (London: Routledge, 1998); M. Hamilton, *Literacy and the Politics of Representation* (Abingdon: Routledge, 2012).

13 See, for example, K. Worpole, 'A ghostly pavement: the political implications of local working class history', in R. Samuel (ed.), *People's History and Socialist Theory* (London: Routledge & Kegan Paul, 1981), pp. 22–32.
14 D. Morley and K. Worpole, *The Republic of Letters: Working Class Writing and Local Publishing* (London: Comedia, 1982), p. 61.
15 A. Biressi and H. Nunn, *Class and Contemporary British Culture* (Basingstoke: Palgrave Macmillan, 2013).
16 E. Janes Yeo, *The Contest for Social Science* (London: Rivers Oram Press, 1996); I. Roberts, 'A historical construction of the working class', in H. Beynon and P. Glavanis (eds), *Patterns of Social Inequality: Essays for Richard Brown* (London: Longman, 1999), pp. 78-95.
17 D. Bertaux, 'Stories as clues to sociological understanding: the bakers of Paris', in P. Thompson and N. Burchardt (eds), *Our Common History: The Transformation of Europe* (London: Pluto, 1982), p. 107.
18 See also P. Burke, *A Social History of Knowledge: From Gutenberg to Diderot* (Cambridge: Polity, 2000) and *A Social History of Knowledge*, vol. 2: *From the Encyclopédie to Wikipedia* (Cambridge: Polity, 2012).
19 For one important example, see R. Samuel, *Theatres of Memory* (London: Verso, 1994).
20 F. R. Leavis, *The Great Tradition* (Harmondsworth: Penguin, 1972/1948); T. S. Eliot, *Notes towards the Definition of Culture* (London: Faber and Faber, 1962/1948).
21 R. Williams, *The Long Revolution* (London: Pelican, 1971/1961); R. O'Rourke, *Creative Writing: Education, Culture and Community* (Leicester: NIACE, 2005).
22 P. Widdowson, *Literature* (London: Routledge, 1999); Williams, *Problems in Materialism and Culture*.
23 Morley and Worpole, *The Republic of Letters*.
24 R. Hoggart, 'The crisis of relativism', *New Universities Quarterly*, 35:1 (Winter 1980/81), 16; J. McGuigan, 'The State and Serious Writing. Arts Council Intervention in the English Literary Field' (PhD dissertation, University of Leicester, 1984).
25 D. Marsden, 'Jam for tea', *New Society* (10 March 1977), 511.
26 R. Hoggart, *The Uses of Literacy: Aspects of Working-Class Life with Special Reference to Publications and Entertainments* (Harmondsworth: Penguin, 1957).
27 C. B. Cox and A. E. Dyson, *The Black Papers on Education* (London: Davis-Poynter, 1971).
28 See Chapter 11.
29 B. Cox, *Literacy Is Not Enough: Essays on the Importance of Reading* (Manchester: Manchester University Press and The Book Trust, 1998).
30 Morley and Worpole, *The Republic of Letters*, p. 43; K. Worpole, *Reading by Numbers: Contemporary Publishing & Popular Fiction* (London: Comedia, 1984), p. 63.
31 R. Williams, 'The role of the literary magazine', *Times Literary Supplement* (6 June 1980), p. 637. Contained in a letter to Melvyn Bragg, Chairman, Literature Panel, ACGB, 16 June 1980, signed by Barbara Shane, Ken Worpole and Ian Bild, FWWCP Archive (in personal possession).
32 The first director of CCCS was Richard Hoggart.
33 S. Hall, 'Notes on deconstructing the popular', in R. Samuel (ed.), *People's History and Socialist Theory* (London: Routledge & Kegan Paul, 1981), p. 239. For these debates see J. Scott, 'The evidence of experience', *Critical Inquiry*, 17:4 (Summer 1991), 773–97; G. Eley, *A Crooked Line: From Cultural History to the History of Society* (Ann Arbor, MI: University of Michigan Press, 2005).
34 T. Eagleton, *After Theory* (London: Penguin, 2004); K. Razmig, *The Left Hemisphere: Mapping Critical Theory Today* (London: Verso, 2014).

35 J. White, 'Beyond autobiography', in Samuel (ed.), *People's History*, p. 37.
36 J. Swindells, *Victorian Writing and Working Women* (Cambridge: Polity, 1985); R. Gagnier, *Subjectivities* (Oxford: Oxford University Press, 1991); see also changes in *History Workshop Journal*.
37 The work of Carolyn Steedman is particularly relevant, for example, *Past Tenses: Essays on Writing, Autobiography and History* (London: Rivers Oram, 1992); 'Enforced narratives: stories of another self', in T. Cosslett, C. Lury and P. Summerfield (eds), *Feminism and Autobiography: Texts, Theories, Methods* (London: Routledge, 2000), pp. 25–39.
38 G. Spivak, 'Can the subaltern speak?', in C. Nelson and L. Grossberg (eds), *Marxism and the Interpretation of Culture* (Basingstoke: Macmillan Education, 1988), pp. 271–313.
39 A. Gorz, *Farewell to the Working Class: An Essay on Post-Industrial Socialism* (London: Pluto, 1982).
40 P. Bourdieu, *Distinction: A Social Critique of the Judgement of Taste* (London: Routledge & Kegan Paul, 1984). S. Bowles and H. Gintis, *Schooling in Capitalist America: Educational Reform and the Contradictions of Economic Life* (New York: Basic Books, 1976).
41 Popular Memory Group, 'Popular memory: theory, politics, method', in R. Johnson et al. (eds), *Making Histories* (London: Hutchinson, 1982), pp. 205–52.
42 Chris Miller quoted in Morley and Worpole, *The Republic of Letters*, p. 94.
43 G. Gregory, '"Working Class Writing, Publishing and Education: An Investigation of Three "Moments"' (PhD dissertation, University of London, 1986), p. 364.
44 K. Worpole, 'The history lark', *Oral History Journal*, 12:2 (1984), 19–20.
45 See Worpole, 'A ghostly pavement', and S. Yeo, 'The politics of community publications', in Samuel (ed.), *People's History*, pp. 42–8.
46 Morley and Worpole, *The Republic of Letters*, p. 43.
47 C. Steedman, *Landscape for a Good Woman* (London: Virago, 1985); R. Fraser, *In Search of a Past: The Manor House, Amnersfield, 1933–1945* (London: Verso, 1984).
48 The phrase comes from M.-F. Chanfrault-Duchet, 'Narrative structures, social models and symbolic representation in the life story', in S. B. Gluck and D. Patai (eds), *Women's Words: The Feminist Practice of Oral History* (New York: Routledge, 1991), p. 89.
49 S. Laing, *Representations of Working Class Life, 1957–1964* (Basingstoke: Macmillan, 1986); S. Rowbotham and H. Beynon (eds), *Looking at Class: Film, Television and the Working Class in Britain* (London: Rivers Oram, 2001); Waters, 'Autobiography, nostalgia, and the changing practices of working-class selfhood'.
50 D. Vincent, *Bread, Knowledge and Freedom. A Study of Nineteenth Century Working Class Autobiography* (London: Europa, 1981); G. Cavallo and R. Chartier (eds), *A History of Reading in the West* (Cambridge: Polity, 1999); J. Rose, *The Intellectual Life of the British Working Classes* (New Haven, CT: Yale University Press, 2001); C. Hilliard, *To Exercise Our Talents: The Democratization of Writing in Britain* (Cambridge, MA: Harvard University Press, 2006); U. Howard, *Literacy and the Practice of Writing in the 19th Century: A Strange Blossoming of Spirit* (Leicester: NIACE, 2012).
51 See, for instance, I. Haywood (ed.), *The Literature of Struggle: An Anthology of Chartist Fiction* (Aldershot: Scolar Press, 1995); I. Haywood, *Working Class Fiction from Chartism to Trainspotting* (British Council, Plymouth: Northcote House, 1997); M. Vicinus, *The Industrial Muse* (London: Croom Helm, 1974); G. Klaus, *The Literature of Labour: Two Hundred Years of Working Class Writing* (Brighton: Harvester, 1985). The trade unionist Michael McGahey was partly self-educated; see V. Allen, 'The red and the black',

Obituary, *Guardian* (1 February 1999), www.theguardian.com/news/1999/feb/01/guardianobituaries2, accessed 25 January 2016. For the USA see also M. Denning, *Mechanic Accents: Dime Novels and Working Class Culture in America* (London: Verso, 1998).

52 R. Williams, *Politics and Letters: Interviews with New Left Review* (London: NLB, 1979); E. P. Thompson, 'Education and experience', in *The Romantics: England in a Revolutionary Age* (Woodbridge: Merlin, 1997), pp. 4–32. See also S. Rowbotham, 'Travellers in a strange country: responses of working class students to the University Extension Movement 1873–1910', in S. Rowbotham, *Threads Through Time* (London: Penguin, 1999), pp. 260–301; L. Goldman, *Dons and Workers. Oxford and Adult Education Since 1850* (Oxford: Clarendon Press, 1995); T. Woodin, 'Working class education and social change in nineteenth and twentieth century Britain', *History of Education*, 36:4/5 (2007), 483–96.

53 G. Hughes, *Millstone Grit* (London: Victor Gollancz, 1976), p. 51.

54 J. F. C. Harrison, *Learning and Living 1790–1960* (London: Routledge & Kegan Paul, 1961), pp. 349–50; Rose, *The Intellectual Life of the British Working Classes*, p. 11; see also Hilliard, *To Exercise Our Talents*.

55 See the survey in Widdowson, *Literature*.

56 Hilliard, *To Exercise Our Talents*, pp. 142–3 and 282–3.

57 Waters, 'Autobiography, nostalgia, and the changing practices of working-class selfhood'.

58 Rose, *The Intellectual Life of the British Working Classes*, p. 11; Goldman, *Dons and Workers*, ch. 11.

59 Worpole, 'A ghostly pavement'.

60 Cf. Howard, *Literacy and the Practice of Writing in the 19th Century*.

61 D. Vincent, *Literacy and Popular Culture* (Cambridge: Cambridge University Press, 1989); see ch. 3, especially pp. 259–67.

62 R. Samuel, E. MacColl and S. Cosgrove, *Theatres of the Left 1880–1935: Workers' Theatre Movements in Britain and America* (London: Routledge & Kegan Paul, 1985), p. xi; Klaus, *The Literature of Labour*; E. Hobsbawm and T. Ranger, *The Invention of Tradition* (Cambridge: Cambridge University Press, 1983).

63 Williams, *Problems in Materialism and Culture*; Hobsbawm and Ranger, *The Invention of Tradition*.

64 Comedia, 'The alternative press', *Media, Culture & Society*, 6:2 (1984), 95–102; C. Atton, *Alternative Media* (London: SAGE, 2002); J. D. H. Downing, 'Audiences and readers of alternative media: the absent lure of the virtually unknown', *Media, Culture & Society*, 25:5 (2003), 625–45.

65 B. Brecht, 'New ages', in B. Brecht, *Poems 1913–1956* (London: Methuen, 1976), p. 386.

66 See new edition, D. Morley, K. Worpole, S. Parks and N. Pollard, *The Republic of Letters: Working Class Writing and Local Publishing* (Philadelphia, PA: New City Community Press/Syracuse University Press, 2009).

67 For instance, G. Gregory, 'Using community-published writing in the classroom'; A. Thomson, 'Community publishing. The Republic of Letters revisited', *Adults Learning*, 2:1 (1990), 15–16; G. Gregory, 'Community publishing as self-education', in D. Barton and R. Ivanic (eds), *Writing in the Community* (Newbury Park, CA: Sage Publications, 1991), pp. 109–42; J. Mace (ed.), *Literacy, Language and Community Publishing: Essays in Adult Education* (Clevedon: Multilingual Matters, 1995); S. Courtman, 'Freirian liberation, cultural transaction and writing from "The Working Class and the Spades"', Society for Caribbean Studies Annual Conference

Papers, 1, 2000, http://community-languages.org.uk/SCS-Papers/, accessed 20 January 2017; N. Coles, 'Joe Shakespeare: the contemporary British worker-writer movement', in J. Trimbur (ed.), *Popular Literacy: Studies in Cultural Practices and Poetics* (Pittsburgh, PA: University of Pittsburgh Press, 2001), pp. 189-208; S. Courtman, '"Culture is ordinary": the legacy of the Scottie Road and Liverpool 8 Writers', in M. Murphy and D. Rees-Jones (eds), *Writing Liverpool: Essays and Interviews* (Liverpool: Liverpool University Press, 2007); S. Parks and N. Pollard, 'The extra-curricular of composition: a dialogue on community publishing', *Community Literacy Journal*, 3:2 (2009), 53–77; S. Parks and N. Pollard, 'Emergent strategies for an established field: the role of the worker writer groups in composition and rhetoric', *College Composition and Communication*, 61:3 (2010), 476–509; N. Pollard, 'Occupational narratives, community publishing and worker writing groups: sustaining stories from the margins', *Groupwork*, 20:1 (2010), 9–33; N. Pollard and P. Smart, 'Making writing accessible to all: the Federation of Worker Writers and Community Publishers and TheFED', in P. Mathieu, S. Parks and T. Rousculp (eds), *Circulating Communities: The Tactics and Strategies of Community Publishing* (Lanham, MD: Lexington Books, 2012), pp. 21–34; M. Ikiugu et al., 'Meaning making through occupations and occupational roles: a heuristic study of worker-writer histories', *British Journal of Occupational Therapy*, 75:6 (2012), 289–95; see also Woodin references in note 74.

68 S. Westwood, 'When class became community: radicalism in adult education', in A. Rattansi and D. Reeder (eds), *Rethinking Radical Education* (London: Lawrence & Wishart, 1992), pp. 222–48; N. Wright, *Assessing Radical Education: A Critical View of the Radical Movement in English Schooling, 1960–1980* (Milton Keynes: Oxford University Press, 1989); Samuel, *Theatres of Memory*.

69 Archive collections now exist at the TUC Library, London Metropolitan University, Mass Observation Unit at Sussex University and the Working Class Movement Library in Salford. Centerprise archives are at the Bishopsgate Institute.

70 See also T. Woodin, 'An Evaluation of the FWWCP' (PhD dissertation, University of Manchester, 2002).

71 See, for instance, P. Corrigan and D. Sayer, *The Great Arch. English State Formation as Cultural Revolution* (Oxford: Blackwell, 1985).

72 T. Woodin, 'Muddying the waters: class and identity in a working class cultural organisation', *Sociology*, 39:5 (2005), 1001–18; '"More writing than welding": learning in worker writer groups', *History of Education*, 39:5 (2005), 551–67; 'Building culture from the bottom-up: the educational origins of the FWWCP', *History of Education*, 39:4 (2005), 345–63; '"Chuck out the teacher?" The pedagogies of community publishing', *International Journal of Lifelong Education*, 26:1 (2007), 89–104; '"A beginner reader is not a beginner thinker": student publishing since the 1970s', *Paedagogica Historica*, 44:1/2 (2008), 219–32; 'Working class writing, alternative publishing and audience participation', *Media, Culture and Society*, 31:1 (2009), 79–96; 'Rethinking society and culture', in S. Parks and N. Pollard (eds), *The Republic of Letters* (Syracuse: New Community Press, 2009), 240–56.

73 D. Patai, 'US academics and third world women: is ethical research possible?', in S. B. Gluck and D. Patai (eds), *Women's Words: The Feminist Practice of Oral History* (New York: Routledge, 1991), p. 147.

74 R. Williams, *Culture and Society* (Harmondsworth: Penguin, 1962/1958), pp. 312–14.

Chapter 1

1. R. Hoggart, *The Uses of Literacy* (London: Penguin, 1992/1957); R. Williams, *The Long Revolution* (London: Chatto & Windus, 1961); E. P. Thompson, *The Making of the English Working Class* (Harmondsworth: Penguin, 1968).
2. R. Williams, *Problems in Materialism and Culture* (London: Verso, 1980).
3. D. Morley and K. Worpole, *The Republic of Letters: Working Class Writing and Local Publishing* (London: Comedia, 1982), pp. 2–3; S. Rowbotham et al., *Beyond the Fragments: Feminism and the Making of Socialism*, 2nd edn (London: Merlin, 1981).
4. R. Miliband, 'A state of de-subordination', *British Journal of Sociology*, 29:4 (1978), 399–409; K. O. Morgan, *Britain Since 1945: The People's Peace* (Oxford: Oxford University Press, 2001), pp. 328–90.
5. R. Hewison, *Culture and Consensus: England, Art and Politics Since 1940* (London: Methuen, 1995), ch. 6.
6. T. Blackwell and J. Seabrook, *A World Still to Win: The Reconstruction of the Post-War Working Class* (London: Faber, 1985), pp. 129–37.
7. B. Hindess, *The Decline of Working Class Politics* (London: MacGibbon and Kee, 1971).
8. S. Rowbotham, *A Century of Women: The History of Women in Britain and the United States* (London: Penguin, 1999), p. 426.
9. See also Morley and Worpole, *The Republic of Letters*.
10. Various, *Stepney Words*, vols 1 and 2 (London: Reality Press, 1971), republished as *Stepney Words I & II* (London: Centerprise, 1973).
11. C. Searle, *None but Our Words* (Buckingham: Open University Press, 1998).
12. Chris Searle, interviewed by Tom Woodin, 2000.
13. Ibid.
14. Ibid.
15. A. Dein, *Document: The Fire Is in Our Hearts*, BBC Radio 4, 20 November 1997.
16. S. Johnson, 'The world is dim and dull', in *Stepney Words I & II*, p. 19.
17. D. King, 'The astonishing world of these East End kids', *Sun* (11 March 1971), pp. 14–15. 'Please don't sack sir!', *Sun* (28 May 1971), front page.
18. Ibid., ch. 5.
19. Searle, *None but Our Words*, p. 77.
20. M. Wilkinson, 'How "the class struggle" is taught in the classroom', *Daily Mail* (15 October 1975), p. 18.
21. J. Rogaly, 'Teaching revolution in the classroom', *Financial Times* (14 October 1975), p. 25.
22. K. Worpole, *Local Publishing and Local Culture: An Account of the Centerprise Publishing Project 1972–1977* (London: Centerprise, 1977), p. 3.
23. K. Worpole, 'Beyond the classroom walls: making available the means of production', *Teaching London Kids*, 1 (1973), 5.
24. V. Usherwood, 'The sun glitters as you look up', in V. Usherwood, *Poems* (London: Centerprise, 1975/1972), p. 5.
25. K. Worpole, Talk at Fed Festival, Co-operative College, Stanford Hall (April 1996).
26. C. Searle (ed.), *One for Blair: An Anthology of Poems for Young People* (London: One World Books, 1989).
27. A. Johnson, interviewed by Tom Woodin, 2016.
28. M. Simmons and M. Raleigh, 'Where we've been: a brief history of English teaching, part 1 1920–1970', *English Magazine*, 8 (Autumn 1981), p. 28. See also N. Wright, *Assessing Radical Education: A Critical View of the Radical Movement in English Schooling, 1960–1980* (Milton Keynes: Oxford University Press, 1989), chs 3–5.

29 See C. Steedman, 'Writing the self: the end of the scholarship girl', in J. McGuigan (ed.), *Cultural Methodologies* (London: Sage, 1997), pp. 106–25. Early in the twentieth century, Sir Philip Hartog had criticised essays in favour of writing from experience; see P. J. Hartog with A. H. Langdon, *The Writing of English* (Oxford: Clarendon Press, 1907).
30 D. Shayer, *The Teaching of English in Schools, 1900–1970* (London: Routledge & Kegan Paul, 1972), pp. 159–66; A. Clegg, *The Excitement of Writing* (London: Chatto & Windus, 1964); see also P. Medway, J. Hardcastle, G. Brewis and D. Crook, *English Teachers in a Postwar Democracy: Emerging Choice in London Schools, 1945–1965* (New York: Palgrave Macmillan, 2014).
31 Ibid., ch. 5.
32 Central Advisory Committee for Education, *Children and Their Primary Schools* (the Plowden Report), vol. 1 (London: HMSO, 1967), pp. 218–23. See also Simmons and Raleigh, 'Where we've been'; Steedman, 'Writing the self'.
33 Simmons and Raleigh, 'Where we've been', 26.
34 N. Keddie, *Tinker, Tailor: The Myth of Cultural Deprivation* (Harmondsworth: Penguin Books, 1973).
35 H. Rosen, 'Out there or where the masons went', in M. Hoyles (ed.), *The Politics of Literacy* (London: Writers and Readers Co-operative, 1977), p. 208.
36 H. Rosen, 'Their language and ours', *Teaching London Kids*, 1 (1973), inside front cover–3.
37 Discussion with Michael Rosen; J. Hardcastle, email 24 January 2017.
38 For example, see G. Thompson, 'Our national cultural heritage' and other contributions to *Britain's Cultural Heritage*, supplement of meeting the previous year on American Threat to British Culture (London: Arena Publication, 1952), pp. 3–19.
39 For example, B. Leeson (ed.), 'Worker writer's special', *Morning Star* (19 October 1978), p. 4.
40 Kate, 'Kate's poem', in C. Searle (ed.), *Elders* (London: Reality Press, 1973), pp. 6–8.
41 G. Wilkinson, 'Understanding Lifetimes', *Oral History Journal*, 4:2 (Autumn 1976), 91.
42 Ibid.
43 Ibid.
44 No author, 'Review' of Lifetimes, *Oral History Journal*, 4:1 (Spring 1976), 107–8.
45 Stephen Yeo, interviewed by Tom Woodin, 2001.
46 For an overview, see G. E. Evans, *Spoken History* (London: Faber, 1987).
47 C. Parker, *Radio Ballads* (London: BBC, 1958–64; republished by Topic Records).
48 J. Berger and J. Mohr, *A Fortunate Man: The Story of a Country Doctor* (London: Allen Lane, 1967); see also J. Berger and J. Mohr, *The Seventh Man: A Book of Images and Words about the Experience of Migrant Workers in Europe* (Harmondsworth: Penguin, 1975).
49 For instance, S.-L. Konttinen, *Byker* (London: Cape, 1983).
50 R. Samuel, *History Workshop: A Collectanea 1967–1991: Documents, Memoirs, Critique and Cumulative Index to History Workshop Journal* (Oxford: History Workshop, 1991), p. 29.
51 Worpole, *Local Publishing and Local Culture*, p. 9.
52 This shift of priorities can be seen in the journal *History Workshop*.
53 Ken Worpole, interviewed by G. Gregory. 1979. 'Worker Writers' (MA dissertation, Institute of Education, University of London), p. 161.
54 K. Armstrong and H. Beynon, *Hello, Are You Working? Memories of the Thirties in the North East of England* (Whitley Bay: Strong Words, 1977); Strong Words Collective, *But the World Goes on the Same: Changing Times in Durham Pit Villages* (Whitley Bay: Erdesdun, 1979). Formally the group remained distant from the Fed although members overlapped.
55 B. Ainley, 'Introductory', *Voices*, 1 (1972), 3. On Ainley, see A. Rowland, *Poetry*

as Testimony: Witnessing and Memory in Twentieth Century Poems (Abingdon: Routledge, 2014), especially ch. 5.
56 Ibid.
57 Rick Gwilt, interviewed by Tom Woodin, 2000.
58 Willis once attended an AGM.
59 Hewison, Culture and Consensus, p. 114. For Centre Fortytwo, see also F. Coppetiers, 'Arnold Wesker's Centre Fortytwo: a cultural revolution betrayed', Theatre Quarterly, 18:1 (1975), 18.
60 A. Sinfield, Literature, Politics and Culture in Postwar Britain (Oxford: Basil Blackwell, 1989), p. 265.
61 Stephen Yeo, interviewed by Tom Woodin, 2001.
62 Thanks to Eileen Janes Yeo for pointing this out, taken up in L. Sitzia, 'Telling People's Histories: An Exploration of Community History Making from 1970–2000' (PhD dissertation, University of Sussex, 2010).
63 C. Kirkwood, 'Adult education and the concept of community', Adult Education, 51:3 (1978), 148–9; see also T. Lovett, 'Community adult education', Studies in Adult Education, 3:1 (1971), 6.
64 Searle wrote Thompson's obituary in C. Searle, 'Life of a seminal black publisher, Glenn Thompson', Morning Star (19 September 2001), p. 9.
65 FWWCP Archive, Centerprise, Annual Report (London: Centerprise, 1992), p. 2.
66 FWWCP Archive, Centerprise, Annual Report (London: Centerprise, 1978), p. 4.
67 Centerprise Archive, Bishopsgate Institute, London (hereafter 'Centerprise Archive'), 'Centerprise: bookshop/coffee-bar/community centre. Report', December 1975.
68 Centerprise Archive, 'Notes concerning the bookshop for the Redcliffe-Maud Enquiry on Arts Patronage', in ibid.
69 Ibid.
70 S. D. Alinsky, Reveille for Radicals (New York: Vintage Books, 1969); Rules for Radicals: Practical Primer for Realistic Radicals (New York: Vintage Books, 1972).
71 See also G. Fofi, 'Danilo Dolci', Wikiradio, www.radio3.rai.it/dl/radio3/programmi/PublishingBlock-0e9b2d8d-4516–42a0–9719-a67fa50e9d9b-podcast.html, accessed 26 December 2012.
72 David Evans, interviewed by Tom Woodin, 2000. See also S. Courtman, '"Culture is ordinary": the legacy of the Scottie Road and Liverpool 8 writers', in M. Murphy and D. Rees-Jones (eds), Writing Liverpool: Essays and Interviews (Liverpool: Liverpool University Press, 2007), pp. 194–209.
73 P. Freire, Pedagogy of the Oppressed, new ed. (Harmondworth: Penguin, 1990) and Education for Critical Consciousness, Education as the Practice of Freedom, Extension or Communication (London: Sheed and Ward, 1973).
74 K. Jackson and B. Ashcroft, 'Adult education and social action', in D. Jones and M. Mayo (eds), Community Work One (London: Routledge & Kegan Paul, 1971), p. 55.
75 T. Lovett, Adult Education, Community Development and the Working Class (London: Ward Lock, 1975), pp. 83–4.
76 J. Edwards, Working Class Adult Education in Liverpool: A Radical Approach (Manchester: The Centre for Adult and Higher Education, Manchester University, 1986).
77 Ibid., pp. 179–80.
78 Liverpool 8 Writers Group, 'To our readers', 19 From 8 (Liverpool: Liverpool 8 Writers Group, n.d., c.1979).
79 See A. Walmsley, The Caribbean Artists Movement 1966–1972 (London: New Beacon Books, 1992).
80 'Bristol Broadsides', in FWWCP, Writing (London: FWWCP, 1978), p. 23.

81 C. Aubrey and C. Landry, 'Breaking cover', *Guardian* (6 September 1980), p. 14.
82 For the history of the campaign, see M. E. Hamilton and Y. Hillier, *The Changing Face of Adult Literacy, Language and Numeracy 1970–2000: A Critical History* (Stoke-on-Trent: Trentham Books, 2006); B. Street, *Adult Literacy in the UK: A History of Research and Practice* (Lancaster: RaPAL, 1997); A. Withnall, 'Literacy on the agenda: the origins of the adult literacy campaign in the UK', *Studies in the Education of Adults*, 26:1 (April 1994), 67–85.
83 Street, *Adult Literacy in the UK*, p. 6.
84 Maureen Cooper, interviewed by Tom Woodin, 2000.
85 Reported in *New Society* (6 March 1975), p. 571.
86 WFT Archive, Ruskin College, Oxford, S. Gardener (published as Shrapnel), 'Can we produce a teaching news-sheet for literacy work', c.1974.
87 WFT Archive, Write First Time, 'Application to Adult Literacy Resouce Agency', c.1974/75.
88 S. Gardener (published as Shrapnel), 'Thoughts on to paper: publications from adult literacy centres, 1974–78', *Adult Education*, 52:2 (1979), p. 93.
89 Ibid., p. 93.
90 J. Mace, *Working with Words: Literacy beyond School* (London: Writers and Readers Co-operative in association with Chameleon, 1979).
91 Withnal, 'Literacy on the agenda', p. 82.
92 S. Gardener (published as Shrapnel), 'They look normal but …', in M. Ben-Tovim and R. J. Kedney (eds), *Aspects of Adult Illiteracy* (Liverpool: Merseyside and District Institute of Adult Education, 1974), pp. 9–13.
93 Jane Mace, interviewed by Tom Woodin, 2001.
94 Worpole, *Local Publishing and Local Culture*, p. 9.
95 See R. Hewison, *Too Much: Art and Society in the Sixties 1960–75* (London: Methuen, 1986), pp. 95–7.
96 W. Benjamin, 'The work of art in the age of mechanical reproduction', in H. Arendt (ed.), *Illuminations* (New York: Schocken Books, 1968), pp. 217–51; W. Benjamin, 'The author as producer', in W. Benjamin, *Understanding Brecht* (London: Verso, 1973), pp. 85–103; G. Gregory, 'Working class writing: breaking the long silence', *English Magazine*, 4 (Summer 1985), 15–17; R. Williams, *Communications* (Harmondsworth: Penguin, 1976/1962); Gregory, *Worker Writers*, p. 161.
97 See, for instance, Keddie, *Tinker, Tailor*; S. Braden, *Artists and People* (London: Routledge, 1978); B. Jackson and D. Marsden, *Education and the Working Class* (London: Routledge & Kegan Paul, 1962).
98 Alan Gilbey and Chris Searle, interviewed separately by Tom Woodin, 2000. Roger Mills by email, 11 February 2016. See also Braden, *Artists and People*, ch. 2.
99 Centerprise Archive, K. Worpole, 'Some questions', 15 March 1979; Chris Searle interview.
100 R. Williams, *Culture and Society: Coleridge to Orwell* (London: Hogarth, 1987); C. Snee, 'Working class literature or proletarian writing?', in J. Clark et al. (eds), *Culture and Crisis in Britain in the 30s* (London: Lawrence & Wishart, 1979).
101 Morley and Worpole, *The Republic of Letters*, pp. 95–7.
102 FWWCP Archive (in author's possession), FWWCP Minutes 10–11 April 1976.
103 Quoted in Searle, *None but Our Words*, p. 58.
104 Keith Birch, interviewed by Tom Woodin, 2000.
105 Jimmy McGovern, interviewed (email) by Tom Woodin, 2001.
106 See also R. Samuel, E. MacColl and S. Cosgrove, *Theatres of the Left 1880–1935: Workers' Theatre Movements in Britain and America* (London: Routledge & Kegan Paul, 1985), p. xi

and G. Klaus, *The Literature of Labour: Two Hundred Years of Working Class Writing* (Brighton: Harvester, 1985), p. 1.
107 Roger Mills, interviewed by Tom Woodin, 2000.
108 K. Worpole, 'Village school or blackboard jungle', in R. Samuel (ed.), *Patriotism: The Making and Unmaking of British National Identity*, vol, 3: *National Fictions* (London: Routledge, 1989), pp. 125–40.
109 Blackwell and Seabrook, *A World Still to Win*, p. 47.
110 Ken Worpole, interviewed by Roger Drury, 1995. On Centerprise, see R. Schling, *The Lime Green Mystery: An Oral History of the Centerprise Co-operative* (London: On the Record, 2017),
111 Roger Kitchen, interviewed by Tom Woodin, 2002.
112 Stephen Yeo, interviewed by Tom Woodin, 2001.
113 Ken Worpole, interviewed by Roger Drury, 1995.
114 Man Alive, 'Alright, we'll do it ourselves', BBC, 11 October 1972, www.youtube.com/watch?v=2nxgsvLXKmA, accessed 20 February 2017.
115 FWWCP Archive, 'Introduction', FWWCP Report, 1979. Various, *Writing* (London: FWWCP, 1978).
116 FWWCP Archive, K. Worpole, postcard to Stephen and Eileen Yeo, c.1979.
117 Ken Worpole, interviewed by Roger Drury, 1995.
118 Alan Gilbey, interviewed by Tom Woodin, 2000.
119 No groups from Wales or Scotland joined the Fed in the early period.
120 FWWCP Archive, K. Worpole, letter to FWWCP groups, 18 November 1980. See also K. Worpole, letter to Stephen Yeo, 13 March 1979.
121 Lydia Meryll, interviewed by Tom Woodin, 2001.

Chapter 2

1 For the background on LATE, see S. Gibbons, *The London Association for the Teaching of English, 1947–67* (London: Trentham, 2013).
2 See T. Woodin, G. McCulloch and S. Cowan, *Secondary Education and the Raising of the School Leaving Age – Coming of Age?* (New York: Palgrave Macmillan, 2013), p. 144.
3 See M. Armstrong, *Closely Observed Children: The Diary of a Primary Classroom* (London: Writers and Readers in association with Chameleon, 1980); and *Children Writing Stories* (Maidenhead: Open University Press, 2006). Also, K. Worpole, 'The politics of writing', *Radical Education*, 12 (Spring 1979), 8.
4 P. Ritchens, 'Let it flow, Joe!', in Various, *Stepney Words I & II* (London: Centerprise, 1973), p. 2.
5 P. Kirk, untitled, in *Stepney Words I & II*, p. 35.
6 M. Balgobin, 'The year ticks by', in *As Good As We Make It* (London: Centerprise, 1982), p. 38.
7 M. Lyon, 'The old school', in *Stepney Words I & II*, p. 20.
8 C. Burke and I. Grosvenor, *School* (London: Reaktion, 2008).
9 C. Graves, 'Soldier', in *Stepney Words I & II*, p. 68.
10 R. Porter, 'Domino', in *Black Ink* (London: Black Ink, 1982/1978), p. 31.
11 Michael Simmons, interviewed by Tom Woodin, 2000.
12 For example, R. Harris, 'Disappearing language: fragments and fractures between speech and writing', in J. Mace (ed.), *Literacy, Language and Community Publishing: Essays in Adult Education* (Clevedon: Multilingual Matters, 1995), pp. 118–44.
13 P. Isword, 'Walcott versus Brathwaite', *Caribbean Quarterly*, 17:3/4 (September–December 1971), 54–7.

14 Alan Gilbey, interviewed by Tom Woodin, 2000.
15 J. Ackerman, *The Kids Are Alright* (London: English Centre, 1979), p. 23.
16 C. Herbert, *In the Melting Pot* (London: English Centre/Ebury Teachers' Centre, n.d), p. 1.
17 John Hardcastle, email, 24 January 2017.
18 See also Worpole, 'The politics of writing'; G. Moss, *Un/popular Fictions* (London: Virago, 1989).
19 Various, *Our Lives* (London: English Centre, 1979); Worpole, 'The politics of writing'; Michael Simmons, interviewed by Tom Woodin, 2000.
20 S. Ing, 'Saroeun's Story', in Various *More Lives* (London: English Centre, 1987), pp. 45–6.
21 M. Patel, 'Rare Bengal Tiger', in *Our Lives*, p. 107.
22 P. George, *Memories* (London: Commonplace, c.1975), p. 5.
23 Thanks to John Hardcastle for making the link to Lamming.
24 George, *Memories*, p. 32.
25 A theme developed in R. Williams, *The Country and the City* (London: Hogarth, 1985).
26 R. Sumal, *Back Home* (London: Commonplace, 1981), pp. 17–18.
27 S. Bandali, *Small Accidents: The Autobiography of a Ugandan Asian* (London: Tulse Hill School, 1976), p 56. See also N. Wilson, *Home in Working Class Fiction* (Farnham: Ashgate, 2015).
28 See mixture of racist and anti-racist sentiments in D. King, 'The astonishing world of these East End kids', *Sun* (11 March 1971), pp. 14–15. B. Richardson, *Tell it Like it Is: How Our Schools Fail Black Children* (Stoke-on-Trent: Trentham, 2007).
29 Z. El Kssmi, 'Families', in *Our Lives*, p. 18.
30 Ibid., pp. 19–20.
31 See also C. Steedman, '"Listen, how the caged bird sings": Amarjit's song', in C. Steedman, C. Urwin and V. Walkerdine (eds), *Language, Gender and Childhood* (London: Routledge & Kegan Paul, 1985), p. 145.
32 L. Mildiner and B. House, *The Gates* (London: Centerprise, 1974).
33 Ibid., p. 9.
34 Ibid., p. 11.
35 Ibid., p. 20.
36 Ibid., pp. 88–9.
37 Ibid., pp. 40–1.
38 Ibid., p. 55.
39 Anonymous, *Jackie's Story* (London: Centerprise, 1984), p. 47.
40 Ibid., p. 61.
41 Ibid., p. 65.
42 C. Steedman, *The Tidy House: Little Girls Writing* (London: Virago, 1982), p. 82.
43 Anonymous, *Jackie's Story*, pp. 1–2.
44 Ibid., p. 15.
45 Ibid., pp. 26, 82. See also ch. 4.
46 Ibid., pp. 55–6.
47 Ibid., p. 55.
48 Ibid., p. 100.
49 Ibid., p. 110.
50 R. Mills, *A Comprehensive Education* (London: Centerprise, 1978), p. 8.
51 Ibid., p. 7.
52 Roger Mills, interviewed by Tom Woodin, 2000.
53 Mills, *A Comprehensive Education*, p. 43.

54 Ibid., pp. 51–2, 56–7.
55 Ibid., p. 94.
56 Ibid., p. 8.
57 Ibid., p. 61.
58 Ibid., p. 27.
59 Ibid., p. 49.
60 S. Todd, The People: The Rise and Fall of the Working Class (London: John Murray, 2015).
61 R. Mills, 'We don't need no ...', in D. Morley et al., The Republic of Letters (Philadelphia, PA: New City Community Press/Syracuse University Press, 2009), pp. 193–5.
62 J. Hardcastle, email, 24 January 2017.
63 Ibid., p. 109.
64 C. Searle, None but Our Words (Buckingham: Open University Press, 1998).
65 Worpole, 'The politics of writing', 8.
66 J. Hardcastle, '"The dramas themselves": teaching English in London in the 1970s', Changing English, 23:2 (2016), 112–27.
67 Chris Searle, interviewed by Tom Woodin, 2000. On Searle, see also B. Davis, 'Teaching tough kids: Searle and Stepney', Race and Class, 51:2 (2009), 18–32.
68 K. Worpole, interviewed by Tom Woodin, 2008.
69 P. Medway, J. Hardcastle, G. Brewis and D. Crook, English Teachers in a Postwar Democracy: Emerging Choice in London Schools, 1945–1965 (New York: Palgrave Macmillan, 2014); The Poetry Society ran 'poets in schools' schemes; Various, Splash! (London: Eastside, 1996); P. Smart (ed.), It's Our World as Well (Liverpool: FWWCP, 1990).
70 Various, Stepney Words III: Poetry by East London Schoolchildren (London: Rich Mix, 2017).
71 R. Lowe, The Death of Progressive Education: How Teachers Lost Control of the Classroom (London: Routledge, 2007).
72 C. Ward, The Child in the City (London: Architectural Press, 1978).
73 M. Thomson, Lost Freedom: The Landscape of the Child and the British Post-War Settlement (Oxford: Oxford University Press, 2013), pp. 224–5; Ward, The Child in the City. It is ironic that the 1970s is now looked back to as a good era for some children.
74 R. Johnson, 'Really useful knowledge', in J. Clarke et al. (eds), Working Class Culture (London: Hutchinson in association with CCCS, 1979), pp. 75–102.
75 For example, J. Piaget, Origins of Intelligence in the Child (London: Routledge & Kegan Paul, 1936).
76 M. Knowles, The Modern Practice of Adult Education. From Pedagogy to Andragogy, 2nd ed. (Englewood Cliffs, NJ: Prentice Hall, 1980) and Andragogy in Action: Applying Modern Principles of Adult Education (San Francisco, CA: Jossey Bass, 1984).
77 Alan Gilbey, interviewed by Tom Woodin, 2001.

Chapter 3

1 G. Gregory, 'Working class writing: breaking the long silence', English Magazine, 4 (1985), 16.
2 F. Davis, Yearning for Yesteryear: A Sociology of Nostalgia (New York: Free Press, 1979); C. Lasch, The True and Only Heaven: Progress and its Critics (New York: Norton, 1991).
3 M. Wood, 'Nostalgia or never: you can't go home again', New Society, 7:631 (7 November 1974), 343. A key text was A. Toffler, Future Shock (New York: Random House, 1970); see O. Hatherley, The Ministry of Nostalgia: Consuming Austerity (London: Verso, 2015).
4 For instance, see D. F. Crew, 'Class and community: local research on working class history in four countries', Historische Zeitschrift, 15 (1986), 279–335.

5   S. Dentith and P. Dodd, 'The uses of autobiography', Literature and History, 14:1 (Spring 1988), 18–19. See also C. Waters, 'Autobiography, nostalgia and the changing practices of working class selfhood', in G. K. Behlmer and F. M. Leventhal (eds), Singular Continuities: Tradition, Nostalgia and Identity in Modern Britain (Stanford, CA: Stanford University Press, 2000), pp. 178–95.; R. Bromley, Lost Narratives: Popular Fictions, Politics and Recent History (London: Routledge, 1988).
6   C. Steedman, Landscape for a Good Woman (London: Virago, 1988); S. Yeo, 'Difference, autobiography and history', Literature and History, 14:1 (Spring 1988), 37–47.
7   J. Bourke, Working Class Cultures in Britain 1890–1960: Gender, Class, and Ethnicity (London: Routledge, 1993). See also R. Williams, The Country and the City (London: Hogarth, 1985).
8   J. Bornat, 'The communities of community publishing', Oral History Journal, 20:2 (1992), 23–31.
9   R. Hewison, The Heritage Industry: Britain in a Climate of Decline (London: Methuen, 1987); P. Wright, On Living in an Old Country: The National Past in Contemporary Britain (London: Verso, 1985); R. Samuel, Theatres of Memory (London: Verso, 1994).
10 D. Lowenthal, The Past Is a Foreign Country (Cambridge: Cambridge University Press, 1985).
11 For a critique of austerity, see Hatherley, Ministry of Nostalgia. For more sympathetic accounts, see S. Boym, The Future of Nostalgia (New York: Basic Books, 2001); B. Williamson, 'Living the past differently: historical memory in the North East', in R. Colls and B. Lancaster (eds), Geordies: The Roots of Regionalism (Newcastle: University of Northumbria Press, 2005), pp. 149–68; the journal Memory Studies 3:3 (2010); T. Strangleman, 'Smokestack nostalgia, ruin porn or working-class obituary: the role and meaning of deindustrial representation', International Labor and Working-Class History [Online], 84 (2013), 23–37.
12 B. Jones, 'The uses of nostalgia: autobiography, community publishing and working class neighbourhoods in post-war England', Cultural and Social History, 7:3 (2010), 355–74; B. Jones, The Working Class in Mid-Twentieth Century England: Community, Identity and Social Memory (Manchester: Manchester University Press, 2012).
13 Some good examples include H. Beynon and T. Austin, Master and Servants: Class and Patronage in the Making of a Labour Organisation: The Durham Miners and the English Political Tradition (London: Rivers Oram Press, 1994); Jones, The Working Class in Mid-Twentieth Century England; see also G. Eley, A Crooked Line: From Cultural History to the History of Society (Ann Arbor: University of Michigan Press, 2005).
14 J. Langley, Always a Layman (Brighton: QueenSpark, 1977), pp. 4–5.
15 Ibid., pp. 9–10.
16 S. Manville, Everything Seems Smaller (Brighton: QueenSpark, 1989), p. 17.
17 Ibid., p. 21.
18 J.-M. Strange, Fatherhood and the British Working Class, 1865–1914 (Cambridge: Cambridge University Press, 2015).
19 On this theme, see A. Johnson, This Boy (London: Corgi, 2013).
20 Manville, Everything Seems Smaller, pp. 9–10.
21 T. G. Ashplant, 'Anecdote as narrative resource in working-class life stories: parody, dramatization and sequence', in M. Chamberlain and P. Thompson (eds), Narrative and Genre (London: Routledge, 1998), pp. 99–113.
22 S. Manville, Our Small Corner (Brighton: QueenSpark, 1994), p. 40.
23 Manville, Everything Seems Smaller, pp. 86–98.
24 O. Masterson, The Circle of Life (Brighton: QueenSpark, 1986), p. 16.
25 Ibid., p. 90.

26 See the classic declinist text, N. Postman, *The Disappearance of Childhood* (London: W.H. Allen, 1983); see also UNICEF 'Report Cards' on child well-being since 2007, www.unicef-irc.org/publications/890/, accessed 15 September 2017.
27 D. Noakes, *The Town Beehive* (Brighton: QueenSpark, 1980/1975), pp. 9–10.
28 Steedman, *Landscape for a Good Woman*; S. Rowbotham, '"Shush Mum's Writing": personal narratives by working class women in the early days of British women's history', *Socialist History*, 17 (2000), 14–15.
29 The school leaving age was raised from twelve to fourteen in 1921 and to fifteen in 1947. See T. Woodin, G. McCulloch and S. Cowan, *Secondary Education and the Raising of the School Leaving Age – Coming of Age?* (New York: Palgrave Macmillan, 2013).
30 Langley, *Always a Layman*, p. 21.
31 E. Benson, *To Struggle Is to Live: A Working Class Autobiography*, vol. 1 (Newcastle: People's Publications, 1979).
32 Alfred Dedman, Lighterman, in Various, *Working Lives*, vol. 1 1905–45 (London: Hackney WEA and Centerprise, c.1976), pp. 94–5.
33 On this point, see Bromley, *Lost Narratives*, p. 27.
34 A. Paul, *Hard Work and No Consideration* (Brighton: QueenSpark, 1981), pp. 28–30.
35 Langley, *Always a Layman*, p. 45; Noakes, *The Town Beehive*, p. 87.
36 M. Ward, *One Camp in the Living Room Chair* (Brighton: QueenSpark, 1988), p. 21.
37 Ibid., p. 46.
38 Noakes, *The Town Beehive*, p. 46.
39 Ibid., p. 50.
40 Rowbotham, '"Shush Mum's Writing"', 13.
41 D. Noakes, *Faded Rainbow: Our Married Years* (Brighton: QueenSpark, 1980).
42 Masterson, *The Circle of Life*, pp. 98–9.
43 Ibid., pp. 88–9.
44 Ibid., pp. 68–9. Cf. Waters, 'Autobiography, nostalgia, and the changing practices of working-class selfhood', 187–8 on the difficulty of handling chronological change.
45 Masterson, *The Circle of Life*, p. 74.
46 Ibid., p. 42. See also I. Grosvenor, '"There's no place like home": education and the making of national identity', *History of Education*, 28:3 (1999), 235–50.
47 See also G. Grout, *The Smiling Bakers* (Brighton: QueenSpark, 1992).
48 Paul, *Hard Work and No Consideration*, pp. 15–19.
49 Healey, *Hard Times and Easy Terms and Other Tales by a QueenSpark Cockney* (Brighton: QueenSpark, 1980), pp. 118–19.
50 Ibid., p. 125.
51 Manville, *Our Small Corner*, p. 49.
52 Thanks to Jackie Lewis for this point. M. Hayler and A. Thompson, 'Working with words: active learning in a community writing and publishing group', in J. Mace (ed.), *Literacy, Language and Community Publishing: Essays in Adult Education* (Clevedon: Multilingual Matters, 1995), p. 53.
53 J. Cummins, *The Landlord Cometh* (Brighton: QueenSpark, 1981), p. 13.
54 Ibid., p. 18.
55 Ibid., p. 21.
56 See T. G. Ashplant, *Fractured Loyalties: Masculinity, Class and Politics in Britain, 1900–30* (London: Rivers Oram, 2007).
57 L. Moss, *Live and Learn: A Life and Struggle for Progress* (Brighton: QueenSpark, 1979), p. 12.
58 Ibid., pp. 21–2.
59 Ibid., p. 9.

60   Ibid., p. 12.
61   Ibid., p. 89.
62   Ibid., p. 74.
63   R. Dunn, *Moulsecoomb Days* (Brighton: QueenSpark, 1990), pp. 64–5.
64   Various, *Of Whole Heart Cometh Hope* (London: Age Exchange, 1983), p. 4. See also N. Wilson, *Home in British Working Class Fiction* (Farnham: Ashgate, 2015).
65   See also, P. Graves, *Labour Women: Women in British Working Class Politics, 1918–1939* (Cambridge: Cambridge University Press, 1994).
66   Masterson, *The Circle of Life*, pp. 68–9.
67   Healey, *Hard Times and Easy Terms*, p. 143.
68   Ibid., p. 113.
69   Paul, A., *Poverty, Hardship but Happiness: Those Were the Days 1903–1917* (Brighton: QueenSpark Books, 1981/1974), p. 27.
70   Cf F. Tonnies, *Community and Society* (New York: Harper and Row, 1957).
71   R. Williams, *Politics and Letters: Interviews with New Left Review* (London: NLB, 1979), p. 159.
72   J. Kirk, *The British Working Class in the Twentieth Century: Film, Literature and Television* (Cardiff: University of Wales Press, 2003); *On the Trail of the Working Class* (London: Palgrave Macmillan, 2007).
73   For instance, see R. Williams, *The Country and the City* (London: Hogarth, 1985); B. Jackson, *Working Class Community: Some General Notions Raised by a Series of Studies in Northern England* (London: Routledge, 1968).
74   QueenSpark newspaper, No. 11, November–December 1975. See also A. P. Cohen, *The Symbolic Construction of Community* (London: Tavistock Press, 1985), pp. 103, 108.
75   Huw Beynon, interviewed by Tom Woodin, 1999.
76   Davis, *Yearning for Yesteryear*; Boym, *The Future of Nostalgia*.
77   K. Worpole and B. Masters, 'Introduction', to A. S. Jasper, *A Hoxton Childhood* (London: Centerprise and John Bunting, 1974/1969), p. 6.
78   D. Hall, *Growing Up in Ditchling* (Brighton: QueenSpark, 1985), p. 7.
79   J. Langley, quoted in Various, *Writing* (London: FWWCP, 1978), pp. 163–4.
80   E. P. Thompson, *Customs in Common* (New York: The New Press, 1993).
81   East Bowling History Workshop, *East Bowling Reflections* (Bradford: East Bowling History Workshop, 1980), p. 19.
82   Rowbotham, '"Shush Mum's Writing"', 12.
83   J. Rose, *The Intellectual Life of the British Working Classes* (New Haven, CT: Yale University Press, 2001), p. 341.
84   Jasper, *A Hoxton Childhood*, pp. 127–8.
85   Ibid., p. 78.
86   D. Marsden, 'Jam for tea', *New Society* (10 March 1977), 511.
87   R. E. K. Catterall, 'Jam for tea', *New Society* (24 March 1977), 622.
88   T. Woodin, 'An Evaluation of the Federation of Worker Writers and Community Publishers' (PhD dissertation, University of Manchester, 2002), p. 163. See also Jones, *The Working Class in Mid-Twentieth Century England*, p. 123; Bourke, *Working Class Cultures in Britain 1890–1960*; R. Colls, 'When we lived in communities: working class culture and its critics', in R. Colls and R. Rodger (eds), *Cities of Ideas: Civil Society and Urban Governance in Britain, 1800–2000* (Aldershot: Ashgate, 2004), pp. 283–307; Williamson, 'Living the past differently'.
89   *East Bowling Reflections*, p. 30.
90   H. Forrester, *Twopence to Cross the Mersey* (London: Jonathan Cape, 1974).

91 See Bornat, 'The communities of community publishing', 24 and E. Roberts, *A Woman's Place: An Oral History of Working Class Women 1890–1940* (Oxford: Blackwell, 1994), p. 184.
92 Elsie, 'A couple from Manchester', *Lifetimes*, 1 (1974), p. 24.
93 Paul, *Hard Work and No Consideration*, pp. 43–4.
94 E. Janes Yeo (published as Yeo) and S. Yeo, 'On the uses of "community": from Owenism to the present', in S. Yeo (ed.), *New Views of Co-operation* (London: Routledge, 1988), pp. 229–58.
95 There has been a shift away from analysing the accuracy of 'evidence' to probing the silences, inaccuracies and myths that help to reveal the historical construction of subjectivity. For the former, see T. Lummis, *Listening to History: The Authenticity of Oral Evidence* (London: Hutchinson Education, 1987). For the latter, see Cohen, *The Symbolic Construction of Community*; L. Passerini, *Fascism in Popular Memory: The Cultural Experience of the Turin Working Class* (Cambridge: Cambridge University Press, 1987); A. Portelli, *The Death of Luigi Trastulli and Other Stories: Form and Meaning in Oral History* (Albany: State University of New York Press, 1990).
96 Langley, *Always a Layman*, p. 65.
97 Noakes, *Faded Rainbow*, pp. 29–53.
98 Various, *The Island* (London: Centerprise, 1979); Various, *Backyard Brighton* (Brighton: QueenSpark, 1988); Various, *Backstreet Brighton* (Brighton: QueenSpark, 1989); Various, *St Philip's Marsh, The Story of an Island and its People* (Bristol: Bristol Broadsides, n.d.).
99 *Backyard Brighton*, p. 27.
100 Gladys Amelia Jane Stenning, in Ibid., p. 37.
101 *The Island*, p. 4; see also Jones, *The Working Class in Mid-Twentieth Century England*, chs 3 and 4.
102 Healey, *Hard Times and Easy Terms*, pp. 55–6.
103 QueenSpark Archive, File 40, SB9, Que box e, S. Yeo, 'QueenSpark Books, selection and comment', South East Arts, c.1979.
104 S. Hall and M. Jacques (eds), *The Politics of Thatcherism* (London: Lawrence & Wishart in association with Marxism Today, 1983).
105 Bornat, 'The communities of community publishing'.
106 Masterson, *The Circle of Life*, p. 5; Healey, *Hard Times and Easy Terms*, pp. 29–30; Manville, *Our Small Corner*, pp. 52–4.
107 Brighton Ourstory Project, *Daring Hearts: Lesbian and Gay Lives of 50s and 60s Brighton* (Brighton: QueensSpark and Brighton Ourstory, 1992). See also, A. Thomson, 'History, writing and community publishing', *Oral History Journal*, 20:1 (1992), 23.
108 Lydia Meryll, interviewed by Tom Woodin, 2001.
109 Various, *More Bristol Lives* (Bristol: Bristol Broadsides, 1988).
110 Liverpool 8 Writers Workshop, *19 from 8* (Liverpool: Liverpool 8 Writers Workshop, c.1979); P. Fryer, *Staying Power: The History of Black People in Britain* (London: Pluto, 1984).
111 S. Bourne and E. Bruce, *Aunt Esther's Story* (London: ECOHP, 1995). See also S. Bourne and S. Kyriacou (eds), *On a Ship and a Prayer* (London: Ethnic Community Oral History Project, 1999); M. Barker, *The New Racism: Conservatives and the New Ideology of the Tribe* (London: Junction Books, 1981).
112 *The Island*, p. 42.
113 Noakes, *The Town Beehive*, p. 41.
114 Hall, *Growing Up in Ditchling*, p. 57.
115 Rose, *The Intellectual Life of the British Working Classes*, ch. 10.
116 Ward, *One Camp in the Living Room Chair*, p. 31.

117 Ibid., p. 15.
118 Manville, *Our Small Corner*, p. 35.

Chapter 4

1. P. Goode, 'A beginner reader is not a beginner thinker', in G. Frost and C. Hoy (eds), *Opening Time* (Manchester: Gatehouse, 1985).
2. For other examples, see M. Hamilton, 'Keeping alive alternative visions: ABE in the UK', in J. P. Hautecoeur (ed.), *ALPHA97: Basic Education and Institutional Environments* (Hamburg: UNESCO Institute for Education Hamburg, 1997), pp. 131–50; M. Hamilton, *Literacy and the Politics of Representation* (Abingdon: Routledge, 2012).
3. Editorial, 'As we see it', *Write First Time*, 4:2 (October 1978), 7.
4. Maureen Cooper, interviewed by Tom Woodin, 2000.
5. J. Anderson, 'Why I write poetry', in Various, *Once I Was a Washing Machine* (Brighton: FWWCP, 1989), p. 84.
6. J. Byrnes, *Never in a Loving Way* (Manchester: Gatehouse, 1994/1977), p. 2.
7. Ibid., pp. 5, 9. See also Anonymous, *Jackie's Story* (London: Centerprise, 1984), discussed in chapter 2.
8. Byrnes, *Never in a Loving Way*, p. 21.
9. Ibid., p. 31.
10. Sue Torr, quoted in Gatehouse, *Book List* (Manchester: Gatehouse, 1996); see S. Richardson, 'Working class women writers – in and out of the Fed', in D. Morley et al., *The Republic of Letters* (Philadelphia, PA: New City Community Press/Syracuse University Press, 2009), pp. 208–9.
11. J. Mace, *Working with Words: Literacy beyond School* (London: Writers and Readers Co-operative in association with Chameleon, 1979) and *Talking about Literacy* (London: Routledge, 1992); B. Street, *Literacy in Theory and Practice* (Cambridge: Cambridge University Press, 1984).
12. Mine work was an alternative to conscription from 1943–8; 'Bevin boy' is a reference to Ernest Bevin, Minister of Labour and National Service 1940–5.
13. Alan, *A Good Life* (Manchester: Gatehouse, 1996/1977), pp. 9–12.
14. 'You and the law', *WFT*, 1:1 (April 1975). The Social Contract was introduced by Harold Wilson's government in the early 1970s to encourage wage restraint and collaboration with the trade unions.
15. R. Carson, 'I know what's going on', *Write First Time*, 6:4 (November 1981), 1.
16. J. Britton et al., *The Development of Writing Abilities 11–18* (London: Macmillan, 1975).
17. WFT Archive, Ruskin College (hereafter WFT Archive), 'Application to ALBSU for grant-aid for a Special Development Project: a Residential Summer School on Writing Development 1984'.
18. General accounts include K. O. Morgan, *Britain Since 1945: The People's Peace* (Oxford: Oxford University Press, 2001); A. Marwick, *British History Since 1945* (Harmondsworth: Penguin, 1990).
19. The Adult Literacy Unit later became the Adult Literacy and Basic Skills Unit and later the Basic Skills Agency.
20. C. Fearnley, 'Mrs Thatcher', *Write First Time*, 7:3, November 1982, p. 1.
21. See discussion in Mace, *Working with Words*.
22. W. Shelton, quoted in S. Freeman, 'Write First Time "getting it wrong"', *Sunday Times* (1 May 1983), p. 5.
23. WFT Archive, WFT Minutes, 7 May 1983.

24 WFT Archive, A. Wells letters to WFT, 21 March 1983 and 7 January 1985.
25 WFT Archive, WFT Minutes, 2 July 1983; Colin Gerrard letter to WFT, 12 March 1984; John Taylor to Colin Gerrard, 7 June 1983.
26 Freeman, 'Write First Time "getting it wrong"'.
27 WFT Archive, Alan Wells letter to WFT, 7 January 1985.
28 Quoted in J. Wallis, 'You can't write until you can spell! Attitudes to writing amongst adult basic education students', in J. Mace (ed.), *Literacy, Language and Community Publishing: Essays in Adult Education* (Clevedon: Multilingual Matters, 1995), p. 66.
29 R. O'Rourke and J. Mace, *Versions and Variety: A Report on Student Writing and Publishing in Adult Literacy Education* (London: Leverhulme Trust, 1992).
30 C. Curley, *The Cardigan* (Manchester: Gatehouse, 1994).
31 Thanks to Joan Woodin for pointing this out.
32 Based on personal memory.
33 G. Conway, *My New World* (Manchester: Gatehouse, 1998); C. Carrington, *The Body Builder* (Manchester: Gatehouse, 1998).
34 Carrington, *The Body Builder*, p. 19.
35 For instance, K. Akter, *Oceans Apart* (Manchester: Gatehouse, 1998).
36 S. Fitzpatrick, *Working Around Words: An Account of Editorial Work for Two Gatehouse Books* (Manchester: Gatehouse, 1988), pp. 1–22; Stella Fitzpatrick interviewed by Tom Woodin, 2001.
37 'William', in Various, *Just Lately I Realise* (Manchester: Gatehouse, 1985), pp. 42–6.
38 See also I. Schwab and J. Stone, *Language, Writing and Publishing Work with Afro-Caribbean Students* (London: Hackney Reading Centre, 1985); J. Craven and F. Jackson, *Versions* (Manchester: Manchester Education Committee, 1987); see also Chapter 2.
39 WFT Archive, WFT, Funding application to the ALU, 12 June 1978; WFT Minutes, 24 April 1976. On reactions within the FWWCP, see S. Gardener's draft for the Republic of Letters, 'Draft for Minority Press book on worker writers'.
40 K. Higgins, *The Seed Is Me* (London: WFT, 1982).
41 H. Walsh, 'My Dad', in Gatehouse, *Working Lives: The Experiences of Fifteen Workers, from the 40s to the Present Day* (Manchester: Gatehouse, 1997), pp. 90–3.

Chapter 5

1 R. Allinson, review of *Union Street*, *Voices*, 28 (Spring 1983), 28–9; A. Cox, review of *Union Street*, *Voices*, 28 (Spring 1983), 29–30.
2 L. Thompson, *Just a Cotchell: Tales from a Dockland's Childhood and Beyond* (London: Basement, 1987).
3 Ibid., pp. 23–4.
4 For a celebrated example, see J. Braine, *Room at the Top* (London: Eyre & Spottiswoode, 1957).
5 A. Thickett, *Deckhand, West Pier* (Brighton: QueenSpark, 1993), pp. 31–2. See also L. Sitzia and A. Thickett, *Seeking the Enemy* (London: Working Press, 2002).
6 Thickett, *Deckhand, West Pier*, pp. 17–18.
7 Ibid., p. 19.
8 Jimmy McGovern, interviewed by Tom Woodin, 2001.
9 E. Barrett, 'I fought Norman Snow', in Various, *Writing* (London: FWWCP, 1978), p. 220.
10 Ibid., p. 219.
11 J. Archer, 'The collector', *Fed News*, 4 (April 1990), 9–10.

12 Ibid.
13 R. Crofts, 'Turning the tables', *Fed News*, 6 (February 1991).
14 B. Shane, 'Another kind of Union', in Various, *Voices of Scotland Road and Nearby* (Liverpool: Scotland Road Writers' Workshop, c.1978).
15 Tower Hamlets Worker Writers Group, *No Dawn in Poplar* (London: THAP, 1980), front cover.
16 P. Dallimore, Knowle West Writing Group, *Shush Mum's Writing* (Bristol: Bristol Broadsides, 1978).
17 G. McGee, 'Empire day', in G. McGee, *Showtin' an Bawlin'* (London: THAP, 1982).
18 Gladys reading a version can be seen at www.youtube.com/watch?v=vzuJHwDx-PYo, accessed 15 April 2017.
19 P. Whittingham, 'An unemployed steelworker in the middle of a zebra crossing stealing a diamond', in Various, *Once I Was a Washing Machine* (Brighton: FWWCP, 1989), p. 3.
20 S. Ashworth, *A Matter of Fat* (Manchester: Commonword, 1991); C. Staincliffe, *Looking for Trouble* (Manchester: Commonword, 1994); M. Duff, *Lowlife* (Manchester: Commonword, 2000); D. Evans, *A Touch of the Sun* (Manchester: Commonword, 2005); for recent work, see www.cultureword.org.uk/, accessed 20 January 2017.
21 K. Worpole, 'The politics of writing', *Radical Education*, 12 (Spring 1979), 8.
22 Jimmy McGovern, interviewed by Tom Woodin, 2001. See also Chapter 10.
23 R. Gwilt, 'Voices', in *Writing* (London: FWWCP, 1978), p. 206.
24 FWWCP Archive, Minutes of FWWCP Executive Committee, 4 November 1978.
25 Worpole, 'Afterword', in *Writing* (London: FWWCP, 1978), pp. 244–5.
26 I. Haywood, *Working Class Fiction from Chartism to Trainspotting* (Plymouth: Northcote House in association with the British Council, 1997); J. Zandy, *Hands: Physical Labor, Class, and Cultural Work* (New Brunswick, NJ: Rutgers University Press, 2004).
27 R. Williams, *Marxism and Literature* (Oxford: Oxford University Press, 1977), pp. 43–54.
28 S. Manville, *Our Small Corner* (Brighton: QueenSpark, 1994), p. 14. See also U. Howard, *Literacy and the Practice of Writing in the 19th Century: A Strange Blossoming of Spirit* (Leicester: NIACE, 2012), p. 121.
29 D. Hall, *Growing Up in Ditchling* (Brighton: QueenSpark, 1985), p. 8; M. Ward, *One Camp in the Living Room Chair* (Brighton: QueenSpark, 1988), pp. 21–2; S. Manville, *Everything Seems Smaller* (Brighton: QueenSpark, 1989), pp. 79–80.
30 J. Bornat, presentation in Nottingham, 'The myth of community', 27 January 1991.
31 Cf. P. Hitchcock, *Working-Class Fiction in Theory and Practice: A Reading of Alan Sillitoe* (Ann Arbor, MI: UMI Research Press, 1989), p. 44.
32 R. Mills, 'Through the mangle', *Voices*, 31 (Autumn 1984), 1.
33 A. Thomson, 'Community publishing. The *Republic of Letters* revisited', *Adults Learning*, 2:1 (September 1990), 15–16.
34 Keith Birch, interviewed by Tom Woodin, 2000.
35 See also S. Fitzpatrick, 'Sailing out from safe harbours', in J. Mace (ed.), *Literacy, Language and Community Publishing: Essays in Adult Education* (Clevedon: Multilingual Matters, 1995).
36 J. Smythe, *Come and Get Me: Poems by Joe Smythe* (Manchester: Commonword, 1979); J. Smythe, *Liberation Soldier* (Manchester: Commonword, 1986).
37 N. Coles and J. Zandy (eds), *American Working Class Literature: An Anthology* (Oxford: Oxford University Press, 2007).
38 See Manville, *Our Small Corner*, p. 9.

39 K. Worpole, *Local Publishing and Local Culture: An Account of the Centerprise Publishing Project 1972–1977* (London: Centerprise, 1977), p. 6.
40 Various, *The Island: The Life and Death of an East London Community 1870–1970* (London: Centerprise, 1979), p. 3.
41 Amber, the film and photography group, had similar debates, Richard Grassick and Sirrka-Liisa Konttinen interviewed by Tom Woodin, 2001.
42 Lydia Meryll, interviewed by Tom Woodin, 2001.
43 Pam Schweitzer interviewed by Tom Woodin, 2001.
44 C. Lynch, 'Worker writer: mantle or manacle?', *Fed News*, 8 (August 1991), 2. Lynch at the time was a literacy organiser and is now a Labour politician in Ireland; see www.ciaranlynch.ie/ accessed 20 January 2017.
45 S. Rowbotham, '"Shush Mum's Writing": personal narratives by working class women in the early days of British women's history', *Socialist History*, 17 (2000), 9.
46 S. Bandali, *Small Accidents: The Autobiography of a Ugandan Asian* (London: Tulse Hill School, 1976), see also Chapter 2.
47 FWWCP Archive, R. Mills, 'Hackney Writers' Workshop lowdown', n.d.
48 J. Kelman, *Some Recent Attacks: Essays Cultural and Political* (Stirling: AK Press, 1992), p. 11.
49 Ibid., p. 14.

Chapter 6

1 M. Hayler and A. Thompson, 'Working with words: active learning in a community writing and publishing group', in J. Mace (ed.), *Literacy, Language and Community Publishing: Essays in Adult Education* (Clevedon: Multilingual Matters, 1995), pp. 41–59; G. McCulloch and T. Woodin (eds), 'Histories of learning in the modern world', special issue of *Oxford Review of Education*, 36:2 (2010).
2 Ken Worpole, interviewed by Gerry Gregory, in G. Gregory, 'Worker writers in the 1970s' (MA thesis, University of London, 1979).
3 G. Gregory, 'Community publishing as self-education', in D. Barton and R. Roz (eds), *Writing in the Community* (Newbury Park, CA: Sage, 1991), pp. 109–42.
4 Ibid., p. 135.
5 S. Hicks, *The Boxer Speaks: Odes and Poems* (London: Basement, 1973). See also C. Searle, *None but Our Words* (Buckingham: Open University Press, 1998), ch. 4.
6 Roger Mills, interviewed by Tom Woodin, 2000.
7 T. Olson, *Silences* (London: Virago, 1980).
8 D. Morley and K. Worpole, *The Republic of Letters: Working Class Writing and Local Publishing* (London: Comedia, 1982), p. 10.
9 Anonymous, *Jackie's Story* (London: Centerprise, 1984), p. 126. See also Chapter 2, pp. 48–50.
10 Ibid., introductory letter.
11 Jack Davitt, interviewed by Tom Woodin, 2001.
12 Fitz Lewis, interviewed by Tom Woodin, 2001.
13 Liz Thompson, interviewed by Tom Woodin, 2001. See also Chapter 5, pp. 94–5.
14 See C. Wright Mills, *The Sociological Imagination* (Harmondsworth: Penguin, 1973/1959).
15 Liz Thompson, interviewed by Tom Woodin, 2001.
16 Ibid.
17 Ibid. See also Man Alive, 'Alright, we'll do it ourselves', BBC, 11 October 1972, www.youtube.com/watch?v=2nxgsvLXKmA, accessed 20 February 2017.

18 Jack Davitt, interviewed by Tom Woodin, 2001.
19 S. Manville, *Our Small Corner* (Brighton: QueenSpark, 1994), pp. 7–8.
20 Eddie Barrett, interviewed by Tom Woodin, 2001. See also W. Benjamin, 'The storyteller', in H. Arendt (ed.), *Illuminations* (New York: Schocken Books, 1968), pp. 83–109.
21 L. Moore, 'The witch in the wardrobe', *Federation*, 1 (1992), 8.
22 K. Ekevall, *Kindling Memories for the Future: Poems and Tributes* (London: London Voices, 1995); see also G. Oxford, 'Thinking of Kay Ekevall', *Federation*, 23 (2002), 22–3.
23 Rick Gwilt, interviewed by Tom Woodin, 2000.
24 Fitz Lewis, interviewed by Tom Woodin, 2001.
25 Roger Mills, interviewed by Tom Woodin, 2000.
26 Alan Gilbey, interviewed by Tom Woodin, 2000.
27 Keith Birch, interviewed by Tom Woodin, 2000.
28 Patricia Duffin, interviewed by Tom Woodin, 2001.
29 Pat Smart, interviewed by Roger Drury, 1995.
30 Fitz Lewis, interviewed by Tom Woodin, 2001.
31 Keith Birch, interviewed by Tom Woodin, 2000; see also J. Mace, *The Give and Take of Writing: Scribes, Literacy and Everyday Life* (Leicester: NIACE, 2002).
32 Keith Birch, interviewed by Tom Woodin, 2000.
33 Eddie Barrett, interviewed by Tom Woodin, 2000.
34 Keith Armstrong, interviewed by Tom Woodin, 2001.
35 Ken Worpole, interviewed by Gerry Gregory, 1979.
36 Alan Gilbey, interviewed by Tom Woodin, 2000; Fitz Lewis, interviewed by Tom Woodin, 2001; Mike Hoy, interviewed by Tom Woodin, 2002.
37 Nick Pollard, interviewed by Tom Woodin, 2001.
38 Keith Birch, interviewed by Tom Woodin, 2000.
39 FWWCP Archive, B. Morrison, 'Report submitted to the Arts Council, December 1979, on the work being done in the field of community arts literature', extract.
40 Pat Smart, interviewed Tom Woodin, 2001. She refers here to the 'Four Marys', which was the comic's most popular feature. The scholarship girl was meant to be an aspirational figure for working-class readers; see M. Gibson, 'What Bunty did next: exploring some of the ways in which the British girls' comic protagonists were revisited and revised in late twentieth-century comics and graphic novels', *Journal of Graphic Novels and Comics*, 1:2 (2010), 127.
41 Pat Smart, interviewed Tom Woodin, 2001.
42 David Evans, interviewed by Tom Woodin, 2000.
43 Ibid.
44 M. Casey, 'A working woman reads history', in Various, *In a Few Words* (Liverpool: Second Chance to Learn Writers Workshop, Liverpool University, 1977–79), back cover.
45 T. Lee, 'Come live with me and be my love', in Various, *Let's Hurry Up and Get This Relationship Over ... So I Can Get on with Decorating the Hallway* (Bristol: Bristol Broadsides, 1987), p. 9.
46 Jack Davitt, interviewed by Tom Woodin, 2001.
47 Rebecca O'Rourke, interviewed by Tom Woodin, 2001.
48 Alan Gilbey, interviewed by Tom Woodin, 2000.
49 David Evans, interviewed by Tom Woodin, 2000.
50 Rebecca O'Rourke, interviewed by Tom Woodin, 2001.
51 B. House and L. Mildiner, *The Gates* (London: Basement and Centerprise, 1974), p. 10, see also, pp. 46–8.

52 Jimmy McGovern, interviewed (email) by Tom Woodin, 2001.
53 Ibid.
54 G. Gregory, 'Working class writing: breaking the long silence', *English Magazine*, 4 (1985), 16.
55 T. Harcup, 'There is no alternative', in B. Franklin and D. Murphy (eds), *Making the Local News* (London: Routledge, 1998), pp. 105–16; T. Harcup, *Never Had it So Good: Poems* (London: Basement, 1974).
56 Jimmy McGovern, interviewed (email) by Tom Woodin, 2001.
57 Ibid.
58 Ibid.
59 Cf. S. Courtman, '"Culture is ordinary": the legacy of the Scottie Road and Liverpool 8 Writers', in M. Murphy and D. Rees-Jones (eds), *Writing Liverpool: Essays and Interviews* (Liverpool: Liverpool University Press, 2007), p. 207.
60 S. Blandford, *Jimmy McGovern* (Manchester: Manchester University Press, 2013).
61 Rebecca O'Rourke, interviewed by Tom Woodin, 2001.
62 Hayler and Thompson, 'Working with words'.
63 On organising, see also B. Jackson, *Working Class Community* (London: Routledge, 1968); J. F. C. Harrison, *Learning and Living, 1790–1960: A Study in the History of the English Adult Education Movement* (London: Routledge & Kegan Paul, 1961), pp. 287–9.
64 Rick Gwilt, interviewed by Tom Woodin, 2000; Keith Birch, interviewed by Tom Woodin, 2000. Cf. R. O'Rourke, *Creative Writing: Education, Culture and Community* (Leicester: NIACE, 2005), p. 79.
65 Keith Birch, interviewed by Tom Woodin, 2000.
66 J. Young, *Getting Ideas* (Connisbrough: Yorkshire Arts Circus, 1984), p. 34, quoted in S. Dentith and P. Dodd, 'The uses of autobiography', *Literature and History*, 14:1 (1988), 10.
67 D. Morley and K. Worpole, 'Writers at work', *New Statesman* (30 April 1982), 19–20. A similar occurrence can be found in J. Allin, 'The oddity in the district', in A. Brighton and L. Morris (eds), *Towards another Picture* (Nottingham: Midland Group, 1977), pp. 209–10. See also Gregory, 'Community publishing as self-education', 128–9.
68 Nick Pollard, interviewed by Tom Woodin, 2001. The Liverpool example was related to me at a conference on multiculturalism and heritage held in Manchester in 2000.
69 Keith Birch, interviewed by Tom Woodin, 2000.
70 Ibid.

Chapter 7

1 K. Worpole, 'A ghostly pavement: the political implications of local working class history', in R. Samuel (ed.), *People's History and Socialist Theory* (London: Routledge & Kegan Paul, 1981), pp. 22–32.
2 T. Blackwell and J. Seabrook, *A World Still to Win: The Reconstruction of the Post-War Working Class* (London: Faber, 1985), p. 89.
3 Q. D. Leavis, *Fiction and the Reading Public* (Harmondsworth: Penguin, 1979/1932).
4 A. Paul, *Hard Work and No Consideration* (Brighton: QueenSpark, 1981).
5 K. Worpole, *Reading by Numbers: Contemporary Publishing & Popular Fiction* (London: Comedia, 1984); Huw Beynon, interviewed by Tom Woodin, 1999.
6 R. Williams, *Politics and Letters: Interviews with New Left Review* (London: NLB, 1979), p.164.

7   QueenSpark newspaper, Spring–Summer 1981. The three books were D. Noakes, *The Town Beehive: A Young Girl's Lot in Brighton* (Brighton: QueenSpark, 1975); D. Noakes, *Faded Rainbow: Our Married Years* (Brighton: QueenSpark, 1980); and G. Noakes, *To Be a Farmer's Boy* (Brighton: QueenSpark, 1977).
8   Stephen Yeo, interviewed by Tom Woodin, 2001.
9   Chris Searle, interviewed by Tom Woodin, September 2000.
10 R. Gray, '"History is what you want to say ..." Publishing people's history: the experience of Peckham People's History Group', *Oral History Journal*, 12:2 (1984), 39.
11 Stephen Yeo, interviewed by Tom Woodin, 2001.
12 Jack Davitt, interviewed by Tom Woodin, 2000.
13 FWWCP Archive, Mike Kearney, 'note 5/7/79'.
14 K. Worpole, 'The hard sell', *Fed News* (5 October 1990), 2–3.
15 Ken Worpole, interviewed by Tom Woodin, 1996.
16 Worpole, 'The hard sell'.
17 Rick Gwilt, interviewed by Tom Woodin, 2000.
18 Sally Flood related this anecdote to the audience at a FWWCP reading, AGM 1991.
19 T. Harcup, 'An insurrection in words: East End voices in the 1970s', *Race & Class*, 51:2 (2009), 3–17.
20 Nick Pollard, interviewed by Tom Woodin, 2001.
21 FWWCP Archive, Mike Kearney, 'Paper 29/6/79'.
22 FWWCP Archive, FWWCP Report 1979.
23 Worpole, 'The hard sell', 2.
24 See Chapter 5.
25 Rick Gwilt, interviewed by Tom Woodin, 2000.
26 Transport Review, 'The people's road', *Transport Review* (20 June 1980), 16.
27 R. Dickinson, *Imprinting the Sticks: The Alternative Press Beyond London* (Aldershot: Arena, 1997); N. Fountain, *Underground: The London Alternative Press 1966–74* (London: Comedia and Routledge, 1988); E. Nelson, *The British Counter Culture, 1966–73* (London: Macmillan, 1989); MPG (Minority Press Group), *Here Is the Other News* (London: MPG, 1980); C. Atton, *Alternative Media* (London: Sage, 2002), p. 14.
28 FWWCP Archive, Ken Worpole, letter to FWWCP, 18 November 1980.
29 ACGB Archive, ACGB62/61, 'Centerprise Bookshop', 'Press release: 10th Anniversary', n.d., c.1981.
30 London Edinburgh Weekend Return Group, *In and Against the State* (London: Pluto, 1980).
31 R. O'Rourke and J. Mace, *Versions and Variety: A Report on Student Writing and Publishing in Adult Literacy Education* (London: Leverhulme Trust, 1992).
32 Rick Gwilt, interviewed by Tom Woodin, 2000.
33 Commonword Archive, Commonword, Report to North West Arts, n.d., c.1986, p. 4.
34 Comedia, 'The alternative press', *Media, Culture & Society*, 6:2 (1984), 95–102; C. Aubrey and C. Landry, 'Breaking cover', *Guardian* (6 September 1980), 14; C. Landry, D. Morley, R. Southwood and P. Wright, *What a Way to Run a Railroad* (London: Comedia, 1985), ch. 9.
35 Commonword Archive, Minutes of Commonword Management Committee, 9 September 1986.
36 Dave Parrish, interviewed by Tom Woodin, 2001.
37 D. Berry, 'Radical book trade turns over a new leaf', *New Statesman* (5 July 1985), 14–15.

38 Alan Gilbey, interviewed by Tom Woodin, 2000.
39 Stephen Yeo, interviewed by Tom Woodin, 2001.
40 Rick Gwilt, interviewed by Tom Woodin, 2000.
41 Dave Parrish, interviewed by Tom Woodin, 2001.
42 This was argued at a marketing training day held by Password in 1998.
43 R. D. Altick, *The English Common Reader* (Chicago, IL: University of Chicago Press, 1983/1957), p. 36.
44 Al Thomson, interviewed by Tom Woodin, 1996. See also ACGB Archive, ACGB/62/93, Federation of Worker Writers, Alistair Niven comments in the *Guardian*, in Federation of Worker Writers and Community Publishers (FWWCP) Development Report, November 1989.
45 MPG, *The Other Secret Service* (London: MPG, 1980).
46 Commonword Archive, Pete Kalu letter to Marc Collett, North West Arts Board, n.d.; Various, *Dim Sum* (Manchester: Commonword, 1997).
47 Personal memory, note from Kadija Sesay (also known as Kadija George) to the author, concerning Rebecca Tagoe's book *Trader* (Manchester: Gatehouse, 1995).
48 A. Lawrie, *The Complete Guide to Business and Strategic Planning* (London: Directory of Social Change, 2001).
49 Bishopsgate Institute, Centerprise Archive, Bernadette Halpin, 'Three Month Report', 4 May 1990.
50 Centerprise Archive, based on a summary of report in Centerprise Annual Report 1997, p. 21.
51 Ibid., p. 21.
52 Centerprise Archive, Centerprise Annual Report 1995.
53 For example, Sir B. McMaster, *Supporting Excellence in the Arts: From Measurement to Judgement* (London: DCMS, 2008).
54 Nick Pollard, interviewed by Tom Woodin, 2001.
55 Dickinson, *Imprinting the Sticks*.
56 N. Osmond, 'What is a market book?', *QueenSpark News* (August 1994).
57 M. Allen, 'Women, "community" and the British Miners' Strike of 1984–85', in S. Rowbotham and S. Linkogle (eds), *Women Resist Globalization: Mobilising for Livelihood and Rights* (London: Zed Books, 2001), pp. 46–69. See also S. Rowbotham, '"Shush Mum's Writing": personal narratives by working class women in the early days of British women's history', *Socialist History*, 17 (2000), 8.
58 Personal memory, took place 1996; see also H. Beynon, A. Cox and R. Hudson, *Digging Up Trouble* (London: Rivers Oram, 2000).
59 See also J. D. H. Downing, *Radical Media: Rebellious Communication and Social Movements* (Thousand Oaks, CA: Sage, 2003).
60 F. Braudel, *Afterthoughts on Material Civilization and Capitalism* (Baltimore, MD: Johns Hopkins University Press, 1979).
61 See E. P. Thompson, 'The moral economy of the English crowd in the eighteenth century', *Past and Present* 50 (1971), 76–136.

Chapter 8

1 Centerprise Archive, Bishopsgate Institute, Centerprise Annual Report 1978, p. 6.
2 P. Freire, *Pedagogy of the Oppressed*, new ed. (Harmondsworth: Penguin, 1990/1970); P. Freire, *Pedagogy of Hope* (New York: Continuum, 1994); P. Freire, *Pedagogy of Freedom* (Lanham, MD: Rowan and Littlefield, 1998).
3 Freire, *Pedagogy of the Oppressed*; P. Freire, 'Education and community involvement',

in P. McLaren (ed.), *Critical Education in the Information Age* (Lanham, MD: Rowan and Littlefield, 1999).

4 H. A. Giroux, *Theory and Resistance in Education* (Westport, CT: Bergin and Garvey, 2001), p. xxix.

5 P. Freire, *Pedagogy in Process* (London: Writers and Readers Co-operative, 1978); I. Shor, *Critical Teaching and Everyday Life* (Montreal: Black Rose Books, 1980); Giroux, *Theory and Resistance in Education*; K. Weiler, 'Freire and a feminist pedagogy of difference', in P. McLaren and C. Lankshear (eds), *Politics of Liberation: Paths from Freire* (London: Routledge, 1994), pp. 12–40; b. hooks, *Teaching to Transgress* (New York: Routledge, 1994).

6 A. Darder, P. B. Marta and R. D. Torres (eds), *The Critical Pedagogy Reader* (London: Routledge, 2017).

7 Ken Worpole, interviewed by Roger Drury, 1996; T. Harcup, 'An insurrection in words: East End voices in the 1970s', *Race & Class*, 51:2 (2009), 3–17.

8 C. Thomas, *Liberating Literacy*, Channel 4, Forum Television, 1990.

9 Freire, 'Education and community involvement'.

10 D. Morley and K. Worpole, *The Republic of Letters: Working Class Writing and Local Publishing* (London: Comedia, 1982).

11 FWWCP archive, Minutes of FWWCP, 1978, n.d.

12 FWWCP archive, FWWCP, Minutes of AGM, Centerprise, 28 January 1978.

13 FWWCP Archive, 'Eamonn', in J. Mace, Paper on writing day, 1980.

14 Based on personal knowledge.

15 See Changing Faces, 'A celebration of John Glynn, 1st August 1957–1st January 2008', www.lancaster.ac.uk/fss/projects/edres/changingfaces/john_glynn_tribute.htm, accessed 25 January 2010.

16 A. Karpf, 'Dear dad, dinner's in the oven, mum's writing sonnets again', *Guardian* (25 July, 1979), p. 11.

17 WFT archive, Ruskin College, WFT, Feedback Notes on Conference, 1977.

18 A. Chapman and J. Mace, article in *Adult Literacy Resources Agency Newsletter*, 11 May 1977, p. 6.

19 WFT, Feedback Notes.

20 S. Gardener (published as Shrapnel), 'No one comes with an empty mind', *ALBSU Newsletter* (3 November 1983), 3.

21 WFT, Feedback Notes.

22 U. Howard, entry in Various, *Paper on the Wind* (Brighton: QueenSpark, 1984), pp. 10–11.

23 Centerprise Archive, Bishopsgate Institute, Centerprise, Annual Report 1978, p. 6.

24 K. Worpole, 'A ghostly pavement: the political implications of local working class history', in R. Samuel (ed.), *People's History and Socialist Theory* (London: Routledge & Kegan Paul, 1981), p. 30.

25 Centerprise, Annual Report 1978.

26 Ken Worpole, interviewed by Gerry Gregory, 1979.

27 K. Worpole, *Local Publishing and Local Culture: An Account of the Centerprise Publishing Project 1972–1977* (London: Centerprise, 1977).

28 On writers' circles, see C. Hilliard, *To Exercise Our Talents: The Democratization of Writing in Britain* (Cambridge, MA: Harvard University Press, 2006).

29 FWWCP Archive, n.d. Setting up and running a writers' workshop.

30 S. Rowbotham, L. Segal and H. Wainwright, *Beyond the Fragments* (London: Merlin, 1979).

31 Stephen Yeo, interviewed by Tom Woodin, 2001.

32 For instance, see B. Morrison, 'Black day for the blue pencil', *Guardian Review* (6 August 2005), 4–6.
33 J. Langley, *Always a Layman* (Brighton: QueenSpark, 1977), p. 66.
34 S. Yeo, 'Whose story? An argument from within current historical practice in Britain', *Journal of Contemporary History*, 21:2 (1986), 259–320.
35 H. Wainwright, *Arguments for a New Left* (Oxford: Blackwell, 1994); L. Meryll, interviewed by Tom Woodin, 2002.
36 See Chapter 7.
37 Maureen Cooper, interviewed by Tom Woodin, 2000.
38 Keith Birch, interviewed by Tom Woodin, 2000; FWWCP Archive, Minutes of FWWCP Executive Committee, 16 November 1985.
39 Keith Birch, interviewed by Tom Woodin, 2000. Writers have continued to meet in Scotland Road since that time.
40 Bishopsgate Institute, Centerprise Archive, Rebecca O'Rourke, 'How we work', October 1983.
41 QueenSpark Archive, Minutes of General Meeting, 29 April 1979; see also C. Waters, 'Autobiography, nostalgia, and the changing practices of working-class selfhood', in G. K. Behlmer and F. M. Leventhal (eds), *Singular Continuities: Tradition, Nostalgia and Identity in Modern Britain* (Stanford, CA: Stanford University Press, 2000), p. 191.
42 A. Stanton, 'Learning from the experience of collective teamwork', in J. Batsleer, C. Cornforth and R. Paton (eds), *Issues in Voluntary and Non-profit Management* (Wokingham: Addison-Wesley, 1991), pp. 95–103.
43 C. Landry, D. Morley, R. Southwood and P. Wright, *What a Way to Run a Railroad* (London: Comedia, 1985).
44 O'Rourke, 'How we work'.
45 Popular Memory Group, 'Popular memory: theory, politics, method', in R. Johnson, *Making Histories* (London: Hutchinson, 1982), 205–52.
46 W. Moss, 'Controlling or empowering? Writing through a scribe in adult basic education', in J. Mace (ed.), *Literacy, Language and Community Publishing: Essays in Adult Education* (Clevedon: Multilingual Matters, 1995), pp. 145–70.
47 QueenSpark Archive, Pauline Jones and Mike Sherred, 'Thoughts about QueenSpark arising from the General Meeting of 11th November 1979'.
48 See P. Dodd, 'Criticism and the autobiographical tradition', in P. Dodd, *Modern Selves: Essays on Modern British and American Autobiography* (London: Frank Cass, 1986), pp. 1–13; Popular Memory Group, 'Popular memory'; J. Freeman, 'The tyranny of structurelessness', *Variant*, 2:20 (2004/1970), 16–19.
49 Jones and Sherred, 'Thoughts about QueenSpark'.
50 M. Hayler and A. Thomson, 'Working with words: active learning in a community writing and publishing group', in J. Mace (ed.), *Literacy, Language and Community Publishing: Essays in Adult Education* (Clevedon: Multilingual Matters, 1995), p. 42.
51 E. Ellsworth, 'Why doesn't this feel empowering? Working through the repressive myths of critical pedagogy', *Harvard Educational Review*, 59:3 (1989), 297–324.
52 FWWCP Archive, R. Mills, Confessions of a Federation worker, 1985.
53 FWWCP Archive, O. Rogers, 1982 Report by Olive Rogers, January 1983.
54 Alan Gilbey, interviewed by Tom Woodin, 2000.
55 Pat Smart, interviewed by Tom Woodin, 2001.
56 *Ibid.*
57 Centerprise Archive, M. Hewitt and R. O'Rourke, 'Centerprise publishing project

report', May 1986; Minutes of FWWCP Executive Committee, 5 September 1981.
58 O'Rourke, 'How we work'.
59 Based on David Evans, interviewed by Tom Woodin, 2000; Eddie Barrett, interviewed by Tom Woodin, 2000; Jimmy McGovern, email interview with Tom Woodin, 2001; B. Blanche and B. Shane, interviewed by Tom Woodin, 2001.
60 Laura Corballis, interviewed by Tom Woodin, 2001.
61 Centerprise Archive, Annual Report 1993.
62 Based on personal experience at Gatehouse and later conversations.
63 Lydia Meryll, interviewed by Tom Woodin, 2002.
64 See https://newhamwriters.wordpress.com/, accessed 20 January 2017.
65 FWWCP Archive, FWWCP Minutes, 3 November 1984; Hayler and Thomson, 'Working with words', p. 54.
66 Al Thomson, interviewed by Tom Woodin, 1996. Tim Diggles interviewed by Tom Woodin, 2001.
67 Based on discussions at Pecket Well College. See also Pecket Well College, 'Forging a common language, sharing the power', in M. Hamilton, D. Barton and R. Ivanic (eds), *Worlds of Literacy* (Clevedon: Multilingual Matters, 1994), pp. 227–36.
68 Pat Smart, interviewed by Tom Woodin, 2001.
69 C. Ross, *Telling It! Our Oral History of Pecket Well College (1985–2014)* (Halifax: Pecket, 2014); M. Hamilton, P. Nugent, N. Pollard and Pecket Learning Community Steering Group, 'Learner voices at Pecket: past and present', *Fine Print*, 37:1 (2014), 15–20.
70 Discussion with Cilla Ross.
71 Eddie Barrett, interviewed by Tom Woodin, 2001; David Evans, interviewed by Tom Woodin, 2000; Jimmy McGovern, interviewed by Tom Woodin, 2001.
72 Keith Birch, interviewed by Tom Woodin, 2000.
73 Worpole, *Local Publishing and Local Culture*.
74 For instance, C. Handy, *The Empty Raincoat: Making Sense of the Future* (London: Random House, 1994).
75 J. Barr, *Liberating Knowledge* (Leicester: NIACE, 1999).
76 Worpole, 'Ghostly pavement', p. 30.
77 R. Mackie, *Literacy and Revolution* (New York: Continuum, 1980).
78 Freire, *Pedagogy of the Oppressed*, p. 29.

Chapter 9

1 J. Smythe, 'Small world', in J. Smythe, *Come and Get Me* (Manchester: Commonword, 1979), p. 4.
2 E. Hobsbawm, 'The making of the working class, 1870–1914', in E. Hobsbawm, *Uncommon People* (London: Weidenfeld and Nicholson, 1999), pp. 76–99; S. Todd, *The People: The Rise and Fall of the Working Class* (London: John Murray, 2015).
3 T. Blackwell and J. Seabrook, *A World Still to Win: The Reconstruction of the Post-War Working Class* (London: Faber, 1985), p. 30.
4 E. Laclau and C. Mouffe, *Hegemony and Socialist Strategy: Towards a Radical Democratic Politics* (London: Verso, 2001); see also E. O. Wright, *Understanding Class* (London: Verso, 2015).
5 S. Hall and M. Jacques (eds), *New Times* (London: Lawrence & Wishart, 1989); E. Laclau, 'Class war and after', *Marxism Today* (April 1987), 30–3; C. Offe, 'New

social movements: challenging the boundaries of institutional politics', *Social Research*, 52:4 (1985), 817–68.
6   A. Gorz, *Farewell to the Working Class* (London: Pluto, 1982); R. Holton and B. Turner, *Max Weber on Economy and Society* (London: Routledge, 1989); J. Pakulski and M. Waters, *The Death of Class* (London: Sage, 1996).
7   E. O. Wright, *Classes* (London: Verso, 1985).
8   C. Steedman, *Landscape for a Good Woman* (London: Virago, 1986).
9   P. Fox, *Class Fictions: Shame and Resistance in the British Working Class Novel, 1890–1945* (London: Duke University Press, 1994); B. Skeggs, *Formations of Class and Gender* (London: Sage, 1997).
10 A. Giddens, *The Consequences of Modernity* (Stanford, CA: Stanford University Press, 1990); U. Beck, *Risk Society* (London: Sage, 1992); G. Marshall, H. Newby, D. Rose and C. Vogler, *Social Class in Modern Britain* (London: Hutchinson, 1988), p. 206.
11 Laclau and Mouffe, *Hegemony and Socialist Strategy*; J. Rutherford, *Identity* (London: Lawrence & Wishart, 1990).
12 Lydia Meryll, interviewed by Tom Woodin, 2001.
13 J. Spence, 'Working class lives and photography', *Fed News*, 2 (1989), 6.
14 FWWCP Archive, R. Mills, 'Confessions of a Fed worker', in FWWCP Annual Report 1985.
15 S. Munt, *Cultural Studies and the Working Class* (London: Cassell, 2000); D. Reay, 'Rethinking social class', *Sociology*, 32:2 (1998), 259–75; Skeggs, *Formations of Class and Gender*; V. Walkerdine, *Growing Up Girl* (Basingstoke: Palgrave, 2001); see also O. Jones, *Chavs: The Demonisation of the Working Class* (London: Verso, 2011); A. Biressi and H. Nunn, *Class and Contemporary British Culture* (Basingstoke: Palgrave Macmillan, 2013).
16 FWWCP Archive, Greg Wilkinson, Discussion paper, 'Worker Writers and Community Publishers – A Federation of Local Groups', May 1976.
17 Rick Gwilt, interviewed by Tom Woodin, 2000.
18 Eddie Barrett, interviewed by Tom Woodin, 2000.
19 The Australian middle-class Fed worker had a similar experience. Al Thomson, interviewed by Tom Woodin, 1996.
20 Scotland Road 83, 'Separatist groups', *Voices*, 30 (Winter 1983/84), 24.
21 FWWCP Archive, cutting, Kath Horseman, interviewed by Sara Gowen, 'Fighting for our own little space', *7 Days: Communist Party Weekly* (19 July 1986), p. 10.
22 Alan Gilbey, interviewed by Tom Woodin, 2000.
23 FWWCP Archive, Minutes of FWWCP Executive Committee, 13 May 1978.
24 FWWCP Archive, Minutes of FWWCP Executive Committee, 2 July 1985.
25 FWWCP Archive, Minutes of FWWCP Executive Committee, 27 July 1985.
26 Ken Worpole, interviewed by Tom Woodin, 1996.
27 See D. Amery, J. Day and S. Taylor, 'Feditorial', *Fed News*, 7 (April 1991), 1; D. Amery et al., 'Feditorial', *Fed News*, 8 (August 1991), 1.
28 Epitomised by the Labour deputy prime minister, John Prescott, denying he was working class.
29 Keith Birch, interviewed by Tom Woodin, 2000.
30 FWWCP Archive, Olive Rogers, 'Final report', 21 July 1984.
31 Huw Beynon interviewed by Tom Woodin, 1999.
32 FWWCP Archive, cutting, R. Gwilt, 'Worker writers lament lost world', *7 Days: Communist Party Weekly* (28 June 1986), p. 10.
33 Information from Nick Pollard, 2000.

34 Bishopsgate Institute, Centerprise Archive, 'Jon', 'Something to think about', Centerprise report, 3 December 1977.
35 Centerprise, 'Introduction', Centerprise Annual Report 1978, p. 5.
36 H. Beynon, 'Alternative and community publishing. Talking blues: life and times in East London', *Head and Hand*, 4 (Spring 1980), 22.
37 FWWCP Archive, FWWCP Minutes, Hulme Library, 22 October 1977. See also R. Bangura, unknown poem, www.youtube.com/watch?v=NaZF1PFZgoE, accessed 15 April 2017.
38 FWWCP Archive, FWWCP Constitution.
39 FWWCP Archive, FWWCP Minutes, 3 December 1977.
40 FWWCP Archive, Minutes of FWWCP Executive Committee, 15 January 1983.
41 S. May and K. Worpole, Press Release, 1981, reprinted in D. Morley and K. Worpole, *The Republic of Letters: Working Class Writing and Local Publishing* (London: Comedia, 1982), p. 15.
42 Patricia Duffin, interviewed by Tom Woodin, 2001.
43 FWWCP Archive, B. O'Connor, Centerprise report in FWWCP Annual Report 1989.
44 See P. Gilroy, *There Ain't No Black in the Union Jack: The Cultural Politics of Race and Nation* (London: Hutchinson, 1987).
45 Commonword Archive, Minutes of Commonword Management Committee, 9 September 1986.
46 Centerprise Archive, Words, Sounds & Power Writers Workshop, Letter/petition, 8 December 1988, commenting on M. Jules, *Wesley, My Only Son* (London: Hackney Reading Centre/Centerprise, 1987). See also FWWCP Archive, Minutes of FWWCP Executive Committee, 27 July 1985.
47 M. Hewitt, 'The invisible hand – working with authors', in FWWCP, *FWWCP Community Publishing Information Sheets, Making Books* (Brighton: FWWCP, 1986), p. 6; P. Wiltshire, *Living and Winning* (London: Hackney Reading Centre/Centerprise, 1985).
48 Centerprise Archive, R. O'Rourke and M. Hewitt, 'Publishing project report', May 1986.
49 A. Thomson, 'The story so far', *Fed News*, 5 (October 1990), 13–14.
50 FWWCP Archive, Minutes of FWWCP Executive Committee, 4 July 1987.
51 FWWCP Archive, Minutes of FWWCP Executive Committee, 17 October 1987. See also L. Sissay, 'Black to black', *Fed News*, 5 (October 1990), 5–6.
52 FWWCP Archive, M. J. Gosney, 'Write up North', c.1988.
53 FWWCP Archive, N. Pollard, 'Black writers day', *FWWCP Newsletter*, n.d., c.1989.
54 FWWCP Archive, L. Hickey, 'How do you stop the self-assured taking over?', *7 Days: Communist Party Weekly* (5 July 1986), p. 10.
55 K. Worpole, 'It's not what you say, it's the way that you say it', *Federation*, 8 (Autumn 1996), 2–5; R. O'Rourke, *Creative Writing: Education, Culture and Community* (Leicester: NIACE, 2005), p. 194.
56 Scotland Road 83, 'Separatist groups', 24.
57 Ibid., 24.
58 Ibid., 25.
59 Eddie Barrett, interviewed by Tom Woodin, 2000.
60 J. Batsleer et al., *Rewriting English: Cultural Politics of Gender and Class* (London: Methuen, 1985), p. 35.
61 L. Thompson, 'Women's writing workshop', *Fed News*, 1 (n.d., c.1989), 4.
62 FWWCP Archive, R. O'Rourke, 'Chair's report', FWWCP Annual Report 1985–86.

63   S. Flood, letter to *Fed News* (6 February 1991).
64   Jimmy McGovern, interviewed by Tom Woodin, 2001.
65   Ibid.
66   See also M. Collins, *The Likes of Us: A Biography of the White Working Class* (London: Granta, 2004).
67   FWWCP Archive, Minutes of FWWCP Executive Committee, 1 September 1986.
68   Jimmy McGovern, interviewed by Tom Woodin, 2001.
69   Fed News, 'Feditorial', *Fed News*, 3 (n.d., c.1990), 1.
70   Patricia Duffin, interviewed by Tom Woodin, 2001.
71   I. Julien, 'Revealing desires', in S. Rowbotham and H. Beynon (eds), *Looking at Class: Film, Television and the Working Class in Britain* (London: Rivers Oram Press, 2000), pp. 173–83; A. Sivanandan, *Communities of Resistance: Writings on Black Struggles for Socialism* (London: Verso, 1990).
72   Federation Training Days, *Fed News*, 11 (August 1992), 6–7.
73   D. Hevey, 'Upright on', *Fed News*, 8 (August 1991), 3–4.
74   Roger Mills, interviewed by Tom Woodin, 2000.
75   Ibid.
76   Nick Pollard, interviewed by Tom Woodin, 2001.
77   FWWCP Archive, Minutes of FWWCP Executive Committee, 18 July 1981.
78   Alan Gilbey, interviewed by Tom Woodin, 2000.
79   Pat Smart, interviewed by Tom Woodin, 2001.
80   'Floyd', Letter to *Fed News*, 2 (n.d., c.1989), 11.
81   Commonword Archive, Steven Waling, 'FWWCP AGM', April 1989.
82   Jimmy McGovern, interviewed by Tom Woodin, 2001.
83   David Evans, interviewed by Tom Woodin, 2000. See also S. Courtman, '"Culture is ordinary": the legacy of the Scottie Road and Liverpool 8 Writers', in M. Murphy and D. Rees-Jones (eds), *Writing Liverpool: Essays and Interviews* (Liverpool: Liverpool University Press, 2007), pp. 194–209.
84   Sarah Richardson, interviewed by Tom Woodin, 2001.
85   Roger Mills, interviewed by Tom Woodin, 2000.
86   See *Federation*, 6 (Autumn 1995); N. Pollard, 'Voices talk, hands write: sustaining community publishing with people with learning difficulties', *Groupwork*, 17:2 (2007), 36–56.
87   Joe Bidder interviewed by Tom Woodin, 2001.
88   R. Sennett and J. Cobb, *The Hidden Injuries of Class* (Cambridge: Cambridge University Press, 1972).
89   D. Campbell, 'On worker writers, workers and writers', *Federation*, 17 (Summer 1999), 8.

Chapter 10

1   Cf. R. O'Rourke, *Creative Writing: Education, Culture and Community* (Leicester: NIACE, 2005), p. 53.
2   FWWCP Archive, Minutes of FWWCP Executive Committee, 9 February 1980.
3   K. Armstrong, 'You will say, no doubt, that "this is not poetry"', in *Worker Writer*, 1 (c.1979), inside front cover.
4   FWWCP Archive, Minutes of FWWCP Executive Committee, 1 February 1980.
5   FWWCP Archive, Minutes of FWWCP Executive Committee, 21 July 1985.
6   FWWCP Archive, Minutes of FWWCP Executive Committee, 16 December 1978.

7   T. Glover, letter, 'Biting the hand that feeds', *Guardian* (21 October 1975), p. 21; K. Worpole, no title, *Guardian* (7 October 1975), p. 16.
8   ACGB Archive, ACGB/62/169, Worker Writers 1978–1982, FWWCP – Sequence of applications and meetings to date, 12 March 1979.
9   Worker Writers 1978–1982, Letter from Charles Osborne to Jane Mace, 19 March 1979.
10 Worker Writers 1978–1982, Report of the hearing by the Literature Finance Committee of the application from the Federation of Worker Writers and Community Publishers, 12 March 1979.
11 This fuelled the resentment of writers, who wrote to regional arts associations 'to ask their national body to stop pissing around'. FWWCP Archive, Minutes of FWWCP Executive Committee, 15 September 1978. The Arts Council also refused to support trade union banners; see J. Ezard, 'Union banners only strange devices', *Guardian* (28 August 1979), p. 3.
12 Worker Writers 1978–1982, Charles Osborne to Jane Mace, 1 December 1978.
13 Worker Writers 1978–1982, Jane Mace to Charles Osborne, 13 June 1979.
14 C. Osborne, *Giving it Away: The Memoirs of an Uncivil Servant* (London: Secker and Warburg, 1986).
15 ACGB Archive, Centerprise Bookshop ACGB62/61, Charles Osborne to Stephen Keynes, 9 April 1973.
16 Worker Writers 1978–1982, Charles Osborne to Rebecca O'Rourke, 14 April 1980.
17 Worker Writers 1978–1982, Greg Wilkinson to Roy Shaw, 14 March 1980.
18 Worker Writers 1978–1982, Charles Osborne to Rebecca O'Rourke, 24 April 1980. See also Rebecca O'Rourke to Charles Osborne, 21 April 1980.
19 Worker Writers 1978–1982, Roy Shaw to Andrew Faulds, 25 June 1980. Shaw was knighted in 1979.
20 Ibid.
21 Worker Writers 1978–1982, Charles Osborne, Handwritten note.
22 Worker Writers 1978–1982, Roy Shaw to Melvyn Bragg, 20 March 1980; see also explanatory letter from Charles Osborne to Roy Shaw, 20 August 1980.
23 M. Bragg, 'Arts Counsel', *Punch* (23 September 1981), 516.
24 Worker Writers 1978–1982, Roy Shaw to Charles Osborne, 12 March 1979; see J. McGuigan, 'The State and Serious Writing. Arts Council Intervention in the English Literary Field' (PhD dissertation, University of Leicester, 1984).
25 Worker Writers 1978–1982, Letter from Arthur Clegg to the Arts Council, 10 May 1979.
26 Worker Writers 1978–1982, Letter from Eric Appleby to Charles Osborne, 8 June 1979.
27 *Morning Star* (10 May 1979); Worker Writers 1978–1982, Eric Robinson to Arts Council, 21 May 1980; Reuben Falber to Roy Shaw, 20 June 1979.
28 Writers and the Arts Council Research Project by Jim McGuigan; J. McGuigan, *Writers and the Arts Council* (London: Arts Council of Great Britain: London, 1981), pp. 96, 103.
29 Ibid., p. 117.
30 Osborne, *Giving it Away*, p. 217.
31 S. Raybould, *The English Universities and Adult Education* (London: WEA, 1951).
32 Worker Writers 1978–1982, Ken Worpole to Roy Shaw, 18 September 1979.
33 Worker Writers 1978–1982, Draft reply from Shaw to Wilkinson, 18 March 1980.

34 Worker Writers 1978–1982, Charles Osborne to Rebecca O'Rourke, 24 April 1980. See also Rebecca O'Rourke to Charles Osborne, 21 April 1980.
35 Worker Writers 1978–1982, Charles Osborne to Rebecca O'Rourke, 24 April 1980.
36 R. Hoggart, 'Sir Roy Shaw obituary', *Guardian* (15 May 2012), www.theguardian.com/culture/2012/may/15/sir-roy-shaw, accessed 10 March 2016.
37 R. Hoggart, talk at conference on 'Literacy is not enough', Manchester Metropolitan University, c.1997.
38 One exception to this group was Raymond Williams, who had previously been involved in the Literature Panel, although he was critical of the Council. R. Williams, 'The Arts Council', *Political Quarterly*, 50:2 (1979), 157–71.
39 Worker Writers 1978–1982, FWWCP – Sequence of applications and meetings to date, 12 March 1979.
40 FWWCP Archive, FWWCP meeting with the Community Arts Panel, Minutes of FWWCP Executive Committee, 6 August 1979; see also 21 March 1980.
41 Email communication with Blake Morrison, 26 November 2015.
42 FWWCP Archive, Blake Morrison, Extract, 'Report submitted to the Arts Council, December 1979, on the Work Being Done in the Field of Community Arts Literature'.
43 Worker Writers 1978–1982, Roy Shaw to Charles Osborne, 15 August 1980; FWWCP, 'Open letter to the Arts Council', in *Voices*, 22 (Autumn 1980), 35–8; Minutes of FWWCP Executive Committee, 10 January 1981.
44 Worker Writers 1978–1982, Josephine Falk to Roy Shaw, 7 February 1983.
45 Worker Writers 1978–1982, Roy Shaw to Josephine Falk and Josephine Falk to Roy Shaw, 7 February 1982.
46 Worker Writers 1978–1982, October 1980, exert from minutes of Literature Panel.
47 Worker Writers 1978–1982, letter to Miss Marsh, 16 December 1980.
48 Worker Writers 1978–1982, Internal memo from Kate Marsh to Charles Osborne and Josephine Falk, 16 February 1980.
49 FWWCP Archive, Ian Bild, Barbara Shane and Ken Worpole to Charles Osborne, 13 January 1980.
50 Worker Writers 1978–1982, David Evans to Kate Marsh, 23 September 1981; Marghanita Laski to David Evans, 6 November 1981; Josephine Falk to Fay Weldon, 14 January 1982.
51 Worker Writers 1978–1982, Olive Rogers to Marghanita Laski, 14 February 1982; see also Olive Rogers to Marghanita Laski, 8 August 1982.
52 Worker Writers 1978–1982, Josephine Falk to Roy Shaw, n.d., responding to a note of 7 February 1982.
53 K. Worpole, 'Who's in the community?', *City Limits* (12–18 March 1982), 51; S. Braden, *Artists and People* (London: Routledge & Kegan Paul, 1978).
54 ACGB Archive, Worker Writers 1978–1982, Marghanita Laski, handwritten note, n.d., c.March 1982.
55 L. Edmunds, The transformation of Olive Rogers, *Daily Telegraph* (3 June 1982), p. 17.
56 J. McGuigan, 'Closed shop, closed minds', *New Statesman* (29 May 1981), 18.
57 Worker Writers 1978–1982, Internal memo from Josephine (Falk) to Kate (Marsh) and Charles (Osborne), 18 December 1980.
58 Worker Writers 1978–1982, Miss Marsh, 16 December 1980. See also Community Publishers and Worker Writers, Interviews for the appointment of a southern development worker for the WWCPs, 1 July 1983.

59 Ibid.
60 ACGB Archive, ACGB/59/149, Writers and the Arts Council Research Project by Jim McGuigan, McGuigan, Writers and the Arts Council, p. 111.
61 The Arts Council of Great Britain became the Arts Council of England in 1994 with separate bodies for Scotland and Wales.
62 ACGB Archive, ACGB/59/188; Correspondence with and papers of Melvyn Bragg, Alistair Niven, A. Niven, National Arts and Media Strategy: Discussion Document on Literature (London: Arts Council, 1991), p. 3.
63 S. Taylor, 'The man from the Council', Fed News, 5 (October 1990), 12; Niven, National Arts and Media Strategy.
64 FWWCP Archive, Tom Woodin to Alistair Niven, 5 December 1995 and Alistair Niven to Tom Woodin, 18 March 1996.
65 V. M. Hughes, Literature Belongs to Everyone. A Report on Widening Access to Literature (London, ACGB, 1991), p. 64.
66 S. Szczelkun, 'Literature Belongs to Everyone, review', Fed News, 9 (December 1991), 10.
67 See A. C. Grayling, 'A question of discrimination', Guardian Review (13 July 2002), pp. 4–6; Sir Brian McMaster, Supporting Excellence in the Arts: From Measurement to Judgement (London: DCMS, 2008).
68 Many voluntary organisations were unable to respond to the need for long-term planning with the demise of the GLC; see J. R. Wolch and E. M. Rocha, 'Planning responses to voluntary sector crises', Nonprofit Management and Leadership, 3:4 (1993), 377–95.
69 Arts Council of England, Appraisal Report. The Federation of Worker Writers and Community Publishers (London: Arts Council of England, 1995), p. 18.
70 Ibid., p. 19.
71 Based on personal memory.
72 C. Landry, The Art of Regeneration: Urban Renewal Through Cultural Activity (Stroud: Comedia, 1996); F. Matarasso, Use or Ornament? The Social Impact of Participation in the Arts (Stroud: Comedia, 1997).
73 P. Kalu, Lick Shot (London: X Press, 1993); I. Benjamin, The Black Press in Britain (Stoke-on-Trent: Trentham Books, 1995).
74 J. Storey, Our Joyce 1917–1939: Her Early Years (London: Virago, 1987); J. Storey, Joyce's Dream: The Post-war Years (London: Virago, 1995).
75 Centerprise Annual Report 1992.
76 C. Newland and K. Sesay, IC3: The Penguin Book of New Black Writing in Britain (Harmondsworth: Penguin, 2000).
77 Discussions and interview with Liz Thompson, 2001.
78 Department for Education and Skills, Skills for Life – the National Strategy for Improving Adult Literacy and Numeracy Skills: Delivering the Vision 2001–2004 (London: DfES, 2001).
79 Voices on the Page, www.nrdc.org.uk/?p=728, accessed 17 March 2016.
80 E. Haythorne, On Earth to Make the Numbers Up (Castleford: Yorkshire Arts Circus, 1988).
81 D. Morley and K. Worpole, The Republic of Letters: Working Class Writing and Local Publishing (London: Comedia, 1982), p. 117.
82 Later the Research Excellence Framework (REF). On the role of academics, see E. Janes Yeo, 'Asa Briggs (1921–2016)', History Workshop Journal, 84:1 (2017), 306–12.
83 Tricia Jenkins, interviewed by Tom Woodin, 2001. See also, from her personal collection of MAWW archive materials, 'Adult Unemployed (Creative Arts) Project', November 1985, p. 6.

84   Ken Worpole, interviewed by Tom Woodin, 1996.
85   J. Perks, *Breaking Through*, Channel 4, 1982.
86   FWWCP Archive, Rebecca O'Rourke, Chair's Report, Annual Report, 1985–86.
87   J. Ward, 'Theatre across generations', *Federation*, 1 (1992), 1–2.
88   Morley and Worpole, *The Republic of Letters*, p. 135.
89   Rebecca O'Rourke, interviewed by Tom Woodin, 2001.
90   Based on personal knowledge and visits to these groups.
91   Based on visits to groups as well as Joe Bidder, interviewed by Tom Woodin, 2001.
92   S. Kyriacou, '"May your children speak well of you, mother tongue": oral history and the ethnic communities', *Oral History Journal*, 21:1 (1993), 75–80; S. Kyriacou, 'Oral history and bi-lingual publishing', in J. Mace (ed.), *Literacy, Language and Community Publishing: Essays in Adult Education* (Clevedon: Multilingual Matters, 1995), pp. 171–83.
93   Based on personal knowledge.
94   Based on discussions and a visit to Youngstown State University, 1999. See Working Class Studies Association, https://wcstudiesassociation.wordpress.com/, accessed 31 January 2016.
95   For instance, Steve Parks from Syracuse University has provided a venue in London to hold the annual event.
96   A. Sachs, *Spring Is Rebellious: Arguments about Cultural Freedom* (Cape Town: Buchu Books, 1990).
97   See, for instance, Ledikasyon Pu Travayer, *Diksyoner Kreol-Angle* (Port Louis: Ledikasyon Pu Travayer, 2004/1985).
98   Cf. Philip Pullman who, in 2016, resigned as patron of the Oxford Literary Festival on these grounds: A. Flood, 'Philip Pullman resigns as Oxford literary festival patron over lack of pay for authors', *Guardian* (14 January 2016), www.theguardian.com/books/2016/jan/14/philip-pullman-resigns-oxford-literary-festival-patron-pay-authors, accessed 16 January 2016.

Conclusion

1   Cf. G. McKay, *Senseless Acts of Beauty* (London: Verso, 1996).
2   R. Walker, 'Instagram helps rekindle a love of poetry and a boom in sales', *Guardian* (7 October 2017), p. 3; in 2017 adverts by Nationwide Building Society and McDonalds both utilised poetry.
3   The History Workshop movement has begun to return to the idea of popular history once again. For example, see History Workshop Online, www.historyworkshop.org.uk/, accessed 20 March 2017. See also the fascinating family history, A. Light, *Common People: The History of an English Family* (London: Penguin, 2014).
4   See, for instance, S. Frith, 'The good, the bad and the indifferent: defending popular culture from the populists', *Diacritics*, 2:4 (1991), 102–15; S. Connor, *Theory and Cultural Value* (Oxford: Blackwell, 1992).
5   See R. Williams, *Problems in Materialism and Culture: Selected Essays* (London: Verso, 1980).
6   Cf. E. P. Thompson, 'Education and Experience', in E. P. Thompson, *The Romantics: England in a Revolutionary Age* (Woodbridge: Merlin, 1997), pp. 4–32; J. Rancière, *The Ignorant Schoolmaster: Five Lessons in Intellectual Emancipation* (Stanford, CA: Stanford University Press, 1991).
7   M. Kass, Bridget O'Connor obituary, www.theguardian.com/books/2010/oct/18/bridget-o-connor-obituary, accessed 25 October 2011; D. Ward, 'Putting down roots: an interview with Levi Tafari', in M. Murphy and D. Rees-Jones (eds),

Writing Liverpool: Essays and Interviews (Liverpool: Liverpool University Press, 2007), esp. p. 255.
8   'Lemn Sissay reads Architecture', www.youtube.com/watch?v=v_Jc6BlW7Qo, accessed 20 March 2017.
9   D. Hevey, *The Creatures Time Forgot: Photography and Disability Imagery* (London: Routledge, 1992).
10 R. Hoggart, *The Way We Live Now* (London: Chatto & Windus, 1995). For a reiteration of his approach, see also ch. 8 of his *An Imagined Life*, vol. 3 (London: Chatto & Windus, 1992).
11 J. Delors, *Learning: The Treasure Within* (Paris: UNESCO, 1996).
12 See T. Woodin, 'Co-operative education, neoliberalism and historical perspectives: the dilemmas of building alternatives', in T. Rudd and I. F. Goodson (eds), *Negotiating Neoliberalism: Developing Alternative Educational Visions* (Rotterdam: Sense Publishers, 2017), 117–28.
13 M. Savage et al., *Social Class in the 21st Century* (London: Pelican, 2015), pp. 114–15; T. Bennett et al., *Culture, Class, Distinction* (Abindgdon: Routledge, 2009).
14 K. de Waal, 'Shut out: where are all the working-class writers?, *Guardian Review*, 10 February 2018, pp. 6–11.
15 R. Hewison, *Cultural Capital: The Rise and Fall of Creative Britain* (London: Verso, 2014), 209–15.
16 C. Smith, *Creative Britain* (London: Faber and Faber, 1998).
17 Sir B. McMaster, *Supporting Excellence in the Arts: From Measurement to Judgement* (London: DCMS, 2008).
18 N. Kirk (ed.), *Social Class and Marxism* (Aldershot: Scolar Press, 1996); A. Biressi and H. Nunn, *Class and Contemporary British Culture* (Basingstoke: Palgrave Macmillan, 2016).
19 T. Woodin. 'Working class education and social change in nineteenth and twentieth century Britain', *History of Education*, 36:4/5 (2007), 483–96.
20 H. Bradley, *Fractured Identities* (Cambridge: Polity, 1997). Theories of 'intersectionality' were a response to the situation of black women, although the concept has a wider applicability; A. Brah and A. Phoenix, 'Ain't I A Woman? Revisiting Intersectionality', *Journal of International Women's Studies*, 5:3 (2004), 75–86.
21 An impressive book in the USA was D. Roedigger, *The Wages of Whiteness* (London: Verso, 1991), but it tended to make a sharp distinction between class and race; see more recently *Class, Race and Marxism* (London: Verso, 2017).
22 J. Pakulski and M. Waters, *The Death of Class* (London: Sage, 1996), p. 2.
23 Interesting recent work includes L. Hanley, *Estates: An Intimate History* (London: Granta, 2008) and *Respectable: The Experience of Class* (London: Allen Lane, 2016); O. Jones, *Chavs: The Demonisation of the Working Class* (London: Verso, 2011); A. McIvor, *Working Lives: Work in Britain since 1945* (London: Palgrave Macmillan, 2013); Sonali Perera makes transnational connections via post-colonial theory in S. Perera, *No Country: Working Class Writing in the Age of Globalisation* (New York: Columbia University Press, 2014); S. Todd, *The People: The Rise and Fall of the Working Class* (London: John Murray, 2015).
24 See Centre for Social Justice, www.centreforsocialjustice.org.uk/about-us/history, accessed 20 December 2016; F. Mount, *Mind the Gap: The New Class Divide in Britain* (London: Short Books, 2004); P. Blond, *Red Tory: How the Left and Right Have Broken Britain and How We Can Fix It* (London: Faber, 2010).
25 Cf. R. D. Putnam, *Bowling Alone: The Collapse and Revival of American Community* (New York:

Touchstone, 2001); T. Skocpol, *Diminished Democracy: From Membership to Management in American Civic Life* (Norman: University of Oklahoma Press, 2003).
26 J. Schumpeter, *Capitalism, Socialism and Democracy*, 5th edn. (London: Routledge, 1976).
27 J. Meek, *Private Island* (London: Verso, 2014).
28 T. Woodin, D. Crook and V. Carpentier, *Community and Mutual Ownership – A Historical Review* (York: Joseph Rowntree Foundation, 2010); see also H. Wainwright with M. Little, *Public Service Reform ... but Not as We Know It! A Story of How Democracy Can Make Public Services Genuinely Efficient* (Hove: Picnic, 2009).
29 T. Woodin, 'Co-operative schools: building communities in the twenty first century', Forum, 54:2 (2012), 327–39; T. Woodin (ed.), *Co-operation, Learning and Co-operative Values* (London: Routledge, 2015), especially the chapter by S. Yeo, 'The co-operative university: transforming higher education'; J. Winn, 'The co-operative university: labour, property and pedagogy', Power and Education, 7:1 (2015), 39–55; M. Neary and J. Winn, 'Beyond public and private: a model for co-operative higher education', Krisis: Journal for Contemporary Philosophy, 2 (2015), 114–19; T. Woodin, 'Co-operative Approaches to Leading and Learning: Ideas for Innovation from the UK and Beyond', in L. Gornall, B. Thomas and L. Sweetman (eds), *Exploring Consensual Leadership in Higher Education: Co-operation, Collaboration and Partnership* (London: Bloomsbury, forthcoming 2018).
30 A few examples include ATD Fourth World, *The Roles We Play: Recognising the Contribution of People in Poverty* (London: ATD Fourth World, 2014) and entries in P. Block, D. Kasnitz, A. Nishida, and N. Pollard (eds), *Occupying Disability: Critical Approaches to Community, Justice, and Decolonizing Disability* (Netherlands: Springer, 2010). Mainly in the USA, see P. Mathieu, S. Parks and T. Rousculp (eds), *Circulating Communities: The Tactics and Strategies of Community Publishing* (Lanham, MD: Lexington Books, 2012); M. Novak, *Coal Mountain Elementary* (Minneapolis, MN: Coffee House Press, 2009); POOR Magazine, www.poormagazine.org/, accessed 12 January 2017; N. Connolly ed., *Know Your Place: Essays on the Working Class by the Working Class* (Liverpool: Dead Ink Books, 2017); for current information on the Fed, see http://www.thefed.btck.co.uk/ and for QueenSpark Books see http://queensparkbooks.org.uk/.

Bibliography

Archives

Arts Council of Great Britain, Victoria and Albert Museum.
Centerprise Archive, previously partly in author's possession, now with Bishopsgate Institute.
Commonword Archive.
FWWCP Archive, in author's possession.
Gatehouse Archive, in author's possession.
Mass Observation Archive of FWWCP publications.
Merseyside Association of Writers' Workshops (MAWW) (materials in possession of Tricia Jenkins).
QueenSpark Archive, since moved to The Keep, www.thekeep.info/. See also https://queensparkbooks.org.uk/.
Working Class Movement Library Archive, collection of FWWCP material.
Write First Time Archive, Ruskin College.
Yorkshire Arts Circus Archive.

Interviews

Keith Armstrong
Eddie Barrett
Huw Beynon
Joe Bidder
Keith Birch
Maureen Cooper
Laura Corballis
Jack Davitt
Tim Diggles
Patricia Duffin
David Evans
Stella Fitzpatrick
Sue Gardener
Alan Gilbey
Richard Grassick and Sirrka-Liisa Konttinen
Rick Gwilt
John Hardcastle (email)

Mike Hoy
Tricia Jenkins
Anne Johnson
Roger Kitchen
Eva Levin
Fitz Lewis
Jane Mace
Jimmy McGovern (email)
Richard McKeever
Lydia Meryll
Roger Mills
Rebecca O'Rourke
Dave Parrish
Nick Pollard
Sarah Richardson
Olive Rogers
Pam Schweitzer
Chris Searle
Barbara Shane and Barbara Blanche
Michael Simmons
Pat Smart
Liz Thompson
Al Thomson
Ken Worpole
Stephen Yeo

Other interviews

Ken Worpole, interviewed by Gerry Gregory, in G. Gregory, 'Worker Writers'.
Chris Searle, interviewed by Gerry Gregory, in G. Gregory, 'Worker Writers'.
Ken Worpole, interviewed by Roger Drury, 1995.
Pat Smart, interviewed by Roger Drury, 1995.

Official documents

Arts Council of England, *Appraisal Report. The Federation of Worker Writers and Community Publishers* (London: ACE, 1995).
Central Advisory Committee for Education, *Children and Their Primary Schools* (Plowden Report), vol. 1 (London: HMSO, 1967).
Delors, J., *Learning: The Treasure Within* (Paris: UNESCO, 1996).
DfES (Department for Education and Skills), *Skills for Life – The National Strategy for Improving Adult Literacy and Numeracy Skills: Delivering the Vision 2001–2004* (London: DfES, 2001).
Hughes, V. M., *Literature Belongs to Everyone. A Report on Widening Access to Literature* (London: ACGB, 1991).
McMaster, Sir B., *Supporting Excellence in the Arts: From Measurement to Judgement* (London: DCMS, 2008).
Niven, A., *National Arts and Media Studies. Discussion Document on Literature* (London: Arts Council of Great Britain, c.1990).

Radio and TV

Dein, A., *Document: The Fire is in our Hearts*, BBC Radio 4, 20 November 1997.
Fofi. G., *Gofredo Fofi Raconta Danilo Dolci*, Rai 3, Wikiradio, www.radio3.rai.it/dl/radio3/programmi/PublishingBlock-0e9b2d8d-4516–42a0–9719-a67fa50e9d9b-podcast.html, 28 June 2012.
Man Alive, *Alright, we'll do it ourselves*, BBC, 11 October 1972, www.youtube.com/watch?v=2nxgsvLXKmA, accessed 20 February 2017.
Parker, C., *Radio Ballads*, London: BBC, 1958–64; republished by Topic Records, 1999.
Perks, J., *Breaking Through*, Channel 4, 1984.
Thomas, C., *Liberating Literacy*, Channel 4, Forum Television, 1990.

Websites

Bangura, R., unknown poem, www.youtube.com/watch?v=NaZF1PFZgoE, accessed 15 April 2017.
Centre for Social Justice, www.centreforsocialjustice.org.uk/about-us/history, accessed 20 December 2016.
Changing Faces, 'A celebration of John Glynn, 1st August 1957–1st January 2008', www.lancaster.ac.uk/fss/projects/edres/changingfaces/john_glynn_tribute.htm, accessed 25 January 2010.
The Fed: A Network of Writing and Community Publishers, http://www.thefed.btck.co.uk/, accessed 20 January 2017.
History Workshop Online, www.historyworkshop.org.uk/, accessed 20 March 2017.
McGee, G., 'Empire Day', www.youtube.com/watch?v=vzuJHwDxPYo, accessed 15 April 2017.
POOR Magazine, www.poormagazine.org/, accessed 12 January 2017.
QueenSpark Books, https://queensparkbooks.org.uk/, accessed 20 January 2017.
Sissay, L., 'Lemn Sissay reads Architecture', www.youtube.com/watch?v=v_Jc6BlW7Qo, accessed 20 March 2017.
Voices on the Page, www.nrdc.org.uk/?p=728, accessed 17 March 2016.
Working Class Studies Association, https://wcstudiesassociation.wordpress.com/, accessed 31 January 2016.

Newspapers and magazines consulted

Daily Mail
Daily Telegraph
English Magazine
Fed News
Federation Magazine
Financial Times
Guardian
Head and Hand
Liverpool Echo
Morning Star
New Society
Radical Education
7 Days: Communist Party Weekly
Sun

Teaching London Kids
Times Literary Supplement
Transport Review

Cited community publications

Ackerman, J., *The Kids Are Alright* (London: English Centre, 1979).
ATD Fourth World, *The Roles We Play: Recognising the Contribution of People in Poverty* (London: ATD Fourth World, 2014).
Ainley, B., 'Introductory', *Voices*, 1 (1972), 3.
Akter, K., *Oceans Apart* (Manchester: Gatehouse, 1998).
'Alan', *A Good Life* (Manchester: Gatehouse, 1996/1977).
Allinson, R., review of Union Street, *Voices*, 28 (Spring 1983), 28–9.
Amery, D., J. Day, A. Scanlon and S. Taylor, 'Feditorial', *Fed News*, 8 (August 1991), 1.
Amery, D., J. Day and S. Taylor, 'Feditorial', *Fed News*, 7 (April 1991), 1.
Anderson, J., 'Why I write poetry', in Various, *Once I Was a Washing Machine* (Brighton: FWWCP, 1989), p. 84.
Archer, J., 'The collector', *Fed News*, 4 (April 1990), 9–10.
Armstrong, K., 'You will say, no doubt, that "this is not poetry"', *Worker Writer*, 1 (c.1979), inside front cover.
Armstrong, K. and H. Beynon, *Hello, Are You Working? Memories of the Thirties in the North East of England* (Whitley Bay: Strong Words, 1977).
Ashworth, S., *A Matter of Fat* (Manchester: Commonword, 1991).
Balgobin, B., 'The year ticks by', in *As Good As We Make It* (London: Centerprise, 1982), p. 38.
Barnes, R., *Licence to Live* (London: Centerprise, 1974).
Barnes, R., *Coronation Cups and Jam Jars* (London: Centerprise, 1976).
Barrett, E., 'I fought Norman Snow', in Various, *Writing* (London: FWWCP, 1978), pp. 218–20.
Benson, E., *To Struggle Is to Live: A Working Class Autobiography*, vol. 1 (Newcastle: People's Publications, 1979).
Bourne, S. and E. Bruce, *Aunt Esther's Story* (London: ECOHP, 1995).
Bourne, S. and S. Kyriacou (eds), *On a Ship and a Prayer* (London: Ethnic Community Oral History Project, 1999).
Brighton Ourstory Project, *Daring Hearts: Lesbian and Gay Lives of 50s and 60s Brighton* (Brighton: QueensSpark and Brighton Ourstory, 1992).
Byrnes, J., *Never in a Loving Way* (Manchester: Gatehouse, 1994/1977).
Campbell, D., 'On worker writers, workers and writers', *Federation*, 17 (Summer 1999), 8.
Carrington, C., *The Body Builder* (Manchester: Gatehouse, 1998).
Carson, R., 'I know what's going on', *Write First Time*, 6:4 (November 1981), 1.
Casey, M., 'A working woman reads history', in Various, *In a Few Words* (Liverpool: Second Chance to Learn Writers Workshop, Liverpool University, 1977–79).
Conway, G., *My New World* (Manchester: Gatehouse, 1998).
Cox, A., Review of Union Street, *Voices*, 28 (Spring 1983), 29–30.
Crofts, R., 'Turning the tables', *Fed News*, 6 (February 1991).
Cummins, J., *The Landlord Cometh* (Brighton: QueenSpark, 1981).
Curley, C., *The Cardigan* (Manchester: Gatehouse, 1994).
Dallimore, P., 'Shush mum's writing', in Knowle West Writing Group, *Shush Mum's Writing* (Bristol: Bristol Broadsides, 1978).
Dedman, A., Lighterman, in Various, *Working Lives, vol 1 1905-45* (London: Hackney WEA and Centerprise).

Duff, M., *Lowlife* (Manchester: Commonword, 2000).
Dunn, R., *Moulsecoomb Days* (Brighton: QueenSpark, 1990).
East Bowling History Workshop, *East Bowling Reflections* (Bradford: East Bowling History Workshop, 1980).
Ekevall, K., *Kindling Memories for the Future: Poems and Tributes* (London: London Voices, 1995).
El Kssmi, Z., 'Families', in *Our Lives* (London: English Centre, 1979), p. 18.
Elsie, 'A Couple from Manchester', *Lifetimes*, 1 (1974).
Evans, E., *A Touch of the Sun* (Manchester: Commonword, 2005).
Fed News, 'Federation training days', *Fed News*, 11 (August 1992), 6–7.
Fed News, 'Feditorial', *Fed News*, 3 (n.d., c.1990), 1.
Fitzpatrick, S., *Working Around Words: An Account of Editorial Work for Two Gatehouse Books* (Manchester: Gatehouse, 1988).
Flood, S., letter to *Fed News*, 6 (February 1991).
'Floyd', letter to *Fed News*, 2 (n.d., c.1989), 11.
FWWCP, 'Open letter to the Arts Council', in *Voices*, 22 (Autumn 1980), 35–8.
George, P., *Memories* (London: Commonplace, c.1975).
Goode, P., 'A beginner reader is not a beginner thinker', in G. Frost and C. Hoy (eds), *Opening Time* (Manchester: Gatehouse, 1985).
Goode, P., *The Moon on the Window* (Hebden Bridge: Open Township, 1989).
Graves, C., 'Soldier', in Various, *Stepney Words* (London: Centerprise, 1973), p. 68.
Grout, G., *The Smiling Bakers* (Brighton: QueenSpark, 1992).
Gwilt, R., 'Voices', in Various, *Writing* (London: FWWCP, 1978), pp. 205–6.
Hall, D., *Growing Up in Ditchling* (Brighton: QueenSpark, 1985).
Harcup, T., *Never Had it So Good: Poems* (London: Basement, 1974).
Haythorne, E., *On Earth to Make the Numbers Up* (Castleford: Yorkshire Arts Circus, 1988).
Healey, B., *Hard Times and Easy Terms and Other Tales by a QueenSpark Cockney* (Brighton: QueenSpark, 1980).
Hensman, S., *Flood at the Door. Poems* (London: Centerprise, 1979).
Herbert, C., *In the Melting Pot* (London: English Centre/Ebury Teachers' Centre, n.d.).
Hevey, D., 'Upright on', *Fed News*, 8 (August 1991), 3–4.
Hewitt, M., 'The invisible hand – working with authors', in FWWCP, *FWWCP Community Publishing Information Sheets, Making Books* (Brighton: FWWCP, 1986).
Hicks, S., *The Boxer Speaks: Odes and Poems* (London: Basement, 1973).
Higgins, K., *The Seed Is Me* (London: WFT, 1982).
Howard, U., entry in Various, *Paper on the Wind* (Brighton: QueenSpark, 1984), pp. 10–11.
Ibekwe, S., *Teenage Encounters* (London: Centerprise, 1978).
Ing, S., 'Saroeun's Story', in Various, *More Lives* (London: English Centre, 1987), pp. 45–6.
'Jackie' (Anon), *Jackie's Story* (London: Centerprise, 1984).
Jasper, A. S., *A Hoxton Childhood* (London: Centerprise and John Bunting, 1974/1969).
Jules, M., *Wesley, My Only Son* (London: Hackney Reading Centre/Centerprise, 1987).
Kate, 'Kate's poem', in C. Searle (ed.), *Elders* (London: Reality Press, 1973), pp. 6–8.
Kirk, P., untitled poem, in Various, *Stepney Words I & II* (Centerprise: London, 1973), p. 35.
Langley, J., *Always a Layman* (Brighton: QueenSpark, 1977).
Langley, J., extract, in Various, *Writing* (London: FWWCP, 1978).
Ledikasyon Pu Travayer, *Diksyoner Kreol-Angle* (Port Louis: Ledikasyon Pu Travayer, 2004/1985).
Lee, T., 'Come live with me and be my love', in Various, *Let's Hurry Up and Get This Relationship Over ... So I Can Get on with Decorating the Hallway* (Bristol: Bristol Broadsides, 1987), p. 9.
Liverpool 8 Writers Workshop, *19 from 8* (Liverpool: Liverpool 8 Writers Workshop, c.1979).

Lynch, C., 'Worker writer: mantle or manacle?', *Fed News*, 8 (August 1991), 2.
Lyon, M., 'The old school', in Various, *Stepney Words I & II* (London: Centerprise, 1973), p. 20.
McGee, G., 'Empire day', in G. McGee, *Showtin' an Bawlin'* (London: THAP, 1982).
Manville, S., *Everything Seems Smaller* (Brighton: QueenSpark, 1989).
Manville, S., *Our Small Corner* (Brighton: QueenSpark, 1994).
Masterson, O., *The Circle of Life* (Brighton: QueenSpark, 1986).
May, S. and K. Worpole, Press Release, 1981, reprinted in Morley and Worpole, *The Republic of Letters* (London: Comedia, 1982), p. 15.
Mildiner, L. and B. House, *The Gates* (London: Centerprise, 1974).
Mills, R., *A Comprehensive Education* (London: Centerprise, 1978).
Mills, R., 'Through the mangle', *Voices*, 31 (Autumn 1984), 1.
Moore, L., 1992, 'The witch in the wardrobe', *Federation*, 1 (1992), 8.
Moss, L., *Live and Learn: A Life and Struggle for Progress* (Brighton: QueenSpark, 1979).
Noakes, D., *The Town Beehive* (Brighton: QueenSpark, 1980/1975).
Noakes, D., *Faded Rainbow: Our Married Years* (Brighton: QueenSpark, 1980).
Noakes, G., *To Be a Farmer's Boy* (Brighton: QueenSpark, 1977).
Osmond, N., 'What is a market book?', *QueenSpark News* (August 1994).
Oxford, G., 'Thinking of Kay Ekevall', *Federation*, 23 (2002), 22–3.
Patel, M., 'Rare Bengal tiger', in *Our Lives* (London: English Centre, 1979), p. 107.
Paul, A., *Hard Work and No Consideration* (Brighton: QueenSpark, 1981).
Paul, A., *Poverty, Hardship but Happiness: Those Were the Days 1903–1917* (Brighton: QueenSpark Books, 1981/1974).
Porter, R., 'Domino', in *Black Ink* (London: Black Ink, 1982/1978), p. 31.
QueenSpark Rates Book Group, *Brighton on the Rocks* (Brighton: QueenSpark Books, 1983).
Ross, C., *Telling It! Our Oral History of Pecket Well College (1985–2014)* (Halifax: Pecket, 2014).
Ritchens, P., 'Let it flow, Joe!', in Various, *Stepney Words I & II* (London: Centerprise, 1973), p. 2.
Sachs, A., *Spring Is Rebellious: Arguments About Cultural Freedom* (Cape Town: Buchu Books, 1990).
Schling, R. *The Lime Green Mystery: An Oral History of the Centerprise Co-operative* (London: On the Record, 2017),
Schwab, I. and J. Stone, *Language, Writing and Publishing Work with Afro-Caribbean Students* (London: Hackney Reading Centre and City and East London College, 1985).
Scotland Road 83, 'Separatist groups', *Voices*, 30 (Winter 1983/84), 24–5.
Scotland Road Writers Workshop, *Voices of Scotland Road and Nearby* (Liverpool: Scotland Road Writers Workshop, c.1978).
Searle, C. (ed.) *One for Blair: An Anthology of Poems for Young People* (London: One World Books, 1989).
Sissay, L., 'Black to black', *Fed News*, 5 (October 1990), 5–6.
Sitzia, L. and A. Thickett, *Seeking the Enemy* (London: Working Press, 2002).
Smart, P. (ed.), *It's Our World as Well* (Liverpool: FWWCP, 1990).
Smythe, J., *Come and Get Me: Poems by Joe Smythe* (Manchester: Commonword, 1979).
Smythe, J., 'Small World', in J. Smythe, *Come and Get Me* (Manchester: Commonword, 1979), p. 4.
Smythe, J., *Liberation Soldier* (Manchester: Commonword, 1986).
Spence, J., 'Working class lives and photography', *Fed News*, 2 (1989), 6.
Staincliffe, C., *Looking for Trouble* (Manchester: Commonword, 1994).
Strong Words Collective, *But the World Goes on the Same: Changing Times in Durham Pit Villages* (Whitley Bay: Erdesdun, 1979).

Sumal, R., *Back Home* (London: Commonplace, 1981).
Szczelkun, S., 'Literature Belongs to Everyone, review', *Fed News*, 9 (December 1991), 10.
Tagoe, R., *Trader* (Manchester: Gatehouse, 1995).
Taylor, S., 'The man from the Council', *Fed News*, 5 (October 1990), 12.
Thickett, A., *Deckhand, West Pier* (Brighton: QueenSpark, 1993).
Thompson, L., *Just a Cotchell: Tales from a Dockland's Childhood and Beyond* (London: Basement, 1987).
Thompson, L., 'Women's writing workshop', *Fed News*, 1 (n.d., c.1989), p. 4.
Thomson, A., 'The story so far', *Fed News*, 5 (October 1990), 13–14.
Tower Hamlets Worker Writers' Group, *No Dawn in Poplar* (London: THAP, 1980).
Usherwood, V., 'The sun glitters as you look up', in V. Usherwood, *Poems* (London: Centerprise, Hackney, 1974/1972), p. 5.
Various, *Stepney Words* (London: Reality Press, 1971).
Various, *Stepney Words 2* (London: Reality Press, 1971).
Various, *Stepney Words I & II* (London: Centerprise, 1973).
Various, *Working Lives, 1905–45* vol. 1 (London: Hackney WEA and Centerprise, c.1976).
Various, *Bristol as WE Remember It* (Bristol: Bristol Broadsides, 1984/1978).
Various, *The Island* (London: Centerprise, 1979).
Various, *Our Lives* (London: English Centre, 1979).
Various, *Writing* (London: FWWCP, 1978).
Various, *Paper on the Wind* (Brighton: QueenSpark, 1984).
Various, *Just Lately I Realise* (Manchester: Gatehouse, 1985).
Various, *More Bristol Lives* (Bristol: Bristol Broadsides, 1988).
Various, *Backyard Brighton* (Brighton: QueenSpark, 1988).
Various, *Once I Was a Washing Machine* (Brighton: FWWCP, 1989).
Various, *Splash!* (London: Eastside, 1996).
Various, *Dim Sum* (Manchester: Commonword, 1997).
Various, *Stepney Words III: Poetry by East London Schoolchildren* (London: Rich Mix, 2017).
Walsh, H., 'My dad', in Gatehouse, *Working Lives: The Experiences of Fifteen Workers, from the 40s to the Present Day* (Manchester: Gatehouse, 1997), pp. 90–3.
Ward, J., 'Theatre across generations', *Federation*, 1 (1992), 1–2.
Ward, M., *One Camp in the Living Room Chair* (Brighton: QueenSpark, 1988).
Whittingham, P., 'An unemployed steelworker in the middle of a zebra crossing stealing a diamond', in Various, *Once I Was a Washing Machine* (Brighton: FWWCP, 1989), p. 3.
'William', in Various, *Just Lately I Realise* (Manchester: Gatehouse, 1985), pp. 42–6.
Wiltshire, P., *Living and Winning* (London: Hackney Reading Centre/Centerprise, 1985).
Worpole, K., Afterword, *Writing* (London: FWWCP, 1978), 241–7.
Worpole, K., 'The hard sell', *Fed News* (5 October 1990), 2–3.
Worpole, K., 'It's not what you say, it's the way that you say it', *Federation*, 8 (Autumn 1996), 2–5.
Worpole, K. and J. Boler, *Hackney Half-Term Adventure* (London: Centerprise, 1972).
Write First Time, 'You and the law', *Write First Time*, 1:1 (April 1975).
Write First Time Editorial, 'As we see it', *Write First Time*, 4:2 (October 1978), 7.
Young, J., *Getting Ideas* (Connisbrough: Yorkshire Arts Circus, 1984).

Select bibliography

Adonis, A. and S. Pollard, *A Class Act* (London: Hamish Hamilton, 1997).
Alinsky, S. D., *Reveille for Radicals* (New York: Vintage Books, 1969).

Alinsky, S. D., *Rules for Radicals: Practical Primer for Realistic Radicals* (New York: Vintage Books, 1972).

Allen, M., 'Women, "community" and the British Miners' Strike of 1984–85', in S. Rowbotham and S. Linkogle (eds), *Women Resist Globalization: Mobilising for Livelihood and Rights* (London: Zed Books, 2001), pp. 46–69.

Allen, V., Michael McGahey: 'the red and the black', Obituary, *Guardian* (1 February 1999), p. 15.

Altick, R. D., *The English Common Reader* (Chicago, IL: University of Chicago Press, 1983/1957).

Archer, M., *The Reflexive Imperative* (Cambridge: Cambridge University Press, 2012).

Armstrong, M., *Closely Observed Children: The Diary of a Primary Classroom* (London: Writers and Readers in association with Chameleon, 1980).

Armstrong, M., *Children Writing Stories* (Maidenhead: Open University Press, 2006).

Ashplant, T. G., 'Anecdote as narrative resource in working-class life stories: parody, dramatization and sequence', in M. Chamberlain and P. Thompson (eds), *Narrative and Genre* (London: Routledge, 1998), pp. 99–113.

Ashplant, T. G., *Fractured Loyalties: Masculinity, Class and Politics in Britain, 1900–30* (London: Rivers Oram, 2007).

Atton, C., *Alternative Media* (London: SAGE, 2002).

Aubrey, C. and C. Landry, 'Breaking cover', *Guardian* (6 September 1980), p. 14.

Barker, M., *The New Racism: Conservatives and the New Ideology of the Tribe* (London: Junction Books, 1981).

Barr, J., *Liberating Knowledge* (Leicester: NIACE, 1999).

Barton D. and M. Hamilton, *Local Literacies: Reading and Writing in One Community* (London: Routledge, 1998).

Batsleer, J., T. Davies, R. O'Rourke and C. Weedon, *Rewriting English: Cultural Politics of Gender and Class* (London: Methuen, 1985).

Beck, U., *Risk Society* (London: Sage, 1992).

Benjamin, I., *The Black Press in Britain* (Stoke-on-Trent: Trentham Books, 1995).

Benjamin, W., 'The storyteller', in H. Arendt (ed.), *Illuminations* (New York: Schocken Books, 1968), pp. 83–109.

Benjamin, W., 'The work of art in the age of mechanical reproduction', in H. Arendt (ed.), *Illuminations* (New York: Schocken Books, 1968), pp. 217–51.

Benjamin, W., 'The author as producer', in W. Benjamin, *Understanding Brecht* (London: Verso, 1973), pp. 85–103.

Bennett, T., M. Savage, E. Silva, A. Warde, M. Gayo-Cal and D. Wright, *Culture, Class, Distinction* (Abingdon: Routledge, 2009).

Berger, J. and J. Mohr, *A Fortunate Man: The Story of a Country Doctor* (London: Allen Lane, 1967).

Berger, J. and J. Mohr, *The Seventh Man: A Book of Images and Words about the Experience of Migrant Workers in Europe* (Harmondsworth: Penguin, 1975).

Berry, D., 'Radical book trade turns over a new leaf', *New Statesman* (5 July 1985), pp. 14–15.

Bertaux, D., 'Stories as clues to sociological understanding: the bakers of Paris', in P. Thompson and N. Burchardt (eds), *Our Common History: The Transformation of Europe* (London: Pluto, 1982), pp. 92–108.

Beynon, H., 'Alternative and community publishing. Talking blues: life and times in East London', *Head and Hand*, 4 (Spring 1980), 22.

Beynon, H. and T. Austin, *Master and Servants: Class and Patronage in the Making of a Labour Organisation: The Durham Miners and the English Political Tradition* (London: Rivers Oram Press, 1994).

Beynon, H., A. Cox and R. Hudson, *Digging Up Trouble* (London: Rivers Oram, 2000).

Biressi, A. and H. Nunn, *Class and Contemporary British Culture* (Basingstoke: Palgrave Macmillan, 2013).
Blackwell, T. and J. Seabrook, *A World Still to Win: The Reconstruction of the Post-War Working Class* (London: Faber, 1985).
Blandford, S., *Jimmy McGovern* (Manchester: Manchester University Press, 2013).
Block, P., D. Kasnitz, A. Nishida and N. Pollard (eds), *Occupying Disability: Critical Approaches to Community, Justice, and Decolonizing Disability* (Netherlands: Springer, 2010).
Blond, P., *Red Tory: How the Left and Right have Broken Britain and How We Can Fix It* (London: Faber, 2010).
Bornat, J., 'The communities of community publishing', *Oral History Journal*, 20:2 (1992), 23–31.
Bourdieu, P., *Distinction: A Social Critique of the Judgement of Taste* (London: Routledge & Kegan Paul, 1984).
Bourke, J., *Working Class Cultures in Britain 1890–1960: Gender, Class, and Ethnicity* (London: Routledge, 1993).
Bowles, S. and H. Gintis, *Schooling in Capitalist America: Educational Reform and the Contradictions of Economic Life* (New York: Basic Books, 1976).
Boym, S., *The Future of Nostalgia* (New York: Basic Books, 2001).
Braden, S., *Artists and People* (London: Routledge, 1978).
Bradley, H., *Fractured Identities* (Cambridge: Polity, 1997).
Bragg, M., 'Arts Counsel', *Punch* (23 September 1981), 516.
Brah, A. and A. Phoenix, 'Ain't I a woman? Revisiting intersectionality', *Journal of International Women's Studies*, 5:3 (2004), 75–86.
Braine, J., *Room at the Top* (London: Eyre & Spottiswoode, 1957).
Braudel, F., *Afterthoughts on Material Civilization and Capitalism* (Baltimore, MD: Johns Hopkins University Press, 1979).
Brecht, B., 'New ages', in B. Brecht, *Poems 1913–1956* (London: Methuen, 1976).
Breines, W., *Community and Organization in the New Left: 1962–1968: The Great Refusal* (New York: Praeger, 1982).
Britton, J., N. Martin, A. McCleod and H. Rosen, *The Development of Writing Abilities (11–18)* (London: Macmillan, 1975).
Burke, C. and I. Grosvenor, *School* (London: Reaktion, 2008).
Catterall, R. E. K., 'Jam for tea', *New Society* (24 March 1977), 622.
Cavallo, G. and R. Chartier (eds), *A History of Reading in the West* (Cambridge: Polity, 1999).
Chanfrault-Duchet, M.-F., 'Narrative structures, social models and symbolic representation in the life story', in S. B. Gluck and D. Patai (eds), *Women's Words. The Feminist Practice of Oral History* (New York: Routledge, 1991), pp. 77–92.
Chapman, A. and J. Mace, article in *Adult Literacy Resources Agency Newsletter* (11 May 1977), 6.
Clegg, A., *The Excitement of Writing* (London: Chatto & Windus, 1964).
Cohen, A. P., *The Symbolic Construction of Community* (London: Tavistock Press, 1985).
Coles, N., 'Joe Shakespeare: the contemporary British worker-writer movement', in J. Trimbur (ed.), *Popular Literacy: Studies in Cultural Practices and Poetics* (Pittsburgh, PA: University of Pittsburgh Press, 2001), pp. 189–208.
Coles, N. and J. Zandy, *American Working Class Literature: An Anthology* (Oxford: Oxford University Press, 2007).
Collins, M., *The Likes of Us: A Biography of the White Working Class* (London: Granta, 2004).
Colls, R., 'When we lived in communities: working class culture and its critics', in R. Colls and R. Rodger (eds), *Cities of Ideas: Civil Society and Urban Governance in Britain, 1800–2000* (Aldershot: Ashgate, 2004), pp. 283–307.

Comedia, 'The alternative press', *Media, Culture & Society*, 6:2 (1984), 95–102.
Connolly, N., ed., *Know Your Place: Essays on the Working Class by the Working Class* (Liverpool: Dead Ink Books, 2017).
Connor, S., *Theory and Cultural Value* (Oxford: Blackwell, 1992).
Coppetiers, F., 'Arnold Wesker's Centre Fortytwo: a cultural revolution betrayed', *Theatre Quarterly*, 18:1 (1975), 18.
Corrigan, P. and D. Sayer, *The Great Arch: English State Formation as Cultural Revolution* (Oxford: Blackwell, 1985).
Courtman, S., 'Freirian liberation, cultural transaction and writing from "The Working Class and the Spades"', *Society for Caribbean Studies Annual Conference Papers*, 1, 2000, http://community-languages.org.uk/SCS-Papers/, accessed 20 January 2017.
Courtman, S., '"Culture is ordinary": the legacy of the Scottie Road and Liverpool 8 Writers', in M. Murphy and D. Rees-Jones (eds), *Writing Liverpool: Essays and Interviews* (Liverpool: Liverpool University Press, 2007), pp. 194–209.
Cox, B. (ed.), *Literacy Is Not Enough: Essays on the Importance of Reading* (Manchester: Manchester University Press and The Book Trust, 1998).
Cox, C. B. and A. E. Dyson, *The Black Papers on Education* (London: Davis-Poynter, 1971).
Craven, J. and F. Jackson, *Versions* (Manchester: Manchester Education Committee, 1987).
Crew, D. F., 'Class and community: local research on working class history in four countries', *Historische Zeitschrift*, 15 (1986), 279–335.
Darder, A., P. B. Marta and R. D. Torres (eds), *The Critical Pedagogy Reader* (London: Routledge, 2017).
Davis, B., 'Teaching tough kids: Searle and Stepney', *Race and Class*, 51:2 (2009), 18–32.
Davis, F., *Yearning for Yesteryear: A Sociology of Nostalgia* (New York: Free Press, 1979).
Denning, M., *Mechanic Accents: Dime Novels and Working Class Culture in America* (London: Verso, 1998).
Dentith, S. and P. Dodd, 'The uses of autobiography', *Literature and History*, 14:1 (Spring 1988), 4–22.
de Waal, K., 'Shut out: where are all the working-class writers?' *Guardian Review*, 10 February 2018, pp. 6–11.
Dickinson, R., *Imprinting the Sticks: The Alternative Press Beyond London* (Aldershot: Arena, 1997).
Dodd, P., 'Criticism and the autobiographical tradition', in P. Dodd, *Modern Selves: Essays on Modern British and American Autobiography* (London: Frank Cass, 1986), pp. 1–13.
Dorling, D., *Inequality and the 1%* (London: Verso, 2014).
Downing, J. D. H., 'Audiences and readers of alternative media: the absent lure of the virtually unknown', *Media, Culture & Society*, 25:5 (2003), 625–45.
Downing, J. D. H., *Radical Media: Rebellious Communication and Social Movements* (Thousand Oaks, CA: Sage, 2003).
Driscoll, L., *Evading Class in Contemporary British Literature* (New York: Palgrave Macmillan, 2009).
Eagleton, T., *After Theory* (London: Penguin, 2004).
Edmunds, L., The transformation of Olive Rogers, *Daily Telegraph* (3 June 1982), p. 17.
Edwards, J., *Working Class Adult Education in Liverpool: A Radical Approach* (Manchester: The Centre for Adult and Higher Education, the University of Manchester, 1986).
Eley, G., *A Crooked Line: From Cultural History to the History of Society* (Ann Arbor, MI: University of Michigan Press, 2005).
Eliot, T. S., *Notes towards the Definition of Culture* (London: Faber and Faber, 1962/1948).
Ellsworth, E., 'Why doesn't this feel empowering? Working through the repressive myths of critical pedagogy', *Harvard Educational Review*, 59:3 (1989), 297–324.

Evans, G. E., *Spoken History* (London: Faber, 1987).
Ezard, J., 'Union banners only strange devices', *Guardian* (28 August 1979), p. 3.
Fitzpatrick, S., 'Sailing out from safe harbours', in J. Mace (ed.), *Literacy, Language and Community Publishing: Essays in Adult Education* (Clevedon: Multilingual Matters, 1995), pp. 1–22.
Flood, A., 'Philip Pullman resigns as Oxford literary festival patron over lack of pay for authors', *Guardian* (14 January 2016), www.theguardian.com/books/2016/jan/14/philip-pullman-resigns-oxford-literary-festival-patron-pay-authors, accessed 16 January 2016.
Forrester, H., *Twopence to Cross the Mersey* (London: Jonathan Cape, 1974).
Fountain, N., *Underground: The London Alternative Press 1966–74* (London: Comedia and Routledge, 1988).
Fox, P., *Class Fictions: Shame and Resistance in the British Working Class Novel, 1890–1945* (London: Duke University Press, 1994).
Fraser, R., *In Search of a Past: The Manor House, Amnersfield, 1933–1945* (London: Verso, 1984).
Freeman, J., 'The tyranny of structurelessness', *Variant*, 2:20 (1970/2004), 16–19.
Freeman, S., 'Write First Time "getting it wrong"', *Sunday Times* (1 May 1983), p. 5.
Freire, P., *Education for Critical Consciousness, Education as the Practice of Freedom, Extension or Communication* (London: Sheed and Ward, 1973).
Freire, P., *Pedagogy in Process* (London: Writers and Readers Co-operative, 1978).
Freire, P., *Pedagogy of the Oppressed*, new ed. (Harmondsworth: Penguin, 1990/1970).
Freire, P., *Pedagogy of Hope* (New York: Continuum, 1994).
Freire, P., *Pedagogy of Freedom* (Lanham, MD: Rowan and Littlefield, 1998).
Freire, P., 'Education and community involvement', in P. McLaren (ed.), *Critical Education in the Information Age* (Lanham, MD: Rowan and Littlefield, 1999).
Frith, S., 'The good, the bad and the indifferent: defending popular culture from the populists', *Diacritics*, 2:4 (1991), 102–15.
Fryer, P., *Staying Power: The History of Black People in Britain* (London: Pluto, 1984).
Gagnier, R., *Subjectivities: A History of Self-Representation in Britain, 1832–1920* (Oxford: Oxford University Press, 1991).
Gardener, S., (published as Shrapnel) 'They look normal but...', in M. Ben-Tovim and R. J. Kedney (eds), *Aspects of Adult Illiteracy* (Liverpool: Merseyside and District Institute of Adult Education, 1974), pp. 9–13.
Gardener, S., (published as Shrapnel) 'Thoughts on to paper: publications from adult literacy centres, 1974–78', *Adult Education*, 52:2 (1979), 92–7.
Gardener, S., (published as Shrapnel) 'No one comes with an empty mind', *ALBSU Newsletter* (3 November 1983), p. 3.
Gibbons, S., *The London Association for the Teaching of English, 1947–67* (London: Trentham, 2013).
Gibson, M., 'What Bunty did next: exploring some of the ways in which the British girls' comic protagonists were revisited and revised in late twentieth-century comics and graphic novels', *Journal of Graphic Novels and Comics*, 1:2 (2010), 121–35.
Giddens, A., *The Consequences of Modernity* (Stanford, CA: Stanford University Press, 1990).
Giddens, A., *Modernity and Self Identity: Self and Society in the Late Modern Age* (Cambridge: Polity Press, 1991).
Gilroy, P., *There Ain't No Black in the Union Jack: The Cultural Politics of Race and Nation* (London: Hutchinson, 1987).
Giroux, H. A., *Theory and Resistance in Education* (Westport, CT: Bergin and Garvey, 2001).
Giroux, H., *Border Crossings*, 2nd ed. (London: Routledge, 2005).
Glover, T., Biting the hand that feeds letter, *Guardian* (21 October 1975), p. 21.

Goldman, L., *Dons and Workers: Oxford and Adult Education Since 1850* (Oxford: Clarendon Press, 1995).
Gorz, A., *Farewell to the Working Class* (London: Pluto, 1982).
Graves, P., *Labour Women: Women in British Working Class Politics, 1918–1939* (Cambridge: Cambridge University Press, 1994).
Gray, R., '"History is what you want to say…" Publishing people's history: the experience of Peckham People's History Group', *Oral History Journal*, 12:2 (1984), 38–46.
Grayling, A. C., 'A question of discrimination', *Guardian Review* (13 July 2002), pp. 4–6.
Gregory, G., 'Using community-published writing in the classroom', in J. Miller (ed.), *Eccentric Propositions: Essays on Literature and the Curriculum* (London: Routledge & Kegan Paul, 1984), pp. 267–78.
Gregory, G., 'Working class writing: breaking the long silence', *English Magazine*, 4 (Summer 1985), 15–17.
Gregory, G., 'Community publishing as self-education', in D. Barton and R. Ivanic (eds), *Writing in the Community* (Newbury Park, CA: Sage Publications, 1991), pp. 109–42.
Grosvenor, I., '"There's no place like home": education and the making of national identity', *History of Education*, 28:3 (1999), 235–50.
Gwilt, R., 'Worker writers lament lost world', *7 Days: Communist Party Weekly* (28 June 1986), p. 10.
Hall, S., 'Notes on deconstructing the popular', in R. Samuel (ed.), *People's History and Socialist Theory* (London: Routledge & Kegan Paul, 1981), pp. 227–40.
Hall, S. and M. Jacques (eds), *The Politics of Thatcherism* (London: Lawrence & Wishart in association with Marxism Today, 1983).
Hall, S. and M. Jacques (eds), *New Times* (London: Lawrence & Wishart, 1989).
Hamilton, M., 'Keeping alive alternative visions: ABE in the UK', in J. P. Hautecoeur (ed.), *ALPHA97: Basic Education and Institutional Environments* (Hamburg: UNESCO, 1997), pp. 131–50.
Hamilton, M., *Literacy and the Politics of Representation* (Abingdon: Routledge, 2012).
Hamilton, M. E. and Y. Hillier, *The Changing Face of Adult Literacy, Language and Numeracy 1970–2000: A Critical History* (Stoke-on-Trent: Trentham Books, 2006).
Hamilton, M., P. Nugent, N. Pollard and Pecket Learning Community Steering Group, 'Learner voices at Pecket: past and present', *Fine Print*, 37:1 (2014), 15–20.
Handy, C., *The Empty Raincoat: Making Sense of the Future* (London: Random House, 1994).
Hanley, L., *Estates* (London: Granta, 2008).
Hanley, L., *Respectable: The Experience of Class* (London: Allen Lane, 2016).
Harcup, T., 'There is no alternative', in B. Franklin and D. Murphy (eds), *Making the Local News* (London: Routledge, 1998).
Harcup, T., 'An insurrection in words: East End voices in the 1970s', *Race & Class*, 51:2 (2009), 3–17.
Hardcastle, J., '"The dramas themselves": teaching English in London in the 1970s', *Changing English*, 23:2 (2016), 112–27.
Harris, R., 'Disappearing language: fragments and fractures between speech and writing', in J. Mace (ed.), *Literacy, Language and Community Publishing: Essays in Adult Education* (Clevedon: Multilingual Matters, 1995), pp. 118–44.
Harrison, J. F. C., *Learning and Living 1790–1960* (London: Routledge & Kegan Paul, 1961).
Hartog, P. J. with A. H. Langdon, *The Writing of English* (Oxford: Clarendon Press, 1907).
Hatherley, O., *The Ministry of Nostalgia: Consuming Austerity* (London: Verso, 2015).
Hayler, M. and A. Thompson, 'Working with words: active learning in a community writing and publishing group', in J. Mace (ed.), *Language, Literacy and Community Publishing* (Clevedon: Multilingual Matters, 1995), pp. 41–59.

Haywood, I., *Working Class Fiction from Chartism to Trainspotting* (British Council, Plymouth: Northcote House, 1997).

Haywood, I. (ed.), *The Literature of Struggle: An Anthology of Chartist Fiction* (Aldershot: Scolar Press, 1995).

Hevey, D., *The Creatures Time Forgot: Photography and Disability Imagery* (London: Routledge, 1992).

Hewison, R., *Too Much: Art and Society in the Sixties 1960–75* (London: Methuen, 1986).

Hewison, R., *The Heritage Industry: Britain in a Climate of Decline* (London: Methuen, 1987).

Hewison, R., *Culture and Consensus: England, Art and Politics Since 1940* (London: Methuen, 1995).

Hewison, R., *Cultural Capital: The Rise and Fall of Creative Britain* (London: Verso, 2014).

Hickey, L., 'How do you stop the self-assured taking over?', *7 Days: Communist Party Weekly* (5 July 1986), p. 10.

Hill, G., 'Rhymes with rail', *New Manchester Review* (December 1979).

Hilliard, C., *To Exercise Our Talents: The Democratization of Writing in Britain* (Cambridge, MA: Harvard University Press, 2006).

Hindess, B., *The Decline of Working Class Politics* (London: MacGibbon and Kee, 1971).

Hitchcock, P., *Working-Class Fiction in Theory and Practice: A Reading of Alan Sillitoe* (Ann Arbor, MI: UMI Research Press, 1989).

Hobsbawm, E., 'The making of the working class, 1870–1914', in E. Hobsbawm, *Uncommon People* (London: Weidenfeld and Nicholson, 1999), 76–99.

Hobsbawm, E. and T. Ranger, *The Invention of Tradition* (Cambridge: Cambridge University Press, 1983).

Hoggart, R., *The Uses of Literacy: Aspects of Working-Class Life with Special Reference to Publications and Entertainments* (Harmondsworth: Penguin, 1957).

Hoggart, R. 'The crisis of relativism', *New Universities Quarterly*, 35:1 (Winter 1980/81), 21–32.

Hoggart, R., *An Imagined Life*, vol. 3 (London: Chatto & Windus, 1992).

Hoggart, R., *The Way We Live Now* (London: Chatto & Windus, 1995).

Hoggart, R., 'Sir Roy Shaw: obituary', *Guardian* (15 May 2012), www.theguardian.com/culture/2012/may/15/sir-roy-shaw, accessed 10 March 2016.

Holton, R. and B. Turner, *Max Weber on Economy and Society* (London: Routledge, 1989).

hooks, b., *Teaching to Transgress* (New York: Routledge, 1994).

hooks, b., *Remembered Rapture* (London: Women's Press, 1999).

Horseman, K., interviewed by Sara Gowen, 'Fighting for our own little space', *7 Days: Communist Party Weekly* (19 July 1986), p. 10.

Howard, U., *Literacy and the Practice of Writing in the 19th Century: A Strange Blossoming of Spirit* (Leicester: NIACE, 2012).

Hughes, G., *Millstone Grit* (London: Victor Gollancz, 1976).

Ikiugu, M., N. Pollard, A. Cross, M. Willer, J. Everson and J. Stockland, 'Meaning making through occupations and occupational roles: a heuristic study of worker-writer histories', *British Journal of Occupational Therapy*, 75:6 (2012), 289–95.

Isword, P., 'Walcott versus Brathwaite', *Caribbean Quarterly*, 17:3/4 (September–December 1971), 54–7.

Jackson, B., *Working Class Community: Some General Notions Raised by a Series of Studies in Northern England* (London: Routledge, 1968).

Jackson, B. and D. Marsden, *Education and the Working Class* (London: Routledge & Kegan Paul, 1962).

Jackson, K. and B. Ashcroft, 'Adult education and social action', in D. Jones and M. Mayo (eds), *Community Work One* (London: Routledge & Kegan Paul, 1971), pp. 44–65.

Janes Yeo, E., *The Contest for Social Science* (London: Rivers Oram Press, 1996).

Janes Yeo, E. Janes E., 'Asa Briggs (1921–2016)', *History Workshop Journal*, 84:1 (2017), 306–12.

Janes Yeo, E. (published as Yeo) and S. Yeo, 'On the uses of "community": from Owenism to the present', in S. Yeo (ed.), *New Views of Co-operation* (London: Routledge, 1988), pp. 229–58.

Johnson, A., *This Boy* (London: Corgi, 2013).

Johnson, R., 'Really useful knowledge', in J. Clarke et al. (eds), *Working Class Culture* (London: Hutchinson in association with CCCS, 1979), pp. 75–102.

Jones, B., 'The uses of nostalgia: autobiography, community publishing and working class neighbourhoods in post-war England', *Cultural and Social History*, 7:3 (2010), 355–74.

Jones, B., *The Working Class in Mid-Twentieth Century England: Community, Identity and Social Memory* (Manchester: Manchester University Press, 2012).

Jones, O., *Chavs: The Demonisation of the Working Class* (London: Verso, 2011).

Julien, I., 'Revealing desires', in S. Rowbotham and H. Beynon (eds), *Looking at Class: Film, Television and the Working Class in Britain* (London: Rivers Oram Press, 2000), pp. 173–83.

Kalu, P., *Lick Shot* (London: X Press, 1993).

Kass, M., Bridget O'Connor obituary, www.theguardian.com/books/2010/oct/18/bridget-o-connor-obituary, accessed 25 October 2011.

Keddie, N., *Tinker, Tailor: The Myth of Cultural Deprivation* (Harmondsworth: Penguin Books, 1973).

Kelman, J., *Some Recent Attacks: Essays Cultural and Political* (Stirling: AK Press, 1992).

Kirk, J., *The British Working Class in the Twentieth Century: Film, Literature and Television* (Cardiff: University of Wales Press, 2003).

Kirk, J., *Class, Culture and Social Change: On the Trail of the Working Class* (London: Palgrave Macmillan, 2007).

Kirkwood, C., 'Adult education and the concept of community', *Adult Education*, 51:3 (1978), 145–51.

Klaus, G., *The Literature of Labour: Two Hundred Years of Working Class Writing* (Brighton: Harvester, 1985).

Knowles, M., *The Modern Practice of Adult Education: From Pedagogy to Andragogy*, 2nd ed. (Englewood Cliffs, NJ: Prentice Hall, 1980).

Knowles, M., *Andragogy in Action: Applying Modern Principles of Adult Education* (San Francisco, CA: Jossey Bass, 1984).

Konttinen, S.-L., *Byker* (London: Cape, 1983).

Kyriacou, S., '"May your children speak well of you, mother tongue": oral history and the ethnic communities', *Oral History Journal*, 21:1 (1993), 75–80.

Kyriacou, S., 'Oral history and bi-lingual publishing', in J. Mace (ed.), *Language, Literacy and Community Publishing* (Clevedon: Multilingual Matters, 1995), pp. 171–83.

Laclau, E., 'Class war and after', *Marxism Today* (April 1987), 30–3.

Laclau, E. and C. Mouffe, *Hegemony and Socialist Strategy: Towards a Radical Democratic Politics* (London: Verso, 2001).

Laing, S., *Representations of Working Class Life, 1957–1964* (Basingstoke: Macmillan, 1986).

Landry, C., *The Art of Regeneration: Urban Renewal Through Cultural Activity* (Stroud: Comedia, 1996).

Landry, C., D. Morley, R. Southwood and P. Wright, *What a Way to Run a Railroad* (London: Comedia, 1985).

Lasch, C., *The True and Only Heaven: Progress and its Critics* (New York: Norton, 1991).

Lauter, P., 'Working class women's literature: an introduction to study', *Radical Teacher*, 15 (December 1979), 16–26.

Lawrie, A., *The Complete Guide to Business and Strategic Planning* (London: Directory of Social Change, 2001).
Leavis, F. R., *The Great Tradition* (Harmondsworth: Penguin, 1972).
Leavis, Q. D., *Fiction and the Reading Public* (Harmondsworth: Penguin, 1979/1932).
Leeson, B. (ed.), 'Worker writer's special', *Morning Star* (19 October 1978), p. 4.
Light, A., *Common People: The History of an English Family* (London: Penguin, 2014).
Liverpool Echo, Back on the (Scottie) Road, www.liverpoolecho.co.uk/news/liverpool-news/back-on-the-scottie-road-3544551, 9 May 2013, accessed 8 March 2017.
London Edinburgh Weekend Return Group, *In and Against the State* (London: Pluto, 1980).
Lovett, T., 'Community adult education', *Studies in Adult Education*, 3:1 (1971), 2–14.
Lovett, T., *Adult Education, Community Development and the Working Class* (London: Ward Lock, 1975).
Lowe, R., *The Death of Progressive Education: How Teachers Lost Control of the Classroom* (London: Routledge, 2007).
Lowenthal, D., *The Past Is a Foreign Country* (Cambridge: Cambridge University Press, 1985).
Lummis, T., *Listening to History: The Authenticity of Oral Evidence* (London: Hutchinson Education, 1987).
McCulloch, G. and T. Woodin (eds), 'Histories of learning in the modern world', *Oxford Review of Education*, 36:2 (2010), 133–40.
Mace, J., *Working with Words: Literacy beyond School* (London: Writers and Readers Co-operative in association with Chameleon, 1979).
Mace, J., *Talking about Literacy* (London: Routledge, 1992).
Mace, J., *The Give and Take of Writing: Scribes, Literacy and Everyday Life* (Leicester: NIACE, 2002).
Mace, J. (ed.), *Literacy, Language and Community Publishing: Essays in Adult Education* (Clevedon: Multilingual Matters, 1995).
McGuigan, J., 'Closed shop, closed minds', *New Statesman* (29 May 1981), 18.
McGuigan, J., *Writers and the Arts Council* (London: Arts Council of Great Britain, 1981).
McKay, G., *Senseless Acts of Beauty* (London: Verso, 1996).
Mackie, R., *Literacy and Revolution* (New York: Continuum, 1980).
Marsden, D. 'Jam for tea', *New Society* (10 March 1977), p. 511.
Marshall, G., H. Newby, D. Rose and C. Vogler, *Social Class in Modern Britain* (London: Hutchinson, 1988).
Marwick, A., *British History Since 1945* (Harmondsworth: Penguin, 1990).
Matarasso, F., *Use or Ornament? The Social Impact of Participation in the Arts* (Stroud: Comedia, 1997).
Mathieu, P., S. Parks and T. Rousculp (eds), *Circulating Communities: The Tactics and Strategies of Community Publishing* (Lanham, MD: Lexington Books, 2012).
Medway, P., J. Hardcastle, G. Brewis and D. Crook, *English Teachers in a Postwar Democracy: Emerging Choice in London Schools, 1945–1965* (New York: Palgrave Macmillan, 2014).
Meek, J., *Private Island* (London: Verso, 2014).
Miliband, R., 'A state of de-subordination', *British Journal of Sociology*, 29:4 (1978), 399–409.
Morgan, K. O., *Britain Since 1945: The People's Peace* (Oxford: Oxford University Press, 2001).
Morley, D. and K. Worpole, *The Republic of Letters: Working Class Writing and Local Publishing* (London: Comedia, 1982).
Morley, D. and K. Worpole, 'Writers at work', *New Statesman* (30 April 1982), 19–20.
Morley, D., K. Worpole, S. Parks and N. Pollard, *The Republic of Letters: Working Class Writing and Local Publishing* (Philadelphia, PA: New City Community Press/Syracuse University Press, 2009).

Morrison, B., 'Black day for the blue pencil', *Guardian Review* (6 August 2005), pp. 4–6.
Moss, G., *Un/popular Fictions* (London: Virago, 1989).
Moss, W., 'Controlling or empowering? Writing through a scribe in adult basic education', in J. Mace (ed.), *Language, Literacy and Community Publishing* (Clevedon: Multilingual Matters, 1995), pp. 145–70.
Mount, F., *Mind the Gap: The New Class Divide in Britain* (London: Short Books, 2004).
MPG (Minority Press Group), *Here Is the Other News* (London: MPG, 1980).
MPG, *The Other Secret Service* (London: MPG, 1980).
Munt, S., *Cultural Studies and the Working Class* (London: Cassell, 2000).
Neary, M. and J. Winn, 'Beyond public and private: a model for co-operative higher education', *Krisis: Journal for Contemporary Philosophy*, 2 (2015), 114–19.
Nelson, E., *The British Counter Culture, 1966–73* (London: Macmillan, 1989).
Newland, C. and K. Sesay, IC3. *The Penguin Book of New Black Writing in Britain* (Harmondsworth: Penguin, 2000).
Oakley, A., 'Interviewing women: a contradiction in terms', in H. Roberts, *Doing Feminist Research* (London: Routledge, 1981).
Offe, C., 'New social movements: challenging the boundaries of institutional politics', *Social Research*, 52:4 (1985), 817–68.
Olson, T., *Silences* (London: Virago, 1980).
Oral History, 'Review' of Lifetimes, *Oral History Journal*, 4:1 (Spring 1976), 107–8.
O'Rourke, R., *Jumping the Cracks* (London: Virago, 1987).
O'Rourke, R., *Creative Writing: Education, Culture and Community* (Leicester: NIACE, 2005).
O'Rourke, R. and J. Mace, *Versions and Variety: A Report on Student Writing and Publishing in Adult Literacy Education* (London: Leverhulme Trust, 1992).
Osborne, C., *Giving it Away. The Memoirs of an Uncivil Servant* (London: Secker and Warburg, 1986).
Pakulski, J. and M. Waters, *The Death of Class* (London: Sage, 1996).
Parks, S. and N. Pollard, 'The extra-curricular of composition: a dialogue on community publishing', *Community Literacy Journal*, 3:2 (2009), 53–77.
Parks, S. and N. Pollard, 'Emergent strategies for an established field: the role of the worker writer groups in composition and rhetoric', *College Composition and Communication*, 61:3 (2010), 476–509.
Passerini, L., *Fascism in Popular Memory: The Cultural Experience of the Turin Working Class* (Cambridge: Cambridge University Press, 1987).
Patai, D., 'US academics and Third World women: is ethical research possible?', in S. B. Gluck and D. Patai (eds), *Women's Words. The Feminist Practice of Oral History* (New York: Routledge, 1991), pp. 137–53.
Pecket Well College, 'Forging a common language, sharing the power', in M. Hamilton, D. Barton and R. Ivanic (eds), *Worlds of Literacy* (Clevedon: Multilingual Matters, 1994), pp. 227–36.
Perera, S., *No Country: Working Class Writing in the Age of Globalisation* (New York: Columbia University Press, 2014).
Piaget, J., *The Origins of Intelligence in the Child* (London: Routledge & Kegan Paul, 1936).
Pollard, N., 'Voices talk, hands write: sustaining community publishing with people with learning difficulties', *Groupwork*, 17:2 (2007), 36–56.
Pollard, N., 'Occupational narratives, community publishing and worker writing groups: sustaining stories from the margins', *Groupwork*, 20:1 (2010), 9–33.
Pollard, N. and P. Smart, 'Making writing accessible to all: the Federation of Worker Writers and Community Publishers and TheFED', in P. Mathieu, S. Parks and

T. Rousculp (eds), *Circulating Communities: The Tactics and Strategies of Community Publishing* (Lanham, MD: Lexington Books, 2012), pp. 21–34.

Popular Memory Group, 'Popular memory: theory, politics, method', in R. Johnson, G. McLennan, B. Schwarz and D. Sutton, *Making Histories* (London: Hutchinson, 1982), pp. 205–52.

Portelli, A., *The Death of Luigi Trastulli and Other Stories: Form and Meaning in Oral History* (Albany: State University of New York Press, 1990).

Postman, N., *The Disappearance of Childhood* (London: W.H. Allen, 1983).

Putnam, R. D., *Bowling Alone: The Collapse and Revival of American Community* (New York: Touchstone, 2001).

Rancière, J., *The Ignorant Schoolmaster: Five Lessons in Intellectual Emancipation* (Stanford, CA: Stanford University Press, 1991).

Rancière, J., *Proletarian Nights: The Workers' Dream in Nineteenth-Century France* (London: Verso, 2012).

Raybould, S., *The English Universities and Adult Education* (London: WEA, 1951).

Razmig, K., *The Left Hemisphere: Mapping Critical Theory Today* (London: Verso, 2014).

Reay, D., 'Rethinking social class', *Sociology*, 32:2 (1998), 259–75.

Richardson, B., *Tell it Like it Is: How Our Schools Fail Black Children* (Stoke-on-Trent: Trentham, 2007).

Richardson, S., 'Working class women writers – in and out of the Fed', in D. Morley, K. Worpole, S. Parks and N. Pollard, *The Republic of Letters: Working Class Writing and Local Publishing* (Philadelphia, PA: New City Community Press/Syracuse University Press, 2009), pp. 204–12.

Roberts, E., *A Woman's Place: An Oral History of Working Class Women 1890–1940* (Oxford: Blackwell, 1994).

Roberts, I., 'A historical construction of the working class', in H. Beynon and P. Glavanis (eds), *Patterns of Social Inequality: Essays for Richard Brown* (London: Longman, 1999), pp. 78–95.

Roedigger, D., *The Wages of Whiteness* (London: Verso, 1991).

Rogaly, B. and B. Taylor, *Moving Histories of Class and Community: Identity, Place and Belonging in Contemporary England* (London: Palgrave Macmillan, 2009).

Rose, J., *The Intellectual Life of the British Working Classes* (New Haven, CT: Yale University Press, 2001).

Rosen, H., 'Their language and ours', *Teaching London Kids*, 1 (1973), inside front cover–3.

Rosen, H., 'Out there or where the masons went', in M. Hoyles (ed.), *The Politics of Literacy* (London: Writers and Readers Co-operative, 1977), pp. 202–11.

Rowbotham, S., *The Past Is Before Us: Feminism in Action Since the 1960s* (London: Pandora, 1989).

Rowbotham, S., *A Century of Women: The History of Women in Britain and the United States* (London: Penguin, 1999).

Rowbotham, S., 'Travellers in a strange country: responses of working class students to the University Extension Movement 1873–1910', in S. Rowbotham, *Threads Through Time* (London: Penguin, 1999), pp. 260–301.

Rowbotham, S., '"Shush Mum's Writing": personal narratives by working class women in the early days of British women's history', *Socialist History*, 17 (2000), 1–21.

Rowbotham, S. and H. Beynon (eds), *Looking at Class: Film, Television and the Working Class in Britain* (London: Rivers Oram, 2001).

Rowbotham, S., L. Segal and H. Wainwright, *Beyond the Fragments: Feminism and the Making of Socialism* (London: Merlin, 1981).

Rowland, A. *Poetry as Testimony: Witnessing and Memory in Twentieth Century Poems* (Abingdon: Routledge, 2014).

Rutherford, J., *Identity* (London: Lawrence & Wishart, 1990).

Samuel, R., *History Workshop: A Collectanea 1967–1991: Documents, Memoirs, Critique and Cumulative Index to History Workshop Journal* (Oxford: History Workshop, 1991).

Samuel, R., *Theatres of Memory* (London: Verso, 1994).

Samuel, R., E. MacColl and S. Cosgrove, *Theatres of the Left 1880–1935: Workers' Theatre Movements in Britain and America* (London: Routledge & Kegan Paul, 1985).

Savage, M., *Class Analysis and Social Transformation* (Buckingham: Open University Press, 2000).

Savage, M., N. Cunningham, F. Devine, S. Friedman, D. Laurison, L. McKenzie, A. Miles, H. Snee and P. Wakeling, *Social Class in the 21st Century* (London: Pelican, 2015).

Sayer, A., *The Moral Significance of Class* (London: Routledge, 2005).

Schumpeter, J., *Capitalism, Socialism and Democracy*, 5th ed. (London: Routledge, 1976).

Scott, J., 'The evidence of experience', *Critical Inquiry*, 17:4 (Summer 1991), 773–97.

Searle, C., *None But Our Words* (Buckingham: Open University Press, 1998).

Searle, C., 'Life of a seminal black publisher, Glenn Thompson', *Morning Star* (19 September 2001), p. 9.

Sennett, R. and J. Cobb, *The Hidden Injuries of Class* (Cambridge: Cambridge University Press, 1972).

Shayer, D., *The Teaching of English in Schools, 1900–1970* (London: Routledge & Kegan Paul, 1972).

Shor, I., *Critical Teaching and Everyday Life* (Montreal: Black Rose Books, 1980).

Simmons, M. and M. Raleigh., 'Where we've been: a brief history of English teaching, part 1 1920–1970', *English Magazine*, 8 (Autumn 1981), 23–8.

Sinfield, A., *Literature, Politics and Culture in Postwar Britain* (Oxford: Basil Blackwell, 1989).

Sivanandan, A., *Communities of Resistance: Writings on Black Struggles for Socialism* (London: Verso, 1990).

Sked, A. and C. Cook, *Post-War Britain. A Political History* (Harmondsworth: Penguin, 1993).

Skeggs, B., *Formations of Class and Gender* (London: Sage, 1997).

Skeggs, B., *Self, Class, Culture* (London: Routledge, 2004).

Skocpol, T., *Diminished Democracy: From Membership to Management in American Civic Life* (Norman: University of Oklahoma Press, 2003).

Smith, C., *Creative Britain* (London: Faber and Faber, 1998).

Snee, C., 'Working class literature or proletarian writing?', in J. Clark et al. (eds), *Culture and Crisis in Britain in the 30s* (London: Lawrence & Wishart, 1979), pp. 165–91.

Spivak, G. C., 'Can the subaltern speak?', in C. Nelson and L. Grossberg (eds), *Marxism and the Interpretation of Culture* (Basingstoke: Macmillan Education, 1988), pp. 271–313.

Stanton, A., 'Learning from the experience of collective teamwork', in J. Batsleer, C. Cornforth and R. Paton (eds), *Issues in Voluntary and Non-profit Management* (Wokingham: Addison-Wesley, 1991), pp. 95–103.

Steedman, C., *The Tidy House: Little Girls Writing* (London: Virago, 1982).

Steedman, C., *Landscape for a Good Woman* (London: Virago, 1985).

Steedman, C., '"Listen, how the caged bird sings": Amarjit's song', in C. Steedman, C. Urwin and V. Walkerdine (eds), *Language, Gender and Childhood* (London: Routledge & Kegan Paul, 1985), pp. 137–63.

Steedman, C., *Past Tenses: Essays on Writing, Autobiography and History* (London: Rivers Oram, 1992).

Steedman, C., 'Writing the self: the end of the scholarship girl', in J. McGuigan (ed.), *Cultural Methodologies* (London: Sage, 1997), pp. 106–25.

Steedman, C., 'Enforced narratives: stories of another self', in T. Cosslett, C. Lury and

P. Summerfield (eds), *Feminism and Autobiography: Texts, Theories, Methods* (London: Routledge, 2000), pp. 25–39.
Storey, J., *Our Joyce 1917–1939: Her Early Years* (London: Virago, 1987).
Storey, J., *Joyce's Dream: The Post-war Years* (London: Virago, 1995).
Strange, J.-M., *Fatherhood and the British Working Class, 1865–1914* (Cambridge: Cambridge University Press, 2015).
Strangleman, T., 'Smokestack nostalgia, ruin porn or working-class obituary: the role and meaning of deindustrial representation', *International Labor and Working-Class History* [Online], 84 (2013), 23–37.
Street, B. V., *Literacy in Theory and Practice* (Cambridge: Cambridge University Press, 1984).
Street, B., *Adult Literacy in the UK: A History of Research and Practice* (Lancaster: RaPAL, 1997).
Swindells, J., *Victorian Writing and Working Women* (Cambridge: Polity, 1985).
Thompson, E. P., 'History from below', *Times Literary Supplement* (7 April 1966), pp. 279–80.
Thompson, E. P., *The Making of the English Working Class* (Harmondsworth: Penguin, 1968).
Thompson, E. P., 'The moral economy of the English crowd in the eighteenth century', *Past and Present*, 50 (1971), 76–136.
Thompson, E. P., 'Education and experience', in *The Romantics: England in a Revolutionary Age* (Woodbridge: Merlin, 1997), pp. 4–32.
Thompson, G., 'Our national cultural heritage', in CPGB, *Britain's Cultural Heritage*, supplement of meeting the previous year on American Threat to British Culture (London: Arena Publication, 1952), pp. 3–19.
Thomson, A., 'Community publishing. The Republic of Letters revisited', *Adults Learning*, 2:1 (1990), 15–16.
Thomson, A., 'History, writing and community publishing', *Oral History Journal*, 20:1 (1992), 22–3.
Thomson, M., *Lost Freedom: The Landscape of the Child and the British Post-War Settlement* (Oxford: Oxford University Press, 2013).
Todd, S., *The People: The Rise and Fall of the Working Class* (London: John Murray, 2015).
Toffler, A., *Future Shock* (New York: Random House, 1970).
Tonnies, F., *Community and Society* (New York: Harper and Row, 1957).
Transport Review, 'The people's road', *Transport Review* (20 June 1980), 16.
Vicinus, M., *The Industrial Muse* (London: Croom Helm, 1974).
Vincent, D., *Bread, Knowledge and Freedom: A Study of Nineteenth-Century Working Class Autobiography* (London: Europa, 1981).
Vincent, D., *Literacy and Popular Culture: England 1750–1914* (Cambridge: Cambridge University Press, 1989).
Wainwright, H., *Arguments for a New Left* (Oxford: Blackwell, 1994).
Walkerdine, V., *Growing Up Girl* (Basingstoke: Palgrave, 2001).
Wallis, J., 'You can't write until you can spell! Attitudes to writing amongst adult basic education students', in J. Mace (ed.), *Literacy, Language and Community Publishing: Essays in Adult Education* (Clevedon: Multilingual Matters, 1995), pp. 60–8.
Walmsley, A., *The Caribbean Artists Movement 1966–1972* (London: New Beacon Books, 1992).
Ward, C., *The Child in the City* (London: Architectural Press, 1978).
Waters, C., 'Autobiography, nostalgia and the changing practices of working class selfhood', in G. K. Behlmer and F. M. Leventhal (eds), *Singular Continuities: Tradition, Nostalgia and Identity in Modern Britain* (Stanford, CA: Stanford University Press, 2000), pp. 178–95.
Weiler, K., 'Freire and a feminist pedagogy of difference', in P. McLaren and C. Lankshear (eds), *Politics of Liberation: Paths from Freire* (London: Routledge, 1994), pp. 12–40.

Westwood, S., 'When class became community: radicalism in adult education', in A. Rattansi and D. Reeder (eds), *Rethinking Radical Education* (London: Lawrence & Wishart, 1992), pp. 222–48.
White, J., 'Beyond autobiography', in Samuel, *People's History* (London: Routledge & Kegan Paul, 1981), pp. 33–41.
Widdowson, P., *Literature* (London: Routledge, 1999).
Wilkinson, G., 'Understanding Lifetimes', *Oral History Journal*, 4:2 (Autumn 1976), 91.
Wilkinson, R. and K. Pickett, *The Spirit Level: Why Equality Is Better for Everyone* (London: Penguin, 2010).
Williams, R., *The Long Revolution* (London: Pelican, 1961).
Williams, R., *Culture and Society* (Harmondsworth: Penguin, 1962).
Williams, R., *Communications* (Harmondsworth: Penguin, 1976).
Williams, R., *Marxism and Literature* (Oxford: Oxford University Press, 1977).
Williams, R., 'The Arts Council', *Political Quarterly*, 50:2 (1979), 157–71.
Williams, R., *Politics and Letters: Interviews with New Left Review* (London: NLB, 1979).
Williams, R., *Problems in Materialism and Culture* (London: Verso, 1980).
Williams, R. 'The role of the literary magazine', *Times Literary Supplement* (6 June 1980), p. 637.
Williams, R., *Culture* (London: Fontana, 1981).
Williams, R., *The Country and the City* (London: Hogarth, 1985).
Williamson, B., 'Living the past differently: historical memory in the North East', in R. Colls and B. Lancaster (eds), *Geordies: The Roots of Regionalism* (Newcastle: University of Northumbria Press, 2005), pp. 149–68.
Wilson, N., *Home in Working Class Fiction* (Farnham: Ashgate, 2015).
Winn, J., 'The co-operative university: labour, property and pedagogy', *Power and Education*, 7:1 (2015), 39–55.
Withnall, A., 'Literacy on the agenda: the origins of the adult literacy campaign in the UK', *Studies in the Education of Adults*, 26:1 (April 1994), 67–85.
Wolch, J. R. and E. M. Rocha, 'Planning responses to voluntary sector crises', *Nonprofit Management and Leadership*, 3:4 (1993), 377–95.
Wood, M., 'Nostalgia or never: you can't go home again', *New Society*, 7:631 (7 November 1974), 343.
Woodin, T., 'Building culture from the bottom-up: the educational origins of the FWWCP', *History of Education*, 39:4 (2005), 345–63.
Woodin, T., '"More writing than welding": learning in worker writer groups', *History of Education*, 39:5 (2005), 551–67.
Woodin, T., 'Muddying the waters: class and identity in a working class cultural organisation', *Sociology*, 39:5 (2005), 1001–18.
Woodin, T., '"Chuck out the teacher?" Radical pedagogy in the community', *International Journal of Lifelong Education*, 26:1 (2007), 89–104.
Woodin, T., '"A beginner reader is not a beginner thinker": student publishing since the 1970s', *Paedagogica Historica*, 44:1/2 (2008), 219–32.
Woodin, T., 'Working class writing, alternative publishing and audience participation', *Media, Culture and Society*, 31:1 (2009), 79–96.
Woodin, T., 'Co-operative schools: building communities in the twenty first century', *Forum*, 54:2 (2012), 327–39.
Woodin, T., D. Crook and V. Carpentier, *Community and Mutual Ownership – a Historical Review* (York: Joseph Rowntree Foundation, 2010).
Woodin, T., G. McCulloch and S. Cowan, *Secondary Education and the Raising of the School Leaving Age* (New York: Palgrave Macmillan, 2013).

Woodin, T. (ed.), *Co-operation, Learning and Co-operative Values* (London: Routledge, 2015).
Worpole, 'Beyond the classroom walls ... making available the means of production', *Teaching London Kids*, 1 (1973), 4–7.
Worpole, K., *Local Publishing and Local Culture: An Account of the Centerprise Publishing Project 1972–1977* (London: Centerprise, 1977).
Worpole, K., 'The politics of writing', *Radical Education*, 12 (Spring 1979), 5–8.
Worpole, K., 'A ghostly pavement: the political implications of local working class history', in R. Samuel (ed.), *People's History and Socialist Theory* (London: Routledge & Kegan Paul, 1981), pp. 22–32.
Worpole, K., 'Who's in the community?', *City Limits* (12–18 March 1982), p. 51.
Worpole, K., 'The history lark', *Oral History Journal*, 12:2 (1984), 19–20.
Worpole, K., *Reading by Numbers: Contemporary Publishing & Popular Fiction* (London: Comedia, 1984).
Worpole, K., 'Village school or blackboard jungle', in R. Samuel (ed.), *Patriotism: The Making and Unmaking of British National Identity*, vol. 3: *National Fictions* (London: Routledge, 1989), pp. 125–40.
Wright, E. O., *Understanding Class* (London: Verso, 2015).
Wright, N., *Assessing Radical Education: A Critical View of the Radical Movement in English Schooling, 1960–1980* (Milton Keynes: Oxford University Press, 1989).
Wright, P., *On Living in an Old Country: The National Past in Contemporary Britain* (London: Verso, 1985).
Wright Mills, C., *The Sociological Imagination* (Harmondsworth: Penguin, 1973/1959).
Yeo, S. 'Whose story? An argument from within current historical practice in Britain', *Journal of Contemporary History*, 21:2 (1986), 259–320.
Yeo, S., 'The co-operative university: transforming higher education', in T. Woodin (ed.), *Co-operation, Learning and Co-operative Values* (London: Routledge, 2014).
Zandy, J., *Hands: Physical Labor, Class, and Cultural Work* (New Jersey: Rutgers University Press, 2004).

Unpublished

Gregory, G. 'Worker Writers' (MA dissertation, Institute of Education, University of London, 1979).
Hoggart, R., talk at conference on 'Literacy is not Enough', Manchester Metropolitan University, c.1997.
McGuigan, J., 'The State and Serious Writing: Arts Council Intervention in the English Literary Field' (PhD dissertation, University of Leicester, 1984).
Sitzia, L., 'Telling People's Histories: An Exploration of Community History Making from 1970–2000' (PhD dissertation, University of Sussex, 2010).
Woodin, T. 'An evaluation of the FWWCP' (PhD dissertation, University of Manchester, 2002).
Worpole, K., Talk at Fed Festival, Stanford Hall (April 1996).

Index

academic research 4, 10, 20, 57–8, 71, 79, 134
academics 4, 6, 7, 10, 19, 20, 21, 22, 57, 134, 146, 160, 188, 198
access courses 27, 188
Ackerman, Joe 40
adolescence 61
Adrian Henri 35
adult education 8, 13, 26–30, 55–6, 134, 180, 196
adult literacy 13, 28–30, 55, 79, 80–93, 106, 107, 116–17, 144, 149, 152, 194
  see also literacy
Adult Literacy and Basic Skills Unit (ALBSU) 86–7, 138
Adult Literacy Resource Agency 28
Adult Literacy Unit 28
aesthetic 8, 13, 75, 82, 82, 91, 105
Africa Centre 184
African-Caribbean 15, 39–40, 43, 90, 91, 191
Aftab, Ahmed 191
Agard, Sandra 195
Agbabi, Patience 187, 195
Age Exchange 69, 108
agit-prop 115
Ainley, Ben 22–3
Akenfield 20
'Alan' 84–5
Alinsky, Saul 25
Allen, Jim 31, 179
alternative press 133
alternatives 134, 139, 141, 142, 161, 170, 186, 197, 199

Amber film 21
anarchism 67, 68
andragogy 55
anecdotes 27, 79, 89, 105
apartheid 27
Appleby, Eric 180
Apples and Snakes 187
apprenticeship 61
Archer, Jean 98–9
Armstrong, Keith 176–7
Arts Council (of Great Britain) 5, 104, 120, 126, 137, 176, 177–86, 189
Arvon Foundation 187
Ashcroft, Bob 27
Ashworth, Sherry 103
Asian women 90
Asian writers 90, 109, 157, 166, 174, 191
Auden, Wystan (W. H.) 23, 31
audience 10, 15, 23, 31, 33, 40, 53, 71, 73, 76, 105, 114, 117, 125, 128–41, 145, 178
  see also readers
authenticity 6, 23, 82, 99, 105
autobiography 1, 7, 18, 19, 24, 25, 52, 57–79, 94–7, 105, 106, 107, 110, 148, 163, 166, 194
  collective autobiography 51
autodidact 7, 8–9, 120
autonomy 12, 54, 167, 196
Avery, Valerie 17
Ayres, Pam 121

Baldwin, James 120
Balgobin, Michelle 36–8

Bafta 195
Bandali, Sabir 45, 109
Bangura, Roberto 195
Barker, Pat 94
Barnes, Ron 5, 73, 116
Baron, Alexander 32
Barrett, Eddie 97, 114–15, 119, 120, 124, 160, 195–6
Basement Writers 15, 18, 31, 32, 34, 40, 53, 56, 113, 121, 129, 132, 152
Battle, Betty 124
BBC 28, 127, 196
Beatles 97
beauty 13, 15, 68, 102, 120, 177, 195
Beckett, Samuel 121
Beckman, Maurice 138
Beck, Ulrich 158
beginner readers 82–3
Belloc, Hilaire 68
Benjamin, Walter 30, 115
Berger, John 20
Berg, Leila 18
Bernstein, Basil 17
Bevin boy 84
Bidder, Joe 174
Big Flame 26, 27
Big Issue Writing Group 191
Bild, Ian 32
Birch, Keith 27, 116, 118, 119, 125, 147–8, 153, 161–2
Birmingham 186
Blackfriars 29
Black Ink Collective 39–40
Black Papers 5
Black People's Writing Group 166
black writers/workshops 1, 17, 39–40, 76, 77, 90–2, 109, 120 127, 135, 139, 151, 158, 163, 164–7, 168, 170, 171, 173–4, 198
  children 51
  and community 162
  and consciousness 25, 164, 166
  and literature worker 173
Blair, Tony 162
Blake, William 31, 91, 190–1
Blatchford, Robert 67
Bleasdale, Alan 196
Blunkett, David 54
Blythe, Ronald 20
body 171

book launches 117, 131
Bookseller 25
bookshops 24, 25, 31, 116, 133, 136, 137, 143
Bornat, Joanna 58, 76
Bourke, Joanna 58, 73
Boys' Brigade 68
Bradbury, Malcolm 187
Braden, Sue 30
Bradford 74, 159
Bragg, Melvyn 179, 180
Braithwaite, Edward 40
Brangwyn, Frank 77
Braudel, Fernand 141
Brazil 143
Breaking Through 188
Brecht, Bertolt 9, 120, 121
Breeze, Jean 'Binta' 191
Brexit 198
Brighton 18, 33, 62, 70, 124, 131
Bristol 77, 158
Bristol Broadsides 28, 30, 32, 75, 77, 100, 144, 151, 186
Britain 42, 44, 51, 57, 77, 78, 174, 176, 194
Britain's Got Talent 197
British Association of Settlements 28
Britten, Benjamin 23
Britton, James 86
Brixton 39
Brookside 195
Bruce, Esther 77
Buchu Books 191
builders' strike (1972) 115
bullying 90
Bunty 120
burden of representation 109
Burge, Maureen 144
business planning 185
Buston, John 181
Butler, Larry 174
Byrnes, Josie 83

Cabral, Amilcar 27
Calabash 138
Cambridge 161
Cambridge House 29
Campbell, Dona 174
Canada 191
canon 4, 195

capitalism 6, 7, 8, 12, 68–9, 141, 176, 199
care in the community 189
care system 48–50
Caribbean 43, 91, 92
Carrington, Charles 90
Carson, Robert 86
cartoons 40–1
Cartwright, Jim 128
Casey, Mary 121, 196
Cassidy, Anne 122, 173, 195
Catholic (Church) 26, 67, 151
CAVE 29
Centerprise 15, 24–5, 28, 30, 32, 33, 37, 46, 51, 54, 55, 73, 75, 82, 106, 107, 108, 116, 120, 134, 137, 138, 139, 142, 145, 151, 162, 163, 166, 178, 182, 186
Centre for Continuing Education 189
Centre for Cultural and Community Studies (CCCS) 6
Centre Fortytwo 23–4
Chanel 4 124, 188
Chaplin, Sid 179
charity 6, 177, 185
Chesterton, Gilbert (G. K.) 68
childbirth 85
childhood 22, 35–56, 58–61, 83–4, 92–3, 114
children's writing 13–18, 35–56, 163
Childwall Writers 27
Chile 143
Chinese 138
Churchill, Caryl 179
cinema 8, 32
  see also film
City Life 182
Civil Rights Movement 25–6, 115, 143
civil society 141
Clare, John 105 179
Clarke, John Cooper 195
classical music 179
classics 5, 9, 31, 96, 195
Clegg, Alec 17
Clegg, Arthur 179
Clyne, Peter 29
coalmining 162, 169
cockney 14, 18, 38–9
Cold War 92
Coleridge, Samuel Taylor 68

collective representation 107–10
collective working 149–51
Comedia 135
Commission for Racial Equality 92
commons 141
Commonword 19, 103, 135, 136, 137, 138, 139, 140, 143, 160, 164, 166, 186
Communist Party 8, 14, 18, 22–3, 69, 75, 88, 140, 158, 180
  communists 68
community 3, 9, 10, 20, 24–6, 44, 69, 70–9, 110, 116, 128, 140, 148, 149, 177, 186, 193, 194, 197
  group 136, 143
  and politics 166
  and working-class community 57
  and writing 104
community arts 104, 181, 182, 189
Community Arts Panel 181
community development 194
community organising 13, 24–6, 30, 151
community publishing 1, 2, 3, 5, 9, 12, 13, 20, 24, 25, 26, 30, 57–79
Community Relations Council 27
comprehensive education 35, 47, 52, 194
Comprehensive Education, A 46
conscientisation 142
consensus, post-war 1, 13
Conservatives 6, 88, 146, 158
Controlled Attack 122
Conway, Georgina 90
co-operative movement 69, 70, 197, 199
co-operatives 7, 69–70, 136, 138, 145, 163, 172, 197
copyright 108
Cork 191
Corridor Press 189
counter-culture 20, 22, 133, 140, 193
Cowley, Harry 67
Cox, Brian (C. B.) 5
creative writing 106, 150
crime fiction 120
critical pedagogy 11, 142–56
Crocus 136
Crofts, Renee 99
culture 1, 4, 5, 6, 8, 9, 10, 12, 17, 18, 22, 23, 25, 29, 30–2, 39, 40, 46, 47, 54, 78, 85, 105, 107, 113, 117–18, 120, 126, 127, 128, 134,

136, 143, 146, 150, 155, 159, 160, 161, 162, 168, 170, 171, 172, 174, 176, 178, 179, 180, 181, 184, 185, 186, 192, 193, 195, 197
  common culture 76, 162
  see also counter culture, popular culture, youth culture
cultural deprivation 17
cultural industry 186, 197
cultural revolution 12, 143, 155
cultural studies 6
Cultureword 139, 166, 186
  see also Commonword
Culzac, Alvin 121
Cummins, Jack 67–8
Curley, Chris 89

Daily Telegraph 182
Dallimore, Pat 101
Darwin, Chris 195
Dash, Jack 14
Davitt, Jack 113, 114, 121, 131
Dedman, Alfred 61
deficit 17, 29, 84, 187, 199
deindustrialisation 103
democracy 1,2, 4, 7, 11, 12, 18, 119, 141, 142, 143, 145, 152, 176, 178, 185, 193, 195, 197, 199
democratic deficit 199
Dentith, Simon 57
Department of Education and Science (DES) 87–8
desktop publishing 139
developmental psychology 55
dialogue 6, 33, 35, 56, 83, 89, 99, 129, 142, 154–6, 194, 198
Dickens, Charles 31, 66, 120
disability/disabled 3, 10, 76, 149, 157, 166, 196, 198
disciplines 4, 6, 105, 120
distribution 130–1, 136–40, 149, 199
dockers 163
docks 41, 84, 85, 113, 114, 162
documentary 31, 35, 48, 54, 104, 105
Dodd, Philip 57
Dolci, Danilo 26
domestic service 62–4
drama 1, 8, 94, 99–100, 106, 109
dreaming 50, 60
Duffin, Patricia 116–17, 164, 168

Duff, Mike 103
Duncan Smith, Iain 198
Dunn, Ruby 69
Dyson, Tony (A. E.) 5

E1 Festivals 33, 114
Earl Marshall School 54
East Bowling History Workshop 22, 32, 76, 108, 152, 159
East End *see* London
Eastside 174
Edexcel 196
editing 7, 23, 31, 48, 66, 76, 79, 94, 112, 122, 146, 188
education 111, 117, 127, 159, 162, 168, 179, 184, 185, 189, 196, 197, 199
  banking concept 142, 155
  and secondary education for all 84, 193
Education Reform Act (1988) 54, 134
Ekevall, Kay 115
Eliot, Thomas (T. S.) 190
elitism/elite 4, 7, 12, 30, 53, 108, 128, 140, 143, 150, 175, 178–83, 185, 196, 197, 199
El Kssmi, Zohra 45
Ellison, Ralph 120
embourgeoisement 160
emotions 10, 46, 49–50, 54, 60, 61, 64, 193
Empire 77–8
Empire Day 77, 101–2
empowerment 2, 3, 149, 154
England 42–5
English Centre 16
English class 113, 117, 144
English department 187
English language 46
English lesson 17, 54
English literature 4
English teachers 15, 17, 42, 103
English teaching 13–18, 42
equality 118–19, 145, 146, 195
equal opportunities 135, 150, 162, 171
Ethnic Communities Oral History Project 77, 152, 191
Evans, David 26, 103, 120, 160, 163, 173
Evans, George Ewart 20
Everyman Theatre 124
exams 53

262 Index

Exell, Arthur 106
experience 1, 2, 4, 6, 7, 8, 9, 10 ,12, 20, 22, 23, 47, 53, 94, 105, 128, 133, 134, 146, 155, 177, 194
Exploring Living Memory 134

Faber and Faber 177
Fair Rent Act 26
fairy tale 54
Falber, Reuben 180
Falklands War 86
family 44–5, 48–9, 52, 53, 58, 59–61, 64–6, 72, 76–7, 79, 97, 107, 114, 125–6, 172, 194
family learning 196
Fanon, Frantz 27
Fantasy 51, 105
fathers 59, 61, 114
Fearnley, Colin 86–7
Federation Book Club 138
Federation Magazine 131, 174
Fed News 170, 185
feminism 6, 30, 101, 163, 168, 169
 black feminism 45
 see also women's liberation
fiction 97–100, 103
film 64, 105–6, 195
 see cinema
first chapter membership 189
First World War 8, 13, 38–9, 65, 67–8
Flanagan, Joe 190
Flood, Sally 108, 131
flower power 96
Floyd 173
Fo, Dario 124
Foley, Bernadette 196
folk music 23
football 32, 33, 113, 197
Forbuoys 136
Forest Artworks 190
Forest of Dean 189
Forrester, Helen 74
Forster, Margaret 178, 180, 181
France 138, 191
Fraser, Ronald 58
Freire, Paulo 27, 29, 142–3, 154–6
friendship 72, 75, 116, 122, 124, 127, 159, 167, 173, 192, 199
Fullman, Janice 187
functional literacy 29

funding/funder 10, 28, 31, 32, 86, 88, 90, 92, 128, 138–9, 150–1, 162, 166, 171, 186, 187, 188, 189, 192, 196, 197, 199, 177, 184, 187, 199
FWWCP executive committee 108, 151, 154, 161, 162, 163, 167, 172, 178, 182

Gardener, Sue 28, 29–30, 144
Garnett, Tony 31
Gatehouse Books 29, 82, 83, 89–92, 107, 116, 117–18, 136, 137, 138, 144, 151, 164, 187, 189
Gates, The 46–8, 122
gay writers 76, 109, 135, 139, 158, 164, 167, 198
GCSE 196
gender 2, 3, 10, 76, 99, 120, 149, 157, 166, 168, 174, 198
generations 6, 9, 12, 27, 31, 32, 55, 57, 58, 60, 65, 78, 79, 95, 96, 109, 146, 166, 180, 193–4
gentrification 75, 113
George, Paul 43–4
Germany 191
ghetto 92, 170
Giddens, Anthony 2, 158
Gilbey, Alan 31, 40–1, 116, 119, 122, 150, 172, 195
Giroux, Henry 143
globalisation 2, 191
Glory of the Garden 183
Glover, Trevor 177
Glynn, John 144
Goode, Peter 80, 92, 159
Gowling, John 164
Gowrie, Alexander (Lord) 186
grammar 17, 92, 117
grammar schools 5
Gramsci, Antonio 27
grants 135, 138, 150
Grassick, Richard 20–1
grass-roots 137, 141, 170, 196, 199
Graves, Colin 38–9
Gray, Richard 32, 129
Greater London Arts Association 31
Greater London Council (GLC) 162, 182
Greek writers 191
Greenwich Community College 186
Gregory, Gerry 111

Grenada 43
Grimsby Writers 152
Guardian 137, 177
Gwilt, Rick 23, 104, 115, 120, 123, 124, 131, 133, 134, 136, 160, 162, 170

Hackney 32, 67, 92, 108, 116, 145, 162
Hackney Downs School 15
Hackney Half-Term Adventure 15
Hackney Reading Centre 25, 29, 30, 85
Hackney Writers' Workshop 25, 152, 153, 164
Half Moon Theatre 132
Hall, Doris 71
Hall, Stuart 6
Hammersmith and Fulham 191
Handy, Charles 154
Hannington, Walter 68
Harcup, Tony 31, 123, 131
Hardy, Thomas 43, 105
Harrison, John (JFC) 8
Hastings 189
Haythorne, Evelyn 187
Hazlitt, William 68
Healey, Bert 66, 70, 75
heavy industry 102, 157
Heeley Writers 99, 102, 119, 124
Herbert, Chelsea 41
heritage 58
Hevey, David, 171, 196
Hewitt, Maggie 166
Hicks, Stephen 111–12
hierarchy 4, 119, 128, 153, 154, 178, 180, 181, 184, 185, 186, 196, 199
Higgins, Kevin 92
higher education 187–8
 see also universities
Hines, Barry 179
hippies 144
Hiroshima 115
history 2, 4, 6, 7–8, 9, 10, 11, 13, 14, 18–22, 24, 27, 30, 42, 55, 58, 62, 65, 57–79, 106, 107, 115, 121, 125, 129, 132, 134, 135, 143, 152, 153, 155, 158, 166, 180, 182, 186, 189, 193, 194, 195
history from below 6, 13
History Workshop 6, 21–2, 106, 134
 see also East Bowling History Workshop
Hoggart, Richard 5, 12, 32, 180, 181, 196

homelessness 191
Holbrook, David 17, 32
Holt, Billy 8
Home Truths 116, 164
homophobia 169
Hourd, Marjorie 17
House, Bill 46, 122
Housing Act (1969) 129
Howard, Ursula 144
Hoxton Café Project 24–5
Hoy, Mike 119
Huddlestone, Trevor 14
Hughes, Glyn 8
Hughes, Langston 91, 120
Hughes, Violet M 184–5
humour 40, 59, 72, 89, 94, 106, 107, 117, 118, 195

Ibekwe, Stella 42
identity 3, 9, 11, 36, 40, 52, 65, 68, 69, 75, 90, 109, 115, 131, 134, 135, 140, 141, 156, 157–75, 174, 183, 184, 195, 197, 199
immigration 13, 27, 42–6, 98
Independent Labour Party (ILP) 68
India 25, 44
industrialism 162
inequality 2, 6, 11, 52, 59, 60, 70, 84, 154, 174, 178, 197, 198, 199, 200
Ingersoll, Robert 67
inner city 13
Inner London Education Authority (ILEA) 17, 24, 35, 134
Institute of Education (London) 17
interdisciplinarity 6
Ireland 158, 177, 191
Irish writers 191
ITV 177

Jackie's Story 46, 48–50, 113
Jackson, Brian 30, 126
Jackson, Keith 27, 30
Jackson, Roy 180
James, Pedr 124
Janet and John books 28
Jasper, Stan (A.S.) 73
jazz 179
Jelley, Dr 67
Jew/Jewish 131, 138, 174
Johnson, Anne 17

Johnson, Linton Kwesi 40, 179
Johnson, Susan 14
Jonathan Cape 186
Jones, Ben 58
Jones, Gethin 140
Jones, Jack 23
judgement 84, 91, 109, 138, 178–83, 195

Kalu, Pete 139, 186, 195
Kearney, Mike 131, 132
Keats, John 68, 182
Keddie, Nell 30
Kelman, James 110
Kensington Welfare Rights Union 191
Kesey, Ken 120
Kinnock, Neil 162
Kirk, Pat 36
Kitchen, Roger 32
Knowle West 144
Konttinen, Sirkka-Liisa 21
Kops, Bernard 32
Kuya, Dorothy 27

Labour government 24, 51
labour history 21–2
Labourism 171
labour movement 8, 13, 22–4, 67–9, 133, 134, 152, 157, 171
Labour Party 13, 22–3, 30, 70, 74, 134, 161–2
labour studies 128
Laclau, Ernest 158
Lamb, Charles 68
Lamming, George 27, 43
Lancashire 191
Langley, John 59, 74, 146
language 17–18, 29–30, 35, 39–40, 46, 54, 81, 85, 89, 92, 97, 98, 116, 158, 168, 171
   standard English 40, 82, 92, 99, 194
language experience 29, 35, 53, 55, 117–18, 134
Lapidus 187
La Rose, John 17
Laski, Marghanita 182
league tables 196
learning 84, 111–27, 195, 196
Leavis, Queenie (Q. D.) 128
Ledikasyon Pu Travayer 191–2

Lee, Terry 121
Leeds Other Paper 31, 123
Leeds University 180
Leeson, Bob 179
Lenin 24
lesbian writers 76, 135, 139, 198
Le Sueur, Meridel 120
Lewis, Fitz 113, 116, 117, 119, 174
Leyland Motors 133
liberalism 169
liberation theology 26
library 33, 129–30, 150
Lifetimes 19–20
lightermen 61–2
literacy 2, 3, 4, 5, 10, 13, 25, 28–30, 35, 55, 79, 80–92, 137, 138, 144, 166, 187
   see also adult literacy
literary criticism 126
literary merit 177–86
literary models 107
literature 4–5, 8, 35, 104, 105, 120, 138, 139, 149, 166, 169 180, 182, 193
   literature development 151, 187, 196
   and literature festival 186
Literature Belongs to Everyone 184
Literature Panel 177–86
Littlewood, Joan 23
Liverpool 26–7, 30, 32, 35, 77, 92, 97, 115, 116, 117, 119, 120, 125, 150, 158, 162, 170, 183, 186
Liverpool and Manchester Railway 133
Liverpool News 28
Liverpool University 26–7, 119, 122
Liverpool 8 Writers' Workshop 27, 32, 77, 163, 173
Loach, Ken 31
local authorities 28
London 13, 14, 33, 35, 40, 48, 74, 94, 97, 113, 114, 116, 131, 138, 162, 174, 183, 184
London Arts Board 139
London Association for the Teaching of English (LATE) 35
London, Jack 96
London Morning 17
London Voices 23
Lovett, Tom 27
Lynch, Ciaran 109

Lyndsey, Jack 179
Lyon, Mary 38

MacColl, Ewan 20, 23, 179
McCormick, Ron 14
Mace, Jane 30, 84, 178
McGee, Gladys 101, 187
McGough, Roger 32
McGovern, Jimmy 31, 97, 104, 107, 118, 119, 120, 122–4, 169–70, 173, 195
McGuigan, Jim 180, 182
McLuhan, Marshall 30
Macmillan 177
Maerdy 140
mainstream 8, 10, 12, 28, 40, 104, 110, 124, 128, 133, 139, 159, 161, 170, 176, 180, 184, 192, 195, 196, 197, 198
Manchester 22, 32, 74, 90, 92, 103, 113, 116, 143, 144, 158, 186
Manchester Union of Secondary School Students 14
Manchester University 196
Mandela, Nelson 191
Manville, Sid 59–60, 66–7, 78, 106, 107
Marchant, Hazel 124
Marchant, Tony 31, 195
market books 140
marketing 135–7, 199
marketisation 138
markets 26, 128, 131, 134–7, 139, 141, 183, 196
Marsden, Dennis 5, 30, 73, 126
Marvell, Andrew 121
Marxism 6, 22, 26, 40, 69
Marxism Today 158
masculinity 65
mass media 3
Masterson, Olive 60, 64–5, 70
Mauritius 191–2
May Day Manifesto 24
May, Sue 164
May, Theresa 198
media 3, 9, 12, 30, 151, 160, 168, 177, 197
memory 18, 42, 58, 78, 94
men 61–3, 65–6, 67–9
mental health 76, 167, 174
mentalism 174
meritocratic 180

Merseyside Association of Writers' Workshops (MAWW) 27, 150, 188
Meryll, Lydia 32
middle class 12, 20, 30, 31, 52, 70, 73, 74, 103, 105, 121, 143, 145, 158, 160, 161, 162, 166, 168, 169, 170–1, 172, 189, 197, 199
migration 42–6, 191, 194
Mildiner, Leslie 46, 122
Miller, Arthur 123
Miller, Chris 7
Mills, C. Wright 114
Mills, Roger 32, 106, 116, 121, 149, 159, 171, 174, 195
Milton Keynes 32
Miners' Strike (1984–85) 86, 162
Minority Press Group (MPG) 138
Mitchell, Adrian 23, 121, 179
Mitford, Nancy 120
Mohr, Jean 20
monarchy 172
Moos, Lottie 119
moral economy 141
Morley, Molly 24
Morning Star 18, 180
Morocco 45
Morrison, Blake 120, 181
Morris, William 67
Morton, Leslie (A. L.) 179
Mosley, Oswald 15
Moss, Les 68, 148
Moss Side People's Writing Group 166
mothers 59–60, 61, 114
Mouffe, Chantal 158
Mount, Ferdinand 198
Mozambique 32

Nairne, Sandy 181
narrative 2, 46, 49
National Association for Literature Development (NALD) 187
National Association of Writers in Education (NAWE) 187
National Committee for Adult Literacy 28
National Federation of Voluntary Literacy Schemes 180
National Health Service 67
national identity 65
National Poetry Day 196
National Portrait Gallery 181

National Trust 72
National Unemployed Workers' Movement 68
National Union of Railwaymen (NUR) 133
Navy 114
neoliberal 1, 141, 146
New Beacon Books 17
Newcastle 113
Newham Writers 152
New Labour 198
New Left 24, 25
new literacy studies 3
New Right 1, 75, 86, 141
Newsnight 196
new social movements 199
New Statesman 182
Newton, Arthur 32
Ngũgĩ wa Thiong'o 120
Niven, Alistair 137, 184
Noakes, Daisy 61, 63–4, 74, 129
Noakes, George 129
Normal, Henry 195
Northern College 125
Northern Gay Writers 164
Northern Ireland 172
Northside Writers 109, 191
north–south divide 162
North West Arts Board 136, 138
nostalgia 6–7, 55, 57–8, 71, 79, 110
Nottingham 30
novel 46–8, 94

occupational therapy 10
O'Connor, Bridget 195
Olson, Tillie 112
Once I was a Washing Machine 137
Open University 187
Opera House 186
oral history 13, 18, 20, 24, 76, 77, 151
O'Rourke, Rebecca 122, 124, 168, 173, 195
Orwell, George 115
Osborne, Charles 177, 178–80
Owen, Wilfred 121
Oxford 162

paid staff 150–4
painting 3, 8, 77, 180

parents 14, 30, 46, 48, 52, 53, 67, 68, 83, 90, 125, 127, 143, 194
Parker, Tony 20
Parrish, Dave 136, 137
Partington 19–20
partnership 187
Password Books 137
Paul, Albert 62, 65–6, 70, 74, 129
payment of writers 33, 149, 151, 192, 199
Peach, Blair 16
Pecket Well College 80, 144, 152, 187, 189, 190
Peckham Bookplace 25
Peckham Publishing Project 29, 32, 82, 129, 163
pedagogy 29, 35, 53, 80, 117–18, 134, 142–3, 154–6
see also critical pedagogy
People's Autobiography of Hackney 22, 25, 71, 145, 153
people's history 18–22, 132
People's Press 32
Penguin 177, 186
performance 3, 40, 48, 77, 97, 101, 117, 131, 139, 186–7, 199
PhD 160
Philadelphia 191
Phnom-Penh 42
photographs 14, 15, 20–1, 55, 83, 140
Piaget, Jean 55
planning 69
Plath, Sylvia 191
play 60
playwriting 122, 196
Plowden Report 17
poetry 1, 8, 13–19, 36–40, 43–4, 54, 81, 82, 86–8, 94, 100–3, 105, 106, 109, 113, 115, 117, 119, 121, 124, 176–7, 191, 199
Poetry Society 187
policy (government) 4, 134, 139, 177, 179, 185, 187, 197, 198 199
political correctness 169
politics 12, 13, 17, 24, 67–70, 75, 79, 85–91, 105, 110, 115, 142, 176, 178, 182, 191, 194, 197, 198, 199
Polish writers 191
Pollard, Nick 119, 131, 166, 172
popular culture 39, 50–1, 54
Popular Memory Group 6, 149

popular music 32, 197
populism 136
Porter, Rose 39
post-modernism 5
power 4, 36, 49–50, 54, 59, 75, 76, 80, 148–9, 152, 155, 166, 193
poverty/poor 13, 14, 26, 48, 58, 67, 72, 75, 83, 97, 106, 107, 194, 197
praxis 142, 155
prefigurative form 145, 148
Prescott Writers 124
printing 3, 30
prisoners 167, 184
professionalisation 140, 143, 152, 199
professionalism 137, 138, 139
professionals 10, 13, 20, 29, 33, 141, 145, 150–4, 170, 185–6, 187
progressive education 17, 54–6
propagandist 109
prisons/prisoners 90
Publications Distribution Co-operative 138
public schools 51, 53, 149
public services 134, 141, 199
publishing houses 126
  see community publishing
punk rock 31, 194, 195
puritan influences 73, 82, 160

QueenSpark Books 20, 22, 24, 26, 30, 32, 58–79, 95, 107, 124, 128–9, 131, 140, 148, 149, 152, 164

race 2, 3, 10, 27, 42–6, 51, 76, 77, 109, 110, 149, 173, 174, 198
  racism 90–1, 110, 119, 155, 157, 166, 168–70
  and anti-racist 173
  and institutional racism 183
  see also African-Caribbean
radio 60, 119, 129
Radio Ballads 20, 30
Ragged Trousered Philanthropists 62, 179
raising of the school leaving age 35
rape 119
Raybould, Sidney 180
Raymond Williams Prize for Community Publishing 184, 186
readers 1, 2, 7, 11, 15, 25, 31, 110
  see also audience

Reader's Digest 104
Reading 189
reading 119, 130
reading public 128–9
readings 97, 131
  see also performance
realism 104
reciprocal membership 189
recording 20, 28, 30, 146
  see also scribing; transcribing
Redcliffe-Maud Enquiry on Arts Patronage 25
Reflections 17
Republic of Letters 7, 10, 31, 113, 143, 181
relativism 5, 8, 185, 196
relevant/relevance 15, 17, 28, 180
Research Academic Exercise (RAE) 188
Resolution 42 23–4
Rhonda 140
Rhonda Community Arts 189
Richards, Ivor (I. A.) 178
Richardson, Sarah 174
Right to Read 28
Ritchens, Paul 36
Robbins, Harold 129
Rodney, Walter 27
Rogers, Olive 149, 168, 182
romance 41–2, 54
Roots 191
Rose, Jonathan 8–9, 181
Rosenberg, Isaac 13
Rosen, Harold 17–18
Rottingdean 62
rough music 72
Rousseau, Jean–Jacques 44
Rowbotham, Sheila 30, 64
Rubaiyat of Omar Khayyam 67
Runcorn 161
Runyan, Damon 120
Ruskin College 21
Russell Committee 29

schools/schooling 13, 28, 35–56, 61, 69, 72, 80, 111, 114, 196, 199
  buildings 38
  and school strikes 13–14
  and Sunday Schools 68, 72
Schools Action Union 14
School Council 86
Scott-Heron, Gil 121

Scotland 110
Scotland Road Free School 32
Scotland Road Writers' Workshop 23, 31, 32, 99, 107, 116, 118, 119, 120, 121, 122, 123, 151, 153, 160, 162, 173, 195
Scottie Road '83 147–8, 151, 160, 167
scribing 3, 29
   see also recording; transcribing
sculpture 179
Seabrook, Jeremy 20
Searle, Chris 13–15, 34, 40
Second Chance to Learn 27
Second World War 8, 57, 65, 69, 74, 96, 138, 194
sectarianism 176, 182
Seeger, Peggy 20, 179
senses 42, 54, 98–9
separatist groups 167–8
serious writing 180
service 62–3
service delivery 151, 184
Sesay, Kadija 186
sex 76
sexism 110, 155, 169–70
sexuality 3, 10, 76, 157
Shakespeare, William 120, 121, 182, 192
shame 29, 59, 72
Shane, Barbara 99
Shaw, Bernard 68
Shaw, Sir Roy 179, 180, 181
Sheba Press 186
Sheffield 99, 119, 186
Shelley, Percy Bysshe 68, 182
Shelton, William 88
shipbuilding 162
shipyards 113, 114
shop stewards 91, 135
Shorelink 189
short stories 1, 94, 97–8
Shrapnel, Sue *see* Gardener, Sue
Shush Mum's Writing 100
Sillitoe, Alan 96
Simon, Brian 23
Sinfield, Alan 24
Sir John Cass School 13
Sissay, Lemn 167, 196
skill 3, 13, 28, 29, 62, 63, 118, 122, 149, 150
Skills for Life 187

Slipman, Sue 88
slums 72, 75
Small, John 92, 161
Smart, Pat 117, 120, 150, 153, 172
Smith, Chris 197
Smith, Ken 190
Smythe, Joe 107, 127, 133, 157
social clubs 153
Social Contract 85
social history 58, 111
socialism/socialist 6–7, 13, 22, 24, 31, 54, 67–9, 75, 115, 162, 163, 168, 171
Socialist Bookfair 166
Social Justice Unit 198
social movements 11, 12, 70, 110, 143, 153, 158, 162, 185, 193, 199
social services 75
social workers 48–50
Society of Authors 180
songwriting/singing 106, 110, 114, 144
Soundsense 189
South Africa 27, 160, 191
South America 27
Southall Riots 16
southerners 162
Spanish Civil War 115
Sparchives 24
speech 17, 29, 28, 100, 105
   see also voice
Spence, Jo 159
Spivak, Gayatri 6
Staincliffe, Cath 103
standards 5, 35, 62, 104, 135, 178, 179, 180, 181, 196
state 26, 128, 142, 199
Steedman, Carolyn 58
Steinbeck, John 120
Stepney 48
Stepney Words 13–14, 34, 35
   Stepney Words III 54
storytelling 43, 97, 98, 105, 110, 115, 118
   Anansi stories 43
Street, Brian 3
Strong Words 22, 71, 114, 129, 162
structure of feeling 71–6
subaltern studies 6
subjectivity 2–4, 25, 35, 47, 74, 107–10
suffragettes 68

Sumal, Ranjit 44
Sunday Times 88
Survivors' Poetry 174, 184, 189–91
Survivors' Poetry Scotland 174
Sussex University 189
Sweden 134
Sweeney, Matthew 190
syndicalism 68
Szczulkun, Stefan 191

Tafari, Levi 195
teachers 13–18, 29, 32, 35, 38, 40, 42, 46, 48, 49, 51, 52, 53, 54, 159, 194, 196
technology 2, 3, 30, 57, 60, 106, 129, 139, 140, 193
television 3, 8, 31, 32, 60, 113, 142, 177, 195, 197
tenants groups 153
Thatcher, Margaret 13, 86–7, 99, 115, 192, 197, 198
　Thatcherism 9, 86–8, 99, 134, 158, 169, 183
　and Dennis 99
theatre 20, 23, 40, 97, 108, 115, 122, 123, 124, 132, 167, 180, 182, 186, 195
theory 7, 20, 31, 57, 155
therapy 6–7, 45, 110, 191
Thickett, Arthur 95–7
Thomas, Dylan 182
Thompson, Edward (E. P.) 12, 72
Thompson, Glenn 24–5, 138
Thompson, Liz 94–5, 113–14, 120, 187
Thomson, Al 106, 166
Tillett, Ben 14
time 59, 65, 78
Times Literary Supplement 181
Tories 140
Torr, Sue 84
Tottenham Writers 187
tower block 98
Tower Hamlets 31, 143, 174
Tower Hamlets Arts Project (THAP) 31
Towpath Press 191
trade unions 8, 13, 14, 23, 62, 75, 91, 99, 133, 134–5, 153, 154, 161, 162, 169, 183, 184, 197
　Association of Cinematograph, Television and Allied Technicians (ACTT) 23

Trades Union Congress (TUC) 23, 180
Transport and General Workers' Union (TGWU) 23
tradition 8–9, 12, 31–2, 54, 59, 158, 160, 176, 181, 184–5, 195
transcribing 26, 79, 92, 146
　see also recording; scribing
Transport Review 133
travel 33, 57, 191
Tressell, Robert 62
truanting 46–50

U and non-U 120
unemployed 13
UNESCO 29, 181, 196
Unity of Arts 23
Unity Theatre 40, 115, 123
universities 3–4, 5, 20, 120, 126, 160, 196, 199
　see also higher education
University of East Anglia 187
USA 13, 24, 25, 172, 191
Usherwood, Vivian 15–16, 116, 178
utopian ideas 45, 57, 67, 196

Vietnam 96
violence 61, 76, 119, 172
Virago Press 186
voice 2, 3, 6, 8, 17, 18, 26, 30, 31, 33, 49, 53, 60, 73, 78, 80, 81–2, 91, 92, 98, 99, 100, 117, 123, 128, 129, 139, 149, 154
Voices 22–3, 104, 115, 123, 124, 134–5, 136, 182, 195
Voluntary Arts Network (VAN) 189
voluntary organisation/group 136, 140, 146–8, 149, 150, 152, 153, 183, 185

Walcott, Derek 40
Waling, Steve 119, 173
Wapping 40, 113
Ward, Colin 55
Ward, Margaret 62, 76, 77
Waterstones 136
WEA (Workers' Educational Association) 22, 27, 28, 30, 120, 134, 144, 145
Wednesday Play 31
welfare 6, 13, 20, 28, 57, 162
　welfare advice 25

welfare state 13, 74, 75, 193
Wells, Alan 88
Welsh, Irvine 103
Wesker, Arnold 23, 128
Wesleyans 137
whiteness 43, 164, 166, 167–9, 174, 198
Whittingham, Peter 102–3
WHSmith 25, 131, 132, 136
widening participation 27, 187, 196
Wilkinson, Greg 19, 160, 179
Williams, Raymond 3, 5, 10, 12, 30, 70, 105, 120, 129, 140
Willis, Norman 23
Wiltshire, Pauline 92, 166
Wimbourne 162
women 62, 69–70, 109
Women and Words 164
Women's Co-operative Guild 69
women's liberation 25, 148, 168
  see also feminism
Women's Press 186
women writers/workshops 26–7, 45, 59, 62, 64, 65, 69–70, 85, 90, 109, 114, 125, 134, 135, 139, 158, 163–4, 167, 171, 173, 182, 198
Wood, Michael 57
Woolf, Virginia 31
Words, Sounds and Power 166
work 61–4, 79
worker priest movement 26

worker writer 159, 161, 174
working-class studies 191
Working Press 191
World Social Forum 191
Worpole, Ken 15, 18, 31, 33, 34, 104, 108, 116, 120, 133, 177, 178, 182
Worsley, Peter 23
Write First Time 28, 29, 80–2, 85–8, 134, 138, 144, 163
Writernet 187
writers' circles 145
Writing 33, 131
writing workshops 5, 7, 11, 22, 23, 26, 55, 93, 94–110, 109, 113, 115, 139, 144, 153, 168, 199
Wyse, Audrey 179

X Press 186

Yarnit, Martin 27
Yeats, William Butler (W. B.) 121
Yeo, Stephen 145
Yorkshire 17, 108
Yorkshire Arts Circus 103, 108, 136, 188
Young Communist League 115
Young, Julia 125
young people 13–18, 24, 32, 34, 35–56, 60, 61, 91, 104, 107
youth culture 40–1, 45
youth work 24–5

EU authorised representative for GPSR:
Easy Access System Europe, Mustamäe tee 50,
10621 Tallinn, Estonia
gpsr.requests@easproject.com

www.ingramcontent.com/pod-product-compliance
Lightning Source LLC
Chambersburg PA
CBHW070236240426
43673CB00044B/1807